PEOPLE

people

Richard T. Stout

HARPER & ROW, PUBLISHERS

NEW YORK, EVANSTON,

AND LONDON

1817

Grateful acknowledgment is made for permission to quote from the following books and articles:

An article by William H. Honan, *The New York Times Magazine*, December 10, 1967; © 1967 by The New York Times Company. Reprinted by permission of the *New York Times* and the author.

A column by Tom Wicker appearing in the *New York Times*, February 8, 1968; © 1968 by The New York Times Company. Reprinted by permission.

An article by Jack Newfield appearing in *The Village Voice*, December 28, 1967. Reprinted by permission of *The Village Voice*. Copyright The Village Voice, Inc., 1967.

The Year of the People by Eugene J. McCarthy. Copyright © 1968 by Eugene J. McCarthy. Reprinted by permission of the publisher, Doubleday & Company, Inc.

"Why I Am Battling LBJ," by Eugene J. McCarthy, *Look* magazine, February 6, 1968. Copyright © 1968, *Look*. Reprinted by permission.

My Brother Lyndon by Sam Houston Johnson. Copyright © 1969, 1970 by Sam Houston Johnson. Reprinted by permission of the publisher, Cowles Book Company, Inc.

Material reprinted by permission of The World Publishing Company from *Frontiers in American Democracy* by Eugene J. McCarthy. Copyright © 1960 by Eugene J. McCarthy.

"Magical Mystery Tour," by John Lennon and Paul McCartney. Copyright © 1967 by Northern Songs Ltd. Used by permission, all rights reserved.

Series of articles by Jay G. Sykes, titled "Jay Sykes' Story of the McCarthy Campaign in Wisconsin," which appeared in the Madison (Wisc.) *Capital-Times* May 26 through June 9, 1968. Copyright © 1968 by Jay G. Sykes. Reprinted by permission of the author.

An article by Robert Healy which appeared in the Boston *Globe* August 28, 1968. Copyright © 1968 by The Boston Globe Newspaper Co. Reprinted by permission.

An interview with Eugene J. McCarthy which appeared in the Miami *Herald* August 28, 1968. Copyright © 1968 by Knight Newspapers. By permission of the Miami *Herald*.

973.924
St 7p
74189
April 1971

FIRST EDITION

LIBRARY OF CONGRESS CATALOG CARD NUMBER: 71-123964

For my children,

Richard, David, Rebecca and Sarah

I am a man who, sauntering along without fully stopping, turns
    a casual look upon you and then averts his face,
Leaving it to you to prove and define it,
Expecting the main things from you.

FROM "POETS TO COME" BY WALT WHITMAN

CONTENTS

VIII. Some Footnotes to This History

1

Headnote

★

The Secretary of Agriculture has said
we will be "only a footnote in history."
But I think we can say with Churchill,
"But what a footnote." And I think
it could be that we will become
part of the main text.

EUGENE J. MCCARTHY, DURING HIS 1968
CAMPAIGN FOR PRESIDENT

1. GRASS ROOTS

It was spring of 1970, but it seemed like 1968 all over again. This time the President was Richard Nixon. The war that had befouled his predecessor now pushed into Cambodia. In response to this and the killing of four students at Kent State University in Ohio by National Guardsmen at an antiwar protest, Americans rose up anew in dissent as they had in 1968 around the presidential candidacy of Eugene McCarthy.

Once more the dissent was spontaneous. Again students were at the forefront. In untold numbers they and concerned adult Americans petitioned Congress to finally stop the war, and they began working with new intensity for political candidates who opposed it.

That the vast majority still chose to work within the system was testimony to the success of the McCarthy campaign. For in 1968 they had seen the possibilities of change through political action. They did not win that year, but a President retired and war policy altered.

This movement of concerned citizens of all ages seemed to many to have faded after the 1968 election. For a time, Nixon's troop withdrawals from Southeast Asia had tempered war opposition. But this citizens movement had not stopped. The people who had supported McCarthy had remained alive and well in politics and protest and social action, whether in national or community endeavors. Their legions grew, and politics was yet in their blood.

In 1969 in Massachusetts, for example, they had evolved into the Citizens for Participation Politics and fielded candidates for school committees, city councils, the state legislature. One of their number, Michael Harrington, was elected to Congress from a district that had been Republican for decades. In Saint Louis, they threw their strength behind a public housing rent strike and elected some township committeemen. In Madison, Wisconsin, they fought construction of a new airport runway they felt contrary to the public interest. They had been on the ramparts of the fight against the antiballistic missile system, the struggle for an improved environment, the effort to make large corporations more responsive to social needs, and the continuing drive to end the war. It would take a small book to list those who helped Mayor John Lindsay of New York to reelection.

In 1970, some ran for the United States Senate or the House of Representatives with little real hope of winning but with a firm intent to keep issues they believed in before the public and the President. In countless precincts and counties, McCarthy people and others who joined them had by 1970 begun to change the politics in their locales. They did not control, and there was backsliding in some places, but political regulars had begun to listen to them solicitously.

"Perhaps we can't yet elect anybody," said Ted M. Warshafsky, who had been cochairman of the Wisconsin McCarthy effort, "but we could defeat anybody."

Thus their strength two years later was what it had been in 1968— a kind of negative muscle, a power of veto, the power they had used on Lyndon Johnson and Hubert Humphrey. It was, in effect, a politics of threat, but with positive goals. Theirs was a latent strength that fed on no fancy national organization but on individual conscience. They had proved that a President could not take the people for granted. They knew they could prove it again.

This movement, up to 1970, had been most pronounced within the Democratic party. And these people were resolved not to let that party become again what it had been in 1968.

"If the party goes in that direction, they can't take us with them," said Midge Miller, another Wisconsin McCarthy leader who had been a hard-working Democrat for many years before 1968. There, then, was the ultimate threat: If the Democratic party did not reform, did not become more responsive to the people by 1972, a new party on the left might arise. That such splinter efforts had never gone far would not necessarily dissuade them.

At the same time, most of these people were dedicated to trying to carry out the reforms they had initiated at the 1968 Democratic National Convention. "We want to make the party work as it was meant to work," said Anne Wexler of Connecticut, who helped devise the reforms.

By the spring of 1970 these reforms had begun in a number of states. Forty had established reform commissions, and each of these had at least a token representation of the 1968 dissidents. The dissidents were not allowed to run things, but they could influence. Rhode Island, where in 1968 only three people had selected convention delegates, decided to do it by vote of the people in 1972. A number of states moved in other ways to democratize their delegate selection process. But many efforts languished. Reform meant that those in power were charged with spreading their power; thus it would not come about easily. Reform portended credential challenges at the 1972 convention that could make the seating fights of 1968 seem mild. But it also presented a potential challenge to Republicans to begin to examine their own party.

This time of struggle in the Democratic party was emerging as the old New Deal coalition of liberals, labor, minorities and the South was falling apart. By 1968, the South was no longer a part of it. The power of big city bosses was dwindling. Labor had become less responsive to its leadership. Political independence, particularly among the young, was increasing. "The old alignment is no longer valid," said party chairman Lawrence F. O'Brien after the 1968 elections. "The importance of political organizations has been diminished."

And as the importance of political organizations diminished, the potential for grass-roots effort increased. Thus, it was wrong to think that what had begun in 1968 had dissipated. McCarthy might have faded; the movement had not.

Even when these people rose up in 1968, it was not only because of the Vietnam war and Lyndon Johnson. Their concerns went much deeper, to a consideration of the very quality of life in America.

When Eugene McCarthy sauntered into New Hampshire in January, 1968, the nation was in many ways in the most enviable position in Western history. Most of its people could live the life they thought they wanted, get a decent job, a car or two, an education, a house. America had gone through nearly twenty-five years without major calamity—no general war, no depression—yet its people were not particularly happy. A new generation had grown up in the perversely good time and saw acutely that America was not what was taught in the classrooms. So, too, had silent adult Americans come to see this, people like the voter in Berlin, New Hampshire, who told McCarthy's wife, Abigail, early in 1968, "We must get on the track again." And Eugene McCarthy saw it. "It's worse than the Depression," he said at the time:

> That was a limited delusion—it wasn't universal. It was largely economic; it didn't run through the whole fabric. Some of the middle class were undisturbed. This one's horizontal and vertical both, and I think we're questioning more significant values. What you get is the feeling that the country's just loose, somehow.

Loose, somehow. So loose that things were happening over which people seemed to have no control. So loose that truth and honesty seemed to be losing what little meaning they still had. So loose that a whole new institution, a thing vaguely called the military-industrial complex, had since World War II assumed a vast and unwholesome influence in the nation. So loose that America itself threatened to become a tragic farce.

The McCarthy campaign did not change this. It did prompt an unknown number of Americans to begin to examine the meaning of their country with an intensity the nation had never seen. It did help create a new resolve to try to start to get on the track—a resolve that did not diminish after the campaign, a resolve that took on new urgency as a new decade unveiled even greater threats to American life than existed in 1968. On the right were the voices not only of Wallace but also of Agnew and Mitchell, who seemed every bit as bent on a politics of reactionary fear. On the far left were new excesses of violence and terror. The times demanded new exertions of leadership in the land, but there seemed to be none. "If the leadership will not lead, then the followers must lead and that's what we're about," Midge Miller said.

That is why the movement that arose in 1968 remained important. These people had rejected fear and violence. They wanted to operate within the political process to make the system work the way it was meant to work. In 1968 McCarthy had given them voice; certain issues had given them focus. They did not delude themselves that what happened that year could happen the same way again. They knew they might never again have the same unity of structure, but they retained a unity of spirit and purpose that was as strong. Theirs was a coalition of conscience that sought the best for America. If their efforts, however inchoate, meant nothing, then perhaps America meant nothing.

As a *Newsweek* reporter assigned to cover the McCarthy campaign, I discovered, as did most reporters, that it had been an error to cover that campaign the usual way: follow the candidates; talk to the established politicians; write the stories; largely ignore the people in the hinterland, except for an occasional feature article. It was known that a large volunteer army had arisen around McCarthy; yet few of us reporters told of it in any depth. Most often we pictured the army as composed almost solely of college students and young people. This was only part of the truth.

To try to correct this, I later went over paths I had missed during the campaign. I wrote and talked to several hundred local McCarthy leaders, people who before had been so many faces at the airport stops and in the cities where the candidate would briefly pause, and I asked them why they had been a part of it. None told more poignantly than Mrs. Frances Morrow, of Bedford, Indiana. She was not an important person as the term is usually thought of in politics. But then none of the most important people in the McCarthy campaign was. Politicians never sought her advice (until after 1968, when she became a recognized force in the politics of her community). She was a thoughtful woman, a member of that group who came to maturity in the 1950's and became known as the Silent Generation, a group very numerous in the McCarthy campaign. A physician's wife and the mother of three young sons, she was a woman who had lived her life without questioning what was going on, until certain things changed her. She became a McCarthy leader in her community, and not just because of Vietnam. Her concerns went much deeper. What she wrote to me was what others like her felt as 1968 came, and as it passed, and it is why the McCarthy movement, in newer manifestations, will affect the American future far more than many can now imagine.

Frances Morrow spoke with honesty and urgency, and in the end she and those like her were the heart of the McCarthy phenomenon. Here, in introduction, is what she said:

Dear Mr. Stout:

Ordinarily I never answer questionnaires, but I am going to make an exception and answer this one and I will tell you why—

I have spent most of my life minding my own business and fending off anyone who showed even a limited interest in my attitudes or affairs. In other words, I regard myself as fairly typical in this respect—and I think this is important because there must be so many like me. I realize now that we must speak up. And I insist that we be listened to. I demand it.

We have become intimidated in this country. We call it modesty when we tremble before the experts. And look what the experts have done for us.

We must stop apologizing for what we don't know—and act upon what we do know.

And what is it that we know? We know that this earth is beautiful and good—and that the generations to come deserve the same crack at life as the generations past—and that in the next few years we are going to decide whether to allow these generations to come into existence.

In the past few years, I have awakened to the terrible realization that we are transferring the wealth and the power to the cinder-makers of this world—I look around and see what has happened in my own little community.

One of the main sources for income here is Crane Naval Base—which gives us proud accounts of the amount of explosives it is producing, and occasional modest reminders of the millions of dollars in payroll it pours into this community. They have even hired a professional public relations man to drop in at the newspapers to give us newsy items about their deer-hunts and their cocktail parties. Their pay scale is such that they make it extremely difficult for owners of small industry here to compete.

They are courted, of course, by the newspaper and by the retail store owners, the service clubs and ladies clubs make wide use of their speakers, and, by and large, I would say that Crane has become one of the dominant economic and social factors of this community.

At a recent dinner party I attended, the commandant of the base was there, and his opening conversation with me dealt with the rightness of our involvement in Vietnam, and by his manner I could tell that this conversational tack was routine with him and that he was accustomed to getting a favorable response. He was a Billy Graham type and had the whole thing tied up somehow with God. He was not prepared for my response. He seemed to become quite agitated.

Now, my point is that the entire military system in this country is being used as a political tool, and we must re-assert that this is a civilian-dominated country. That captain is in my employ, and I do not appreciate knowing that the propaganda he is putting out is financed with money out of my own pocket.

Now, to get back to my original point, when I first tried to seek out people to help me in the McCarthy campaign, a common conversation would go like this, "We must consider how we feel about the war, and if you find that you don't support it then we must give help to the man who has based his campaign upon this opposition." The response would be, "Well, I can't rightly say I like the war, but somebody up there must know more than we do about it, and since they have access to information we don't have, we'll just have to accept their judgment." In other words, it is amazing to me how many people have lost confidence in their own judgment. They are afraid to trust their own reactions.

As I see it, this faith must be restored. And though it pains me to admit it, I think that George Wallace successfully articulated this even better than Gene McCarthy did. Do you remember how many times Wallace said, "Don't trust the experts, *you* know something about life, *trust yourself,*" or words to that effect, and do you recall seeing the look on peoples' faces when he said it? It was *hope,* hope of regaining some measure of control over their own destinies that brought that light to their eyes, and I must say that I found it very touching, much as I disagreed with the candidate himself. But I am saying that people want to be reassured that their opinions and judgments have value.

You wanted to know when I first became politically active, and after some hard thinking I have decided it was long before the McCarthy campaign. The event that influenced me the most and the real turning point was the assassination of John Kennedy. My anguish was so deep and so stunning that the only remedy for the shock was to resolve to do something—to change my life in some way that enabled me to tell myself that this horrible loss was not for nothing.

And so, I reasoned, that since physical memorials are useless and silly, that if hundreds of thousands of people across this country would resolve to speak up about the things that really bothered them, what a memorial that would be, and it would be the kind of thing John Kennedy would have liked.

And so I planted an oak tree in the yard on the day of his funeral, and I resolved that every time I looked at the tree I would remind myself of this promise.

Not long after that a column by George Crane, the Worry Clinic, appeared in the local paper in which disparaging remarks were made about the Negro race and they were referred to in a little anecdote as "Rastus" and "Sambo." I had seen this type of thing before and it had angered me but I had never done anything about it. I went to the telephone and called the publisher of the paper, who happened to be my neighbor, and I sensed the shock at the other end as I told him that I thought this column was a disgrace and that we were entitled to expect better things from his newspaper.

This was my first overt act that set me on the direction that I find myself now. I have been as vocal as I can reasonably be and still be effective in the community since that time. I have overcome the embarrassment I used to feel. I have spoken out frequently since that time on the John Birch Society (which is *very strong* here), also civil rights, and the Vietnam war.

I notice that you ask what I think we accomplished in our state and local organization. What we have done, at least locally, is to change the atmosphere so that dissent, though still very reluctantly acknowledged, is at least accepted. Now I know that our local campaign cannot claim all the credit for this, that the national mood is also changing, but what is the national mood but Bedford many times over?

When I was growing up the nature of this country was different than it is now. What a comfort, what a luxury it was to think, to know, that my country stood for everything that in my childish heart I thought was right.

My children have been robbed of this happy circumstance. They hear me and my husband discuss the foreign policy and domestic developments of the past few years and know that we question it most bitterly. How can it help but affect their thinking? I resent the fact that we have had to raise our children in an atmosphere of alienation from their government, and I wonder what the effect will be.

I am angry because my children are being denied this experience of growing up *believing*. I cannot honestly tell them that I believe myself in what we are doing in Southeast Asia. And I certainly cannot do what many of my friends do; that is, tell their children that it doesn't matter whether we are right or wrong, that patriotism demands that we mindlessly follow commands and do as we are told.

But then I try to take a larger view. Sometimes I think when I was growing up the country was in the last throes of its boisterous youth, innocence was sweet; but with Vietnam we have experienced sin, guilt, responsibility, and the country is developing in the way that a human being develops. Perhaps after this we will be more mature, use better judgment. Our country is not a lusty apple-cheeked boy now, and never will be again.

And that is the reason I am answering you. I want to be counted. I want it to be known that I did not submit willingly.

I want my country to be rededicated to its original principles and purpose, for the good of all mankind, and I want my children to regain that faith and trust which should not have been taken from them, the right to *believe* in their country.

And so, in your book, tell the world that we are here.

—FRANCES J. MORROW

Along the campaign trail, Eugene McCarthy often said 1968 was a year in which involvement of people like Frances Morrow might help keep America from an Orwellian 1984 and that in years to come a citizen might well look back on 1968 and ask himself where he was then and what he did.

Mrs. Morrow was with McCarthy, and although 1968 did not turn out as she had wished, it was, I think, a beginning of something more significant. This is the story of that beginning, of Eugene McCarthy's place in it, and, more important, of the role played by the Frances Morrows of America.

11

The Unmaking of the President, 1968

★

We knocked Johnson off.
No matter what he or anyone else says
different, we knocked him off.

FRANK BUTLER, SOUTH DAKOTA
MCCARTHY FOR PRESIDENT LEADER

2. REBELLION

On a clear Sunday afternoon, Waukesha, Wisconsin, is a Norman Rockwell portrait of the Midwestern College Town: the simple beauty of old, used buildings; a look of what might be contentment on the faces of townfolk; an Up-With-People freshness in the faces of the students at Carroll College, a small Presbyterian school where not much has happened since September 5, 1906, when St. Louis University quarterback Brad Robinson threw the first forward pass in football history—seven years before Knute Rockne of Notre Dame hurled to Gus Dorias—while leading S.L.U. to a 22-20 victory over the Carroll Pioneers. Each year Carroll sends some two hundred graduates into the main stream, all but a few of them white middle-class. Town people live their lives, rising early to man the four large foundries and the other enterprises in town or to get in their cars and shoot out Interstate 94 to jobs in Milwaukee fifteen miles away. As 1968 arrived it was a Brigadoon, as removed as almost any place in America could be from the issues on the minds of many people across the country—race and war; or so it seemed outwardly. There were few Negroes in town, and no one, not even from the college, had felt compelled to picket the Amaron Corporation plant near campus, which made 20- and 40-millimeter shell cases and projectiles for Vietnam.

But something was happening in Waukesha and at Carroll as spring of 1968 approached. Political activity was building with an intensity reminiscent of the 1800's, when Waukesha was a center of abolitionist activity and a citadel of early Republicanism. To portray Waukesha properly at this point in 1968, Norman Rockwell would have had to include a living-room scene of adult Americans discussing how to get rid of their President, or a store-front political headquarters with college students issuing forth with canvassing kits while, inside, others worked telephones or distributed blue and white buttons and bumper stickers heralding a man called Eugene J. McCarthy.

The scene was repeated throughout the country that spring.* Across the street from the Von Castle Theater in Greencastle, Indiana, students from DePauw University, a school with as conservative a history as that of Carroll, worked out of a headquarters under the direction of English Professor Thomas Merrill and student leader John Evans. In Columbus, Ohio, Martin Seltzer, thirty-one, a metallurgist, and his blossoming Franklin County organization were working with history Professor Clayton Roberts and his new Ohio State group. Greg Jergeson, just seventeen, and with no direction from anyone, was drumming up support in Chinook, Montana, and with great success. Dr. James R. Cook, thirty-one, a Springfield, Missouri, physician who never before had found himself compelled to political action, was doing the same in Greene County, but with less success. In Asheville, North Carolina, Mrs. Demaree Bess, seventy, widow of a foreign correspondent, was as active as a woman a third her age, and in Topeka, Kansas, such a woman, Mrs. Karen Schectman, was trying to put together a Topekans-for-McCarthy group. In Erie, Pennsylvania, the name was Ted T. Buczik, fifty-three, a union organizer; in Mount Clemens, Michigan, it was Warren G. Mock, forty-seven, a high-school princi-

---

* Rereading the manuscript after writing it, I found that perhaps I'd mentioned more of the McCarthy people than a reader's patience could stand, and with great reluctance I deleted many of their names. The reader will meet the rest in these pages and may be tempted to skip over them. But to do so will be at the risk of missing what is, I believe, the heart of this story. For the names themselves, not only of the people but also of the places, evoke a cumulative sense of the grass-roots movement, an impression of that various and mystically vital force that the Constitution calls "We the People."

pal; and in the thirteenth precinct of Hermosa Beach, California, it was Ray Banks, forty-nine, executive secretary of a professional association. (Later he would claim persuading perhaps twenty voters in the California primary.) All were working. All were part of the same political movement. Many, if not most, had never been politically active before; but this year they were, and nowhere was this movement more in motion on the crisp Sunday afternoon of March 31 than in Waukesha.

That evening at Carroll College, Eugene McCarthy was to make what had been billed as his last major speech of the Wisconsin primary election campaign. At the same time, 750 miles away in Washington, D.C., President Lyndon B. Johnson was preparing to go before television cameras in the White House to discuss the Vietnam war. No one in Waukesha knew that the President that night would also announce his decision not to run for reelection. So the bustle and excitement had nothing to do with awareness that Waukesha and the college would soon share vicariously in a historic moment due to the presence in town of the man who had given voice to Seltzer and Bess, Schectman and Banks, and many others.

There had been talk in Waukesha, as there had been all over the country, that the President might not run again. On March 25, the Waukesha *Freeman*, a good newspaper that long ago got over its chagrin for playing the Abraham Lincoln assassination on page 2, printed a speculative article by managing editor G. H. Koenig about the possibility that Johnson might drop out. But Koenig felt this possible only at, or shortly before, the national convention in August. On March 28 the *Freeman*, which had never endorsed a Democrat for President, endorsed Eugene J. McCarthy. On the twenty-ninth, in the Carroll version of the national "Choice '68" campus presidential election, McCarthy won, although the Carroll student body was usually as Republican as the Congressman from that district, Representative Glenn Davis. Over that week end, the reports of the hundreds of out-of-state students—mostly from Ann Arbor and Flint, Michigan—who had come to canvass indicated that McCarthy would win heavily in the Democratic primary in Waukesha County and make substantial inroads on Richard M. Nixon among Republicans. Thus excitement was at a peak the afternoon of March 31. No one had dreamed it could ever come this far in conservative Waukesha County.

Until 1967 in this part of America, sentiment against the war and the President, while certainly there, was mostly below the surface, and only a few actively sought to do anything to stimulate it. There was Harriet B. Steel, a respected sixty-eight-year-old retired art teacher and one of about fifteen active members of a small unit of the Women's International League for Peace and Freedom. There was Robert L. Kealy, of nearby Oconomowoc, a former attorney for the U.S. Department of Agriculture in Milwaukee. For some time he had been involved in a chapter of SANE. There was Thomas J. Miglautsch, of nearby Delafield, owner of an advertising business. A Democrat, he had for two years heatedly deplored President Johnson's betrayal of the 1964 Democratic platform. And there were others involved with the Unitarian Fellowship and the Friends. Each in his way worked for peace. One of Miss Steel's ways was to regularly walk over to the *Freeman* office and drop her copy of I. F. Stone's Washington newsletter on Koenig's desk.

In 1967, Miss Steel and many of the others who had been working separately began to get together as the Waukesha County Citizens for Peace in Vietnam. They opened a store-front office and began to distribute literature in shopping centers, to provide a speaker for any group that wanted one, to hold meetings for anyone who would come. There were certain limits to what they would do—limits imposed by their collective sense of what they thought their community would tolerate. It would not tolerate, it was felt, any demonstration at the Amaron plant. (Amaron, after all, was the second largest employer in the area.) For some, it was even going a bit far to allow the young conscientious objector sent by a Friends group to offer draft counseling at their store front. But by mid-1967 they were, in a very small way, becoming radicalized. They joined in the national effort known as Vietnam Summer and went to the police for a permit to hold vigils each Friday evening in a downtown park. The police refused them the location they wanted, a park right in the center of Friday evening traffic. Instead, they were allowed use of a portion of Cutler Park by the library. They were instructed not to come too far forward in the park, but in one of the least blatant examples of civil disobedience not on record, these people gradually did move their vigils into a part of the park where they did not have permission to be, but where motorists could see them, and weekly about twenty of them would gather there for about a half-hour and stand silently in a circle and pray and try to ignore the few motorists who would tell Miss Steel, a slim, gray-haired woman, and the rest, to go to hell. Thus, when on November 30, 1967, Eugene J. McCarthy announced his challenge to President Johnson, the nucleus of an organization was awaiting him or anyone else who would come forth.

Growth occurred rapidly around that nucleus. Robert Hoskins, a young Delafield high-school teacher ousted as Waukesha County Democratic chairman by three votes late in 1967 because of his anti-administration views, joined the group. Carroll religion professor Milo Milanovich, fifty-nine, who in January, 1968, had offered a noncredit course on the "Now Generation" (he had been on sabbatical at Berke-ley at the height of the Free Speech protest), moved on two fronts: he became an early official of a state educators-for-McCarthy com-mittee, and he also tried to start a campus organization. One night he ran into a senior, David Lust, at a campus appearance by Reed Benson, national executive of the John Birch Society, and noticed Lust's wife was wearing a McCarthy button. And so Lust was enlisted. As a sophomore, Lust had tried to revive a Young Democrats group at Carroll, but only six students had showed up for an organizational meeting, compared to four hundred for a similar Young Republican meeting. In early 1968, another young student, David Krings, who like Lust was from Kaukauna, Wisconsin, was having better luck as head of Carroll's Young Democrats, and he joined in the McCarthy effort. At the same time, Don Wolfe, the college publicity director, who also had contact with what there was of the Waukesha County Democratic organization, placed an ad in the paper seeking McCarthy supporters. Through the ad, word of mouth, and chance acquaintances, a Waukesha County McCarthy-for-President Committee, with Miglautsch as chairman, evolved—town and gown, campus and county in the happiest marriage of endeavor that had ever occurred. By March 31, the group numbered almost 250. Also at work were a handful of young full-time coordinators, like Mr. and Mrs. David McLaren, from Yale, sent by the national McCarthy headquarters to help local volunteers coordinate efforts of the throng of out-of-state college canvassers who poured in during the final three week ends before the primary. And that afternoon the town and the college were bustling with preparation.

Don Wolfe, for example, scared up two television sets, one for a pressroom at the rear of Shattuck Auditorium, another for the chaplain's office adjacent so that McCarthy could pause there to watch the President before his own address. David Lust, meanwhile, knuckled down to figuring out just how he would introduce McCarthy that night. He figured he would start with Daniel Webster's reply to Hayne, in which Webster said that when a mariner has been lost at sea in a storm, at the first opportunity he fixes his position, locates his port, and finds where he is. Then Lust jotted down his next line: "Today our nation is beset by a storm of the worst proportions." Bob Hoskins checked final arrangements with local police, who seemed nervous about the whole thing. Others arranged a McCarthy dinner in the main dining room of the College Union Building. The trouble was, no one knew whether McCarthy would be able to be at the dinner. No one knew precisely when or how McCarthy would come to Waukesha, but rooms were ready in the Avalon Motel, and Miglautsch and Hoskins were ready with rented cars to pick him up at the airport, if, as rumored, this is where he would arrive.

While these things were going on, McCarthy was thirty-three miles away in Whitewater, Wisconsin, concluding a campaign appearance at Whitewater State University. Most of the faces in the crowd of 3,500 were young, but there was a notable portion of adults from the community. It was not a special speech, and reporters traveling with McCarthy who had deadlines approaching were beginning to wonder

3. REEVALUATION

How long Lyndon Johnson had considered not running again obviously was not generally known March 31, 1968. Even when Johnson gave his version of how and when he came to his decision, his tragedy was such that many Americans did not believe him. In a television interview with Walter Cronkite, of CBS, on December 27, 1969, Johnson declared he had never wanted to be President in the first place and that in May of 1964 he discussed with his wife whether he would run for a full term. Johnson said he was inclined not to, but Lady Bird, after deep consideration, determined he should and wrote a memo which, according to Johnson, said: "Yes, you've got to run again. But if you do, you've got to do it with the understanding and in the knowledge that three years and three months from the time you take the oath—and that would make it March, 1968—you can say to the people that . . . you're not going to succeed to another term." The day of his nomination at the 1964 Democratic National Convention, Johnson declared in the 1969 interview, he had prepared a statement withdrawing from the race, but again Lady Bird convinced he must not. He said he had spoken at that time with some close friends about his doubts over whether he should be a candidate. But none of this leaked to the press. Every public word and deed of what they might be able to write for their early editions. In retrospect, the only significant statement came during a question and answer period after McCarthy's talk. Perhaps it was simply that it was a very nice day, or perhaps McCarthy had some prescient notion of what the President would do that night, but he remarked offhandedly in answe to a question about what he expected the President's message to co tain: "I don't mean to sound overconfident, but I think the tes between me and Mr. Nixon now." He dismissed Robert F. Ken/ as but "a problem along the way."

Kennedy, at this moment on March 31, 1968, was about to fl' Phoenix, Arizona, to New York City, where an aide was to m with the text of the President's message.

In Washington, D.C., President Johnson stopped by the a of Vice-President Hubert Humphrey, who was about to Mexico City to represent the United States at the signing Johnson told Humphrey what he would say that night ab and also told him of the special ending he might include stunned, urged the President not to retire. He left W really knowing what the President would do.

Lyndon Johnson seemed to reflect only a lust for the power of the presidency.

Perhaps the first public indication he might be considering only a single four-year term occurred during the Selma, Alabama, civil rights march in 1965. He told several reporters then that he looked forward to returning to Texas, perhaps to teach a course in government at the university. In 1965, he spoke to his staff of "how little time" he had and urged even more intense efforts to bring the Great Society to reality. From this, speculation arose that the President might be worried about his health. Not so, he told a visitor. The fact was, he said, he might be but a one-term President, either by choice or because his mandate might run out.

As 1967 neared an end, Johnson's mandate clearly was running out, and faster than he and most of the professional politicians in the land imagined. It was, as John Kenneth Galbraith remarked, "a year when the people are right and the politicians are wrong." Johnson was certainly a politician who was very wrong when he told one interviewer that year: "The movement against the war makes headlines because it is composed of beatniks and so-called 'intellectuals' and newspaper columnists. But the real American, though he hates war, is not prepared to let his country down. Of that I am sure. If you get out among the ordinary people you will find it to be the case."

Tom Miglautsch, Robert Hoskins, Don Wolfe, and others in Waukesha were ordinary. Anita Frenkel, of Lynn, Massachusetts; and Michael C. Reynolds, head of Rockford (Illinois) College's history department; and a lawyer, H. David Blair, of Batesville, Arkansas; and William R. Remington, forty-nine-year-old chemist of Wilmington, Delaware; and Robert R. Wolanske, twenty-seven, a Greenfield, Massachusetts, pharmacist; and Lee Matt Smith, Jr., of El Paso, Texas, were ordinary people. None was a beatnik, an intellectual in the way that the President meant it, or a newspaper columnist. All were part of the movement against the war and ultimately leaders in the McCarthy campaign. Each was a real American. Each hated the war and was not prepared to let his country down. The President's notion of patriotism, however, was something else. He held with the "my nation right or wrong" idea that had crippled so many consciences for so long. Speaking in Los Angeles that June, Johnson had said: "Whatever the prophets may write, no President has ever been turned upon when he was engaged in trying to protect his country and its interest against a foreign foe."

That, of course, was the whole point. People of absolutely no influence felt that their country, rather than being protected from a foreign foe, was illegally and immorally involved in a senseless war. McCarthy happened along, and they were no longer so many voices. Until then it wasn't fully apparent how tragically out of touch with his people President Johnson had become.

Certainly he realized his popularity was on the skids. In August, 1967, after the riots in Detroit and Newark, it reached its lowest ebb. With several close friends and advisers, the President began to discuss the possibility of withdrawing from the 1968 campaign. George C. Christian, the President's press secretary, jotted down these words of the President: "I want to give 14 months notice . . . no man is indispensable . . . we must have unity." The President asked Christian to draft a retirement statement with Texas Governor John Connally, and the emphasis of that draft was national unity. In January, 1968, Johnson almost appended such an annoucement to his State of the Union address. Yet he did not. Obviously the timing would have been wrong, for that night the President was presenting to the Congress outlines of a program he felt was vitally needed. A political bombshell at the same time would have overshadowed this. Other considerations may have been important. The President's popularity as reflected in the polls was undergoing a slight resurrection from the lows of 1967: up ten points to 48 per cent since October, Gallup said. The threat of the McCarthy candidacy seemed at that time minimal, if even that, or so the professionals and expert observers thought. McCarthy was still an aberration, a jouster with windmills, a new kind of Harold Stassen. Reports from New Hampshire had him destined to get about 8 to 12 per cent of the vote in that state's primary, first in the nation, March 12. And reports of McCarthy on the stump across the nation were almost unanimously dreary: he wasn't turning people on. Thus did things appear in mid-January, when the view from the White House was rosier than in a long time. But a few days later, what remained of the roof began to fall in on Lyndon Johnson's presidency.

On January 23, North Korea seized the United States spy ship *Pueblo,* unboxing fresh outrage at Lyndon Johnson from both right and left. Seven days later, the Tet offensive was launched. Saigon and the United States embassy as well as numerous other supposedly secure cities in South Vietnam came under heavy, co-ordinated attack, and all the questions that had been raised in the streets and on the campuses, in the quiet meetings in countless living rooms across the country like those in Waukesha, in statements and letters and debate in the Congress, and finally in the candidacy of Eugene McCarthy—these questions began to be considered with a new urgency in the White House. Were those with most influence on the President regarding Vietnam wrong—men such as Rusk, Rostow, Ambassador Ellsworth Bunker, and General Westmoreland in Saigon? Before Tet broke out they had drawn together elaborate charts and statistics to prove that the huge United States commitment indeed was paying off. If it were paying off, how in the world could the enemy, even considering his heavy losses, mount so great a simultaneous attack on so many cities? The hawks and doves would dispute long after Tet who was really the loser, but it clearly had brought sobering new doubts about the United States Vietnam strategy to men close to the President. As February ended, an intensive review of Vietnam policy was launched inside the administration.

In this atmosphere resounded the results from New Hampshire and of Robert Kennedy's reassessment of whether he would run for President; they exposed the depth of dissent and Johnson's political vulnerability. Moreover, Johnson received in this period a private poll indicating he would likely get no more than 35 per cent of the vote in the Wisconsin primary April 2. Johnson would subsequently insist the political developments of early 1968 had absolutely nothing to do with his March 31 decision, but he would be doubted. For the facts as they were visible in the early spring of 1968 suggested nothing but ill for Lyndon Johnson. The Democratic party was divided; the country was divided; Congress was intractable; the President's honesty was suspect.

As the debate in the administration progressed, a suggestion of a new commitment for 206,000 more troops for Vietnam was rejected and various versions of a bombing halt were put forth. By all indications, however, Johnson seemed ready to escalate again during this period. "From American responsibilities, God willing, we shall never retreat," Johnson defiantly told a Veterans of Foreign Wars gathering in the aftermath of New Hampshire. In a surprise visit to the National Farmers Union meeting March 17 in Minneapolis, Johnson declared: "We will—make no mistake about it—win." (As the President was introduced, television cameras dutifully panned on Mrs. Anton J. Miller, a Chippewa Falls, Wisconsin, McCarthy leader, glowering from a front-row seat, her two McCarthy buttons prominently on display).

White House aides began drafting a new presidential statement on Vietnam to be delivered the night of March 31, and as late as March 28 it carried an unrelenting hard line. Yet various presidential advisers continued to argue strongly for a partial bombing halt, and somehow, sometime in the next days, Lyndon Johnson decided to turn around United States policy in Vietnam.

All through this period, the President did not indicate he would add an ending that would rock the nation more than would his modification of Vietnam strategy. At a press conference on March 29 he flatly denied reports he had made a decision on when he would announce his candidacy for reelection. "I will cross that bridge when I come to it," he said. On Sunday, March 31, the fateful day, only a a handful of men on his staff and the President's immediate family knew his intent, and even they, to the last moment, were not absolutely sure he would go through with it.

At about 6:30 P.M. White House aide James R. Jones and a Signal Corps technician, alone in the President's office, put the withdrawal statement into the Teleprompter the President would use. Just after 9 P.M.—8 P.M. Waukesha time—the President went before the nation.

4. RETIREMENT

"Tonight, I want to speak to you of peace in Vietnam and Southeast Asia."

Across the United States, the people who had rallied to the McCarthy candidacy watched and listened, brought together in a kind of electronic mass meeting by the man whose actions had spurred them to individual action months, in many cases years, before.

". . . No other question so preoccupies our people . . ."

In Concord, New Hampshire, Mrs. David Underwood III, a young mother, sat in her home before her television set. She had had a role in the decision almost two months earlier that student McCarthy canvassers in New Hampshire should not have beards, long hair, or very short skirts.

In Oroville, Washington, Wilbur G. Hallauer, fifty-four, a factory manager and the state McCarthy leader, settled before his set after preparing a political speech he would give later.

Benjamin E. Smith, forty-one, a New Orleans lawyer, and his wife were at the big wooden table in their kitchen having a snack of cheese sandwiches as they listened.

David J. Fries, thirty-eight, a Watertown, Wisconsin, lawyer and local McCarthy leader, usually would not watch Lyndon Johnson on television, so deep was his distase for the leader of his country. This night he did. He felt something special might be said.

In Albuquerque, New Mexico, Rudy A. Ortiz, thirty-five, a life-insurance executive and a Kennedy partisan, watched, and in Warwick, Rhode Island, State Senator Eleanor F. Slater, another Kennedy worker, lay in bed and watched. After the death of Kennedy, both would become state McCarthy leaders.

In Honolulu, Allen Trubitt, thirty-seven, a music professor and McCarthy leader there, listened. In Alaska, Wendell Kay, fifty-five, an Anchorage lawyer and McCarthy leader in the state, listened.

Robert Kennedy was flying to New York.

Hubert Humphrey was in the United States embassy in Mexico City, glued to a short-wave radio.

McCarthy was arriving at Shattuck Auditorium in Waukesha. Without comment he eased through a knot of reporters demanding reaction to Johnson's Vietnam announcement (the contents of the speech, without the withdrawal statement, were already in newspaper offices across the country), up some stairs to the office of College Chaplain Robert E. Buzza, where one of Don Wolfe's television sets waited on Buzza's desk. The door closed behind McCarthy and Buzza. Outside only muffled words of the President could be heard over the commotion in the corridor and the din of the capacity crowd of 1,400 waiting in the auditorium. The gymnasium and another hall were also filled.

"*. . . We are prepared to move immediately toward peace through negotiations.*

"*So tonight, in the hope that this action will lead to early talks, I am taking the first step to de-escalate the conflict. . . .*"

In Washington, Jack Valenti, former White House aide who became famous for his assertion that he slept better each night knowing Lyndon Johnson was his President, watched quietly. He had been with the President until shortly before the address.

In San Francisco, Ann Alanson, California Democratic National Committeewoman, received a call from California committeeman Gene Wyman telling her Lyndon Johnson would not run again, or so the caller from the White House had just told him. A few hours later she would become the first major California political figure to announce her support of McCarthy.

"... *Tonight, I have ordered our aircraft and naval vessels to make no attacks on North Vietnam, except in the area north of the Demilitarized Zone....*"

Donald Peterson, leader of the Wisconsin Dump Johnson movement and in everyday life a pizza wholesaler, reclined on a couch in his Eau Claire home, fighting to stay awake. The campaign had exhausted him.

In the office of the President, assistant press secretary Tom Johnson stood listening to Lyndon Johnson's words. The young assistant glanced at the President's signing table behind the desk where the President spoke. The table was bare. Tom Johnson could not remember ever seeing that table without something on it waiting to be signed.

Speaker John McCormack of the House of Representatives answered his phone. It was the White House, notifying him to be sure to watch the end of the speech.

"... *Now, as in the past, the United States is ready to send its representatives to any forum at any time, to discuss the means of bringing this ugly war to an end....*"

On the auditorium stage at Carroll, David Lust polished his introduction: "... We are in need of courage. The courage to disagree when necessary in an effort to find the honest answers.... The man I am about to introduce is indeed one of the very courageous. When all others were silent, he was the man who stepped forth and asked the crucial questions. He was the man who sought the honest answers...."

McCarthy did not stay in Buzza's office to hear the President complete his address. He came down an aisle of the auditorium amid the cheering and the chant of that time: "We want Gene, we want Gene!" The applause was long and warm. On the stage, Richard Lee, a guest of honor, clapped heartily. He had been among the first contingent of soldiers shipped to Vietnam in July, 1965, after Lyn-

don Johnson escalated the war. Now he was home in Waukesha working for McCarthy during spring break from Far Eastern graduate
studies at Columbia.

There is little to say about McCarthy's speech. The prepared text
dealt with education, but McCarthy, who followed a prepared text
infrequently, discarded that. Instead, he went through one of his
standard talks that traced reasons for the heavy involvement of
students and the rest of the academic community in his campaign.
And, as he had done even more often, he traced how justification
for United States involvement in Vietnam escalated seemingly as a
product of military escalation until the administration was giving
as its reason for being there just what Lyndon Johnson was saying
over television at about the same time:

"... Throughout this entire, long period, I have been sustained by
a single principle: that what we are doing now, in Vietnam, is vital
not only to the security of Southeast Asia, but it is vital to the
security of every American. ..."

As McCarthy was bringing his talk to a close in Waukesha, the
President was reaching the point in his talk where he would either
close it with the words, "may God be with you," or move into his
sta ment of withdrawal. He raised his right hand in the direction
of his wife as if to say this is it, and at 9:27 P.M., White House time,
he began:

"Throughout my entire public career I have followed the personal
philosophy that I am a free man, an American, a public servant and
a member of my party, in that order always and only. ..."

Senator Everett Dirksen, who had a text of the speech in front of
him in his Virginia home as the President spoke, looked but could
not find these words or the words that came after.

In the Philadelphia McCarthy headquarters, a young volunteer
looked at the TV set and snarled: "I'm going to get that son-of-a-
bitch if it's the last thing I do."

Milton Schneider, a fifty-eight-year-old plumbing and electrical
supply wholesaler who served as the McCarthy chairman in the
Wisconsin Rapids area, half seriously told his family Johnson was

going to drop out. "To me he sounded a lot like Harry Truman when he announced his decision not to run again in 1952," Schneider said later.

In Waukesha, the applause for McCarthy was dying down, and he was about to take questions from the audience.

At that moment, President Johnson was telling the nation: ". . . *I shall not seek, and I will not accept, the nomination of my party for another term as your President. . . .*"

In Eau Claire, Don Peterson snapped out of a slumber and tried to orient himself.

In Concord, Barbara Underwood raced upstairs and awakened her husband, babbling, "I think I heard the President say he's not running again."

In New Orleans, Ben Smith jumped up from his kitchen table, stuck it in elation, and cheered, "We did it; we did it!"

"You did it; you did it!" shouted Ted Warshafsky, Wisconsin vice-chairman, to other campaign workers gathered around a television set in Milwaukee's Sheraton Schroeder Hotel. One young staffer, Barry Satlow, ran out of the room into the corridor singing, "The war is over," as volunteers poured out of other rooms and sang and danced and kissed and hugged.

In New York City, Ellen Perlmutter, a student volunteer who had just returned from a week end of canvassing in Wisconsin, ran down Fifth Avenue crying out the news.

In Oroville, Wilbur Hallauer began revising the speech he would give later.

In the Carroll College auditorium in Waukesha, what seemed a battalion of reporters charged from the television-equipped press-room. Others in the front of the auditorium quickly got the drift of what had happened and all vaulted onto the stage like maddened buffalo, startling the usually placid candidate into one of the few speechless moments of his life. Above the clamor, McCarthy asked for a text. Someone thrust a scribbled version of Johnson's withdrawal statement in front of him; someone else began replaying a tape of the statement. McCarthy said into the microphone: "We have some problem here about what the President said."

"He's not running," shouted a student in the back of the hall. Cheering erupted.

From amid the gaggle of reporters, McCarthy again spoke into the microphone. "This is a surprise to me," he said, as the noise in the auditorium grew. He was finally ushered to a car waiting to take him back to his Milwaukee headquarters. "Where are you going?" a reporter shouted to Paul Gorman, a McCarthy speech writer then serving as a press aide, who had climbed into the car. "To the White House," declared Gorman.

In cities across the land, on campuses, celebrations broke out.

In the University of Chicago Quadrangle, students staged an hour-long celebration, climaxing it by watching *All the King's Men* on television.

In Philadelphia, a mob of students marched down Chestnut Street past McCarthy headquarters carrying American flags and continued to Independence Hall, where a crowd of five thousand sang "The Star Spangled Banner" and chanted, "Thank you, LBJ. . . ."

A small parade gradually grew in size as it wormed out of Harvard Square in Cambridge, Massachusetts, and to the cadence of a snare drum and rattles wound past the Massachusetts Institute of Technology campus, then down Boston's Commonwealth Avenue, and as it reached the Common it numbered a thousand. Those in the front ranks linked arms and shouted, "Peace Now, Peace Now!" and when they reached the State House they sang "God Bless America" and shot off Roman candles. They stayed until rain chased them away.

In Washington, rain fell softly as about a hundred persons gathered outside the White House and sang, "We Have Overcome. . . ."

Even in this moment, many were skeptical of the President's motives. The reaction of Rudy Ortiz in Albuquerque was typical: "I felt he would find a way to change his mind later." There also was sincere feeling for what the President had done. "Truly magnanimous," were Robert Kennedy's words. "I look upon this as a personally sad and difficult moment," said Eugene McCarthy, "for a man who has given so many years to the service of his country."

The White House phones rang into the early hours of Monday, April 1. Friends, colleagues, many persons who had disagreed sharply with the President's policies, felt the need to register their feelings. Abigail McCarthy was among the very first to call. Each caller undoubtedly wondered why, precisely, the President had moved when he did. Despite his later explanations, he could never erase the assessments that arose.

Certainly he was a proud man who did not want to do what, finally, he felt he had to do that night. After the New Hampshire primary, the thought of making the move distressed him even more, aides would say. The entry of Robert Kennedy was an important consideration, they would add. The Tet offensive and the debate in the White House that followed and the decisions that followed that debate were even more important. And to make the new moves toward peace he announced that night he must, as he indicated to the nation, operate free from a political campaign with the certain charges that his moves were inspired by political expediency. Perhaps the overriding consideration—one inseparable from all the others—could be found in one of the phrases George Christian jotted down nearly five months earlier: ". . . we must have unity. . . ." Lyndon Johnson came to see this could never happen so long as he was President.

Certainly the movement that Eugene McCarthy gave focus to could be said to have helped bring the President to this realization. In New Hampshire, it showed once and for all the breadth of opposition to the war and to the President himself. It pushed open the door behind which Robert Kennedy had been standing in uncertainty. Whether he really would have opened it himself had New Hampshire turned out differently will never be known. Thus, in a sense, Frank Butler, of South Dakota, was correct when he said, "We knocked Johnson off." It was neither McCarthy nor Kennedy alone, but the Butlers, the Morrows, the Underwoods, the Bankses, the Petersons, and all the rest.

The President's decision not to run demanded the bigger headlines, though the more important story lay in what he said before.

That night McCarthy assessed it this way: "His announcement that he would not seek reelection has significance, but I think the more important thing is the indication that he has in mind to proceed to try to bring the war to an end . . . and if I have contributed anything, it was probably to bring it to this point somewhat earlier than it would otherwise have come."

But it had finally come. That night Lyndon Johnson had initiated the most significant change in United States policy on Vietnam since Saturday, February 6, 1965.

I I I

The Making of a Movement

★

We are not about to send American boys
nine to ten thousand miles away from home
to do what Asian boys ought
to be doing for themselves.

PRESIDENT LYNDON B. JOHNSON,
AKRON, OHIO, OCTOBER 21, 1964

5. BOMB

At about 2:45 P.M. Saturday, February 6, 1965, a messenger bearing bad news hurried from the Situation Room of the White House to the Cabinet Room and interrupted a conference President Johnson was having with several top security advisers. The message he carried was from General William C. Westmoreland, United States military commander in South Vietnam. It informed the President that Viet Cong guerillas had attacked the United States military advisers' compound at Pleiku in Vietnam's central highlands, and Camp Holloway, a United States helicopter base, four miles away.

In the next seven hours, the character of the Vietnam war changed. The events that would propel Mrs. Frances Morrow, of Bedford, Indiana, into a movement to topple the President of the United States were in motion.

Further dispatches poured in through the afternoon and evening as White House, Pentagon, State Department, and CIA officials gathered at crisis stations. Casualties mounted as the Viet Cong attacked at least three more locations. By 7:30 P.M. the President had in his hands a recommendation from Westmoreland to hit North Vietnam. Fifteen minutes later President Johnson placed the recommendation before a hastily assembled session of the National Security Council.

Pentagon military officers had urged retaliation in the past. Christmas Eve, a bomb exploded at a United States officers billet in downtown Saigon, killing two and wounding sixty-three. October 31, four days before the 1964 presidential election, Viet Cong killed four Americans and destroyed $10 million in war planes at Bien Hoa airfield. Both times the President resisted advice to strike back. This night he did not. At about 9 P.M. he ordered into execution one of the many intricately detailed, limited responses ready for months for such a contingency. In the crowded Pentagon War Room, someone placed a red arrow on a wall map of Vietnam. The arrow pointed at Dong Hoi on the North Vietnam coast, one of the intended targets. Next to the arrow was placed the number of the plan. A teletype order, scrambled through a coding machine, soon began clattering halfway around the world. A short time later Navy A-4 Skyhawks and F-8 Crusaders from the carriers *Coral Sea, Hancock*, and *Ranger*, on station in the South China Sea, were streaking to their targets. The Vietnam war in those moments moved from a sublimited, or guerilla, conflict to the early stages of a Korea-type limited war. It had escalated.

In June, the first Army combat troops landed, and a month later Richard Lee, of Waukesha, would be headed to Bien Hoa, a member of the expanding new colony of American immigrants to South Vietnam. When 1965 began, 23,000 United States "advisers" were in South Vietnam. When it ended, 181,392 troops were there. In between, the United States fought a little war in the Dominican Republic wih a string of tailored justifications that stretched belief. But that war quickly went away. Vietnam wouldn't. It began doing things to America.

6. PROTEST

Protest has been a part of almost every war the nation has fought. Tens of thousands of Tories huffed off to Canada rather than sever their allegiance to the British Crown during the Revolution. Most of New England opposed the War of 1812—to the point of almost seceding. The worst draft riots the nation has experienced wracked New York City during the Civil War. In 1917, six Senators and fifty Congressmen voted against declaring war on Germany. Antiwar Socialist party candidates polled well in the subsequent election. World War II was an exception. The sneak attack on Pearl Harbor produced a united America. But just six months after the Korean war began, a poll showed that two-thirds of the country wanted American troops brought home. Dissent over Vietnam grew apace with the American commitment. It was there before February 6, 1965, but it escalated dramatically with each military escalation thereafter.

The new peace movement's initial growth after President Johnson initiated the bombing came predominantly from the campuses. On April 17, 1965, fifteen thousand students from across the country demonstrated in front of the White House. At Amherst, Defense Secretary McNamara became the first administration official to be walked out on as he gave an address.

A new institution called the Teach-In arose almost overnight.
It began at the University of Michigan with men like Professor
Arnold Kaufman, who three years later would become a McCarthy
leader. A New York activist by the name of Allard K. Lowenstein
also became associated with the Teach-In movement. The people
of this movement, which spread to more than fifty campuses in this
country and more in Canada and abroad, were trying to do what
the administration seemed constrained not to do: let the people
know what was happening. Walter Lippmann wrote October 26,
1965:

> There is only one way that a democratic people can be won over and
> convinced, and that is by enabling this people to hear informed debate
> by its responsible leaders. . . . There has been a radical change of policy
> for the war in Vietnam. It has occurred without serious, thorough, inform-
> ing, and candid discussion and responsible debate in Washington. That
> is why there have been teach-ins. They have been attempts by educated
> but not fully informed teachers to fill the void left by the absence of official
> debate.

But public attention fastened more on the often boisterous protesters in the streets who borrowed civil disobedience tactics from
the waning civil rights crusade and the campus protest movement
spawned in 1964 at Berkeley, California. The week end of October
15–16, 1965, some 100,000 marchers staged the largest demonstrations against the war to that time in dozens of American cities.
Others protested in Canada, London, Dublin, Brussels, Stockholm,
Tokyo.

Though some well-groomed adults could be seen among the
ranks of marchers, more who had begun to feel deeply against the
war held back. The protest had not become "respectable" enough
as yet. Many would not even join a peace group because, as Mrs.
Charlotte Jones, of Keokuk, Iowa, would explain later, "I have a
tendency to be wary of such groups." She would come forth when
the movement entered the realm of traditional politics.

Many who shunned demonstrations began to protest in individual,
unimportant little ways. That year Eric Schnapper, a summer con-

gressional intern, suddenly found himself popping up at a meeting of interns with Hubert H. Humphrey, challenging administration speakers to let more than one side of the war be explained during their discussion session. Schnapper was booed down. (He became the first out-of-state student to appear in New Hampshire in the winter of 1968 to work for McCarthy.) George Marrow, an aging New Hampshire certified public accountant, felt driven to write a letter to Senator George Aiken, Vermont Republican, commending Aiken's criticism of administration actions. That December he organized a public forum on Vietnam in his community. A year later he took to wearing a black tie as a symbol of his opposition. William G. Rice, then seventy-one, a Madison, Wisconsin, lawyer, began denouncing the war before any group that would listen to him—almost from the time the White House released word of the retaliatory air strikes on North Vietnam. Rice and Marrow would be McCarthy delegates at the Democratic National Convention in 1968.

The administration did not see Marrow or Schnapper or Rice, or the others like them in Bedford and Waukesha, in San Mateo, California, and Alfred, New York. The administration focused on the blossoming draft protest movement, the Students for a Democratic Society, and other radical campus groups such as the Maoist-oriented May 2nd Movement as the major elements of dissent. Inevitably, some alleged Communists were found there. An investigation that fall by the Senate Internal Security Subcommittee concluded that "the control of the anti-Vietnam movement has clearly passed from the hands of moderate elements . . . [to those] who are openly sympathetic to the Viet Cong and openly hostile to the United States." Actually, the anti-Vietnam movement was beginning to pass from the radicals to the moderates. Attorney-General Nicholas Katzenbach disclosed an investigation of the antidraft movement with a hint of possible Communist involvement. President Johnson, through an aide, criticized the demonstrators and expressed surprise that "any one citizen would feel toward his country in a way that is not consistent with the national interest and that wrongfully portrays to our adversaries a picture that does not exist with the general public." He did have a point; the Louis Harris poll that fall showed that 66 per cent of the people supported the President's conduct of the war. The motto "My country, right or wrong" still seemed viable. Indeed, the New York City Council proclaimed October 30, 1965, "Support American Viet Nam Effort Day." Some 25,000 persons marched down Fifth Avenue under that banner.

The year 1965 had without question become one of upheaval. Vietnam aggravated dislocations already under way elsewhere.

Following the example of the Berkeley Free Speech movement, students on other campuses began to protest over an assortment of issues. At the same time, the civil rights movement was beginning to crumble. A new type of black leader arose out of the flames of Watts that summer. His tactic was not patience and nonviolent disobedience. He viewed the white liberal not as an ally but as a "honky" whose know-it-all superiority rendered the black man as servile as if still in chains. The following summer—1966—the focus would be on Stokely Carmichael, a young man who screamed "Black Power," and the civil rights movement as it had been known would be dead.

Politicians found themselves stumbling over the new issue of Vietnam. At the Annual Governors Conference held the summer of 1965 in Minneapolis, George Romney, of Michigan, declined to join in a resolution backing President Johnson's support of the war. Accurate information seemed to be lacking, he declared. Then, dramatically, Johnson flew the governors to the White House for a special Vietnam briefing. When he emerged, Romney declared: "Based on the additional information received today, I support the President's action . . . and I urge all Americans to do the same. We have a commitment in South Vietnam . . . We must stop Communist aggression." It was as if he had been brainwashed.

Vice-President Hubert Humphrey seemed bent on unveiling a politics of joy regarding the issue. At a black tie dinner at the governors conference, Humphrey gave a rip-snorting "guns and butter" speech, a phrase just then coming into use. "We face no choice between guns and schools, ammunition and medical care. We face necessities which are within our power to meet," his voice rang out. "We can have both in abundance."

Late in 1965, one more major demonstration occurred—the November 27 March on Washington for Peace in Vietnam. It was a milestone in the development of the force that ultimately rallied to the presidential candidacy of Eugene McCarthy.

At first, it had the earmarks of just another demonstration; certainly better financed than most: more than one full-page ad appeared in the *New York Times*. The list of sponsors was impressive. It included authors Saul Bellow, John Hersey, and Michael Harrington; James Farmer, then national director of CORE; John Lewis, then of the Student Non-Violent Coordinating Committee; and Mrs. Martin Luther King, Jr. There were Norman Thomas, Bayard Rustin, Dr. Benjamin Spock, and Erich Fromm; playwrights William Gibson and Arthur Miller; actors Robert Ryan, Ossie Davis, and Tony Randall; cartoonist Jules Feiffer; and a number of peace group leaders, including Mrs. Dagmar Wilson, of Women Strike for Peace, Dr. Bernard Feld, of the Council for a Livable World, Dr. Dorothy Hutchinson, of the Women's International League for Peace and Freedom, Edward P. Gottlieb, of the War Resisters League, Stewart Meacham, of the American Friends Service Committee, Dana McLean Greeley, of the Unitarian Universalist Association. Three years later many of these would support Eugene McCarthy. A worker behind the scenes for the march, Curtis Gans, then an Americans for Democratic Action staff member, would play an important and little-noticed role in the Dump Johnson movement of 1967 and a major role in the McCarthy campaign. Another figure behind the march, later influential in organizing McCarthy groups in the West, was Jack Gore, an economics professor at the University of Colorado, who was active in SANE and the Teach-In movement. The coordinator of the march was Sanford Gottlieb, of SANE, who was close to the McCarthy campaign, though not a staff member.

Some twenty thousand marchers came to Washington, D.C., that day, from as far away as Washington State, the great majority of them neatly dressed, educated, middle-class Americans. Countless of them, too, would work in the campaign of Eugene McCarthy. Don Peterson and Robert Kealy, of Wisconsin, met on the chartered bus that carried a Wisconsin contingent from Milwaukee, and two years later, in the fall of 1967, when Peterson began organizing a state-wide drive to get Wisconsinites to reject Johnson in the Wisconsin primary, Kealy was one of the first persons Peterson called. "A lot of contacts and acquaintances grew out of that march that were useful later," said Jack Gore. In a sense it was the first meeting of what McCarthy came to call the "government in exile." They met again electronically March 31, 1968.

The day of the November march President Johnson was in Texas, and so Norman Thomas and Sanford Gottlieb and several other march representatives were granted an audience with second- and third-level White House assistants. March organizers, in a studied effort to mantle the march in the most respectable of robes, appointed monitors to deal with disrupters and to make sure only authorized signs were carried. The fourteen approved slogans included: "Stop the Bombings," "Respect 1954 Geneva Accords," "War Erodes the Great Society," "Self-Determination—Vietnam for the Vietnamese." As the marchers filed to the outdoor Sylvan Theater at the foot of the Washington Monument for an afternoon of speeches, the quiet protesters deposited their signs in specially fenced-off enclosures set up for that purpose to prevent unnecessary littering. Their decorum astounded police. Orderliness for this middle-class throng was a way of life, but that day it was also a political tactic. In 1968, the same kind of thing would be called going "Clean for Gene." In both instances, it was the thing to do for the cause.

This subdued gathering of concerned Americans sat on the slope of the Washington Monument as Norman Thomas addressed them, the wind blowing his wisp of white hair and the small American flag he held in one hand. And in a voice like a reed he told them: "I'd rather see America save her soul than her face."

The tone of that quiet protest made one wonder whom J. Edgar

Hoover had been speaking about. That week end the FBI director made public a letter he had written to a Vietnam veteran telling just who was involved in the dissent in this country. Hoover wrote: "The small, but highly vocal minority which is staging these anti-Vietnam demonstrations is, for the most part, composed of halfway citizens who are neither morally, mentally nor emotionally mature."

7. DEBATE

Dr. Benjamin Spock also addressed the demonstrators that November afternoon. He deplored the "virtual absence of debate in Congress" on Vietnam and urged the listeners to begin to work for political candidates "who will refuse to be silenced."

George McGovern had been the first Senator to question United States Vietnam involvement; he did so as far back as 1963. Wayne Morse and Ernest Gruening, Democratic Senators from Oregon and Alaska, had also been speaking out; they had been the only Senators to vote against the Gulf of Tonkin resolution in August, 1964, which President Johnson frequently used to justify subsequent escalations. So, too, had Senators J. W. Fulbright, Frank Church, Gaylord Nelson, and others. In the House, California Democrat George E. Brown, Jr., another speaker at the November protest, had been making antiwar statements. But when the first chance to oppose Vietnam with a vote came in 1965, only seven representatives and three Senators did so.

In May of 1965, both chambers agreed to appropriate a supplemental $700 million for Vietnam, in response to the first of a string of presidential requests for more money for the war. Johnson clearly sought to have the vote read as a mandate for his escalation. He declared: "This is not a routine appropriation. For each member of

Congress who supports this request is also voting to persist in our effort to halt Communist aggression in South Vietnam. Each is saying that the Congress and the President stand united before the world in joint determination that the independence of South Vietnam shall be preserved and Communist attack shall not succeed."

Eugene McCarthy and Robert Kennedy voted for the appropriation.

McCarthy had not come to the point of open opposition, though he was beginning to have doubts about the escalation and the railroading of the Gulf of Tonkin resolution. Kennedy, who as Attorney-General had shared in responsibility for Vietnam policy and once declared that "we are going to win and we are going to stay [in Vietnam] until we win," would begin to speak out in a contrary fashion several months later.

Through 1965 dissent in the Congress was as ill-formed and tentative as anywhere else, but as the year ended it seemed that there had been some effect. On Christmas Eve the President called a thirty-hour bombing pause, and then he extended it into January. On top of that, the administration disclosed that it had dispatched envoys to several countries in a widespread diplomatic effort to open the door to peace talks. By mid-January, however, it became obvious that the peace offensive was not succeeding and the bombing would resume.

In the Congress, this was a period of private discussions among groups of Representatives here, Senators there. In the House, seventy-seven members sent the President a letter urging him to continue the peace effort despite lack of encouraging response. And on January 27, 1966, fifteen Democratic Senators, led by Indiana's Vance Hartke, signed a letter urging the President to continue the bombing halt. Robert Kennedy was tempted, but he declined to sign. He had begun to have questions about the war, but at that time he was wary of an open split with Johnson and not especially unsympathetic with over-all policy. And he regarded the bulk of the peace movement with a disdain approaching that of J. Edgar Hoover.

Kennedy's signature on the letter would have raised it to a higher level of import. Nevertheless, the letter was significant in that it included names of a number of Senators not previously identified as willing to differ with the administration, and one was McCarthy, usually, to that time, considered a sufficiently regular administration man. Thus, on January 27, 1966, McCarthy publicly began his break, if that can be said to have been the word for it then.

That same day he stood up on the Senate floor to explain why he felt the bombing halt should be continued. Some of the phrases and themes McCarthy used would come through repeatedly in 1968. He spoke of "an intellectual judgment" and "moral commitments"; he raised questions about the role of the State and Defense Departments; he saw the discussion of Vietnam as part of a larger examination of America that was needed. He strung this all together with his frequent connectives: "with reference to . . ."; "a kind of . . ."; he used words precisely, carefully. He opened, for example, by saying that the growing discussion in the Senate on Vietnam, "if it cannot properly be described as a debate, is nonetheless a significant discussion with reference to our involvement in Vietnam." He continued:

This is a proper point for the beginning of a much deeper and much more extensive discussion not only of Vietnam, but also of the whole function of America in history during this second half of the 20th Century.

Our commitment in Vietnam is different from our commitment in the Korean War. It is also different from our commitment in World War II, when our objectives were clearly definable. On the basis of that kind of understanding and comprehension and intellectual judgment, we were able to make a quite full moral commitment to the achievement of those objectives.

The Vietnamese situation is quite different. It calls for a national debate, a national discussion, and a real searching of the mind and soul of America. It includes everyone who is concerned about the future of this country and its role. It concerns the people responsible for political action. It involves those responsible for making an intellectual judgment on the extent of our moral commitments.

I am encouraged by the growing response to this challenge throughout America today. We need to be on guard against being caught and committed to certain figures of speech, to a kind of ideological commitment which prevents us from making a fair and continuous and objective judgment. If we find ourselves in the position of trying to prove or disprove a metaphor, our position is little different from that of the historical determinists with reference to communism and any other ideology.

The particular point with reference to bombing North Vietnam comes to this: When the decision was made to begin the bombings, the argument was that it would accomplish two purposes—first, a military purpose, but, more important, a political or a diplomatic achievement.

Bombings have been stopped. The question now is whether they should be resumed. It is my position that the burden of proof is on two branches of the Administration. The burden is on the Defense Department to prove, if it can, that the bombings in the past have had any significant military effect. The burden is also upon the State Department to prove that the bombings have had some kind of beneficial political or diplomatic effect. If the bombings have not had these benefits in the past, then at least it should be demonstrated to us that the resumption of such bombings would have a desirable military or political effect, or both.

It is my judgment that this has not been demonstrated with reference to the bombings in the past; and I have not yet been convinced that the resumption of bombing in North Vietnam would advance the military objectives, or that they would advance our political objectives.

The serious problem today is that we are called upon to make a kind of moral commitment to an objective or to a set of purposes which we do not clearly understand. There is a kind of imbalance between the understanding and the comprehension of the objective on the one hand and, on the other, the moral commitment which we are called upon to make.

I do not believe that a balance between those two can be restored only by Senate debate. This problem requires the attention of mind and spirit, the thoughts and prayers of the entire nation.

This was McCarthy's reasoned judgment at that time. He indirectly questioned the war's morality, but seemed more concerned that the bombing was not working. He did not criticize the President, and in fact pointedly added after his remarks in a brief colloquy with Senators McGovern and Nelson:

I think we should note that the fact that many Senators have spoken out on the side of not resuming the bombing is not necessarily to be interpreted in any way against the Commander in Chief. . . . The President is trying to make a hard decision. By letting him know the position taken by members of the Senate in support of withholding bombing or of resuming bombing, we are being, in my judgment, of service to the President of the United States.

In an interview with a reporter for the Saint Paul *Pioneer-Press* that same day, McCarthy went a step further than urging continuation of the bombing halt. Without being definite, he suggested that the United States accept the Viet Cong as a force in the war. Almost three weeks later Kennedy, in more specific terms, suggested much the same thing, and his remarks were misunderstood and misinterpreted by the press, hawks and doves alike. Kennedy was widely seen as proposing guarantee of a role for the Communists in a coalition government in advance of negotiations. To hawks, it seemed a sellout; to doves, something just short of pull-out. Kennedy was forced to clarify what he thought was clear, and some commentators inevitably interpreted this as backpedaling. McCarthy, meanwhile, was not noticed. The focus was on Kennedy because he was Kennedy. The position was enviable, but also terrifying. No matter what Kennedy said, it would be read as something more.

Segments of the peace movement immediately latched onto Kennedy as a new savior. Soon after he gave his views, the California Democratic Council, having passed a wide-ranging antiwar resolution, greeted his statement with plaudits. Told of the CDC support, Kennedy was unimpressed. Lumping the CDC with the far left, he muttered to a friend: "Those are the people with picket signs and beards, aren't they? They used to picket me."

In the same vein, he had deliberately avoided an alliance with Senator Fulbright, despite urging from liberal friends who wanted him to move to the front of Senate Vietnam dissent. "I'm not their Wayne Morse," he remarked. But he was nevertheless becoming the darling of those people with the picket signs and beards, and more importantly of the people like those who had marched in front of the White House the previous November.

Between the McCarthy comments of January 27, 1966, and the Kennedy statement of February 19, the debate Dr. Spock and others

the illusion that Kennedy seemed to be breaking with the administration. Even the headlines on the vote for another authorization were illusory. They registered the fact of the overwhelming vote in favor of the authorization. The stories largely missed the depth of feeling that was growing in both houses against the war. Clearly, the tenuous consensus in the Congress behind the war was rent; Johnson's relations with some of his congressional leaders were deteriorating; the façade of unity had evaporated; the Democratic party, to the glee of the Republicans, was, if not divided, "badly bruised," in the words of McCarthy.

Out of this milieu, Hubert Humphrey began to stake a new position for himself as administration pitchman supreme, effectively at first. His championing of administration war policy became something of a vehicle to boost him out of the obscurity of his first year as Vice-President. He made an inspection of Vietnam and came back burbling that the "tide of battle . . . has turned for the better." His statements, in public and in briefings with Congressmen, seemed to suggest the American objective had become outright military victory, rather than the objectives stated by Dean Rusk and Maxwell Taylor in the Fulbright hearings: to stop North Vietnamese aggression and bring about negotiations. At a press conference in the White House February 24, 1966, Humphrey declared: "We have a right to have restrained optimism and confidence in the outcome of the struggle. It is fair to say that there is plan of action . . . militarily to thwart the aggression, to defeat the Viet Cong . . ."

In retrospect, the words sounded as empty as they were proven, but at the time, Humphrey was downright persuasive to many who were as yet unsure of what was happening. He seemed hardly able to constrain himself on hearing news of the initial bombing attacks on North Vietnamese oil depots that June, another leg up in the escalation. "The precision and accuracy of our bombing of oil installations in North Vietnam was nothing short of a military miracle— unbelievable," he crowed. This success together with headway he discerned on other fronts amounted to "good news" that "must be spread throughout the land where there are too many doubters."

8. BALLOT

There were indeed doubters in 1966, and as election time neared Humphrey saw them while he campaigned for Democratic congressional candidates. At campus after campus, hecklers greeted Humphrey; but once safely inside, his performance was often compelling, if not convincing, to young listeners.

Watching Robert Kennedy on the stump that year was something else. Squealers and jumpers of all ages, though mostly young, mobbed him at every stop. The polls, both Harris and Gallup, found him the preferred candidate over Lyndon Johnson. Kennedy insisted repeatedly he wouldn't be a candidate for President in 1968 "under any foreseeable circumstances"—words that would come to haunt him.

He touched on Vietnam barely if at all in his campaign speeches, and in fact that issue did not seem to be on the minds of the people who came to see him. They came to see Bobby. As one Iowa woman declared: "I can't hear what he said; but whatever it was, was right."

At the same time here and there across America, individual citizens concerned over Vietnam began inchoate efforts to draft Robert Kennedy for President in 1968. In New Mexico, Robert Harris, of Albuquerque, organized a small draft committee and spread "Kennedy for President 1968" bumper stickers around Bernalillo County.

Harris persisted until he was convinced Kennedy would not run, then became Bernalillo County McCarthy chairman. When Kennedy finally entered the race, Harris, in one of the countless ironies of 1968 that contributed to the Kennedy tragedy, sold his 1966 Kennedy bumper stickers to the new, hastily formed Kennedy organization and used the money to help finance McCarthy operations.

In Bloomington, Indiana, James Dinsmoor, Indiana University psychology professor, who ran unsuccessfully for the Democratic nomination for Congress in Indiana's Seventh District in the 1966 spring primary, talked up a Kennedy candidacy at university teach-ins. But late in 1967, when Kennedy had made clear he would not run, Dinsmoor helped establish the Indiana McCarthy organization, resurrecting the group in Bloomington that had worked in his 1966 campaign. This became the core of the McCarthy organization in the Bloomington area, one of the more successful in McCarthy's losing effort in that state.

It was a year of numerous peace candidacies like Dinsmoor's. In most instances, the remnants of the organizations that backed these candidates rallied to the McCarthy candidacy two years later. Though there were demonstrations in 1966, the emphasis was on political organization in the peace movement—for 1966 initially, but with 1968 in mind.

The race that gained greatest national attention was in Oregon. Howard Morgan, a critic of Vietnam policy, challenged Representative Robert B. Duncan, who supported it while insisting he was not a Johnson man, in the Democratic primary for United States Senator. Morgan, a member of the Federal Power Commission under President John F. Kennedy, received 34.5 per cent of the vote in a three-man race won by Duncan, later defeated in the general election by Republican dove Mark Hatfield. The Morgan vote, however, was an indicator of the deepening antiadministration feeling at that time. In late 1967 and early 1968, Morgan and his campaign manager, Blaine Whipple, helped build the McCarthy Oregon organization. Their initial core of support was drawn from the 1966 campaign.

In Connecticut's Fourth Congressional District, Mrs. Anne Wexler managed the unsuccessful peace campaign for the Democratic nomination of John Fitzgerald, a biophysicist. At the same time, she developed the canvassing and volunteer-organizing techniques used statewide in 1968 to force primaries throughout Connecticut for the McCarthy effort. Mrs. Wexler would also be the prime originator of the effort for party reform that would result in formation of the special Democratic party commission headed by Senator George McGovern in 1969.

In Maine, Delaware, Kentucky, Washington, Hawaii, California, in almost every state, some movement was afoot. And though there were no peace candidate victories that year except for reelection of a handful of dove Congressmen, a loose, grass-roots political structure for 1968 had begun to develop.

At the top levels of the growing antiwar movement, a communications network was developing among people like SANE's Sanford Gottlieb, Jack Gore, of Colorado, and Arnold Kaufman, of Ann Arbor, both alumni of the Teach-In movement, and Allard Lowenstein, who was becoming convinced Lyndon Johnson must be replaced (but in 1966 was thinking in terms of a third party of some kind). Curtis Gans was increasingly involved in antiwar efforts beyond his ADA duties and had moral support from such ADA leaders as Don Edwards and John Kenneth Galbraith. Incidents of minirevolt increased. They meant little in themselves in 1966, but a lot when they were finally added up in 1968. Frederik Pohl, forty-eight, of Red Bank, New Jersey, a writer-editor and a Democratic committeeman in his locale, resigned in disgust over Lyndon Johnson. James Dinsmoor was arrested while picketing Johnson at an appearance in Indianapolis. (He was acquitted.) In Watertown, Wisconsin, David J. Fries, thirty-eight, a lawyer and a long-time Democrat and former Wisconsin ADA chairman, took out a membership in the Socialist party because of his opposition to the war and the administration. New national committees of doctors, lawyers, businessmen, clergy, and laymen in opposition to Vietnam began to flourish. Students used tactics other than demonstrations. Cynthia

Samuels and Abby Erdmann, of Smith, Greg Craig, of Harvard, and
Dave Hawk, of Union Theological, lobbied the Americans for
Democratic Action regarding draft law revision and selective conscientious objection. Ferment was there in 1966. It was building.
People of little importance were beginning to act as the Constitution
tells them is their right. Their numbers would grow significantly in
the next year. Then, all they would need would be a candidate.

9. SEARCH

The candidate most of these people dreamed of was Robert Kennedy. He seemed the only alternative to Lyndon Johnson. Short of that, most antiwar people thought in terms of a third-party effort, perhaps headed by Dr. Martin Luther King, Jr., or Dr. Benjamin Spock. No one was thinking of Eugene McCarthy as 1967 came except for a handful of supporters in New York and Washington, people as anti-Kennedy as they were antiwar. They were part of the dwindling remnant of what was loosely known as the Stevenson crowd, a group whose political victories had been limited for the most part to New York reform battles. They had been supporters of Adlai Stevenson through his two presidential campaigns and in the eleventh-hour attempt in 1960 to gain him the Democratic nomination. Since his death on a London sidewalk July 14, 1965, they had been without a horse. They viewed the man who provided the most stirring moment of the 1960 Democratic convention as their potential new horse. That was Gene McCarthy, who in 1960 had nominated Adlai Stevenson. The thought of Robert Kennedy's picking up the Kennedy standard bothered them. Their anti-Kennedyism sprang from 1960; was intensified by what they considered a shallow Kennedy campaign against Richard Nixon, one that played on a blatantly phony missile gap (though most worked for John F. Kennedy and some received appointments); hardened when Kennedy declined to name Stevenson Secretary of State, then treated him shabbily as United Nations ambassador; was reinforced as they observed Kennedy's handling of foreign policy, which they considered a tired continuation of Dulles.

The negative feeling was reciprocated. Since the 1956 Democratic National Convention, when nominee Stevenson threw the choice of a running mate to the convention in the face of an energetic bid by young John Kennedy, the Kennedys had been able to withstand the Stevenson appeal with absolutely no trouble. When Robert Kennedy was told of the sudden praise showered on him by the California Democratic Council after his February 19, 1966, Vietnam statement, he not only jokingly tossed the CDC off as "those people with picket signs and beards." He thought of them as, essentially, "Adlai's people," and so, for practical purposes, to be discounted. They were never practical. They did not seem to get it through their heads that the name of the game in politics was winning; principles later. Jesse Unruh, not the CDC, was California politics to Kennedy. Decisive action was the proper style, not contemplative hesitation. Words that stirred the emotions were the real words, not the cerebralisms of a Stevenson. The feeling was mutual. Kennedyites and Stevensonians could take each other, with a hard swallow, or leave each other alone.

As the presidential election year of 1968 neared, a handful of the Stevenson crowd determined to try to put into operation a contingency in the event Lyndon Johnson should die in office, or resign, or if, for some other unforeseen reason, there would be a contest for the nomination in 1968. They did not want to be left with the alternative of Robert Kennedy and Robert Kennedy only. And so a quiet dinner was planned March 22, 1967, in the East 79th Street Manhattan apartment of Thomas K. Finletter, New York lawyer, Harry Truman's Secretary of the Air Force, founder of the New York Democratic reform movement with Eleanor Roosevelt and Herbert Lehman. Among those invited were Wall Street lawyers and Stevensonians John Shea and Larry Levine (who was unable to attend), and Russell Hemenway. A handsome former diplomat, Hemenway was director of the National Committee for an Effective Congress (NCEC), which funneled money from the rich people in the Stevenson crowd to liberal candidates for Congress, like McCarthy. The object of the meeting was clearest in Hemenway's and Shea's minds. It was, simply, to try to persuade McCarthy to use the Senate in such a way as to become better known around the country and a bigger voice in the Democratic party, so that, if some opening toward a presidential candidacy should develop, McCarthy would be in a better position to move out front. It had nothing to do with rising clamor over Vietnam. They were prepared to help him financially by agreeing to pay the salary of added staff. They even had a young lawyer tentatively lined up to carry out the mission.

McCarthy doubtlessly was aware what was coming before he sat down to dinner. (Hemenway had been in touch with McCarthy friends in Washington.) As participants later reconstructed the evening, before Hemenway and Shea could make their presentation McCarthy launched into a monologue about Johnson's handling of the Vietnam war. Hemenway recalled: "McCarthy said that night the only way to get Johnson to change would be for someone to run against him, and that he just might do it if no one else would. No matter how much the Senate might do, Lyndon Johnson would not be moved unless someone challenged him electorally. Gene felt that was the only thing he would understand."

The conversation was essentially hypothetical, similar to many McCarthy had through 1967. Perhaps more significant is what didn't happen as a result of the dinner. When Hemenway and Shea suggested their build-up campaign, McCarthy seemed receptive. Later in the evening, they contacted the young lawyer, who agreed to make himself available. But two days later McCarthy told them to lay off. "He was saying, 'Well, maybe the time isn't right; play it by ear; live off the land; let's see what happens,'" recalled Hemenway. These were phrases familiar to Shea and Hemenway. Live off the land. Let's see what happens. They were McCarthy litany. Had he decided to go ahead he would have said, "You take care of it," a phrase some campaign aides would find familiar in 1968. Thus by March of 1967, the horse had been led to water, or, perhaps more exactly, had led itself to water, but had not drunk—yet.

Nevertheless, McCarthy was walking a path that in a few months would converge with countless others, many more than just that narrow path bearing a few Stevensonians. Eventually McCarthy would find himself walking with Mrs. Virginia Rand, of Chicopee, Massachusetts, a nurse and a mother of six, one of them a son in Vietnam, who each Saturday at noon stood with a small group in silent vigil in the center of town, just as Harriet Steel's group did on Friday evenings in Waukesha, Wisconsin, as Joan Chaney's group would do week ends in Tiffin, Ohio. He would walk with Mrs. Robert Jessup, wife of an Indianapolis lawyer; A. B. Conner, sixty-three, a retired personnel executive from Portland, Maine; Sheldon Stark, a young hardware store owner in Port Huron, Michigan, backer of a 1966 peace candidate. There would be the Reverend Lowell Johnson, thirty-eight, a Methodist minister in Seymour, Connecticut, and Dr. David W. Bentley, thirty-two, of Chicago, Illinois, a physician, and Gordon Reed, forty-five, of Strathmore, California, who shunned peace groups, but not political action. There would be Mrs. Owen Wiley, of Spokane, Washington, a long-time regular Democrat, and Dr. Ben I. Heller, fifty-two, of Oklahoma City, Oklahoma, a medical school professor who years earlier had been involved in Democratic-Farmer-Labor politics in Minnesota with Hubert Humphrey. Untold numbers of those who marched in the largest antiwar demonstration yet—on April 15, 1967, in New York and San Francisco—would find McCarthy's path, including many young people who became members of the McCarthy campaign staff: Joshua Leinsdorf, Wendy Anne Robineau, Bill Brewer, Leith Hammond Spieden, John McIlwain, Michael Churchill, Ellen Perlmutter, Dee Knight, Tom DeVries, to name but a few. Some who marched on the Pentagon on October 21 would also come to McCarthy and join his staff: Lance Dublin, Rick Merrill, Sam Ostrow, Thomas W. Farrell, George D. Roberts, to name but a few more.

· · ·

In the months before all of these paths merged in 1967, antiwar activity accelerated. The tactics of the preceding years—all the peaceful demonstrations, the statements and letters, the debate in Congress, draft card burnings, peace vigils—had failed to influence policy. In the search for the right lever, differences over tactics developed. At one end, leaders of some of the demonstrations became more radical in their denunciation of the administration and American society generally. At the other were dissenters who among themselves argued much as McCarthy did in Finletter's apartment: Johnson would have to be attacked at the polls.

Antiwar political activity thus increased. The California Democratic Council adopted a resolution calling for a special convention to determine whether to run a special slate of "peace delegates" in the 1968 California presidential primary—the first action by a major political group concerning the election year to come.

In Michigan, a new political organization called the Michigan Conference of Concerned Democrats formed in opposition to Johnson's war. And Zoltan Ferency became the first state Democratic chairman to denounce Vietnam policy.

In over two hundred communities, including Waukesha, vacationing college students and local citizens undertook a loosely structured organizing effort under the aegis of "Vietnam Summer." Their initial slogan: "Everyone does his own thing." As the project was launched, Dr. Benjamin Spock said prophetically: "We have in this country today a large number—millions—who are disenchanted with the Johnson administration because of the war. This group could well make the difference at the polls." A Harvard divinity student involved in the project, a young man named Sam Brown, said: "We have the potential to translate demonstrations into a strong political force."

Kennedy-in-'68 organizations began to pop up around the nation, and though Kennedy insisted again he had no plans to run, activity continued. It persisted even in the face of Humphrey-like praise of the President by Kennedy. At a New York Democratic fund-raising dinner June 3, Kennedy declared that Johnson had "borne the burdens of the world as few other men have ever borne them" and that the President had

poured out his own strength to renew the strength of the country . . . he has sought consensus but he has never shrunk from controversy . . . gained huge popularity but he has never hesitated to spend it. In 1964 he won the greatest victory of modern times and with our help will do so again in 1968. And with our help he will again have at his side the best vice-president since his predecessor, Hubert H. Humphrey."

Eugene McCarthy, meanwhile, was traveling the country speaking quietly about Vietnam, dissent, and other matters. He was not trying to capture headlines and doing a very good job of not capturing them. And no one speculated about Eugene McCarthy's challenging the President.

In June, a number of antiwar leaders who had been conversing informally through the year met in Washington, D.C., in the conference room of the Friends Committee on National Legislation, and what came to be known as the Dump Johnson movement was born. Those at the meeting included Allard Lowenstein, then thirty-eight, a man who had dedicated his life to a peripatetic pursuit of causes. There was Curtis Gans, thirty, an intense, lean man, almost Rasputin-like in appearance, who would, in a few weeks, begin crisscrossing the country asking Americans disgusted with the war the unheard-of question: "Will you join in an effort to depose the President of the United States?" There were Sanford Gottlieb of SANE; Paul Gorman, a young staff man for a number of liberal Democratic Congressmen; Professors Jack Gore, of Colorado, and Arnold Kaufman, of Michigan, pioneers of the Teach-In movement; Bella Abzug, of Women Strike for Peace; Ed Schwartz, of the National Student Association; and David Hartsough, of the Friends Committee on National Legislation.

At the meeting, they resolved to try to start setting up organizations across the country modeled generally on the Michigan Conference of Concerned Democrats. And Lowenstein offered to try to find a presidential candidate.

Few truly believed Johnson could be dumped as they left their meeting that June. The possibility of fielding slates of peace delegates, as was about to happen in California, seemed more realistic. And, if nothing else, perhaps dissent in the Democratic party might prompt the Republicans to nominate a dovish candidate. If none of these things happened, well, the National Conference for New Politics had planned a fall convention. Maybe a peace party could be started. (But the convention disintegrated in a wild jumble of Black Power rhetoric and white liberal masochism, setting the peace movement back, if anything.)

Within the Americans for Democratic Action, a debate over what stand to take began developing. Rejecting the arguments of those who wanted to refute President Johnson, the ADA executive board adopted a compromise by former chairman Joseph Rauh to push for a peace plank at the 1968 Democratic convention and to back slates of peace delegates where that seemed appropriate. "If the effort can be made on the peace issue alone without any personal overtones of any sort, there are very real possibilities of success," Rauh said at the time.

But the Dump Johnson leaders knew that dislike of Lyndon Johnson would be as potent for them as antiwar sentiment.

On September 1 Gans and Lowenstein launched the official Dump Johnson effort under the name of the National Conference of Concerned Democrats in the living room of Gans's Southeast Washington apartment. At the start it had a telephone answering service, a secretary, two credit cards, Lowenstein and Gans, and very little money. Donald Peterson and Gerald Hill were named cochairmen with Lowenstein. Harold Ickes, Jr., a New York law student and son of President Franklin D. Roosevelt's Secretary of the Interior, also became involved.

In the meantime, a student group called the Alternative Candidate Task Force for 1968, or ACT-68, had been formed after a rousing appearance by Lowenstein at the Twentieth Annual Congress of the organization he once led, the National Student Association. Its purpose: to begin mobilizing students for the 1968 election. Though it never became the organizing force Lowenstein envisioned, a loose network of contacts and Dump Johnson chapters was established, many of them quite spontaneously, by the time of McCarthy's announcement of candidacy. ACT-68's leader was Sam Brown, Harvard divinity student from Council Bluffs, Iowa. He was helped by such other future McCarthy staffers as Clint Deveaux, a one-time University of Buffalo student body president; Stephen Cohen, a former Amherst student president; Marge Sklencar, Mundelein College student president; Cindy Samuels, of Smith; David Hawk, of Union Theological; Sue Hestor, formerly of Wheaton College.

And finally, Lowenstein began a search for a candidate in earnest. Lowenstein had kept his friend Robert Kennedy informed of plans of the antiwar movement and had spoken with him frequently about a potential Kennedy candidacy. "But he would constantly close it out," said Lowenstein. As time passed, Lowenstein bluntly told Kennedy: "I've got to let you know you're destroying everything by hovering. It keeps us from doing anything else."

So Lowenstein went to others. He had no neat list of whom to see in what order after Kennedy. His conversations often occurred by chance. Wherever he went the answer was no, for one reason or another. General James M. Gavin, somewhat naïvely, said he felt he had a better chance with the Republicans. John Kenneth Galbraith, very agreeable to the idea, found he was constitutionally prohibited from running because he had been born in Canada of Canadian parents. Representative Don Edwards, of California, and Senator Frank Church were considered, but nothing resulted. Senator George McGovern felt a challenge of the President might damage his chances for reelection to the Senate in 1968. Senator Lee Metcalf of Montana said no. Eugene McCarthy of Minnesota did not, for he had already been thinking along the same lines. But when they first met, in September, McCarthy told Lowenstein that Bobby Kennedy would be the strongest candidate.

And so it seemed. In New Hampshire, an outspoken lawyer-politician, Eugene Daniell, three-time mayor of Franklin, was pulling together an RFK-68 organization. In Oregon, Charles O. Porter

refused to halt his own Kennedy organizing activity. Calling Johnson a "political zombie," Porter said he would desist only if Kennedy
campaigned for Johnson in New Hampshire. At the end of September, the Citizens for Kennedy claimed chapters in twelve cities and
held a convention in Pittsburgh. But in countless other cities, there
were organizations without any current favorite. All they wanted
was a candidate.

More than any of those Lowenstein had talked to, McCarthy had
seemed to recognize the possibilities of the moment. McCarthy had
not mentioned he previously had been contemplating such a move,
though some of his statements suggested it. For all through 1967 he
had been progressing toward this point.

10. McCARTHY

On February 1, 1967, speaking in Washington to the Clergy and Laymen Concerned About Vietnam, McCarthy began to outline his objections to Vietnam war policy in phrases that would become familiar in 1968. He did not suggest a specific plan to try to end the war or bring negotiations, as Kennedy did a month later. McCarthy's message was educative, not prescriptive; a lecture, not a "major policy address." As he proved later, his style did not change greatly from one kind of audience to another. That February 1 he could have been speaking to the Hog Butchers Concerned About Vietnam, and he would have delivered his message little differently. He said the justice of a war depended on three general considerations: the morality of its purposes and objectives, its methods and means, and the proportion between means and objectives. He reviewed the stated objectives, or justifications, for Vietnam—to protect the United States, to contain China, to oblige treaty commitments, to preserve national honor—and declared: "In every other war we have had the support of what is generally accepted as the decent opinion of mankind. We do not have that today. . . . Certainly our objectives and purposes are not clear, are not precise."

As for the means of this war, such as civilian bombing and the use of napalm, he did not attack them directly (as "Bombing of hamlets and use of napalm is immoral and ought to be stopped"); rather, he said these tactics were "much more difficult to defend" than in past wars.

Whether the proportion between means and ends was moral depended on the meaning and possibility of victory, the cost of victory, and whether there was some assurance "a better world or a better society will emerge in Vietnam following that victory." He said:

The answers should be positive on each of these three counts. I do not believe that the answers are positive and since they are not, we must be prepared to pass a hard and harsh moral judgment on our actions in Vietnam.

We should hesitate to waste our strength—economic, military, and moral —in so highly questionable a course.

When caught in this kind of balance of uncertainty, we should be willing to make mistakes because of an excess of trust, rather than because of an excess of mistrust; because of an excess of generosity, rather than because of an excess of suspicion and narrow self-concern.

We must not do the wrong things for the right reasons, nor succumb to what T. S. Eliot called the ultimate temptation, described by Thomas à Becket as he faced martyrdom: "The last temptation is the greatest treason: to do the right deed for the wrong reason."

There was little there; yet there was a lot. It demanded something of the listener; or did it? There was a delicate line of difference. Reporters, not to mention supporters and detractors, would find themselves tripping over other such delicate lines throughout the McCarthy campaign: the line between arrogance and humility; the line between compassion and demagoguery; the line between substance and shadow. The Clergy and Laymen Concerned got a sneak preview that day.

A month later McCarthy did get a bit prescriptive. Speaking at Edina, Minnesota, he proposed disengagement from an area in Vietnam as a test "to see what happens." He also proposed that the U.S. look "very strongly" at possible other action on its own, with other nations or through the United Nations. He had already urged, in 1966, a "greater willingness" to talk to the National Liberation Front.

He stressed he was not proposing that the United States "cut and run"; only that it ease its efforts to see if the situation could be stabilized. His statements were growing bolder, but what he said was little noticed beyond Minnesota.

In April, when President Johnson called General Westmoreland home to state the administration case for the war publicly and before the Congress, McCarthy considered the move as dangerous an "escalation of language, method and emotions" as escalation of the war itself. He questioned the appropriateness of using "a field commander on active duty to make a case which is not only military, but also political." It was one of McCarthy's early discourses on the President's misuse of the institutions of government, something he would come back to again and again in the campaign.

In May, he discussed the right of dissent. It was, he said,

a kind of removed right. It is a protection to insure us and to encourage us to exercise what is a fundamental human obligation and the duty to speak one's mind; to tell the truth or to state one's best moral judgment whenever the conditions and the demands of the time require it.

Thus dissent was a duty more than a right, and he concluded:

What we are really asking today from the people of this country is heroic virtue and no one really has the right to ask for heroic virtue unless he has done everything to prevent conditions from developing in which that kind of virtue is called upon.

McCarthy did not, at that time, call on his audience to expend "heroic virtue." He himself had not yet done all he could.

During this prepresidential part of 1967, he also discussed domestic problems on occasion. As the worst riots of the year broke out late in the summer of 1967, McCarthy sought to place their cause in perspective in a Senate speech. He said in part:

Riots may be inspired by leaders who view themselves as patriots or by self-seeking men stirring up the people for unscrupulous purposes. But it is clear from history that the leaders—regardless of their personal motives —do not receive a hearing unless there are large numbers of citizens who are frustrated and aggrieved, who have long been oppressed or deprived of decent jobs, homes, and food; people who have been subject not only to serious injustice but also to needless and daily irritations in minor matters; and finally, people who have lost hope in the traditional and ordinary legal means of securing improvements in the conditions of life or work.

The poor, of whatever color, are themselves a minority in the United States today. The indifference of an insensitive majority heightens the frustration of the minority poor.

But Vietnam and the thrust of foreign policy generally were the subject of most of McCarthy's statements as the months progressed.

On August 17, McCarthy walked in disgust from a Senate Foreign Relations Committee hearing where Under Secretary of State Nicholas Katzenbach had just asserted that the speed of events in modern times gave the President the right to make war, if not to declare it, without consulting Congress. Congress was "compelled" to support administration foreign policy, Katzenbach said. "This is the wildest testimony I ever heard," McCarthy told E. W. Kenworthy, of the *New York Times.* "There is no limit to what he says the President can do. There is only one thing to do—take it to the country."

McCarthy had said essentially the same thing over cocktails and dinner at Tom Finletter's in March. Yet even in August he was not thinking especially of himself as the one to "take it to the country," though the thought had certainly occurred to him. Now duty was beginning to hover; someone had to do something. It was Dean Rusk, however, at a press conference on October 12, who jarred McCarthy into accepting that the someone might have to be he. Answering criticism about Vietnam policy, Rusk warned that within the next decade or two there would be a "billion Chinese on the mainland, armed with nuclear weapons, with no certainty about what their attitude toward the rest of Asia will be."

Four days later, McCarthy, in one of his rare Senate speeches, criticized Rusk for obscuring Vietnam debate with his statements. McCarthy said Vietnam "may well be a costly exercise in futility." He declared that the administration was trying to "establish and maintain an anti-Communist bastion in South Vietnam," and he berated Rusk for raising the "ancient fear of the Yellow Peril" in his mention of Chinese with nuclear weapons. "If this is the specter that is haunting Asia, it is difficult to see how we will rid Asia of it even though we achieve an unpredictable and total victory in South Vietnam," he said.

McCarthy was close now. There was the Katzenbach testimony, which, if analyzed, "was nothing short, really, of a kind of prescription for a four-year, we hope, benevolent kind of dictatorship in foreign policy," as McCarthy put it. There were the constant calls for "unity." "Nearly every administration spokesman has called for it: the President, the Secretary of State, the Vice-President—who made a civil rights speech in 1948 where there were those who said we ought to have unity." There was the "erosion of institutions" for which McCarthy held Johnson responsible. "As majority leader, he used his power to destroy the Democratic National Committee . . . to turn the Senate into another House of Representatives . . . the Senate Foreign Affairs Committee into sort of a stock pen." And there was the Yellow Peril, which brought McCarthy to the conclusion that the cause of peace would be better served if Dean Rusk would tender "a quiet resignation."

On October 26, 1967, in Berkeley, McCarthy spoke of these things, but, more important, he said for the first time publicly that the issue of Vietnam ought to be put to a political test within the Democratic party:

We have to be prepared to send instructed delegates to the Democratic National Convention, if one has any power to influence these choices. We should be prepared to support favorite sons who may be committed to a position on Vietnam and on some issues that concern me and the country. And be prepared, I think also, where there are primaries, to support those men who may be willing to carry the flag against the incumbent President of the United States.

When he answered questions after that talk, he did not say *who* should challenge the incumbent President. He seemed to suggest that Robert Kennedy should; he intimated that he himself might have to:

I am not prepared to nominate anybody today, but I think that we have to establish that this responsibility does exist. There come certain times in

politics when the individual, I do not think, really, has the right to antici-
pate how things are going to be better for him in 1972. . . . I am not sure
that Bobby is going to wait until '72. There may be others who will challenge. I really think that really a kind of broader challenge—at least at this
stage of the campaign—is much preferred to a kind of individual challenge
or a grasping of the banner and an effort to rally people around. As I said,
I think everyone in high office in the Democratic Party has to, at least
theoretically, accept that there may be a call that he may have to answer.

This was Robert Kennedy's very feeling, but he had advice.
Advice out of the ears. Certainly Kennedy was hearing the call,
and his every inclination was to answer. But he was a man with
many advisers. He agonized—a word that became a travesty before
it was over—and he hovered. His young, idealistic aides such as
Adam Walinsky, Jeff Greenfield, and Peter Edelman wanted him
to run. Lowenstein dreamed he would. But in the end he listened to
"pros" who had been young idealists when his brother ran for President, and they, for the most part, told him what all the experts were
saying: you can't knock over an incumbent President in your own
party; you'll be ripe for 1972; don't chance lousing yourself up.
Kennedy's political philosophy had been built around the god of
winning. Too many people, including brother Ted, told him he
couldn't win, even though he half felt that that was not what was
most important at that moment in American history. Courage was
important at that moment, and 71 per cent of the public, as polled
by Louis Harris that year, agreed with the statement that Robert
Kennedy was "courageous and unafraid to follow his convictions."

"It is time to act . . . those who do nothing are inviting shame as
well as violence. Those who act boldly are recognizing right as well as
reality." Words in 1963 from the author of *Profiles in Courage*.
Robert Kennedy's time to act came, and passed. He would try to
retrieve this lost moment, but it would never be the same. Only the
ultimate tragedy would be greater than this error in judgment, a
decision he made against all his instincts.

About the time of Dean Rusk's October 12 press conference,
McCarthy began telling people close to him he probably would

become a candidate, and the word was soon known well enough for colleagues to rib him good-naturedly. One day in the Senate dining room, Abraham Ribicoff jokingly asked McCarthy to save him a spot on the ticket. Senator James B. Pearson, a Kansas Republican, stopped at McCarthy's table and asked for a place in the Cabinet. (In the summer of 1968, McCarthy named the kind of men he would like to have in the Cabinet if elected. Pearson was listed as Agriculture Secretary.) On November 2 McCarthy publicly confirmed he might run. At a press conference, he said: "You must take it to the people. . . . When you say who's going to do it, I have to say that I don't know, but I might have to respond myself."

Though many people urged him along the way, no single person can be said to have influenced him ultimately. His decision to run was a private one. His daughter Mary had been suggesting it for months. Didn't he want to be remembered in history for some nobler act than support of Lyndon Johnson's reelection? she would say to her father. Some friends like the Reverend Francis Sayre, Woodrow Wilson's grandson and dean of the National Episcopal Cathedral across Woodley Road from McCarthy's home in Washington, told him he should run. People who didn't know McCarthy personally urged him to run. One week end when McCarthy was in Saint Paul, Donald Peterson and Karl Andresen of Eau Claire, leaders of the Wisconsin Dump Johnson forces, arrived to implore McCarthy to make the challenge. Some McCarthy friends sternly counseled the opposite, pointing out he would hurt either himself or the party and probably both. An aide of Hubert Humphrey suggested that to run might sever McCarthy's pipe line to the White House, and McCarthy noted wryly that if there was one suggestion he had made that Lyndon Johnson had ever accepted he would not run. But the weight of opinion was to run. That was what the several hundred letters a day that came into his office, many containing five or ten dollars, were saying. And that was the message to be drawn from certain seemingly unimportant political activity around the country.

In Michigan, James Harrison, a county chairman and also public relations director for the Democratic State Committee, announced the first McCarthy for President Committee.

On the West Coast, the California Democratic Council adopted a resolution urging McCarthy to run.

In Wisconsin, a campaign urging Democrats to exercise their newly legislated right to vote "No" in the Democratic primary began turning into a "vote McCarthy" drive.

On October 29, seventy-five persons in Salem, Oregon, turned out to hear Lowenstein.

On November 11, Notre Dame Professor James Bogle, Indiana Professor James Dinsmoor, Purdue Professor Robert Toal, the Reverend James Armstrong, the Reverend Harvey Lord, Arthur Fasig, a lawyer, and several others met in the basement of the Merchants National Bank on 38th Street in Indianapolis, heard Lowenstein, and formed a group that would become the state McCarthy organization.

Lowenstein and Gans stepped up their crisscrossing of the country, dropping the yet unofficial word that McCarthy was going to run. The message made their organizing efforts suddenly easier.

Gans stayed about a week ahead of Lowenstein, setting things up. He worked from lists of ADA leaders, SANE members, known peace supporters, persons who had been recorded as speaking out against Johnson. He would arrive with a few phone numbers and lots of dimes and go on from there.

Wisconsin was an example. Gans contacted Wisconsin Democratic chairman Louis Hanson, national committeeman David Carley, and former Lieutenant Governor Patrick J. Lucey, state chairman for John F. Kennedy in 1960. Lucey was sympathetic to an effort to organize a "no vote" campaign against Johnson and encouraged Gans, but was unwilling to play a role himself. (Later he worked in the Robert Kennedy campaign and in the summer of 1968 became an important member of the McCarthy campaign staff.) Carley was also unwilling to take part, though he was against administration war policy. Hanson would have nothing to do with it, though he suggested that Gans talk to Karl Andresen, a University of Wisconsin professor and county Democratic official in Eau Claire. Andresen, Hanson recalled, had been the only delegate to the 1964 Democratic National Convention recently to sign a petition urging a Kennedy-Fulbright ticket. Gans had other phone numbers with him. Since he was in Madison, he got out a phone number Jack Gore, of Colorado, had given him, that of Michael N. Bleicher, thirty-three, a University of Wisconsin math professor and chairman of the Dane County Democratic organization. Gore and Bleicher were acquaintances from the Teach-In movement and had conversed frequently during the summer about what to do about Vietnam. Bleicher had also been discussing the same thing with several other persons, including two university colleagues, Professors Ted Finman and Edgar Feige, and the state ADA chairman, Donald Peterson, who was acquainted with Lowenstein through ADA. When Gans phoned Bleicher, they found they were already on the same wave length. Peterson (who ultimately became state chairman for McCarthy), Bleicher, Feige, Finman, Andresen, and Jack Nikolay, an Abbotsford lawyer and a former county chairman, were suddenly the core of an organization launched officially some weeks later called Wisconsin Concerned Democrats.

Peterson and the others began rounding up persons of similar outlook on Vietnam. Ted M. Warshafsky, a Milwaukee lawyer, had achieved some publicity for urging at a party meeting that Johnson be replaced. Peterson called him. (Warshafsky ultimately became McCarthy's state vice-chairman.) Peterson remembered Robert Kealy, whom he had met on the chartered bus to the November 27, 1965, march on Washington. He called him. The group grew. It soon included Anthony Fisher, chairman of Ozaukee County Democrats at the time; Diana Green, Winnebago County Democratic chairman; and Marilyn Taylor, Outagamie County chairman, who later dropped out. There were Bert Murch, seventy-two, social security pensioner and turkey feeder from Bloomer who had long been active in the Democratic party and was a one-time Progressive party worker; Mrs. Mary Berg, wife of a Sturgeon Bay drugstore owner and an active party worker; Richard K. Darr, an economist at the River Falls state university branch, who later helped found Veterans for McCarthy; R. W. Brandt, of Janesville, an engineer, who stirred from "the apathetic middle class I previously represented" after McCarthy entered the campaign. By the New Hampshire primary, Wisconsin would have a solid organizational skeleton, mostly home-grown, fertilized a bit by Gans's dimes and Lowenstein's salesmanship, cultivated by contact with people like Gore and Gerald Hill of California, finally harvested with the help of Eugene McCarthy and thousands of students.

All over the nation, people like these were reaching the same point as November 30 neared. About thirty states had some degree of organization. If McCarthy had lingering doubts, the political activity, the mail, the turnout wherever he traveled throughout November, should have dispelled them. In Detroit, he was met at the airport by a band of well-wishers carrying posters saying "Peace with McCarthy" and "We Want Gene." Nearly a thousand of the students gathered from across the nation in Boston for the national College Young Democrats meeting, many of them already involved in Dump Johnson efforts and more excited than ever by rumors McCarthy would announce his candidacy that early November week end, greeted McCarthy with the most enthusiastic response yet. Blue and white McCarthy buttons left over from his 1964 Senate race began popping up. In Minnesota, eager young Democrats pasted the word "President" on 1964 "McCarthy for Senator" placards.

The euphoria shielded the fact, which McCarthy knew, that the most he could hope for was perhaps to help bring pressure to change policy; he could not win. Even if he did well in some primaries, Kennedy was sure to jump in and try to pick up all the marbles, friends would tell him. McCarthy would nod in agreement, and they would go their way and he would go his. McCarthy had waited for others to step forward first. He personally informed Kennedy beforehand what he probably would do. William H. Honan related their conversation in the *New York Times Magazine* of December 10, 1968. McCarthy, he wrote, said: "I told him [Kennedy] I was considering entering the primaries myself. I didn't ask him what he was going to do. I just said, 'I'm not worried as to whether I'm a stalking horse for you,' meaning that if Bobby were to enter later on I would not say I'd been tricked. I left it open to him. He didn't give me any encouragement or disencouragement. He just accepted what I'd said."

Kennedy finally said he thought a McCarthy entry would be a "healthy" development. He stepped back from an earlier endorsement of Lyndon Johnson to a position of neutrality, though Kennedy said he expected the nominee to be Johnson, whom Kennedy was then leading in every major poll. "I think I would remain out of it until the time of nomination," he remarked hypothetically late in November. "Perhaps I'll have something further to say."

In Fayetteville, Arkansas, they could not wait for whatever it was Kennedy might say later on. November 29, Mrs. Eloise Jones, wife of a University of Arkansas professor, after scurrying around getting thirty-five cosigners, fired off a telegram to Senator Eugene McCarthy in Washington, D.C., urging him to announce his candidacy. In Fayetteville, they were ready to go.

McCarthy was ready, too. The next day he told the world that he and Eloise Jones were going to tilt a windmill.

IV

An Uncommon Man

★

I count it one of my more desirable pleasures
to say good words—at any time—
about Gene McCarthy. He's one of those
uncommon men who puts his courage
in the service of his country,
and whose eloquence and energy are
at the side of what is right and good.

PRESIDENT LYNDON B. JOHNSON, 1964

11. SAINT JOHN'S

Shortly before 10 A.M. Thursday, November 30, 1967, Eugene McCarthy walked from his office, Suite 411, in the Old Senate Office Building, and headed to the Senate Caucus Room on the floor below to announce to Eloise Jones and the rest of the nation that he would challenge the President. He could have been stepping out to lunch, so casual seemed his stride. He walked with a slight lilt, the result of a bursitis condition in one foot. He wore a gray suit. His hair was gray, his eyes were gray, and his face seemed to have a grayness to it. He was all gray, like some kind of essence, trotting down the stairs now, moving toward the Senate Caucus Room where John Kennedy had announced his candidacy for President, where Estes Kefauver had uncloaked the mob, where another McCarthy in another day had brought disgrace on America. A few more steps now and his path would join that of Eloise Jones and all the rest, a path that began March 29, 1916—Wednesday of the third full week of Lent—in Watkins, Minnesota, which is not much bigger than the White House grounds.

Eugene Joseph McCarthy was the first son and third of four children of Michael John McCarthy and Anna Baden McCarthy, both of whom had been born and reared by immigrant parents in the heavily Irish area of Meeker County, Minnesota; he of Irish descent, she of German. Michael was known as "Mike," and Mike made a good enough life for his family in farming and livestock, though the family was by no means rich; and the cream-colored clapboard two-story home he built in Watkins on a street with no name was a place of comfort, when the winter wind did not blow too hard. Young Eugene's parents and their parents before them had found an openness in this northwest country that the immigrants who settled in the crowded eastern cities did not. Whether Lutheran or Presbyterian or Roman Catholic, Scandinavian or German or Irish, all arrived in Minnesota about the same time and grew hand in hand, not fist to fist—not as in the Irish slums of Boston, where newcomers were reviled, where they found shame of their heritage the safest attitude to achieve America, where the church and its demagogic wearers of the cloth smothered as many as it spurred on. Those who made it to the Midwest, to Minnesota, found America without having to shed their heritage. They brought their cultures and their languages and their churches and their schools and replanted them proudly in the new soil and achieved an independence that was the true wonder of the Melting Pot. In the East, politics became an important vehicle out. It had no exalted place in the Minnesota farm country seventy miles northwest of the Twin Cities where Gene McCarthy was born. No one needed a way out. Life was already in hand, not around some corner or in another neighborhood across the tracks, God be willing. Life was here; do with it what you may. It was a good place to grow up, Watkins.

There were four things important in Eugene McCarthy's early life: baseball, hockey, reading, and school in the basement of Saint Anthony's Church. When he graduated from high school at the age of sixteen it was already assumed he would go on to college, no question about it, even though the Depression had brought some belt tightening to the McCarthy home. "He was the smartest young man in the county," Elmer Werner, a distant relative, would tell strangers after McCarthy had gone off on his challenge of Lyndon Johnson. McCarthy chose Saint John's University, Collegeville,

twenty-five miles due north of Watkins. Saint John's was established
by the Benedictine Monks in 1856 to serve the German immigrants.
The Benedictine Order, or the Black Monks, as they were also called
centuries ago (from the habit they once wore), had traditionally
been short on asceticism, long on humanism, and indulgent of social
ferment, though it had never been identified with a special social
or political program. It placed a premium on individuality and freedom. Its members were noted for their learning and teaching. This,
essentially, was what the sixteen-year-old McCarthy found in Collegeville, and there he began shaping his life. He came under the
influence of Virgil Michel, a founder of the Liturgical Movement,
a social philosopher concerned with the laboring man and migrant
workers. "He knew where it was, you know," McCarthy said many
years later of Michel. Under the influence of Michel and the Benedictines, McCarthy became a progressive Catholic. "McCarthy was
a John XXIII Catholic twenty years before John," a long-time friend
said. His deep religiosity was not generally known when he announced his candidacy for President. It was probably the most
important thing to know about McCarthy.

Just as Watkins was a good place to grow up, Saint John's was
a good place to go to school. It was as open and as free for intellectual inquiry as the countryside was for living. Gene McCarthy
lived the life fully. He was first baseman on the baseball team,
center on the hockey team, clarinetist in the band, on the staff of
the school paper, and at the top of his class with all A's except in
trigonometry. The Saint John's *Record* printed reams of copy about
McCarthy. When he nearly lost his cool in a baseball game, the
Record reported:

> For once in a millennium the even temper of Gene McCarthy was dis-
> turbed. It happened during the St. Cloud baseball game when a St. Cloud
> man bowled Gene over. He hopped up and in a low voice earnestly asked
> the offending party, "What's your name?" The fellow was so affrighted at
> this that he stole a base in his effort to get away from Gene.

June 15, 1935, the Saint John's *Record* waxed laudatory over Mc-
Carthy's academic accomplishments. With a major in English and

minors in economics, education, and philosophy, he had accumulated 363 points in only three years, 243 more than needed for a degree, which McCarthy earned that spring at the age of nineteen.

McCarthy would return to Saint John's five years later. Meanwhile he took a Master of Arts degree at the University of Minnesota, served as principal at high schools in Tintah and Kimball, Minnesota, and taught at Mandan, North Dakota, High School. At Mandan he met a pretty young teacher named Abigail Quigley who had grown up in Wabasha, Minnesota, on the Mississippi River, southeast of Minneapolis–Saint Paul. "He was too handsome to be true. I don't think I ever met anybody who was so unconscious of it," she recalled later.

The engagement of the two attractive young teachers was choice gossip among the students at Mandan. At that time, though, something else also burned in the young man. McCarthy found himself in a dilemma one thinks of happening only in movies: he was the young Catholic torn between the church and a woman, and so he put himself to the test to discover whether his vocation was strong enough to become a monk or a priest. He returned to Saint John's in 1940 to teach economics and education and two years later entered the Benedictine novitiate. He was no longer Eugene J. McCarthy. For nine months he was Frater Conan, a young novice working in the fields at hard labor, studying, meditating, praying, examining his life and the meaning of life, and moving to a decision. The philosophers and saints he had been introduced to as a Saint John's student now became his life: Aquinas, Thomas More, Saint Augustine, Jacques Maritain, Emmanuel Mounier, Charles Péguy, Georges Bernanos. They were important to him then and later, as were others. And he entered into a special relationship with the poets.

Biographies handed out by his Senate and campaign offices never mentioned that McCarthy spent nearly a year as Frater Conan or a summer after that in Saint Francis Seminary, Milwaukee. Yet in that period seeds were planted that developed the moral and philosophic forces that in large measure brought McCarthy to the point of challenging the President. He found no vocation as a Black Monk.

He became instead a kind of Gray Monk in a United States Senator's well-tailored habit. Later, when asked why he found no vocation, McCarthy would say: "Oh, I dunno. It was a mixed sort of case. I was inclined to give it a test. On the other hand, if it didn't really prove out, it doesn't really hurt to spend nine or ten months drawn away from it all."

"I think Gene missed me," Abigail said in 1968. "I did not urge, or even ask him to come out of the monastery, but I think I had something to do with it."

The official biographical sketches next pick up Eugene McCarthy in 1944. He is no longer at Saint John's Abbey. He is now in Washington, D.C., in the Military Intelligence Division of the War Department, a civilian code breaker—he had a small role in helping break the Japanese code—rejected from military service (though he tried three times to get in) because of the unusual bursitis ailment that developed in 1939. (It affected the tilt of his hips and forced him to wear a back brace.) Next it is June, 1945. McCarthy is twenty-nine years old. He has married Abigail Quigley. About seven years have elapsed since they met. A movie would end here. It was only the beginning.

They settled first on a farm near Watkins and began to grow a crop of books and papers and ideas and little else. One idea, to start some sort of spiritual life movement for young people on their farm, died on the vine. Money did not seem to be coming in. Abigail wrote and sold some short stories to national magazines in their early married years. Gene became interested in the consumer-cooperative movement that was flourishing in Minnesota. He felt it could be a tool to attack poverty. He talked to needy farmers about their problems and about co-ops. Talking to needy farmers did not pay well. He taught briefly at Grand Rapids (Minnesota) High. In 1946, returning war veterans swamped the nation's colleges, and the president of Saint Thomas, a small men's college in Saint Paul, persuaded McCarthy to join the staff and teach sociology and economics. Abigail joined the faculty of Saint Catherine's. They lived in a converted basement, then a campus, Navy-type surplus hut, traveling many week ends to their farm. They had full lives. To some degree this helped ease the pain when their first child, a son, was born dead. (They subsequently had four children: Ellen in 1947, Mary Abigail in 1949, Michael Benet in 1951, and Margaret Alice in 1955.)

At that time, the young mayor of Minneapolis, Hubert Humphrey, and a circle of friends were beginning to unveil a dynamic new day in Minnesota politics. They had knitted together the Democratic and the Farmer-Labor parties of Minnesota. In late 1946, though, their efforts appeared to be unraveling. That November, Republicans made mincemeat of the new alliance in general elections that brought significant GOP gains nationally. The GOP took both Twin Cities congressional seats, previously held by Democrats, and a Republican was elected to the United States Senate. The only Farmer-Labor Congressman bolted to the GOP in disgust over the DFL merger. In the DFL itself, a bloc of Communists was becoming troublesome. Politics was the Number 1 topic all over Minnesota. Gene McCarthy, who had never contemplated a career in politics, began to listen. He and some other Saint Thomas professors began to discuss what they might do. Someone suggested they get in touch with Humphrey. "Humphrey urged us to move into the party in Ramsey County [Saint Paul] with as many like-minded friends as we could muster," McCarthy colleague Marshall Smelser wrote in *Harper's* in 1964. The muster was a sneak preview of what happened nationally in 1968 among professors, housewives, students, concerned citizens of all kinds.

The first step was to take control. In 1947 Smelser nominated McCarthy as chairman of the anti-Communist "right wing" caucus of the Ramsey County DFL. Smelser recounted how he did it:

In my spirited nominating speech I hit the Irish Catholic Democrats with McCarthy's still hush-hush career in Army Signals (Patriotism), and harvested the flinty-eyed Farmer-Labor types by offering them "a plain dirt farmer from Watkins, the only candidate who owns a walking plow"

(Populism). We had only one opponent, and a lady nominated him with the peroration, "I haven't got anything against professors, but I think we ought to have a man who works for a living." We drones won handily, and the "right wing" (mostly AFL leaders, professors, and soreheads) were elated.

But a few days later at the county convention, the left wing clobbered the McCarthy group's attempt to take over.

McCarthy had begun his political career with a defeat. It did not set well, and he and his friends launched a series of precinct training sessions to school his supporters in the art of taking over a county DFL meeting. In the spring of 1948, they succeeded. Professor Eugene McCarthy, acting head of Saint Thomas' sociology department, was installed as the new Ramsey County DFL chairman, and almost before he knew it, he had agreed, reluctantly, to run for Congress.

His chances did not look good in 1948. All over the country Democrats were moaning that Harry Truman's sagging popularity portended defeat of other candidates. Some party officials, including Hubert Humphrey, joined in a short-lived effort to dump Truman in favor of General Dwight D. Eisenhower, a heretical thing to do since no loyal party man ever challenged the incumbent President.

At first McCarthy seemed to have no organization. Gradually, an army of professors and students developed. They canvassed the Fourth Congressional District door to door, and McCarthy drove up and down the streets in a 1937 Chevrolet, passing out literature. A Saint Thomas colleague, J. Herman Schauinger, became nominal chief of volunteers, but there never was any real direction. Things just happened. The people took to this tall, handsome man whose black hair fell into youthful, tight curls, this young man who did not shout, a city fellow who owned a walking plow, and they elected him.

McCarthy was reelected to the House four times by wide margins. Of those races, 1952 was the most interesting. It was the year of the Eisenhower landslide. McCarthy polled 61.7 per cent of the vote in his district. His opponent was Roger G. Kennedy, twenty-six, a recent law school graduate. (Active in management of Kennedy's campaign was an attorney named Warren E. Burger, who in 1969 would be named Chief Justice of the United States by President Richard Nixon. McCarthy would be one of three Senators to vote against Burger's confirmation.) Kennedy sought to distort McCarthy's voting record, which was decidedly liberal, and accused him of being soft on Communism. Kennedy thought he had a lot to work with. That year, McCarthy had introduced a bill that would have allowed security risks to be hired for nonsensitive government work. And, despite advice of friends who feared he would hurt himself politically, McCarthy had been the only Democratic Congressman to accept a face-to-face radio debate with Senator Joseph R. McCarthy. Kennedy seemed to be making so much headway that some McCarthy advisers spent $1,100 to produce a pamphlet smearing Kennedy. McCarthy, though, refused to allow its distribution. "It is not worth winning, to have to win in that fashion," McCarthy told one of his aides, religion professor Robert McAfee Brown, who headed a campaign among clergymen as he would nationally for McCarthy in 1968.

12. CONGRESS

The House of Representatives is a burial ground for most of the men and women who make it there. Only a few ever achieve access to the secret levers that operate the House. One of them promised to be McCarthy. Speaker of the House Sam Rayburn took a liking to him. Rayburn found that the young Congressman was no holier-than-thou liberal, and he knew as much about cattle as any Texan. McCarthy had sound political instincts, and you could sit down and reason with him. Rayburn saw that McCarthy soon moved to the House's most powerful committee, Ways and Means, and he introduced McCarthy to a Senator named Lyndon Johnson.

Though indeed a liberal, McCarthy was never overwhelmed by the philosophy. He once said:

In many cases, liberals are really doctrinaire in their way, and issue by issue are inclined to be as doctrinaire as anyone else. I think it would be helpful if the word liberal could somehow be copyrighted and used only under carefully circumscribed conditions. Perhaps its use as a noun should be outlawed so that henceforth no one would be simply a liberal, but would have to be a liberal something. In politics he would be a liberal Democrat or a liberal Republican or a liberal Vegetarian. . . . This, it seems to me, would make things simpler for those who are called liberals as well as for the critics of liberals and liberalism.

McCarthy gradually became something of a leader among liberal House Democrats. He helped organize an alert system to insure that liberals were informed of key votes and to guard against unexpected moves by conservatives. The group of Congressmen known as McCarthy's Marauders was a forerunner of the Democratic Study Group, sounding board for more than a hundred House liberals.

As a congressional representative to a number of international meetings, McCarthy became grounded in foreign affairs. In all ways, McCarthy seemed destined for bigger things, and on February 1, 1958, a month before his forty-second birthday, McCarthy announced his candidacy for the United States Senate despite advice of friends that he was sure to lose to the popular Republican incumbent, Edward Thye.

McCarthy's first hurdle in 1958 was to get the DFL endorsement. A number of party leaders, including Hubert Humphrey, were opposed to a McCarthy candidacy, partly because they feared that a Catholic in a state 60 per cent Lutheran was sure to lose. They favored instead Mrs. Eugenie Anderson, former ambassador to Denmark. McCarthy snatched the endorsement from Mrs. Anderson on the second ballot at the DFL state convention May 25, then trampled former Governor Hjalmar Petersen in the September 9 primary. Political experts, though, still gave McCarthy little chance of winning in November.

What had happened in the Fourth District in 1948 began happening all over Minnesota in 1958. With little direction, organizations sprang up, supplementing DFL units. Abigail McCarthy launched a state-wide Women-for-McCarthy group and, an effective speaker in her own right, took to the platform in out-of-the-way hamlets. When the returns came in, McCarthy defeated Republican incumbent Edward Thye with 52.9 per cent of the vote, thus becoming Minnesota's first elected Catholic United States Senator.

Some political experts viewed McCarthy's victory as a sign that perhaps the country had changed enough that a Catholic could be elected President. Mindful of John Kennedy's desire for the presidency, a McCarthy aide twice sought campaign contributions from

Kennedy, but without success. McCarthy never shared the view that his 1958 election was a barometer for 1960. He knew the historic reality of Minnesota better than the commentators who invariably put Catholicism and politics into the bag labeled Boston or Al Smith. He knew what his grandparents and parents had found: that in Minnesota no one much cared how you prayed. Ecumenism was a home-grown product, like soybeans, and prejudices were few.

13. ADLAI

Of all the bright stars among the new Democratic Senators who were part of what came to be called "The Class of '58," none was viewed by senior liberal Senators to have more promise than Gene McCarthy. He started with an enviable advantage: the high regard of Democratic Senate leader Lyndon Johnson, who immediately assigned McCarthy to two choice committees: Finance and Public Works. He was also named chairman of a special committee on unemployment problems. With McCarthy's Saint Thomas friend Larry Merthan as staff director, the special committee a year later turned out a report with recommendations for alleviating poverty, two-thirds of which were similar to proposals by the National Commission on Civil Disorders, the Kerner Riot Commission, in 1968.

As McCarthy took his seat in the back of the Senate early in 1959, attention was already fixing on the countdown to the 1960 presidential nominating conventions. In writing about the Democrats, reporters found their fingers typing over and over again five names: John F. Kennedy, Stuart Symington, Hubert H. Humphrey, Lyndon B. Johnson, and, always with hesitation and qualification, two-time loser Adlai Stevenson. On July 14, 1959, the fingers were busy with Humphrey, because Eugene McCarthy in Washington, and

Governor Orville Freeman in Saint Paul, that day had held simultaneous press conferences linked by telephone to announce formation of a Humphrey-for-President organization with Freeman and McCarthy serving as cochairmen. Each new political move was already being viewed in terms of Kennedy, who had been working toward 1960 for two years, and so the questions began to take on a Kennedy tinge: Yes, McCarthy conceded, the "pace is undoubtedly being set" by Kennedy; that's one reason Humphrey was launching his campaign out in the open so soon. Yes, Humphrey had " a long way to go." No, said McCarthy, the Humphrey announcement was not an anti-Kennedy move. What about Humphrey's finances; where's he going to get enough money? "I suppose I could be mean and say I know he won't be financed by his father," McCarthy said.

It was a comment in passing, but illustrative of McCarthy's feeling for John Kennedy. To McCarthy, Kennedy was a pleasant enough person, but in no way qualified for the presidency. His convictions did not seem to have much substance to them. Just because he was rich didn't entitle him to be President. And if a Catholic were going to be elected President, why not McCarthy? "I'm more liberal than Humphrey, and more Catholic than Kennedy," McCarthy commented that year. This was an understatement regarding Kennedy. "Kennedy was a Catholic by birth," noted a liberal Catholic bishop who knew both Senators. "He was not a product of the Church, he was the product of a Catholic family. McCarthy, on the other hand, is a root-and-branch radically and completely formed Christian. His has been a gradual deepening of the things he has read and in his personal life of the application of these things."

Kennedy, thus, was the first President who was Roman Catholic, rather than the first Roman Catholic President. Indeed, John Cogley, then religion editor of the *New York Times*, schooled Kennedy on his own religion when it became an issue in the 1960 campaign.

McCarthy's first brush with the Kennedy ambitions came at the 1956 national convention, where McCarthy served as floor manager for Hubert Humphrey's attempt to get the vice-presidential nomination. Kennedy, who showed surprising first-ballot strength, dispatched Ted Sorensen to ask Humphrey's support. Sorensen asked McCarthy to relay the request, but McCarthy cut him off. Estes Kefauver had come in person to plead with Humphrey. Kennedy seemed condescending, and McCarthy didn't like it. Kefauver won what proved to be an empty nomination.

McCarthy's lack of regard for the Kennedys intensified as a result of ruthless tactics against Humphrey in the 1960 West Virginia presidential primary, when the Kennedy camp implied that Humphrey had been a draft dodger in World War II. When he went to Los Angeles in July for the 1960 national convention, McCarthy favored Lyndon Johnson over John Kennedy for the presidential nomination. There was the possibility that if Kennedy could be stopped and Johnson put over, McCarthy might be in line for second spot on the ticket. McCarthy, though, did have reservations about Johnson. "I thought he had the capacity to get as much out of a situation— a Congress—for example, as there was in it, but I doubted his ability to inspire or move the nation on to new or greater achievements," he noted later. McCarthy felt Johnson would make a better prime minister than a President, given the greater restraints on a prime minister in the British parliamentary system. But, given a choice between Kennedy and Johnson, there was no need for McCarthy to flip a coin. "To Gene, Kennedyism is like a chronic disease," a close friend would remark in 1969, after McCarthy voted for Senator Russell Long, of Louisiana, to retain the post of Senate Democratic whip over the successful challenge of Edward M. Kennedy.

Then the Adlai Stevenson boomlet began. Over the summer it had grown, Mrs. Eleanor Roosevelt adamantly refusing to accept Stevenson's equally adamant assertion he would not be a candidate. Under the direction of a young New York television producer, David Garth, results of a nationwide petition drive that acquired a million signatures were dumped on the delegates.

Outside the Los Angeles Sports Arena in July, thousands—mostly students—carrying placards for Stevenson materialized, the result of much planning by the Stevenson group. An intricate plan to pack the galleries with Stevenson supporters went into effect. The display began to move the still reluctant Stevenson. The day the convention began it was rumored Stevenson would nominate Kennedy; by late the next day it was accepted that he was running. The question became who would place his name in nomination.

Minnesota was a natural place to look. Hubert Humphrey, during his brief candidacy in the primaries, had been the choice of the Stevensonians. Now, at the convention, Humphrey had freed the Minnesota delegates of loyalty to him and told them to vote their consciences. The Kennedys moved quickly for the Minnesota support by tapping Governor Orville Freeman to nominate Kennedy. (Freeman's so dumb he thinks he's going to be Vice-President, McCarthy told Humphrey.) Stevenson asked Humphrey to nominate him. Humphrey wavered briefly, then said no. Gene McCarthy quickly said yes. He explained in a *Look* magazine article:

I was aware that the chances of Stevenson's nomination were remote, possibly only if a deadlock developed between Johnson and John F. Kennedy. But it seemed to me that the Democratic Party had the responsibility of providing an opportunity for consideration of this man who had brought such great vision and honor to our party, even though it might turn out to be no more than a tribute.

McCarthy's motives would not go unchallenged. Many politicians felt that he was really trying to help Johnson stop Kennedy. Certainly McCarthy was not blind to the opportunity the situation presented.

McCarthy spoke from a few jotted notes, his baritone voice ringing through the arena and from millions of television sets across the country. The voice and the words commanded silence and attention:

Mr. Chairman [he began], Democratic delegates at this great convention, we now approach the hour of all-important decision. You are the chosen people out of 172 million Americans, the chosen of the Democratic Party, come here to Los Angeles not only to choose a man to lead this Democratic Party in the campaign of this fall and this November, but to choose a man who we hope will lead this country and all of our friends and all of those peoples who look to us for help, who look to us for understanding, who look to us for leadership. . . .

Let me ask you at this time to put aside all of your prejudices, to put aside any kind of unwarranted regional loyalties, to put aside for the time being preferences which are based purely upon questions of personality. Put aside, if you can, early decisions—decisions which were made before all of the candidates were in the race, decisions which were made when the issues were not clear, as they are today.

I say to those of you candidates and spokesmen for candidates who say you are confident of the strength that you have at this convention, who say that you are confident and believe in democracy—let this go to a second ballot.

I say let this go to a second ballot, when every delegate who is here will be as free as he can be free to make a decision.

Let us strike off the fetters of instructed delegations. Let governors say to their people: This is the moment of decision and we want you to make it as free Americans, responsible to your own conscience and to the people of the state that sent you here, and to the people of this country.

This I say is the real test of democracy. Do you have confidence in the people of this convention to make a fair and responsible choice, or do you not have that confidence? . . .

There's demagoguery abroad in the land at all times, and demagoguery, I say to you, takes many forms. There's that which says "Here is wealth and here is material comfort." We suffer a little from that in the United States.

There's demagoguery which promises people power, which is used for improper purposes and ends. And we have seen in this century and in this generation what happens when power is abused.

I say to you there's a subtle kind of demagoguery which erodes the spirit. And this is the demagoguery which has affected this United States in the last eight years. . . .

And I say to you that the time has come to raise again the cry of the ancient prophet, and what did he say? He said, "The prophets prophesy falsely. And the high priests," he said, "rule by their words. And my people love to have it so. But what will be the end thereof?"

I say to you the political prophets have prophesied falsely in these eight years. And the high priests of government have ruled by that false prophecy. And the people seem to have loved it so.

But there was one man—there was one man who did not prophesy falsely, let me remind you. There was one man who said: Let's talk sense to the American people.

What did the scoffers say? The scoffers said: Nonsense. They said: Catastrophic nonsense. But we know it was the essential and the basic and the fundamental truth that he spoke to us.

This was the man who talked sense to the American people. There was one man who said: This is a time for self-examination. This is a time for us to take stock, he said. This is a time to decide where we are and where we're going.

This, he said, is a time for virtue. But what virtues did he say we needed? O, yes, he said, we need the heroic virtues—we always do. We need fortitude; we need courage; we need justice. And everyone cheers when you speak out for those virtues.

But what did he say in addition to that? He said we need the unheroic virtues in America. We need the virtue, he said, of patience. There were those who said we've had too much patience.

We need, he said, the virtue of tolerance. We need the virtue of forbearance. We need the virtue of patient understanding.

This was what the prophet said. This is what he said to the American people. I ask you, did he prophesy falsely? Did he prophesy falsely?

He said, this is a time for greatness for America. He did not say he possessed it. He did not even say he was destined for it. He did say that the heritage of America is one of greatness.

And he described that heritage to us. And he said the promise of America is a promise of greatness. And he said this promise we must fulfill.

This was his call to greatness. This was the call to greatness that was issued in 1952. He did not seek power for himself in 1952. He did not seek power in 1956.

He does not seek it for himself today.

This man knows, as all of us do from history, that power often comes to those who seek it. But history does not prove that power is always well used by those who seek it.

On the contrary, the whole history of Democratic politics is to this end, that power is best exercised by those who are sought out by the people, by those to whom power is given by a free people.

And so I say to you Democrats here assembled: Do not turn away from this man. Do not reject this man. He has fought gallantly. He has fought courageously. He has fought honorably. In 1952 in the great battle. In 1956 he fought bravely. And between those years and since, he has stood off the guerrilla attacks of his enemies and the sniping attacks of those who should have been his friends. Do not reject this man who made us all proud to be called Democrats. Do not reject this man who, his enemies said, spoke above the heads of the people, but they said it only because they didn't want the people to listen. He spoke to the people. He moved their minds and stirred their hearts, and this was what was objected to. Do not leave this prophet without honor in his own party. Do not reject this man.

I submit to you a man who is not the favorite son of any one state. I submit to you the man who is the favorite son of fifty states.

And not only of fifty states but the favorite son of every country in the world in which he is known—of every country in which he is unknown but in which some spark, even though unexpressed, of desire for liberty and freedom still lives.

This favorite son I submit to you: Adlai E. Stevenson of Illinois.

As McCarthy concluded, pandemonium erupted. Stevenson supporters packing the galleries spilled into the aisles. On the convention floor, delegates opposed to Kennedy's nomination snaked among the delegations, snatching state standards and cheering deliriously, "*We Want Stevenson, We Want Stevenson!*" Swept up, Hubert Humphrey marched at the front, tears streaming from his eyes. Balloons poured down from above, and a huge papier-mâché ball bearing the words DRAFT STEVENSON bounded over the crowd. Columnist Joseph Alsop forced a swig of whisky from his pocket flask on McCarthy. Bobby Kennedy rushed to the floor to survey what was happening and quickly saw that the demonstration was confined to an unusually large number in the galleries and to delegates not identified with his brother's cause. He reported to John Kennedy that the noise was a brief aberration. Stevenson knew it as the outpouring continued for twenty-five minutes, ignoring the convention chairman and McCarthy as they pleaded for order.

Then it was over. Ted Sorenson later called McCarthy's speech "cynically brilliant." In it, McCarthy had not only paid tribute to Stevenson; he had provided a valve for the pent-up emotions of his supporters, and he had plunged a velvet stiletto into the Kennedys as he underscored their relentless pursuit of the nomination. "Power is best exercised by those who are sought out. . . ." "Let us strike off the fetters of instructed delegations. . . ."

The Kennedys, especially Robert, would not forget the man who besmirched the nomination for the world to see. "We have never liked Gene McCarthy very much," Robert Kennedy would say to a friend soon after McCarthy announced his candidacy for President. McCarthy did campaign for Kennedy that fall. He made sixty speeches in sixteen states, but his regard for Kennedy remained low. It did not change until near Kennedy's death. "I believe we were coming to a point where we could have been friends," McCarthy would say. They were a long way from that point as the pandemonium of the Stevenson celebration subsided in 1960.

The beneficiary of that moment was McCarthy, and McCarthy alone. Overnight, he became something of a national figure. He became the darling of the Stevensonians. Speaking requests flooded his office. His Senate role, however, took on an ambiguity. The first days of promise after his 1958 election were now behind; yet he remained inevitably in the shadow of Hubert Humphrey who as Democratic whip was *de facto* Democratic leader in the Senate. He settled into his role as junior Senator and for the next three years did little that brought attention.

Only a few things he did stand out in retrospect. There was the landmark unemployment investigation. He also pioneered in efforts to improve living conditions of imported Mexican farm laborers. He pressed in the Senate the lonely crusade he began in 1954 in the House: to provide congressional supervision of the Central Intelligence Agency. And he was proposing limits on gun shipments to foreign nations long before it became a popular cause. He did these things without the fanfare most Senators try to conjure to call attention to their good works. In all these matters, McCarthy was ahead of the times, just as Hubert Humphrey was on civil rights, medicare, the Peace Corps, and the Job Corps. But there seemed no future for McCarthy beyond his place in the Senate. The talk was of dynasty, a succession of Kennedys that would certainly close out any subsidiary role on a national ticket for a second Catholic, particularly McCarthy.

November 22, 1963, changed this.

14. CAROUSEL

Even in the first hours after John Kennedy's death, friends of McCarthy began to talk about McCarthy's chances to be Lyndon Johnson's running mate in 1964. Eventually a campaign for the nomination was mounted. It was much more extensive than McCarthy ever told, which was somewhat ironic in view of his assertion in 1968 that he had no physical need to be President—that he was *willing* to serve, but did not *want* the office. He spent at least $39,000 in the quest, much of it provided by the late philanthropist Stephen Currier, whose admiration of McCarthy dated from the Stevenson nominating speech.

McCarthy clearly had White House encouragement. Lyndon Johnson assigned two aides, Walter Jenkins and Hobart Taylor, to keep in close contact with a circle of McCarthy supporters and advisers who began meeting almost weekly in February, 1964, to plot strategy. Moreover, Lady Bird Johnson let McCarthy know he was her favorite.

At various stages, these McCarthy backers took part in the meetings: Larry Merthan and Jerry Eller, of McCarthy's Senate staff; Jenkins and Taylor and yet another White House representative, James Quigley, Health, Education and Welfare assistant secretary; McCarthy neighbor and real estate developer John Safer; Richard

Ravitch, a young New York real estate developer and son of Sylvia Ravitch, a wealthy New York Stevenson contributor; George Agree and Maurice Rosenblatt, of the National Committee for an Effective Congress; the late John Courtney, House Armed Services Committee counsel and a former Saint Paul politician; Thomas D. Finney, Jr., a Washington lawyer and Stevenson's convention floor leader in 1960; Michael Janeway, young son of economist Eliot Janeway, a McCarthy friend; and Stephen Currier.

The group soon opened a secret headquarters in Southwest Washington in a townhouse donated for the cause. Mayne Miller, at that time executive secretary of the Wyoming Democratic party, was hired at $2,000 a month to begin trying to build a base of support. A Twin Cities newsman, Arthur Michelson, was also hired.

Their hopes rested on several premises: Johnson knew and liked McCarthy. McCarthy had no real enemies in the party, nor was he a specter to the amorphous Establishment. He had qualities Johnson might find useful in a running mate, such as his style, and if it were felt a northern Catholic would help the ticket, McCarthy provided an alternative to Robert Kennedy.

"Of course we were all anti-Bobby," one participant said. "We felt we needed to begin to build an alternative to Kennedy for the post-Johnson days."

What developed amounted to a southern strategy buttressed by northern city bosses, people McCarthy would challenge in 1968. The group felt they could count on Texas Governor John Connally, Louisiana Governor John McKeithen, and Georgia Governor Carl Sanders in the South. The northern strength, they felt, included Brooklyn boss Eugene Keough, a former House colleague of McCarthy, Representative Abe Multer, of New York, Philadelphia boss Frank Smith, and, hopefully, Mayor Richard J. Daley, of Chicago.

But McCarthy began to seem an enigma to the circle who met in Washington. "Gene didn't seem to care as much as the rest of us," one participant recalled. At the luncheon meetings he seemed indifferent, never discouraging the effort but never vocally encouraging it.

In June a special poll by John Kraft showed that Lyndon Johnson didn't need a northern liberal Catholic on his ticket to win, and hopes of the McCarthyites sagged. Even when Johnson ruled out Robert Kennedy and the rest of his Cabinet there was no real cause to rejoice, for it was obvious Hubert Humphrey's own intense campaign for the nomination was having greater success.

Walter Jenkins, nonetheless, continued to insist McCarthy had a chance. With that one encouragement, Mayne Miller set up a secret convention week headquarters ten miles north of Atlantic City at the ocean-front Carousel Motel in Brigantine, New Jersey. Miller told the proprietor he was renting the space for an Indiana group and signed on the motel register the name Marshall Smelser, who was then teaching at Notre Dame.

Almost from his arrival at the convention, McCarthy evinced a growing frustration with the game he felt Lyndon Johnson was playing with him. He was unhappy with arrangements for a "Meet the Press" appearance with Hubert Humphrey. He became annoyed when asked about a newspaper poll showing his odds plummeting. He cut short a publicized family stroll down the Boardwalk when the crowds became too annoying. He lied to reporters regarding his whereabouts to avoid their questions. Jenkins still maintained Lyndon Johnson wanted to keep his options open. But it was discovered that placards for a Humphrey victory celebration were already printed. And if even after that McCarthy had any lingering hopes, they would have been dashed utterly had he overheard Lyndon Johnson talking about him at that time. In his book, *My Brother Lyndon,* Sam Houston Johnson quoted the President as saying of McCarthy: "He's not exactly what I'm looking for. There's something sort of stuck up about Gene. You get the impression that he's got a special pipeline to God and that they talk only Latin to each other."

On August 26, the day Johnson would have made his selection known, McCarthy ended the charade. He wrote a telegram to Lyndon Johnson, sent it about 6:30 A.M., and then had the press informed of its contents. If anyone were to do the rejecting, McCarthy would do it. The telegram read:

The time for your announcement of your choice of your vice presidential running mate is very close. I have, as you know, during this convention and for several weeks not been indifferent to the choice you must make. The action that I have taken has been to this end and to this purpose: That your choice would be a free one and that those whom you might consult, or who might make recommendations to you, might be well informed. The great majority of the delegates here are, as you know, ready to support your choice. It is my opinion the qualifications that you have listed or which you are said to have listed as most desirable in the man who would be vice president with you would be met most admirably by Senator Humphrey. I wish, therefore, to recommend for your primary consideration Senator Hubert H. Humphrey.

McCarthy felt that the wording did not foreclose altogether the possibility Johnson could still select him. "I've not withdrawn; but I've stepped aside," McCarthy remarked later in the day.

When Jerry Eller informed Walter Jenkins of McCarthy's action, Jenkins exploded in anger and demanded that the press not be told. It was too late. The story would soon be on the streets.

"McCarthy and some of us swam in the ocean that morning, sort of to get rid of the frustrations," Larry Merthan recalled. Finally, Johnson phoned. Merthan said the conversation went something like this:

JOHNSON: Hello, Gene, I've got your message.

McCARTHY: I figured you'd get it. I sent it through a reliable source.

JOHNSON: I've followed your advice. I'm picking Hubert. I love you and respect you. Here, Lady Bird wants to speak to you.

LADY BIRD: You were my candidate. I love you. Hope to see a lot of you.

Inexplicably, Johnson put Arthur Goldberg on the phone. Goldberg did not seem to know what to say. Then the conversation ended, and McCarthy returned to the ocean.

Many months later, Jenkins admitted to a McCarthy worker that Johnson had made his choice well before this time. He had merely wanted to inject some suspense in an otherwise dull convention. The scenario would have gone like this: McCarthy and Humphrey would have been ordered to fly to the White House in the afternoon from Atlantic City. Later, Johnson's decision still close to his vest, the three would have flown to Atlantic City together and marched to the podium, and then and there for the first time Johnson would have revealed his choice. "Had he told Gene this is what he wanted to do, he would have gone along with it. He would have seen the humor in the thing. But stringing him on like that was too much," said a participant. When the scenario collapsed, Johnson quickly substituted unsuspecting Senator Thomas J. Dodd, of Connecticut, to fly to the White House with Humphrey, but made his choice known before going to Atlantic City.

Thus, Humphrey was nominated, and McCarthy descended into a bitterness against Johnson that would last. Later in one of his poems he spoke indirectly of how Johnson would seek to domesticate deer on his Texas ranch so they could more easily be shot by visitors he wanted to please. Johnson would then have the heads mounted and given to his visitors, as he did with John Kennedy and Hubert Humphrey. "There was a story," McCarthy told poet Louis Simpson, "that Lyndon had the taxidermist put *his* eyes in the deer heads to watch Kennedy and Humphrey."

McCarthy rejected the eye transplant. Humphrey did not. Had McCarthy's campaign for the nomination succeeded, he most likely would not have played the role he did in 1968. He would have been a different kind of Vice-President than Humphrey, though. "I think I would have been quiet," he said later.

The Atlantic City caper did give McCarthy some publicity helpful to his 1964 Senate campaign, though he didn't need it. That November McCarthy swamped Republican Wheelock Whitney III by the widest margin in Minnesota history: 931,353 to 605,933.

15. ECLIPSE

McCarthy was senior Senator now, but with even less likelihood of going farther than after the 1960 convention. And he seemed to change. Many Senate colleagues thought he began to withdraw in a way different from his usual independence. In fact, Eugene McCarthy became almost as quiet as if he had become Vice-President.

This may have been partly due to two illnesses. In the winter of 1960–1961, McCarthy suffered pneumonia. In 1965, he was stricken with a urinary infection. Prostate surgery was ultimately required. Recovery was prolonged. Part of the verve seemed to drain from him, some friends said. Senate aides felt his work was not unduly hampered. More of a bitterness crept into his wit. He seemed to give less attention to the Senate.

Critics point primarily to the period beginning in 1965 in assessing McCarthy as a not particularly exemplary Senator. His attendance seemed as indifferent as John Kennedy's had been while in the Senate. He was not at the center of any great issues. He began to tire of the Senate as he had of the House.

Liberals who had viewed him with such hope were often dismayed. In 1964, he had cast a vote in favor of maintaining the oil depletion allowance at its then current level. His reason, he said, was that Treasury Secretary Douglas Dillon felt opposition would jeopardize the much-needed tax cut bill, of which a reduction in the depletion allowance was an amendment. Though the vote came early in the year, John Connally was reminded of it when McCarthy became interested in the vice-presidency. Disgruntled liberals overlooked McCarthy's explanation and the fact that in other situations he had opposed the depletion allowance, as he would in the future. (Ironically, McCarthy considered his work on the tax cut one of his most significant senatorial performances.) He was also faulted on his vote against repeal of the poll tax as a condition to voting in the 1965 Voting Rights Act. Again, McCarthy explained, he acted at the behest of a Cabinet official, this time Attorney-General Nicholas Katzenbach, who feared legislative repeal might not be constitutional and preferred to do it by court action, which ultimately succeeded. And he said he acted at the request of the Department of Health, Education, and Welfare in voting to kill an amendment that would require the government to pay the generic rather than the higher trade-name price for drugs purchased for federally aided programs. These votes would be raised against McCarthy in the 1968 campaign by Kennedy backers.

So it was that his liberalism began to offend some stalwarts, despite his nearly 100 per cent performance on civil rights, urban renewal, welfare, and labor matters. In 1967, he voted with his party 49 per cent of the time on straight party line votes, compared to a 61 per cent average for all Democratic Senators. Only Frank Lausche, of Ohio, had a lower per cent among northern Senate Democrats. McCarthy did not respond, obviously, as a knee-jerk liberal, especially on lesser issues. For example, he did not consider federal controls in such areas as labeling and packaging to protect the consumer particularly commendable. Similarly, McCarthy saw no need to do away with the virtually nonfunctioning Subversive Activities Control Board, another favorite target of liberals; or to curtail the practice of federal subsidies for rifle clubs; or to end the age-old tradition of the government's footing the bill for printing the report of the Daughters of the American Revolution, an annual mini-issue among liberals; or to pass regulated utilities' savings to consumers; or to make research discoveries made with federal aid available to the public and not patentable. During his ten years in the House, McCarthy displeased the ADA on only three votes. In the three years before his presidential candidacy, nine of fifteen votes he cast were called antiliberal by the ADA. Some saw sinister motives in his support of measures of potential benefit to mutual funds, particularly in view of the heavy financial support from fund executives during his presidential campaign. He had never seen merit in stringent congressional ethics measures and procedural reforms. Thus it was natural that he was named a member of the Senate Committee on Standards and Procedures, or Ethics Committee, at its creation in 1965. He was recognized as honest; yet he wasn't a crusader for the Senate to launder its dirty linen publicly.

As McCarthy said in 1966: "The judgment passed on politicians should not be a kind of pure and absolute one in which you set up a standard or define a principle and then judge all politicians in a most stringent manner against that particular standard. If you purify the pond, the water lilies die." He thus found one of the Senate's chief purifiers, Senator Clifford Case, New Jersey Republican, someone to ridicule in private. "If they have much more of this ethics thing they'll eliminate everyone but Clifford Case. Can you imagine the Senate with just Clifford Case?"

While Senate colleagues increasingly viewed McCarthy as an enigma, when they bothered to consider him at all, he could still be a dogged fighter. The campaign against the CIA begun in 1954 finally resulted in 1967 in at least a partial victory: three members of the Senate Foreign Relations Committee were added to the group of Appropriations and Armed Services Committee leaders charged with overseeing CIA activities. McCarthy also led a 1967 fight by liberals to abolish the Pentagon's revolving fund for financing arms sales. When a measure particularly interested McCarthy, he would forcefully be there. Otherwise he might not. His schedule of speaking engagements kept him busy, and he needed the $1,000 fees he usually got to finance the costly life of being a Senator. (At the time of his 1968 campaign, McCarthy estimated he had assets worth $30,000.)

But the appeal of that life was rapidly fading. McCarthy commented about this time: "I came to the House in the Truman years when there were six or seven major areas that required legislative action. Now the basic work has been done. You just fight for the administration of the programs. It isn't the same any more."

His withdrawal could not be charted in his social life. He never did enter into the full whirl of Washington society available to a Senator. He preferred evenings with intellectually stimulating friends, such as poets Reed Whittemore or James Dickey, journalists like Gilbert Harrison or Walter Lippmann, progressive clergymen of all faiths. In Minnesota, people didn't seem to mind that McCarthy appeared to have become less active. They had never looked to him for favors in the first place. They loved him for his style. He looked like a Senator and, most important, he seemed to have integrity. "He is our Saint Thomas Aquinas in a dinner jacket," one Minnesotan remarked. Said a Minnesota lawyer: "He's the statesman of the Free World—not the guy who gets a post office for Gonvick."

And so McCarthy drifted through his new term in the Senate, unquestioned at home, something of a curiosity to his Senate colleagues. They considered him brilliant but lazy; dependable when it came to lending his vote to most major liberal causes, but otherwise unpredictable; his opinion was valued, yet sometimes he ridiculed his Senate colleagues: Birch Bayh couldn't be found "in a stubblefield"; Charles Percy was a "Hobbitt—he never leaves a shadow, he never stands between the sun and a wall"; Wayne Morse and William Proxmire hassling in the Senate were "trouble in the leper colony." "It was always fun to listen to one of his monologues," said a friend who eventually cooled on McCarthy. "But you never would know what he would say about you once you left the room." One well-known politician sought out for a major role in the McCarthy presidential campaign refused, saying: "In twenty years in politics, McCarthy has cut up virtually every politician in this country. No matter what you did, there would be enough delegates who just wouldn't have him."* Said Minnesota National Committeewoman Geri Joseph, a Humphrey backer not sympathetic to McCarthy: "He won't let you believe in him." He came by friends only if he liked a person. "You can't embrace him, he embraces you; he makes the determination," said his friend Maurice Rosenblatt. People who would become his friends and remain friends rarely would argue with him. "You start to argue and you're out," said a long-time acquaintance. "He surrounds himself with people who are never going to make him unhappy or say an unkind thing." This trait became very obvious in the 1968 campaign.

Even as doubts about McCarthy grew, he climbed the Senate hierarchy. Eventually he would become a member of the Senate Democratic Steering Committee, and in 1965 he was assigned to the Foreign Relations Committee seat vacated by the new Vice-President, Hubert Humphrey, a committee post McCarthy had long wanted. He had desired a similar committee post in the House, where as often as not he had supported Eisenhower foreign policy (though not on the Mideast), helping, in a very small way, John Foster Dulles compile the record McCarthy would disdain in 1968 as the work of "the dead hand of the past." McCarthy couldn't have sounded more like Dulles when, in *Frontiers in American Democracy*, published in 1960, he wrote: "Our policy must be to assist within possible means the liberation of people who are subject to communist tyranny." His views obviously had modified by 1968, when he produced *Limits of Power;* he wrote that if the book had a personal mark "it is that which I believe Adlai Stevenson would have made on foreign policy." An important ingredient in whatever

---

* McCarthy was somewhat sensitive about this impression of him. He once told me that he could think of only a handful of Senators he had ever criticized, and listed more that he had complimented. "More guys in the Senate have said bad things about me than I have said about them," he said. He was also sensitive about statements by some writers that he had no "close friends." "You guys quote unnamed 'close friends' or 'friends' as saying things about me, then you say I have no close friends," he once complained to me. "Maybe you should use the phrase 'close enemies.' "

change evolved in his views was the Dominican Republic intervention which, McCarthy felt, "called into question some of the basic precepts of our foreign policy." Not many months later, he arrived at the same point about Vietnam, and moved on from there to November 30, 1967.

16. ANNOUNCEMENT

In the days before that Thursday, and in the months that followed, a new game arose in Washington: trying to figure out what made McCarthy run, for, as *Newsweek* columnist Kenneth Crawford put it, "Within the political fraternity, McCarthy's own explanation of what he is up to is too lofty to be credited."

Some felt McCarthy was no more than nursing a smoldering grudge against Johnson for dallying with him in 1964. Others felt he found it satisfying to seize a movement that should have been Robert Kennedy's. Some, who felt he ran for Vice-President in 1964 only to get publicity for his Senate race, believed he was embarking only on a rather esoteric campaign for another Senate reelection in 1970. Yet others felt the candidacy was simply McCarthy's response to his own boredom with the Senate. Run for President; it's an interesting way to spend several months. The Students for a Democratic Society had just as plausible a notion: McCarthy was part of an involved CIA plot to quell campus disorder by luring dissatisfied students from growing radicalism to the lotus blossoms of the existing political process.

Certainly he was concerned about the growing tendency of protestors to use extralegal means to put across their point and said as much, and he hoped his candidacy would in some way counteract this. Indeed, he was bored with the Senate and would not deny that this might have been an indirect consideration. "How do you ever know what all goes into a decision?" he said to me after the campaign. "Maybe boredom did have something to do with it." Certainly his regard for Johnson and Kennedy was low. That he put both in an uncomfortable position by his candidacy was, if anything, a fringe benefit of his decision. Part of his reasoning lay in what had happened to Adlai Stevenson as United Nations ambassador. Said McCarthy: "I was determined not to put myself in a position where I could be expended, or expendable, on somebody else's determination." Frank Wright, of the Minneapolis *Tribune,* had an opinion shared by several who were close to McCarthy: "[He] has a sense of history. He believed this was one of those times when the future demanded more than political consideration—that historians would look back on this Vietnam war as a kind of watershed in the history of this country. People said: he's doing it just to get his name in the history books. That wasn't it at all. I think McCarthy would have deeply wished Bobby Kennedy to do this."

And after the campaign, in one of the rare times he allowed himself to be interviewed about the campaign (he would not, for example, discuss substantive matters with me or with Theodore H. White, or other authors of books on the campaign), McCarthy told a team of Boston *Globe* reporters: "What my intentions were, which I think I knew better than some of the people who are telling what they were, in any case, they didn't know what they were. And if I'm not saying what they were, why nobody knows." McCarthy himself stated very clearly why he was running at his announcement of candidacy, and nothing he said or did throughout the campaign suggested his motives were any greater or less than he stated, no matter that the political fraternity considered them too lofty. It was more a shortcoming of the auditors of his campaign that what he had said long before was not examined more thoroughly for a key, however imperfect, to trying to explain McCarthy. In *Frontiers in American Democracy* (1960), McCarthy as much as outlined why he would have to act as he did in 1968. He wrote:

It is generally accepted that there are two conditions under which obedience to the government may be withheld. First, in the event that the state has extended its authority into fields of life which do not properly belong to it; if, for example, it usurps the authority of the family, or religion, or if it trespasses on areas reserved for the individual and personal decision and choice; and second, when the government, acting in its proper sphere, orders actions which would be either an unjust war or an unnecessary one.

The thought was not original. He had cribbed from Socrates, Saint Augustine, and Saint Thomas More, among others. What was important was that he considered their lessons directly relevant to American politics. And when such a condition arose, one was obliged to speak up—the duty of dissent, not just the right of it, as he defined it in the spring of 1967.

McCarthy's long-time legislative assistant, Emerson Hynes, a quiet, pipe-smoking man approaching his sixties, who, like McCarthy and Jerry Eller, was a Saint John's product, knew the dominant strains in McCarthy's thinking better than anyone else. One predominant theme, he said, was "personalism," a regard for the dignity of each individual which, sliced in slightly different ways, might be called humanism, existentialism, populism. Whatever the label, what McCarthy felt was particularly apt to the nation in 1967 and 1968 and beyond. It had meaning to those who saw themselves losing control of their own lives, whether by arbitrary government action or by burgeoning technology. McCarthy would speak of this in one of his first speeches after the assassination of Robert Kennedy:

Technical progress threatens to become the source of values and thus does away with the norms which man had believed in for thousands of years: that one *ought* to do what is true, beautiful and conducive to the unfolding of man's soul. . . .

America stands today at a critical point of decision: it can go in the direction of continued war and violence and further bureaucratization and automation of man, or it can go in the direction of personalism and reason and spiritual renewal.

McCarthy's thought, said Hynes, was also influenced by a deep feeling that the individual has a higher duty to man or God. The obligation to act in given situations follows from this, but not precipitous action; rather, through "right reason" gradually, particularly when authority is to be challenged. It was not the approach of the revolutionary or the crusader, for McCarthy was neither. McCarthy touched on this slightly in discussing the Christian politician in *Frontiers*:

The ideal Christian politician is not necessarily the one who is first and most vociferous to claim that his position is the Christian one and who attempts to cover himself and his cause with whatever part of the divided garment that is within reach. He is not necessarily the one who makes of every cause a "crusade," presenting himself like Carlyle's crusader as "the minister of God's justice, doing God's judgment of the enemies of God." He should himself avoid unwarranted appeals to religion. He has a very special obligation to keep the things of God separate from those of Caesar.

When he does act, McCarthy said, the Christian politician "should shun the devices of the demagogue at all times, but especially in a time when tension is high, when uncertainty prevails, and emotion tends to be in the ascendancy."

Tensions in the nation were high, emotion soaring, when McCarthy walked through the door of the Senate Caucus Room to fulfill his self-determined responsibility to challenge the President. His action did not require quite the same courage as had been required of More in rebuking Henry VIII. McCarthy realized this. "I have a measure of courage," he would say. It would, to some, seem boastful to say even this. It was but another example of the difficulty of gauging on which side of so many delicate lines McCarthy would stand at any given moment. "I suppose I'm the only member of the Senate who knows what the eighth degree of humility is," he would say. "They say the last degree of humility is very close to the ultimate in pride, in the same way that the pale horse of death and the white horse of victory are virtually indistinguishable." The eighth degree of humility was detachment, the Benedictine rule said. And never had a more detached presidential candidate appeared on the scene. McCarthy's was a detachment that often seemed the ultimate in pride, that often seemed a jarring lack of compassion. "I have never thought of compassion as an active virtue," McCarthy would say after George McGovern during the campaign would suggest McCarthy had a "compassion gap." McCarthy would not display "active compassion" when he discussed race or when he assessed the Soviet invasion of Czechoslovakia in August, 1968. Sorrow for the plight of the Czech people should be obvious; it need not be stated, he felt. The injustice of prejudice and poverty did not have to be dwelt upon; by this time we knew the score. Robert Kennedy was compassionate and displayed it; McCarthy would not. He would not have been a suitable mourner at an Irish wake. It did not mean he felt less because he did not display what he felt. At the same time, it was difficult to determine just what he did genuinely care about. Reality was somewhere in the grays of things, as McCarthy well knew.

Many men are at their most demagogic or self-revealing when addressing college graduating classes. They sometimes impart a glimpse of the life lessons they consider important, even if they do not follow those lessons themselves. On June 4, 1967, McCarthy addressed the Notre Dame University graduating class and received an honorary Doctorate of Laws. He gave his listeners some "negative counsel" to consider as they met their responsibility in the world as educated men. The words are useful in trying to perceive McCarthy.

—Do not yield to the temptation to compromise methods in pursuit of acceptable purposes, to consider persons as expendable, or to do what T. S. Eliot has described as the worst treason—to do the right thing for the wrong reason.

—Of all passions the passion for the Inner Ring [an allusion to the self-explanatory title of a C. S. Lewis essay] is most skillful in making a man who is not yet a very bad man do very bad things.

—Do not corrupt language, and be attentive to protecting its integrity: first, as to the obvious obligation to speak the truth; and second, in the more subtle commitment to preserve and protect the meaning of words.

—And finally, this is a kind of ultimate test, be not overly concerned as to what the record may have to say about you if to make that record you must be false. Seek that high state of secular humility which leaves man free to speak and act without fear and without concern for the judgment the world may pass upon him. I suggest two models: Harry Truman in politics, and Pope John XXIII in religion.

And so the game was played: what makes McCarthy run. Once the crowd in the Senate Caucus Room quieted down, McCarthy, standing at the podium now, would tell them. Finally, at 10:07 A.M., November 30, 1967, McCarthy spoke.

"I intend to enter the Democratic primaries in Wisconsin, Oregon, California and Nebraska," were his opening words—a curious way to announce that one is seeking the presidency of the United States.

"The decision with reference to Massachusetts and New Hampshire will be made within two weeks. Insofar as Massachusetts is concerned, it will depend principally upon the outcome of the meeting of the Democratic State Committee this week end."

Nothing could have been drier, more matter-of-fact. McCarthy's quiet voice sounding more nasal than usual, he continued:

Since I first said that I thought the issue of Vietnam and other related issues should be raised in the primaries, I have talked to Democratic Party leaders in twenty-six states, to candidates—especially Senate candidates—who will be up for reelection next year, and to many other persons.

My decision to challenge the President's position, and the Administration's position, has been strengthened by recent announcements out of the Administration—the evident intention to intensify the war in Vietnam and, on the other hand, the absence of any positive indications or suggestions for a compromise or for a negotiated political settlement. I am concerned that the Administration seems to have set no limits to the price that it is willing to pay for a military victory.

Let me summarize the cost of the war up to this point: the physical destruction of much of a small and weak nation by the military operations of the most powerful nation in the world; 100,000 to 150,000 civilian casualties in South Vietnam alone, to say nothing of the destruction of life and property of North Vietnam; the uprooting and the fracturing of the society of South Vietnam, where one-fourth to one-third of the population are now reported to be refugees; for the United States, as of yesterday, over 15,000 combat dead and nearly 95,000 wounded through November;

a monthly expenditure in pursuit of the war running somewhere between $2 and $3 billion.

I am also concerned about the bearing of the war on other areas of United States responsibility, both at home and abroad:

—the failure to appropriate adequate funds for the poverty program here, for housing, for education and to meet other national needs, and the prospect of additional cuts as a condition to the possible passage of the surtax bill;

—the drastic reduction of our foreign aid program in other parts of the world;

—a dangerous rise in inflation and one of the indirect and serious consequences of our involvement in Vietnam—the devaluation of the British pound which in many respects is more important east of Suez today than is the British navy.

In addition there is growing evidence of a deepening moral crisis in America; discontent and frustration, and a disposition to take extra-legal— if not illegal—action to manifest protest.

I am hopeful that this challenge I am making . . . may alleviate to at least some degree this sense of political helplessness and restore to many people a belief in the processes of American politics and of American government. On the college campuses . . . and among adult thoughtful Americans it may counter the growing sense of alienation from politics which I think is currently reflected in a tendency to withdraw from political action, and talk of non-partisan efforts; to become cynical and make threats for third parties or other irregular political movements.

I do not see in my move any great threat to the unity and the strength of the Democratic Party—whatever that unity may be today and whatever strength it may be.

I am not—as I'm sure I will be charged—for peace at any price, but for an honorable, rational and political solution to this war.

The issue of the war in Vietnam is not really a separate issue but one which must be dealt with in the configuration of other problems in which it is related. And it is within this broader context I intend to take the case to the people of the United States.

McCarthy was in the race officially. Now in the Caucus Room it was time for questions, and for the first time he seemed to warm to the occasion.

Did he think he had a chance to win?

"I think the President is the leading candidate for the Democratic nomination right now," he deadpanned.

Did he have enough money?

"Two-thirds of a candidate's money usually goes to talking about your opponent, and I won't have to do that."

When, exactly, did he make up his mind to run?

"There was no really precise moment. It was nothing like Saint Paul being knocked off his horse." It had occurred, he added, somewhere in the period spanning the Katzenbach testimony in August, the Rusk press conference in October, and his appearance at Berkeley two weeks later.

Hadn't the administration been seeking a rational solution and offered to meet with Hanoi?

"To suggest a meeting anytime anywhere is not an offer. An offer would be, 'Let's meet next Tuesday morning in Warsaw.'"

Inevitably, questions began to dwell on Robert Kennedy. Did McCarthy think he might turn out to be a stalking-horse for Kennedy? "Coaltown was supposed to be a stalking-horse for Citation but Coaltown didn't quit." Might Kennedy fall heir to this movement? "He might. . . . It certainly wouldn't be illegal or contrary to American politics. . . . I have no commitment from him to stand aside all the way." And if he didn't succeed, he said, he would be "glad" to see Kennedy get the nomination. McCarthy's aides were groaning at this point. They felt he should begin to soft-pedal talk about Kennedy. Kennedy had had his chance. Now he was out of it.

Really, though. Wasn't this political suicide?

"I don't think it will be a case of suicide. It might be an execution."

What kind of an organization did he have?

"It will be pretty much a volunteer's army," said McCarthy.

As his words that morning were transmitted across the country the army rose up. Eloise Jones, Frances Morrow, and the rest had been awaiting only a leader. They were ready to fight the unbeatable foe, despite the fact they didn't really quite know how to go about it, other than to follow their convictions.

V

An Improbable Dream

★

Success follows on a lot of little people,
in a lot of little places, doing a lot
of little things.

REMINDER ON A WALL IN THE OFFICE
OF MCCARTHY CAMPAIGN MANAGER BLAIR CLARK

17. PEOPLE

Just where and in what profusion the volunteer army began to rise up those first few days after Eugene McCarthy's announcement of candidacy cannot be charted completely. It did not happen militarily, with huge wall maps in some headquarters being marked to show each newly activated battalion. It was more like so many guerilla uprisings, connected by an idea but with no central discipline, detailed battle plan, or sophisticated weaponry. In the less warlike allusion Abigail McCarthy used throughout the campaign: "It was as if the rains came and then stopped, and suddenly you saw the mushrooms sprouting up all over the place."

I could write hundreds of stories about where these people came from and why and how in so many cases faster than you could say Gene McCarthy they would suddenly rise to positions of responsibility. There was David L. Brye, thirty, of Coon Valley, Wisconsin, a history professor on leave from Luther College just across the state line in Decorah, Iowa. He wandered into the McCarthy headquarters in Madison, Wisconsin, in December to offer his services. So they put him to work painting the walls, and when that was finished they sent him out to help organize the state. He had never organized a state before.

Whom do you leave out? Whom do you include? Do you leave out Marge Frank, the wife of an English professor in Albuquerque, New Mexico, a veritable whirlwind of the organization there? Do you include Geoffrey Cowan, a Yale law student and a mainstay of the Connecticut organization who discovered a state law, never used before, that allowed his group to force primaries in a number of communities? Do you ignore Mrs. Ann E. Raynolds, of Springfield, Vermont, who one day found herself walking through the rain with Curtis Gans to recruit Eugene Winslow, president of Windham College in Putney, to be Vermont chairman? Do you play up Mrs. Audrey Rood, of Westlake, Ohio, who simply quit her job to go into full-time, unpaid political action? What about Mrs. Myron Nussbaum, of Highland Park, Illinois, whose main protest before McCarthy had been to take part in Saturday peace vigils in front of the library like the ones they held Friday evenings in Waukesha, Wisconsin?

To professional politicians, the first signs of the existence of this mushroom revolution were nothing to regard with any seriousness. Just because people like Raymon Gerard, forty-seven, an engineer from Framingham, Massachusetts, or Martin Dworkin, forty, a professor of microbiology from Saint Paul, Minnesota, or Dr. William J. Norman, forty-six, a Missoula, Montana, neurologist, were suddenly building up new political organizations, one didn't go off half-cocked and believe that they could do anything. And certainly one didn't join up. So it was that the day McCarthy became a candidate he could count the halfway important professional politicians behind him on the fingers of one hand. There was a California Congressman, Donald Edwards. There was the recently ousted Democratic state chairman from Michigan, Zoltan Ferency. And there was a former Oregon state chairman, Howard Morgan. There were also a few lesser politicos, but in rather pathetic quantity.

What McCarthy did have at the beginning was a broad group of well-educated people, mostly liberal in outlook, though aware the old liberalism needed revamping. Eventually, certain aspects of McCarthy's personality would begin to have appeal, but at first

McCarthy's volunteers were people concerned about Vietnam and the flaws in the country that had allowed Vietnam to develop, and the flaws they saw in Lyndon Johnson.* And even when the style of the man began to be appreciated, the movement never took on aspects of a cult, except in isolated instances. ("Personally, I would not have worked harder for Jesus," Mrs. Joan Chaney, of Tiffin, Ohio, said after the campaign.)

This made the McCarthy movement different from the following of Adlai Stevenson, though many of the same impulses of the Stevenson supporter were found in the McCarthy supporter. This is what made it different from the presidential campaigns of both Kennedys and from the campaigns of Barry Goldwater and George Wallace. What began November 30, 1967, was not a McCarthy movement, unless you placed the word "McCarthy" in parentheses. "I don't come to you as someone who is leading a cause, but as someone who is participating in a common effort," McCarthy would sometimes say in his speeches. "This movement is more important than Eugene McCarthy," Frank Hodall implored at a meeting of the Allegany-Hornell McCarthy Committee in Alfred, New York. Said Frederik Pohl, of Red Bank, New Jersey, a McCarthy leader in his community: "To me, and to most of the scores of McCarthy supporters

* In 1969 some writers suggested that much McCarthy support had *voted* for George Wallace in November, 1968. This was an oversimplification of an excellent study by the Survey Research Center of the University of Michigan. That study found, in effect, that a *partial* "plurality" of early McCarthy support later preferred Wallace, though only 7 per cent of this group actually voted for Wallace in the presidential election, a fact usually overlooked in stories on the study. The study specifically excluded the "hard-core" McCarthy support who make up the bulk of the people I discuss in this book—people initially concerned more with issues than with the man, people who contributed effort and money and not simply preference. To be sure, in New Hampshire antiadministration feeling was more prevalent in the McCarthy vote than antiwar feeling, as I state in my account of New Hampshire and as the SRC study found. To be sure, there were McCarthy-Wallacites, like one man who helped write farm position papers, first for McCarthy and later for Wallace. To be sure, the McCarthy and Wallace supporters were similar in rejecting politics-as-usual in 1968. But, I suggest, the McCarthy and Wallace supporters were in the main no more similar than the SRC study found the 1968 Wallace and the 1964 Goldwater supporters to be, despite whatever "preferences" might have been stated during the year by some voters.

I know well, McCarthy was almost incidental to the movement. I admire him personally, but he did not lead me, or most of the others I know in the sense he changed my views in any way. I have been involved in scores of campaigns. In all but one of them I was working for a candidate. In the McCarthy campaign I felt that he was working for me."

But these were views yet to be developed in the late winter of 1967. The people were there and waiting, a group with remarkably similar views, backgrounds, and tastes. Some of the students who worked throughout the campaign would remark at how alike the homes of many McCarthy supporters were from one end of the country to the other. The observation was accurate. Donald Peterson's home in Eau Claire, Wisconsin, could have been David and Barbara Underwood's home in Concord, New Hampshire, or Eleanor Slater's home in Warwick, Rhode Island, the Albert Saenger home in Alburtis, Pennsylvania, or Midge Miller's home in Madison. They were big, old houses that had been refurbished, or were in the process of being fixed up, to something approaching their one-time splendor. They were on tree-lined streets, and they reflected a casual comfort that split-level developments never achieve. The rooms were large enough, and books and magazines were plentiful and very similar from house to house. The houses looked lived in. You could tell that their inhabitants were active and thoughtful and, as Stanford Professor Michael Macoby found in a study of Mc-Carthy people, had a "love of life." They were idealists concerned about mankind and American life and would do what they could to improve things, knowing their efforts might be futile. They did not have any burning thought they would win when they set out in the McCarthy campaign. Winning was not really what it was all about. "We were not ones to seek power for its own sake," said Mrs. Albert Saenger after the campaign. "This made it much easier to face defeat, provided we were getting through to more and more people."

"They do not have to win," Walter Lippmann wrote at the start of the campaign. "In a democratic country everybody cannot always be a winner. But in a healthy democracy everybody can believe, even when he loses, that he has been honestly heard, has made himself felt, has had a fair chance to take part in the give-and-take of debate and of voting."

Thus it was a very homogeneous group. This was their strength, and also their flaw. For the most part, theirs was a movement of a single socioeconomic peer group, not a coalition in the classic sense. At the start, Negroes numbered very few among them, though the longer the campaign progressed the more this changed—a change affected largely by McCarthy's approach, or nonapproach, to the race issue. The students and young people who worked in the campaign—the Children's Crusade—were little different in outlook from the adult volunteers.

Among the adults the largest age group was made up of members of the Silent Generation. These were people born during or near the Depression. Their childhood flowered with such American institutions as the Saturday afternoon movie, Jack Armstrong, and Captain Midnight and his Secret Decoder. World War II interrupted their adolescence. Joe McCarthy and Korea and organization-man morality clouded their early adulthood, and the initial skirmishes of the civil rights revolution and the voice of Adlai Stevenson stirred something in them. Their books were *The Catcher in the Rye* and *The Affluent Society*. They detested tail fins on cars and the phoniness that seemed to proliferate all around. They had come to the same state of mind as that of the young people they coalesced with in the McCarthy campaign, but more gradually. They evolved with America's increasing problems; the young were born into them. They had their beatniks; the young their hippies. They were products of a decade—the thirties—whose graphics and fashions the young of the sixties reincarnated in altered shapes and forms. There was no generation gap between these two groups.

In 1968, with like-minded people of all ages, they combined into a potent political force. The young got all the headlines, which was something of a journalistic oversight. In New Hampshire, the Children's Crusade was, perhaps, vital. In Wisconsin it was helpful.

Thereafter, it had diminishing practical effect, though it remained an important symbol of the spirit of the campaign. But, throughout, the adult volunteers were the foundation of the McCarthy effort. And what they did was mostly spontaneous. The tight, centrally controlled organizing of the 1964 Goldwater effort, and even of the 1968 Wallace effort, was never present in the McCarthy campaign. It was a phenomenon a reporter traveling with the candidate could not fully appreciate or assess.

To try to portray it with some degree of accuracy, I sent a questionnaire to almost every volunteer McCarthy leader in the country, some 800 persons in the fifty states who were city, county, district, and state leaders. About 100 or so letters were returned because of faulty addresses. But slightly more than half of the rest replied, some at great length. The results show that the average local McCarthy leader was a man or woman in his or her late 30s, as likely as not involved in education, a possessor of two or more college degrees, a salary of somewhere around $15,000, not necessarily a member of an antiwar organization, irregular in church attendance, and with little or no political experience. The tables below show the full picture. Because not all respondents answered each question, I have stated my findings in percentages.

AGE OF VOLUNTEER McCARTHY LEADERS

15–20	5.3%
21–25	3.9
26–30	14.8
31–35	13.3
36–40	18.9
41–45	13.0
46–50	13.0
51–55	5.3
56–60	4.7
61–65	2.4
66 and up	2.4

Thus, some 40 to 45 per cent of the McCarthy volunteer leaders were from the Silent Generation, those, roughly, in their early thirties to mid-forties.

EDUCATIONAL LEVEL OF VOLUNTEER McCARTHY LEADERS

Doctoral degrees of all kinds and law degrees	42.7%
Master's degree	17.8
Bachelor's degree	24.2
Some college	10.8
High school and/or Secretarial school	4.5

Thus, 60.5 per cent of the adult McCarthy volunteer leaders had two or more college degrees. Only one person who responded to the questionnaire had not gone to high school.

OCCUPATIONS OF VOLUNTEER McCARTHY LEADERS

(Husband's occupation given for women leaders who listed no occupation of their own)

College professor or administrator	30.7%
High-school or elementary teacher or administrator	13.7
Law	11.4
Medicine and dentistry	5.0
Clergy	4.6
Business and banking	8.8
Engineering and research	7.2
Arts, communications, publishing	1.3
Students	9.2
Miscellaneous	8.1

Though I can't substantiate it with statistics, I believe that a broader sampling of volunteers below the nominal leaders would show higher percentages of physicians, lawyers, and clergymen than my figures. The "students" category refers to young people who achieved leadership roles in their own communities and not to the army of student canvassers and envelope stuffers in the primary elections who came from other states.

ANNUAL INCOME OF VOLUNTEER McCARTHY LEADERS

0–$ 4,999	8.0% (mostly students)
$ 5,000–$ 9,999	17.3
$10,000–$14,999	26.5
$15,000–$19,999	22.4
$20,000–$24,999	8.6

$25,000–$29,999	5.4
$30,000–$34,999	4.5
$35,000–$39,999	3.2
$40,000–$44,999	1.3
$45,000–$49,999	0.3
$50,000 and up	2.5

RELIGION OF VOLUNTEER McCARTHY LEADERS

Protestant	30.7%	
Catholic	13.1	
Jewish	11.9	
Unitarian	12.8	
Quaker	3.3	
Other	2.1	(includes three Humanists)
No religion	26.2	(includes three atheists and three agnostics. Most had discarded former religious activity as irrelevant)

The major Protestant denominations were Presbyterian, Episcopalian, and Methodist. Slightly over 43 per cent fell into the group that either claimed no religion or were from the more secular Unitarian, Quaker, or Humanist beliefs. A 1968 Gallup poll indicated that only 43 per cent of all Americans attend church weekly.

MEMBERSHIP IN ANTIWAR ORGANIZATIONS

No	50.6%
Yes	49.4

Thus, the McCarthy campaign provided an outlet for innumerable persons who found even a moderate organization like SANE too radical.

PREVIOUS POLITICAL ACTIVITY

None	33%
Very Little	29
Often	38

All but about 10 per cent of those with little or no prior political activity vowed to be regular participants in the future.

. . .

I also surveyed some 150 members of the young national campaign staff by mail after the fall election. Only forty responded, so my findings can't be regarded as the last word. However, they do substantiate what was well known during the campaign: that McCarthy attracted very intelligent young people. Median I.Q. of those who responded was 140, with a range of from 122 to 160. (From about 100 to 115 is average for the population at large.) The average age was between twenty-four and twenty-five. They came from families with an average annual income of $31,500. The professions of their fathers ranged from policeman to symphony orchestra director, though nearly a third were businessmen, many of them executives. Few came from academic families. Religious score: 27.5 per cent, Protestant; 25 per cent, Jewish; 10 per cent, Catholic; 2.5 per cent claimed other beliefs; 35 per cent claimed no religious preference. Many had been involved in National Student Association activities, the civil rights movement, and anti-Vietnam war protest, though most did not become especially concerned about the war until late in 1966 or early 1967. A minority took part in the April 15, 1967, peace marches in New York City and San Francisco and the Pentagon demonstration the following October. Many were obviously becoming ripe for radical activity, but then on November 30, 1967, Eugene McCarthy announced.

Thus, McCarthy did not so much pull students off the streets, as some of his campaign advertising suggested. He attracted a quieter, more thoughtful, and more plentiful group in such numbers and spirit as to dilute attention to and growth of the legions of radical demonstrators, at least for a season.

This, then, was the face-to-be of the McCarthy army as his campaign began. It could be seen in preview the day after his Washington announcement at a meeting of the Conference of Concerned Democrats, the Lowenstein-Gans organization, in Chicago. Some 450 people from forty-two states representing an assortment of organizations in various degrees of readiness were there, and it was obvious they were not way-out peaceniks. They were respectable, like the multitude at the November, 1965, march on Washington.

"I was struck by the solid citizen look," said Joe Gross, fifty-seven, a delegate from Georgia who became that state's McCarthy leader.

The delirious disorganization of the McCarthy campaign was apparent at the meeting: written pledges for contributions of nearly a million dollars simply disappeared. And the candidate displayed himself with all the ambiguity his supporters would try to learn to live with: while he informed the Massachusetts contingent he would run in their primary, he told the New Hampshire people he was still undecided about theirs. And when he addressed the full meeting he seemed devoid of life, of any acknowledgment of the pent-up emotions in the room. In his way, he was telling his supporters: Here I am, your candidate. Take me, but you must take me warts and all. I will not burn them away to please you.

Clearly, McCarthy took some getting used to.

18. DOLDRUMS

Many people never did get used to McCarthy or to his quiet style. At first the doubts about him seemed almost universal.

"The people here are turned on. Please don't let them down," a woman in Newark pleaded before a McCarthy speech. He did not accommodate her.

"He failed to take advantage of the emotional fervor," Representative George E. Brown, Jr., complained after an early 1968 McCarthy visit to California. "These people want to feel they're part of a Holy Crusade."

Supporters in Oregon told McCarthy he was not being forceful enough, and McCarthy told them: "This is a test of an issue, not an individual's campaign. I did not want to run."

Arnold Hiatt, a Boston shoe company executive, and two other Massachusetts backers confronted McCarthy in his Washington office. Hiatt, who had been in politics about a month, told McCarthy: "You're not in focus."

McCarthy responded: "What do you expect me to do? Light bonfires on the hills?"

"Some people can only see by that kind of light," Hiatt said. As he left McCarthy's office, Hiatt handed him a letter from his twelve-year-old daughter, begging McCarthy not to let the people down.

Joe Rauh began to wonder if McCarthy's emotional Adlai Stevenson nominating speech had been an aberration. "Maybe he's the kind of guy who can do it only once," Rauh said.

"I really don't intend to shout at anyone," McCarthy told more than one person. "I don't think the issues are served by that kind of emotion."

He didn't shout; therefore, some people reasoned with curious logic, he was not a serious candidate.

They also judged him against traditional standards of presidential campaigns, and McCarthy did not measure up. He seemed unable to build or uninterested in building a campaign staff. It was simple knowledge that any serious candidate had a staff before he announced. McCarthy did not travel with a retinue. A serious candidate always traveled with a retinue. He was seen eating alone in a restaurant or conversing with a poet. Serious candidates don't allow themselves to be caught in such situations. He would not cater to the press and sometimes considered them an annoyance. A serious candidate wooed them and even took advice from them at times.

"The seriousness of my effort will become apparent," McCarthy would say.

But it was not apparent through December and January and even into February that campaign season.

In California, McCarthy's entry seemed to have hurt the antiwar cause. A poll showed Lyndon Johnson favored 63 to 18 per cent over McCarthy among the state's Democrats. Shortly before McCarthy launched his candidacy, Johnson outpolled support for a slate of antiadministration peace delegates in the 1968 primary by only 42 to 39 per cent. In New York, the Coalition for a Democratic Alternative lost its eagerness to run a slate of peace delegates pledged to McCarthy. Instead, it was proposed they run pledged simply to the issue.

Supporters found themselves speaking of McCarthy defensively. "He may not be the best man in the world," George Brown said, "I mean, I've got my disagreements with him. But he's the best man we've got to give us a choice."

As December passed, Allard Lowenstein, recuperating from gall-bladder surgery, found his phone ringing constantly. McCarthy leaders all over the country wondered what they had gotten into with this curious candidate, and some began to wonder whether they should repudiate him.

It was little wonder the press began to write off the candidacy. "No one at this early point can really know the sentiment of the country," McCarthy said at this time. But the press, for the most part, did not consider that the tone McCarthy was trying to establish might be the approach needed for this particular moment in history.

Press criticism became its most damning in an article by New Left writer Jack Newfield, a Robert Kennedy admirer then anguished over Kennedy's failure to act. In the December 28, 1967, *Village Voice*, Newfield wrote: "Let the unhappy, brutal truth come out. Eugene McCarthy's campaign is a disaster. It has been run as if King Constantine was the manager. McCarthy's speeches are dull, vague, and without either balls or poetry." Newfield charged that McCarthy was weakening the peace movement and urged "Resistance" people and the antiwar movement to disavow McCarthy—sentiments shared by Lowenstein. And do what? "Start organizing now for disruption of the Democratic convention in Chicago next August," wrote Newfield. As an alternative: "Make Robert Kennedy run."

Newfield suggested that McCarthy might well be a stalking-horse for Lyndon Johnson, a speculation that was one of the curious phenomena within the McCarthy phenomenon, for right after he became a candidate, it was widely suggested that McCarthy was a stalking-horse for Robert Kennedy. Newfield even hinted that McCarthy might purposely be blowing the campaign to get some reward from Johnson, perhaps appointment as Secretary of State—a notion about McCarthy that Kennedy himself did not reject. McCarthy himself was fully aware that if he failed, Johnson might feel vindicated to wage an even wider war. But he felt it was a risk that had to be taken.

Newfield's criticism wandered into this misassessment: "I fear the campaign will not energize the middle and thus will under-represent the actual feeling in the country against the war." He was thinking in terms of someone leading dynamically, as he felt Robert Kennedy would. He did not consider that the people could in large measure lead themselves, a faith McCarthy had. The "middle" that Newfield spoke of was becoming energized in a way he did not see. The real story was not so much the "disaster" of the McCarthy campaign to that time, but the fact so much was happening anyway. A lot of little people in a lot of little places were doing a lot of little things.

Probably there was no one more inconsequential in the McCarthy effort than Wilma van Dusseldorp, sixty-eight, who lived on a small farm in Roswell, Georgia. "I was too busy to do much, so I attended organization meetings now and then to swell the crowd," she said. No one had to lead her or urge her to these meetings.

In Westfield, New Jersey, Richard I. Samuel, twenty-eight, a patent attorney, had been trying to put together an anti-Johnson delegate slate for the primary even before McCarthy announced his candidacy. And he didn't wait for help from the national head-quarters to get enough literature to distribute. He rented a printing press, put it in the basement of another McCarthy supporter, Saul Harrison, and they printed 300,000 pieces. McCarthy did not lead Samuel. He didn't have to. McCarthy's campaign could have been in even worse shape when Newfield wrote his article. Samuel would not have stopped.

And in Coos County, New Hampshire, in the Berlin-Gorham area, Otto Oleson, fifty-three, a steam turbine operator, past master of of the Grange and a state representative, was seeing clearly what was happening while regular New Hampshire Democrats weren't facing up to it, and it had nothing to do with how dynamic Mc-Carthy was or wasn't being late in 1967. Oleson found himself sub-stituting for the county Democratic chairman at a meeting with Governor John King to assess Lyndon Johnson's strength around the state. One by one, the county chairmen reported that the President should have no trouble with an unknown like McCarthy, should McCarthy enter the state's primary. Oleson's turn came. He said his county chairman, Dennis Kilbride, agreed with the rest, but Oleson didn't. "To make it as simple as I can," he said, "the party can be sure of those who don't go beyond the funnies and sports pages, but of those who reach the editorial page and those in my age group who have sons reaching the draft age, the party can't be certain of them. A friend of mine lost a son in Vietnam and he asked me for what reason. I couldn't tell him, but maybe someone present can so that I can carry back the word."

No one came up with an answer.

As the premature obituaries were being written, a campaign staff of sorts began to develop, in much the way a pickup baseball game develops.

John Safer was first on board. He was a well-to-do Washington-area real estate developer and former neighbor of McCarthy. Sometime before McCarthy announced his candidacy, Safer opened a small campaign office in the Colorado Building in Washington, hired a secretary, and waited for things to happen. In mid-December, Safer, then in general charge of campaign financing, did a curious thing for a top campaign aide to do at the start of a presidential campaign: he went on vacation, clear to Barbados. While there he became ill and almost died and was never able to rejoin the campaign.

The initial money came from June Oppen Degnan, a wealthy California divorcee who drove a Rolls Royce and was a rabidly anti-Johnson member of the ADA executive board. She opened a small campaign office in the Capitol Hill Hotel, near McCarthy's Senate office. She also brought along Tom Page, a Californian and former information director of the Peace Corps, which did nothing to reassure Lowenstein. Lowenstein had once persuaded some returned Peace Corps volunteers to run an antiwar ad in the *New York Times,* and Page had called newspapers to raise questions about Lowenstein's loyalty to the United States. (Page, who was to have acted as press secretary, soon left McCarthy and worked for Robert Kennedy in California.)

The search for a campaign manager took several weeks. About a dozen persons were approached or discussed. The list included Kenneth O'Donnell, the long-time Kennedy family friend; Defense Secretary Robert S. McNamara; Fred Dutton, who ultimately directed Robert Kennedy's campaign; Thomas D. Finney, Jr., a law partner of McNamara's successor, Clark Clifford; former Governor Terry Sanford, of North Carolina (McCarthy's office mistakenly called former Georgia Governor Carl Sanders at first); J. Edward Day, John Kennedy's Postmaster General; Harry Roth, a West Coast clothing executive who, in 1967 before McCarthy's announcement of candidacy, ran a *New York Times* ad urging someone to run against Johnson; Senator Vance Hartke; Representative Don Edwards; and long-time friends Joe Gabler, of Minnesota, and Larry Merthan. And in McCarthy's files was a letter from someone named Blair Clark.

Clark was a Harvard classmate and friend of John Kennedy. He was a pleasant fellow who had had successful careers in newspaper work and television. Apart from brief minor service as a press aide in the 1952 New York gubernatorial campaign of W. Averell Harriman, his practical political experience was nil. He had been concerned about the war for some time. While in London in the fall of 1967, he read that McCarthy might challenge the President. On November 11 he wrote McCarthy offering his services. Clark arrived back in the United States the week end of the Chicago meeting, unaware that McCarthy had announced his candidacy. He flew to Chicago uninvited. With a press badge borrowed from his friend Theodore H. White, author of *The Making of the President* books, Clark wandered through the Conference of Concerned Democrats meeting and finally up to McCarthy's suite in the company of another friend, newspaper columnist Mary McGrory. Again he said he wanted to help. A week or so later, over lunch in Clark's Manhattan apartment, he suddenly heard McCarthy saying that perhaps Clark ought to be campaign chairman. "No," Clark replied, "we'll save that for Herb Lehman." Lehman, of course, was dead, but it was the kind of *non sequitur* McCarthy appreciated. "If you want me to run it, call me campaign manager, without capitals," Clark said.

There Clark was in mid-December, sitting in the Capitol Hill Hotel with June Degnan, Tom Page, and McCarthy's Senate administrative assistant, Jerry Eller, as they held long, inconclusive brainstorming sessions. All were well-meaning, but they were in over their heads. No one in his right mind would have picked them to run a campaign.

Soon after the Chicago meeting, Sam Brown, a Harvard divinity student, began calling Washington from Cambridge to talk about the student role in the campaign and wanting to go to work. For ten days he tried to get through to someone. John Safer spoke to him once. Safer said that McCarthy had him tell Brown: "Don't drop out of school. It's more important to stay in school." Brown finally drove to Washington about the third week in December. He had to wait three hours before Clark would see him, and then Brown laid out his case. "I told him what was happening with the students of America, that they were about to rise up against their President and that he needed me. I was ready to go to work that day." Clark nodded and said little. "I told him there was a conference in Cleveland of the University Christian Movement coming up and McCarthy should be represented." Clark reached into his pocket and pulled out $200, which he handed to Brown. "Go, my son," said Clark. Sam Brown, who would become youth coordinator, had joined the McCarthy campaign.

Meyer "Sandy" Frucher, twenty-two, of New York, and his wife, Floss, met Safer by accident in a Chicago airport limousine while en route to the CCD meeting. Afterward he, too, began calling Washington and finally convinced Clark he could be of service. In the early stages of the campaign, Frucher was, in effect, deputy campaign manager.

Marge Sklencar, from Mundelein College, came aboard about the same time. Peter Barnes, who became fascinated with the McCarthy effort while covering the preannouncement story for *Newsweek*, took a leave and on the first of the year joined the campaign staff as a writer and researcher. Sue Hestor, who had been involved in ACT-68, moved from New York to Washington to join the staff. Seymour M. Hersh, a young Associated Press Pentagon reporter, signed on as new press secretary. Mary Lou Oates, a lively young United Press International reporter, became Hersh's assistant. Ultimately Curtis Gans and his wife, Genie, joined the staff.

A growing number of women volunteers, meanwhile, began attacking the mountains of mail that piled up after McCarthy's announcement of candidacy. They worked in the Senate office and in the attic of the McCarthy home under the direction of Abigail McCarthy, Mrs. Barbara Haviland, and Mrs. Arlene Hynes, wife of McCarthy's legislative assistant, and in the suburban Bethesda home of Mrs. Arthur Mason, a friend of Safer's. (A headquarters for this letter-writing activity was soon established in the Alban Towers apartment building near the McCarthy home.)

McCarthy viewed this mounting activity skeptically. When Sandy Frucher went out and found a bigger headquarters in the Transportation Building on Seventeenth Street, a block and a half from the White House, McCarthy called in a long-time friend, Grace Bassett, a former congressional correspondent for the Washington *Star,* and told her to get over there and hold things down. "He said the staff was getting too big," she said later. "I think he thought he could campaign by just traveling around all alone like some medieval minstrel singing his song."

"He thought it should be inchoate, floating. It wouldn't fit his style otherwise," said John Safer after the campaign.

"McCarthy never wanted any structure," said Blair Clark.

And he didn't really seem to want a campaign manager. Blair Clark quickly found that McCarthy was difficult to deal with.

"You're going to have to make decisions because Gene's not going to make them," Clark was told by Russell Hemenway, of the National Committee for an Effective Congress.

"You've got to hold Gene's feet to the fire," another McCarthy friend told Clark.

Clark would listen, puff on his pipe, and nod. This response would be the trademark of this tall, fifty-one-year-old, duck-footed, ruddy-nosed man who sometimes rode motorcycles and could play the harmonica. He was as unflappable as an aristocrat. It barely fazed him when, once, a young campaign aide pointed out that smoke was issuing from Clark's coat pocket. "You're right, old man," Clark said, and pulled out his pipe, which he had placed in his pocket still lighted.

In the end, Clark was probably the only kind of campaign manager McCarthy could have lived with. Clark was not much on decision, direction, or organization. He was, unavoidably, perhaps, a long-suffering but amiable fainéant. But as McCarthy noted in this period: "Organization is not that important to the kind of campaign I plan to run because the issues are more important than the person."

Nonetheless, Clark did two things in this early period of the campaign that proved vital. He helped persuade McCarthy to enter the New Hampshire primary. And he approved Sam Brown's request for a $25,000 budget for student operations. Clark also understood immediately the television potential of McCarthy's style. But he was never able to hold McCarthy's feet to the fire, and so he never became a strong leader. In fact, he succeeded so well in not taking control that as December waned the leadership of the campaign seemed a several-headed monster. It was being run by McCarthy, Jerry Eller, Blair Clark, Sandy Frucher, Abigail McCarthy, with a dash here and there of Tom Page, June Degnan, Allard Lowenstein, Maurice Rosenblatt, or just about whoever else happened by. Mary McGrory, as a friend of Clark and McCarthy, found herself in the unavoidable position of listener and sometime adviser who, to many on the staff, seemed as much a campaign manager as anyone else.

But Clark did exert enough leadership to almost bring the California organization crashing down on top of him. In an effort to broaden the base of McCarthy support beyond the California Democratic Council, Clark began, with McCarthy's approval, to recruit campaign leaders among regular party politicians who had been identified with the Stevenson campaigns. CDC leaders, already perturbed over McCarthy's failure to make his campaign more emotional, angrily told Clark they might withdraw support. They also demanded that McCarthy take specific stands on certain issues.

"I was pilloried," Clark said later. "I almost began to think it might be better if they renounced him." They did not renounce McCarthy. But Clark had experienced what would be the common condition: central control would become impossible in the McCarthy campaign. Just about everyone came to consider it his right to do his own thing.

After the campaign was over, McCarthy explained what, generally, he had in mind when he started out. In an interview with the Boston *Globe,* McCarthy said:

I thought we could test the media with the campaign and then also test the people, as being better informed, better educated. The two don't necessarily go together. That was the early conception of the campaign, and I thought I could do it, probably in four or five states. . . . And not really run a traditional campaign. If we had been able to hold to that, the test would have been more significant. But then it began to expand. We got more money than I thought we'd have. What you get next is Parkinson's Law.

He had expected to spend about a million dollars, McCarthy said. But it cost more than eleven times that. And most of the money came from people who had never been involved in politics before. A dozen contributors alone gave a total of more than $2 million, and this same group raised even more than they gave. As significant was the breadth of the donor list. Over all, McCarthy received perhaps 250,000 individual contributions of all sizes. Contributions of five, ten, or twenty-five dollars came in by mail at the rate of about $50,000 a day at the peak. Herbert E. Alexander, director of the Citizens' Research Foundation of Princeton, New Jersey, who conducts a quadrennial study of presidential campaign financing, said the number of contributors to McCarthy and other moderate candidates in 1968 was unique for candidates considered "left of center." In 1964, Barry Goldwater drew some 600,000 individual contributions. At the time, Alexander wrote it off as a "right-wing phenomenon." (In 1968 George Wallace received about 750,000 individual contributions.) The big McCarthy money, Alexander found,

was unusually free of special interests. One notable interest, however, was mutual funds. Among the major contributors were Howard
Stein, forty-one, president of the Dreyfus Fund, and the company's
retired chairman, Jack Dreyfus. Stein became one of McCarthy's
major fund raisers. A number of executives of other mutuals contributed. Two other major contributors were Martin Peretz, a
bearded young ultraliberal Harvard professor, and his wife, who
was rich in her own right. Blair Clark, a member of the Clark
Thread family, put a considerable amount of his own money into
the campaign. Other big contributors included Stewart R. Mott, a
thirty-year-old philanthropist from Flint, Michigan, and New York
City, whose family controlled considerable General Motors stock;
William Clay Ford, of Detroit, largest stockholder in the Ford Motor
Company and owner of the Detroit Lions; Ellsworth Carrington, a
New York stockbroker; Bruce Robert Gimbel, of the department
store family; Henry Niles, a Baltimore insurance executive; Martin
Fife, a New York leather-goods manufacturer; Alan Miller, a retired
patent attorney; Harold Willens, a Los Angeles manufacturer and
real estate developer; Arnold Hiatt, chief executive of the Green
Shoe Company of Boston; Dan A. Kimball, of Los Angeles, chair-
man of the executive committee of Aerojet-General; Martin Stone,
Los Angeles manufacturer.

A number of other major contributors were relatively young men
who had created successful businesses of their own. Their ideology
might be called conservative humanitarianism, if it could be classified at all. McCarthy struck a chord. Their giving was essentially
altruistic. Some may have thought McCarthy had a chance of winning, but all knew he was a desperate long shot. It was not the
kind of giving that expected a tangible benefit.

These new contributors filled the void in the lagging early stages
of the campaign and were the financial heart of it throughout.

19. ASSESSMENT

That the McCarthy campaign came out of this period of doldrums intact and with growing strength was stark proof of the virulence of antiadministration sentiment. Yet the idea of challenging an incumbent President seemed so implausible that McCarthy's Senate colleagues who felt as he did about the war declined to stand up with him. Each worked his conscience into an uneasy accommodation with this contradiction. Senator Joseph Clark demanded that the Philadelphia ADA cancel McCarthy as a speaker at a dinner honoring Clark, who was supporting Lyndon Johnson's renomination, though he opposed the war. McCarthy never asked the support of a single Senator, for he knew his candidacy put many of them in a difficult position. But he thought at least a few might rally to him, and he became bitter when they didn't. It was doubly aggravating to him that some seemed to hold back in the expectation that Robert Kennedy might yet enter the race.

Pressures on Kennedy to become a candidate intensified when it appeared McCarthy was going nowhere. He would not do it. It would split the party and perhaps cause the defeat of liberal Senators who might back him, he reasoned. A challenge might give the White House to the Republicans, who might be more inclined to nominate a conservative if the Democrats seemed in disarray. Maybe Lyndon might defiantly intensify the war if he entered the race, Kennedy thought. And above all, Kennedy felt he could not win.

Nor would he support McCarthy. He might as well run himself if he were to do that, he reasoned. He did not like McCarthy and could not understand his calm acceptance that he would be defeated. To join that suicide leap, Kennedy felt, would play right into Lyndon Johnson's hands. "If he beats Kennedy-McCarthy instead of just McCarthy, then he will have destroyed all of his opposition in the Democratic party," Kennedy said at the time in a private conversation. "That is what all these great, well-meaning people who would have me support him don't see. They don't mean any harm. They just don't see it. They only see that I am not doing what they want me to. If they would really think about it they would understand the why. I can't tell them. Maybe they'll understand later. Because after the primaries the issues will still be there and I will still be discussing them."

The pressure for him to support McCarthy if he would not run himself became stinging. Columnist Murray Kempton wrote that Kennedy was making it easier for other politicians to remain uncommitted:

> To define Senator Kennedy's place in the history of the American cop-out, we have to remember Sydney Smith's place in the *History of English Humor*. It was said of Sydney Smith that he was the cause of wit in others; let it now be said of Senator Kennedy, the highest-ranking adolescent since Alexander Hamilton in 1794, that he is the cause of excuses in others.

The signs that greeted him at college campuses were similar. "Vacillation Kills," "Bobby Bird," "Who's Pulling Your Strings?," "Stop Pussy Footing Around," "War Won't Wait for '72," said some at Brooklyn College on January 12, 1968. Student-faculty committee president Lynn Rossman, nineteen, stated the students' complaint simply: "He's come out against the war and he hasn't done anything to back up what he says. Within the Democratic party he's been given a choice. Once you decide your stand you must take action. Kennedy's support of McCarthy would help the party."

McCarthy did not let Kennedy's dilemma go unnoticed. With obvious relish, he told the New York Coalition for a Democratic Alternative on January 6: "There seems to be a disposition to wait for a kind of latter-day salvation, like four years from now. . . . Four years are too long."

Kennedy spoke caustically of McCarthy and his campaign. In a background session with reporters January 30, Kennedy said, "His campaign has been very helpful to President Johnson." And he noted: "McCarthy has hurt me by his taunting, and he hasn't helped himself. He's made it impossible for any Kennedy people to work for him. A couple of months ago he probably could have put something together if he had done it right."

And Kennedy lapsed into the same lack of understanding Jack Newfield reflected in his article a month earlier. Said Kennedy: "The war is one of the great disasters of all time for the United States. But Gene McCarthy hasn't been able to tap the unrest in the country. You have to be able to touch this uneasiness."

Kennedy was wrong. The people did not need to be stirred up. All they needed was for someone to offer himself as a candidate.

Kennedy's wife wanted him to enter the race. The idealistic young men on his staff urged him to. Students on campuses across the land demanded that he run. Allard Lowenstein talked to him some more, and Kennedy replied that Mayor Richard J. Daley, of Chicago, had told him he would be foolish to try to challenge the President. "You'll see that it doesn't matter what Daley says," Lowenstein stormed. But Kennedy would not budge. On January 30 he made it known once more that he would not run in 1968 under "any foreseeable circumstances."

The phrase was not Shermanesque; it left the door open a smidgen. But most of the people who had hoped for a Kennedy candidacy considered the matter closed, and many viewed him in a new light. He had already begun to lose the young and the intellectuals to McCarthy, two of the groups that, it was always said, would help form his base in 1972. Their disillusionment with Kennedy sharpened after January 30. Dianne Dumanoski, twenty-three, a pretty blonde from Gardner, Massachusetts, who had dropped out of her Ph.D. studies at Yale to work for McCarthy in New Hampshire, declared: "That statement. That was when the man of integrity was separated from the politician. I wouldn't work for Kennedy now under any circumstances."

In Hanover, Dartmouth history professor David Roberts, forty-five, one of the original members of the New Hampshire RFK-68 organization that launched in October, 1967, didn't even wait for Kennedy's supposedly final word on not running. By the end of December, he was working for McCarthy, trying to persuade Kennedy backers to make the same break.

Eugene S. Daniell, Jr., sixty-five-year-old lawyer-politician from Franklin, New Hampshire, was chairman of the New Hampshire RFK-68 effort. He doggedly continued plugging for Kennedy until Ted Sorensen traveled to the state in mid-February to put a stop to efforts by Daniell and others. "Any citizen of New Hampshire who votes in this year's presidential primary either for Kennedy as a write-in candidate or for a slate of delegates favoring Kennedy is simply throwing away his vote," Sorensen told a press conference. Within days, Daniell filed papers to become a McCarthy delegate, and in an ad in the Manchester *Union Leader* he urged other Kennedy supporters to back McCarthy.

Had Kennedy not discouraged the RFK-68 group, it conceivably might have secured a large enough Kennedy write-in to have dampened the McCarthy showing. The death of the Kennedy movement was one in a string of events over which McCarthy had little influence that contributed to the unimaginable New Hampshire outcome.

20. HAPPENING

The New Hampshire primary is a happening. There is no pattern to it. As often as not it produces a surprise. People who talk like experts learn a new lesson from it every four years. Of course, the most important fact about New Hampshire politically was that its primary was the *first*. An upstart candidate could hardly avoid it. McCarthy, however, fully intended to.

McCarthy and people he sometimes listened to felt his best bet would be to start in Wisconsin, a progressive midwestern state not too unlike Minnesota where his appeal was unquestioned. He was known to some degree in Wisconsin; he would feel at home there. At the same time, he wanted to conduct his test of Vietnam policy and the political process in each region of the United States. To do this he would have to enter at least one eastern primary. Massachusetts seemed more attractive because its primary fell after Wisconsin's; a large segment of its population was highly sophisticated; it did not have the reputation of "hawkishness" that New Hampshire did; a broader base of support was apparent in Massachusetts, both financially and organizationally, than in New Hampshire. Complicating Massachusetts were the Kennedys, whom McCarthy ultimately disregarded.

Other factors were considered. At his announcement of candidacy, McCarthy had said he might visit Vietnam after the first of the year. This would leave little time to campaign in New Hampshire. The Democratic party in New Hampshire was relatively small (about 89,000 registered Democrats at the time of the primary), thus a high per cent of the party workers were probably pretty well controlled. (When he learned a bit more about the party, however, he would say: "The regular Democratic organization in New Hampshire is like the hierarchy of the Presbyterian church: There really isn't much of it.") The nature of the state—cold, population scattered—would require a lot of uncomfortable travel which might put a strain on the candidate that would handicap him later. Some advisers reasoned that starting in Wisconsin and succeeding there would make it even harder for Kennedy to enter. There was also the possibility that the Kennedy New Hampshire write-in movement might turn into something. Moreover, it was not perfectly clear what the administration planned to do in New Hampshire, though a write-in effort seemed certain. A write-in campaign would give McCarthy an opportunity to confront the President, even though Johnson wouldn't campaign personally. However, a contest against a favorite son, such as Senator Thomas McIntyre or Governor John King, which was also conjectured at that time, might tend to blur the issue. Thus, there were plenty of reasons not to go into New Hampshire.

"We agreed it was totally impractical to go there," said John Safer. "When I left [on vacation] I thought it was all settled."

Obviously it wasn't, for it became apparent McCarthy had to counteract his campaign's early listlessness. His daughter Mary explained it succinctly:

"He went into New Hampshire to prove he meant what he was talking about. It was not a heroic gesture. It was a campaign. You can't avoid a fight. And there was some feeling if you're going to get crushed, let's get it over with."

The New Hampshire McCarthy effort started October 26, 1967. Curtis Gans showed up at a Democratic workshop at Colby Junior

College in New London and spoke to David C. Hoeh, thirty, who had worked in a number of New Hampshire campaigns and was currently at odds with Governor John King. Might Hoeh and some of the others there like to take part in an anti-Johnson effort? Gans asked. "Yes," said Hoeh with little hesitation. "I'm not happy with Vietnam. I feel the war is an albatross to the nation, and not just to the party." Hoeh's wife, Sandy, Second District Democratic chairman, and Gerry Studds, thirty, a master at Saint Paul's School, were also agreeable. Dr. David Underwood III, Concord Democratic chairman, said: "I have nothing to lose, but I think you're nuts." Gans also got the support of Vincent Dunn, state banking commissioner, and Charles Sheridan, Jr., an attorney. Gans traveled the state, talking to people Hoeh had suggested. Allard Lowenstein flew in two weeks later for a pep meeting.

On November 19 the state Democratic committee dropped its façade of neutrality and voted "to take all steps necessary to bring about the renomination and reelection of Lyndon Johnson." That night in Bedford a group of thirteen, headed by Hoeh and Studds, constituted itself as the New Hampshire McCarthy for President Steering Committee, not knowing whether McCarthy would indeed enter their primary.

The disappointment from their inability to sway McCarthy at the Chicago meeting was deepened when the New York Times said a few days later McCarthy probably would not campaign in New Hampshire. But they were not about to give up. Perhaps they could persuade McCarthy, on December 14, when he was scheduled to come to New Hampshire to lecture on human rights. The steering committee drummed up a big crowd for the event, at the Sheraton-Wayfarer outside Manchester. The crowd applauded heartily as McCarthy stepped to the podium. When he finished his talk there was virtual silence. McCarthy had delivered his lecture as a lecture. Its chutzpa quotient was zero. Was this their tiger? Ye gods!

Afterward, McCarthy met with sixty supporters in the Bedford home of Philip and Sylvia Chaplain. He fully intended to tell them he would not run in New Hampshire. McCarthy rarely told anyone

no personally. He might agree to a personal appearance, then instruct a staff person to get him out of it. He could let Lowenstein
think he would announce his candidacy at the Chicago meeting,
then have Joe Rauh pass along the change in plans. It was as if he
did not like the unpleasantness of saying no. Thus he sometimes
strung people along. He could not bring himself to say no this
night.

The group subdued their disappointment over the McCarthy
speech, for they did not want to offend their guest. "This is a government in exile," McCarthy told them. Mild chuckles. They weren't
attuned to the McCarthy wit as yet. Once again, they went through
their arguments for a McCarthy challenge in New Hampshire.
John Teague, a New Hampshire student from Amherst, added his
own with passion: "Students are tired of protests and marches, sit-ins
and draft card burning. They don't get us anywhere. We want to do
it in the system, push the system to the limits of its capacity."

McCarthy seemed more attentive, but left still having made no
commitment. Newspaper stories continued to say McCarthy had no
plans to enter the New Hampshire race. Just before Christmas,
Hoeh and Studds put their arguments into a memo and sent it to
McCarthy. Some of its points:

—The nucleus of an "experienced, broadly representative, and
committed organization" existed, and there was a large volunteer
stock to draw on for canvassing and envelope stuffing.

—Campaigning in Massachusetts and New Hampshire was in
many ways a "package." More populous southern New Hampshire
contained bedroom communities for people who worked in Boston,
with large numbers of new, independent voters. This is where Hoeh
envisioned concentrating the campaign.

—The media always focused on New Hampshire. The exposure
McCarthy would get would help his later efforts.

—A New Hampshire campaign would reaffirm the seriousness of
McCarthy's effort.

—The campaign would be relatively cheap, about $50,000. (The
final cost was close to $300,000.)

"If we are to move," the memo stated, *"we must get going yester-day."*

But as late as December 28, the *New York Times* reported that McCarthy felt New Hampshire was "not particularly significant" for his purposes, though he might consent to a write-in campaign. The memo seemed to have had little effect.

It was always difficult to engage McCarthy in prolonged discussion on any matter, but Clark got an opportunity at that time. Bad weather forced McCarthy to take a train to New York instead of flying, and Clark took the long ride with him. Most of the way Clark, every bit as low-key as McCarthy, reviewed all the arguments for a New Hampshire race. By the time they reached New York, McCarthy was ready to announce he would run. A few days later, he made his decision public.

McCarthy's announcement stirred excitement among the small group Hoeh had put together, but did not immediately allay criticism elsewhere of his seemingly lifeless campaign to that point. His effort was still very much in the doldrums when he made his first campaign foray into New Hampshire January 26. Party officials felt McCarthy would be lucky to get 10 to 12 per cent of the vote; some estimates were lower. Thus when McCarthy stopped by Governor King's office after filing his candidacy papers at the State House in Concord, King greeted him with a catbird amiability.

"You'll find the people here will treat you with courtesy," he told McCarthy. "I think you'll like campaigning in New Hampshire."

Those New Hampshiremen he met that day were courteous enough, but they were few and far between, and not many recognized him. At times he almost had to plead with people to stop and shake his hand. "Don't run away from me," he called wistfully, his hand outstretched, as two teenage girls hurried by on a Nashua sidewalk. He entered the stores on Nashua's Main Street reluctantly and with an apology. "Sorry to disrupt your store," he would say as the reporters and cameramen trooped in behind him. Schedulers placed him in Manchester's second largest restaurant at the busiest part of the lunch hour so he could shake a lot of hands, but he refused. He did not want to disturb anyone's meal. A young man who was to have arranged a stop outside the Brookshire Knitting Mill in Manchester for a change of shifts simply disappeared. The campaign entourage got to the plant thirty minutes early and had to stand around in the cold doing nothing. When the shift finally changed, only fifteen middle-aged women walked past McCarthy, but so quickly that he was lucky to touch an arm, let alone a hand. Moreover, it was discovered the plant was nonunion. "Well, that's enough of that," McCarthy muttered when he saw how dismal the stop had turned out.

To that point, the day had been a failure, but it was a failure with an engaging quality to it. Some of the reporters who covered it had previously been exposed to the huffing, puffing scurrying of George Romney, and this was a pleasant, if curious, diversion. McCarthy put on a happy face. "It's been a good opening day," he said. "A good response." And he wryly added: "Well organized, too." He was so ebullient he told volunteers in the Concord headquarters that he would settle for 55 per cent of the vote from what he'd seen that day. "I have never had as encouraging a response, even in my own state."

He had seen something that no one else saw that day, and his euphoria lingered into the evening when he addressed seven hundred persons at Saint Anselm's College in Manchester. The setting was perfect. McCarthy was never flat when addressing an audience at a Catholic college. Moreover, Saint Anselm's was operated by the Benedictines, and so he could start off with a dig at the Jesuits, whom the Benedictines looked down on as connivers, among other things. One of McCarthy's running jokes would get a better response before Catholic audiences: how the Pentagon had seemed to pick up everything the Vatican Council tried to give up for the church. "The idea of grace of office is running strongly among the generals now (laughter). . . . They have picked up the idea of holy wars (laughter). . . . They're greatly concerned about heresy (laughter). . . .

They're beginning to use more Latin words in the Pentagon (laughter). . . . all their important words now have Latin roots, like escalation, and rectification, and pacification, and—this may be an overstatement—when you see their first release come out in Latin, then you'll know that the time (laughter) has come to really and genuinely be alarmed (laughter)."

He chided Dean Rusk who "has denounced dissension because, in one of his more original phrases, it causes 'joy in Hanoi,'" said McCarthy. Again he told how he came to speak out against the war. And he spoke of deeper hopes for his campaign:

I'm here in New Hampshire in this, the last part of January, to initiate a campaign in which I challenge a Democratic President, and I challenge a particular policy in Vietnam. But beyond that, I would hope that—I'm not so much challenging as suggesting, really, a change of course for America. I suggest that we look to what we are, really, and to look again and consider what our new responsibilities are in a world which is very different from that which existed after World War I and even at the end of World War II. And this suggested change will really not come in response to what I have to say. It will come in part, I hope, from that.

I suppose it will really not come in response to what you may say or do here in New Hampshire and how you may vote. But I think that, in part, that change can be influenced by what does take place here in New Hampshire in March. And I ask you . . . when you go out from this hall tonight, into the streets of this city and into the other cities of New Hampshire, the towns and the villages, and the farms, and this state, that you are aware at least of that share of the burden of citizenship which you carry in the United States, that what you say in some way will be heard, and that what you do—even though it may seem to be unimportant and minimal—will also be noted.

The trend which we now see in America and the policy which we are following need not be continued. This need not be an America which is on the edge of despair. It can, again, be an America of confidence. This need not be an America in which suspicion becomes a growing characteristic. This can be an America, again, in which trust is the mark of individual and general disposition.

This need not be an America in which fear seems to hang as a cloud. It can be an America which is characterized, again, as our country always has been, by an openness and by a hope. It need not be an America which seems to be guided by a kind of narrow expediency. It can, I think, be an America which pursues and which follows our traditional principles.

It need not be an America which seems to be dominated by military considerations. It can be an America which responds in the fullness of our past and, also, in the fullness of our potential to the future. This can be, I think, an America again which is singing; an America which is full of confidence, which is full of trust, and which is full of hope. Not just an example to the world, but a genuine help to the world.

It's within this general conception that I would call upon all of you here to respond in this campaign of 1968 with the fullest possible commitment of your intellect and with, also, the fullest willingness on your part to commit your will to this task. This is the burden of responsibility for each of us as Democrats and Republicans. It's the burden of responsibility which we carry even more significantly, I think, as citizens of this country, and fundamentally and ultimately, it's a burden we carry if we are willing to say, as we all must, that we are patriots in the United States.

The applause was long and warm, for his meanings had got through that evening. He was telling them that in this little place, doing their little things, they might make felt what was crying out inside them, and it is certain that deep down many of them knew, as Francis Morrow, of Bedford, Indiana, knew, that it wasn't just Vietnam that was the matter.

Here's Otto Oleson up in Coos County, having had his say at the special session of county chairmen and in early January not thinking he can do much about it when a phone call from Gerry Studds comes and Studds wants Oleson to file as a McCarthy delegate. They have never met. Channing Evans, a liberal Republican in Berlin, has told Studds that Oleson is a good man. "I'll get the beating of my life," Oleson tells Studds. "All I can offer is limited time and dubious advice and my own expenses and I'll do it only to give the people a chance to voice their dislike of the Administration policies in Vietnam, though I have no quarrel with the President's domestic policies, except that he's squandering money promoting an outmoded foreign policy, and if that's acceptable I'll do it." "Okay," says Studds. And soon Oleson finds himself working with a young student from Yale named Marc Kasky and one other Democrat, which is just about the McCarthy organization in that part of New Hampshire at that time. Soon it grows. Kasky tediously gets to know and win the respect of every wielder of power in the area, knocking on doors, jawing for hours in Ruth's Bar where some Berlin people discuss things, and dealing with the mother superiors (he forgot what you call them; "head nuns" was all he could think of until he asked Abigail McCarthy), organizing the high-school students and dispatching the college kids who can speak French into the French-speaking areas of Berlin and Coos County and finally pulling off perhaps the biggest upset of the New Hampshire campaign when Berlin goes for McCarthy, 1,636 to 1,524. (When the vote from Berlin comes in, things will start getting better, the President's man would vow election night, so sure was he of the vote from the dingy upstate mill town.)

Here's David Roberts, the history professor, climbing up a ladder at the new McCarthy headquarters in Lebanon to put the big sign in place, then climbing back down and going inside and sitting in a chair and looking out the window, butterflies suddenly fluttering in his stomach as he wonders how in the world he'll ever get a vote for McCarthy, for he feels suddenly as if he were in a foreign country. His world is Dartmouth five miles north, an academic oasis nourished on the *New York Times*, not the Manchester *Union Leader*. He doesn't know Lebanon, though he's lived in the area eleven years. "I felt more at home in London the year before," he says. When it is over, after that rather brash but effective student, Fred Wilman, is sent in to help, after all the other students come, after all the work is done, Lebanon comes within twelve votes of going McCarthy.

Here are William Johnson, a New York publisher, and his pretty TV-actress wife, Sandy, flying from New York to New Hampshire in their private plane to try to find the McCarthy campaign because they think maybe, just maybe, this might be the answer. They are angry, frustrated about the war and the mood it has brought to the country, and it has come to the point where they are thinking of packing and leaving altogether. But first they'll look at the Mc-

Carthy thing in New Hampshire. They have a hard time finding it at first; then they do, and they hear the man and they have a "strong positive reaction," so positive they offer to help, and pretty soon Johnson is flying actor Paul Newman around in his airplane and Sandy is working with Sandy Silverman from Chicago on scheduling all the celebrities whom people like Barbara Handman and Frances Leer and Mrs. Robert Loggia in New York are lining up to appear for McCarthy in New Hampshire. (Later, the Johnsons tell their New York friends Frank and Eleanor Perry all about the campaign. The Perrys made the award-winning film *David and Lisa,* and pretty soon they find themselves making a film for McCarthy about the Children's Crusade called *All the Way to Jerusalem.*)

Here's John Meloney, forty-five, eastern regional director of American Youth Hostels, convinced the nation is on a straight path toward nuclear devastation, disgusted with Robert Kennedy, whom he had been ready to support, for not acting. Then Sandy Hoeh calls to get several Claremont people together. Claremont. That's very conservative. Five or six couples show up. Meloney's wife, Virginia, a pretty ex-journalist, ex-commercial pilot, current real estate manager, is there. Meloney hadn't really ever heard of McCarthy till a short time earlier. No one is willing to be McCarthy leader, so Meloney says they can use his name, though he can't do much work since his job keeps him on the road. So he and Virginia become cochairmen of Sullivan County. Before they know it, there's McCarthy in their home for the first coffee hour of the New Hampshire campaign. All the television people are in the Meloney house, too, and all the photographers and reporters, and McCarthy slips and nearly falls on the ice outside the Meloney home. When McCarthy goes to speak to the Claremont Rotarians, Rodney Brock, the president, bars the television cameras, to much indignant howling. McCarthy does not mind. The club sings "Li'l Liza Jane" and "Smile, and the World Smiles with You," and pretty soon McCarthy is telling them how the country must "turn aside from the war in

order to attend to the most pressing problem at home": the problem
of the Negro held like "a kind of colonial people in our own country." No one walks out during the speech as Rotarians sometimes
do in Claremont. Tom Wicker, of the *New York Times,* is there, and
he writes:

It is possible that Rodney Brock was legally off base in turning out the
cameras, and it is possible that Gene McCarthy is wrong in his stand on
the war. Some might question Brock's judgment and others challenge
McCarthy's motives, but during luncheon at the Rotary Club nobody could
accuse either of showing an image rather than a self. That is probably not
good politics; all the pros will tell you that. But in an age when the image
is the idol, the old values are inspected by avid tourists, and the flagrant
falsities and pretensions of American life deride verity, two men stubbornly
being themselves must be worth something.

The Meloneys believe so. They have a hard time convincing many
Democrats. Republican friends begin to listen. One, Mrs. Betti
Learned, turns her house into a headquarters. Another, whose husband is publishing anti-McCarthy editorials in his newspaper, opens
her home to a party of fifty Republicans thrown by Virginia Meloney. The students come, and Mrs. Meloney finds them sleeping
all over the floor after long days of work. Suddenly the day after
election comes and Meloney discovers he has been elected a delegate to the convention in Chicago, and he hasn't even campaigned
except for a short spell one day when Paul Newman dropped
through and said nice things about McCarthy and Meloney, two
men who lent their names.

Here's Barbara Underwood explaining to her husband, David,
who still has doubts about the whole thing, why he should go ahead
and take on cochairmanship of the Concord effort with Marsha
Macey. Barbara Underwood, something of a professional since she
worked in the Louis Lefkowitz campaign in New York, is saying,
"Look, David, I know you're busy. But do it anyway. You're not a
peacenik. People regard you around here as an intelligent young
professional man whose opinion they respect. They may not agree
with you, but McCarthy needs people like you in his campaign to

focus attention on the fact that he isn't some kind of kook. It may also focus attention on the fact he's a serious candidate for the presidency." So David does it, and so here is Barbara with Marsha Macey and the Hoehs and Studds in the old Ralph Pill electrical appliance shop on Pleasant Street Extension in Concord sweeping the place out while their children are running around playing with discarded light sockets and wires, and this is the state headquarters which opens January 14 to curious stares from the people hanging around the taxi office next door.

Now here's Barbara Underwood working on some way to draw attention to McCarthy. George Romney has driven a Snow-Mobile. Even tipped over once. The pictures were printed all over. "It's too bad you don't ski," she tells McCarthy. "Well, I skate," he tells her. "I'm a very good hockey player." Barbara Underwood feels a little thrill shoot through her. "That's wonderful. That's better than skiing. You can skate at the Douglas Everrett Memorial Arena in Concord." There is an Old Timers Hockey League that plays there. "You'd better practice," she tells McCarthy. "Oh, I'm a good player. You don't have to worry about my practicing." All she has to worry about is whether he'll actually do it. Then one evening the telephone rings, and suddenly Barbara Underwood finds herself listening to her husband on the telephone saying yes, McCarthy *will* play hockey tonight, so borrow some skates, size eleven and a half or twelve. It is February 6 and when the pictures of McCarthy skating like crazy, holding a hockey stick and wearing a helmet, get across the country it proves he's alive, and this is when the campaign starts to pick up. The skates come from a fellow named Bower, and during the hockey game McCarthy gives Bower a vicious body check sending him sliding across the ice with a curious look on his face; and finally McCarthy's campaign aides, fearing he's going to injure himself or drop dead of a heart attack, implore Underwood to exert his physician's wisdom to get McCarthy off the ice, which he does, much to McCarthy's relief. In a few days all over New Hampshire McCarthy workers are passing out windshield scrapers with an etching of McCarthy playing hockey and the words "McCarthy Cuts Ice."

.   .   .

It is going on elsewhere. In Monmouth County, New Jersey, for example, a letter to the editor in the local paper says so few people will show up at the McCarthy organizing meeting late in February the meeting should be held in a phone booth. Peter Lumia, thirty-seven, an attorney, has scheduled the meeting in the First Unitarian Church in Lincroft, which turns out to be standing-room-only, and the church is much bigger than a phone booth. Mrs. Jeanne Galazan in Milwaukee invites fifteen persons to an organizing meeting of a Wisconsin McCarthy women's group, and sixty show up. In Sioux City, Iowa, Carrol McLaughlin works for McCarthy and gets the bug to run for school board, and the opposition smears him as a pinko and he loses, but he has a strange satisfaction he's not had before. In the mornings, Mrs. Linda M. Nichols' husband delivers milk, and in the evenings there's Mrs. Nichols tramping the streets of Middletown, Connecticut, even when it's snowing, getting signatures on a petition that will force a primary election in her town.

In Washington, D.C., the McCarthy headquarters in the Transportation Building is filling up with young volunteers. There is a bustle reminiscent of the early days of the Peace Corps or the early days of the poverty war, and there is obviously more motion than production, but this is where the action is. It is a bit more staid at the Alban Towers apartment building where another group works, mainly women. They are sorting mail, answering it, preparing mailings to New Hampshire and elsewhere, zip-coding the envelopes. The mailing is one of Abigail McCarthy's largely unseen contributions. Here are these women poring through alumni directories from their respective colleges, sending personalized form letters in plain envelopes hand-addressed and hand-stamped so the recipient will be sure to open them and find that it's from a fellow alumna talking about McCarthy. Later, Abigail expands the technique to special groups such as teachers, lawyers, doctors, ministers, accountants. My gosh, now these women are addressing the whole Berlin phone directory, ripping out pages and sending some of them to the Mc-Carthy group in Baltimore to address. A shuttle system is developing. They're also going through the Nashua and Manchester phone books identifying nationality groups by name and sending them personalized letters. Now they've run out of money for stamps again and so they send the teenagers who are hanging around, like Kathy Grogan and Steve Klein, to Georgetown to sell McCarthy buttons and bumper stickers to get money to keep the mail going—more than a million hand-addressed pieces out of Alban Towers before the campaign ends.

People do these things in every campaign, but it was different this time. It was not for a man or a party, but for themselves and their country, and it happened with little direction, which was the way McCarthy wanted it. Nashua Mayor Dennis Sullivan saw astutely what was going on from that first McCarthy visit on January 26, though he didn't think it would work. "[They] wanted him to tell them what to do and he wants them to find out for themselves." Richard Goodwin, an off-again, on-again McCarthy campaign aide who had been a White House assistant in the Kennedy and Johnson administrations, said it much the same way. "He doesn't want to tell people what to do but to illuminate what should be done. He doesn't believe in heroes." McCarthy implied this last point to writer Gloria Steinem, who produced an article titled "Trying to Love Eugene" (which McCarthy did not like) for *New York* magazine. She asked McCarthy if there were any time in history he might have preferred to live in. After some hesitation, he replied: "Perhaps England when there were no heroes. And no nationalism. Sometime between the 11th and 16th Centuries. That's when the English language was being developed by men like Chaucer and Langland and Shakespeare. And Erasmus, don't forget Erasmus. That would have been an interesting time to live. A good time for intellectuals."

In thought and action, McCarthy was antihero, which was one of the reasons he caught on with the young. Of course, the young were no more aware of this or McCarthy's other traits as the New Hampshire campaign got under way than were John and Virginia Meloney or any of the other New Hampshire McCarthy leaders. When the students began pouring into New Hampshire from colleges along the eastern seaboard and elsewhere, they were responding to an issue and a situation. This Children's Crusade, as it became known, was, essentially, as spontaneous as everything else in the campaign. Lowenstein and some of the young people at the National Student Association Congress in August of 1967 had envisioned it and set some machinery going to get it launched, once there was a candidate. But most of the students who went to New Hampshire earliest did so more on their own than because of some master plan that had been developed the previous summer. "It would have happened anyway," said Stephen Cohen, one of the students closest to Lowenstein.

Before his announcement of candidacy, McCarthy had said a dissident campaign should be more than a Children's Crusade. Nonetheless, involvement of college students became the first landmark in his effort.

Eric Schnapper, twenty-four, a bespectacled, ordinary-looking young man from the Yale Law School, was the first out-of-state student to join the campaign in New Hampshire. He did not get involved for purely idealistic reasons. He wanted to get some political experience. Moreover, he was still a Bobby Kennedy admirer, even though Kennedy had not become a candidate. Schnapper, son of a Washington, D.C., publisher, got to New Hampshire in a roundabout way. He had worked briefly with Sandy Frucher's wife, Floss, for New York Mayor John Lindsay. Early in 1968, while in New York, Schnapper mentioned to Floss that he would like to work in the McCarthy campaign. She told her husband. A few days later, Frucher phoned Hoeh who phoned Schnapper who was instructed to phone Studds who said to come ahead, and on January 14 Schnapper found himself driving through the sleet from New Haven to Concord. It took eight and a half hours to get there, the weather was so bad. "All the way there I kept thinking that this is a real campaign. But when I got there it was just Studds and Hoeh and a list of people who were interested."

Schnapper's first task was helping get the new Concord headquarters on Pleasant Street Extension in order. Studds found him a place to sleep in the Saint Paul's School infirmary, which became the hostel of many of the earliest students in the campaign. (Later they slept on floors in churches and homes and the various head-quarters across the state.)

Schnapper drove back to New Haven briefly late that week, and when he returned the following week end brought three students from the Connecticut College for Women with him. (He had had a girl friend at the school put up a notice that student volunteers were needed in New Hampshire.) The three were Ann Kibling, Lee Van Kirk, and Naomi Fatt. In the meantime, Dan Dodd arrived from Union Theological Seminary. (He eventually spent most of his time recruiting students from New Hampshire colleges.) Schnapper by now had agreed to stay on full time. Both Studds and Hoeh could devote only part time because of the demands of their jobs. Thus Schnapper was the first full-time campaign worker in New Hampshire. Dodd was the second. Schnapper hired Dianne Dumanoski, who had dropped out of graduate literature studies at Yale, and she was the third. Steve Landers, of the University of Michigan, arrived at about this time, and by January 25, Cindy Samuels, who organized a number of students from Smith and other campuses, was on the scene. Nicki Sauvage, Sue Solenberger, and Sara Elston, from Smith, and Chris Howells, from the Connecticut College for Women, responded. As the first "McCarthy girls," they traveled in the candidate's cavalcade, passing out buttons and pamphlets. Schnapper launched a "Yalie of the Week" program at the law school: a different law student traveled to New Hampshire every week. The parade included Stewart Deutsch, Gerald Sumida, Ed Shaw (he stayed on and worked with Schnapper, taking care of advance preparations for McCarthy visits), Michael Raiss, Matthew Zwerling, and Marc Shantz, who brought his wife.

But Schnapper was alone at first, trying to absorb the orders Hoeh and Studds gave him a few days after his arrival: Go to Manchester and open up a headquarters; have it ready by January 26, because McCarthy is scheduled to visit then.

"I had never rented a room or anything," Schnapper said later. "I had thought I would get up there and do something like lick stamps and all of a sudden I'm supposed to open a headquarters, because McCarthy is going to visit it. Here we were the greatest country in the world and there we were, only me to open up a headquarters. A presidential campaign!"

It had already struck him as fantastically ridiculous, the way they would have to call Blair Clark two or three times a day to make sure there would be money for this or that, or sometimes write checks of their own. But without too much trouble, Schnapper found an empty store-front office at Bridge and Elm streets in Manchester. But what did you put in it? Some chairs, a desk, a typewriter, what else? Making calls from a pay phone in a grocery store, Schnapper rented equipment for the office. At one point, between calls, the phone suddenly rang. It was Blair Clark calling from Washington. "I understand things are going swell," he told Schnapper, who suddenly felt enveloped in unreality. "You're doing a fine job, my good man." And Clark hung up. The headquarters opened on time.

On February 6, Stephen Cohen, of Harvard, shaved off his mustache, put on a neat blue pinstripe suit, picked up Arlene Popkin and Mary McCarthy, daughter of the candidate, at Radcliffe, and headed for New Hampshire. They took a loaf of French bread, a large can of Hawaiian Punch, and extra pairs of socks, since Cohen's Valiant did not have any heat. They had to stop at a Howard Johnson's en route to thaw out.

It was beginning to build now, though even by the second week end in February fewer than a hundred students were going to New Hampshire. On February 11 Sam Brown arrived as student leader. Curtis Gans came a week or so later. Ann Hart, twenty-one, pert little daughter of U.S. Senator Philip Hart, had been managing the Saint Alban's office in Washington, but now she too disappeared to New Hampshire to help manage student volunteers. John Barbieri, twenty-three, just back from the Peace Corps in India, signed on and began trying to organize a mass mailing campaign. Joel Feigenbaum, twenty-five, a Cornell graduate student in nuclear physics, supervised canvassing, dispatching thousands of students about the state. Ben Stavis, a twenty-six-year-old Ph.D. candidate at Columbia studying Chinese politics, obtained detailed maps of every city and town to be canvassed from the state highway department, cut them into sections, and duplicated each section by the dozens so that canvassers, also armed with street directories, would be able to find their assigned canvass areas with no difficulty. From a New York law firm came Charles Negaro, primarily out of curiosity, and found that his first task was taking down folding chairs after a McCarthy speech. A twenty-two-year-old social worker, Katie Odin, hurried east from Portland, Oregon. Jessica Tuchman, twenty-one, daughter of historian Barbara Tuchman, moved to New Hampshire shortly after joining the Washington staff (she became a close aide to Gans). Harold Ickes, Jr., came up from New York. Richard G. Stearns, twenty-four, of Fresno, California, one of many who had known Lowenstein and Gans through the National Student Association, joined the crusade. Lance Dublin, sixteen, a suburban Washington high-school student, finding himself with free time when teachers at his school went on strike, went to work in the Washington headquarters, but traveled twice to New Hampshire, once on a volunteer-packed chartered bus with Senator McCarthy's sixteen-year-old son Mike. Parker Donham and Mary Davis arrived in New Hampshire from their eastern colleges and stayed on as press aides through Chicago, as did Nancy Perlman and Alice Krakauer.

Three week ends before the election more than five hundred students went to New Hampshire. The final two week ends the invasion accelerated. Somewhere around a thousand poured in for the final week end's surge, and, campaign officials said, more than twice that were told not to come because there wasn't housing or work enough for them. In all, the students and young people canvassed some sixty thousand New Hampshire homes, about two-thirds of the total. They got out twice that many pieces of mail and distributed an untold number of leaflets.

The mailings encountered some trouble. Steve Cohen figured at one point that at the rate the outgoing mail was being prepared, the whole mailing of 120,000 pieces wouldn't get out until shortly before the 1984 election. More volunteers were called, and the pace was immediately stepped up. A mailing crisis also developed in Washington. After tens of thousands of envelopes had been stuffed, it was suddenly discovered each piece was an eighth of an ounce overweight. To send them would cost about $10,000 more than expected or than was on hand. The envelopes were emptied, the letters redone on lighter paper, the envelopes restuffed, and the mailing sent off to New Hampshire.

The outpouring of student help—Schnapper and the five thousand who followed him—succeeded despite fears among David Hoeh and Blair Clark and many others that it might backfire. Said Hoeh: "We did not want hippies or flower children." In Concord, Barbara Underwood had overheard some New Hampshire women chatting in the bank about the miniskirts on some of the earliest arrivals. Betty Eberhart had thought a couple of the McCarthy girls smoking outside Saint Paul's was unattractive. Barbara Underwood discussed the matter with Steve Cohen, who, having already shaved his mustache, was searching for new rims for his glasses to replace the mod gold wire rims he used. They agreed that students making personal contacts or on public display should look as neat as possible. "The boys should look like Brooks Brothers and the girls like Peck & Peck," Cohen told Mrs. Underwood. The "Clean for Gene" precepts were put down on paper.

"Be Neat and Clean for Gene," the memo read. "No beards. Wear a coat and tie, 'nice pants.' NO BLUE JEANS OR WORK SHIRTS."

The memo instructed women: "Absolutely no slacks, no miniskirts. . . . EXTREME DRESS OF ANY KIND—EXOTIC JEWELRY, MAKE-UP, ETC.—SHOULD BE AVOIDED. . . . Neat hair-do. Long flying tresses should be restrained in a barrette."

Bus leaders were instructed: "It is extremely important that you turn away (as politely and tactfully as possible) any person who fails the 'neat and clean' test before they leave for New Hampshire. If they come, there may not be any work for them. They will be unhappy; we will be unhappy."

Unhappiness was very rare in New Hampshire. The bearded ones who did come worked out of sight in the Concord headquarters basement with zest. It was all for the cause. Besides, working for McCarthy rapidly became as much the thing to do among some students as growing a beard.

Said Richard Goodwin of the student effort: "They were like the Viet Cong. They couldn't be fought in the traditional way." Nor were they organized in a traditional way. Lines of authority blurred even more than in the helter-skelter of the usual campaign. A Kennedy headquarters in the primaries had some form and structure. A McCarthy headquarters didn't. In New Hampshire, there were "nominal leaders" and "coordinators" supposedly in charge of one thing or another, but most of these "led" because they simply happened to be there first. The demarcation between chiefs and Indians was obscure. Everyone pitched in to do anything. This spirit during the summer would disintegrate into something like *Lord of the Flies,* but in New Hampshire it was as fresh and clean as the snow.

The Children's Crusade emerged just as the candidacy of George Romney died, and reporters from across the country began to focus on it as a new curiosity. And, indeed, it was one of the most dramatic phenomena in the history of American politics. But the reporters paid so much attention to the young people that they missed the broader story of the McCarthy effort, just as they had missed the story of the Goldwater movement in 1964 most of the way.

Generally speaking, the campaign was still not going visibly well at the end of January. A very simple strategy had evolved: to make a good showing in New Hampshire. (Otherwise it would be all over, even though McCarthy had vowed to continue to the end, no matter what.) This obvious strategy required the candidate to spend as much time in New Hampshire as possible, or so most McCarthy people thought. After his announcement, the indications were that he would campaign perhaps twelve days in New Hampshire. But he abruptly cut this to eight. No one in the campaign staff was able "to hold his feet to the fire," as Clark had been told he must. Sandy Frucher, late in January, took it upon himself to plead with Mary McCarthy to get her father moving and her mother even more involved. At one point, Mary McCarthy stormily told her father, in effect: If you aren't going to get up there and campaign I'll quit school and do it myself. (Even after the problem was settled—McCarthy added fourteen more days to his New Hampshire schedule in mid-February—she did drop out for the duration of the campaign, as did many other students.) Even Abigail McCarthy, originally against the candidacy, felt a stronger effort ought to be made if one was going to be made at all.

Like every member of the McCarthy family, Abigail is intelligent, strong-minded, and individualistic, qualities that could engender combativeness as well as respect. She played a large role early in the campaign. She organized Women-for-McCarthy groups which included wives of some politicians who to then had withheld support from McCarthy, such as Mrs. Philip A. Hart, wife of the Senator, and Mrs. Henry Reuss, wife of the Wisconsin Congressman. In five months she made ninety speeches, illness sending her to the hospital three times and finally forcing her from the campaign. As in past campaigns, she took countless phone calls from staffers and supporters her husband did not want to talk to. Inevitably, her concern with the campaign rankled some staffers, rightfully or not. They thought it unnecessary for her to review campaign literature before it was used. They became angry when, on one occasion, they understood she had objected to use of a picture in a supplement to be distributed with New Hampshire newspapers two Sundays before the election. "It was a picture of the Senator shaking hands with an incredibly fat woman with incredibly fat arms," said Peter Barnes, who edited the supplement. "Abigail said women voters don't identify with fat women." Abigail said later that one of the major contributors had objected to the picture, not she. Nonetheless, enough of a hassle arose that some staffers got the definite impression the candidate's wife believed they were trying to sabotage McCarthy. The fat-arms incident was small, but illustrated the leadership void at the top of the McCarthy campaign.

Especially in the early days, many young staffers were reluctant to make suggestions to McCarthy. He tended to convey the feeling they were bothering him, imposing on him, or so many of them felt. Aides quickly learned how unpredictable McCarthy's moods could be. During his first visit to Wisconsin, in January, an aide led McCarthy through a large crowd, thinking McCarthy would want to shake hands. When the crowd was behind, McCarthy icily told the aide, "Don't ever lead me through a crowd again." (At first, at least, McCarthy, rather than barrel into a crowd à la Kennedy, would drift around its outer limits, shaking a few hands, as a fish edges around a rock nibbling lichen, then move swiftly on. He eventually learned to live with crowds and seemed almost pleased the first time he was actually grabbed at and touched in March at the Detroit airport, though he did not lose one cuff link the whole campaign, nor try to.)

He was often just as disconcerting to more experienced persons involved in the campaign. Howard Stein had enlisted Julian Koenig, of the New York advertising firm of Papert Koenig Lois Inc., to help in the New Hampshire effort. The firm had handled, among other campaigns, Robert Kennedy's successful race for the Senate in New York in 1964. Koenig traveled to New Hampshire at the time of McCarthy's January visit to discuss promotional ideas he had cooked up. McCarthy avoided Koenig most of the day, and when Koenig finally got a chance to make his presentation, McCarthy ignored him, tossing off jokes to others present while Koenig tried to make sense. The only explanation for his rudeness was that McCarthy did not like high-powered advertising men, though Koenig was relatively low-key, and what they represented in politics. He did not like packaging of a candidate in any way. "When he would see a piece of campaign copy laudatory of him he'd wince a little," said Russ Hemenway.

"I just don't like slogans," he told me in New Hampshire. "I would just rather have a picture and maybe a few adjectives: integrity, experience. . . ."

But he got slogans. "There *Is* an Alternative" was the first. "New Hampshire Can Bring America Back to Its Senses" was another that sprouted from billboards. And they were pretty good, though the latter came about only after long hassles over whether the campaign should focus primarily on Vietnam ("Peace Begins in New Hampshire" was one idea discarded) or be broader. The broader approach won the day.

Howard Stein, primarily, and also Arnold Hiatt were the financial saviors of the New Hampshire campaign. The New York Coalition for a Democratic Alternative was another big contributor. Stein, who had met McCarthy in passing at a cocktail party two years earlier and was impressed, became better acquainted early in January at a New York conference arranged by economist Eliot Janeway, a McCarthy friend. At that time, Stein promised to pick up much of the tab for media in New Hampshire. It is estimated that he produced about $100,000 for New Hampshire, from his own and other sources, and naturally he cared about how the money was used. This brought Stein into an early clash with Blair Clark. Stein agreed to Russell Hemenway's suggestion that a political-demographic survey by a professional firm be made of New Hampshire. Clark didn't think it was needed. Stein got his way. One suggestion of the computerized survey was that McCarthy consider coming out in favor of a free Quebec because of the large number of French Canadians in New Hampshire. It did not take much wisdom to reject the idea. The survey was interesting, but essentially useless.

Other pressures were building upon the easygoing Clark. A revolt was brewing in the lower ranks in Washington to try to get him fired. Abigail ordered copies of all his mail sent to the McCarthy home so she could keep track of things. Hiatt also had misgivings about Clark. Jerry Eller thought him a lightweight. It seemed that everyone was trying to fill the void that Clark had not, nor could very easily under the circumstances. McCarthy ultimately gave one of his few direct orders of the campaign, one he would regret in later primaries. He told Curtis Gans to take charge of the New Hampshire campaign during the final weeks. Gans arrived in New Hampshire late in February. (Clark did not go back to New Hampshire until election eve and did not have a room in the headquarters hotel until Hiatt got one for him.) Inevitably, Clark uttered some doubts about the candidate in this period of stress. "I think we've got a fraud on our hands," he told a young campaign aide over lunch one day.

These unseen intramural wranglings paled into insignificance as the campaign in New Hampshire progressed. For in everything that mattered to the voters, McCarthy did just right. Toward the end, the once fumbling effort went off with a professional precision unthinkable just weeks earlier. And what had been portrayed as a powerful administration effort, which had got under way more than four months before the primary, faltered at every turn.

The first mistake of the New Hampshire regulars was distribution of a pledge card to be signed by registered Democrats asserting they would write in the President's name on the primary ballot. "The closest thing there could be to denying people the right to a secret ballot," declared McCarthy, grabbing a gift issue.

By mid-February, the New Hampshire Johnson men, led by Governor John King, Senator Thomas McIntyre, and Bernard Boutin, had abandoned their original strategy of simply ignoring McCarthy and extolling Johnson as "A Strong Man for a Tough Job." They decided to attack. McCarthy, stated King, was "a spokesman for the forces of appeasement" and was advocating "a policy of surrender." It was time, King asserted, for administration Democrats "to stand up and be counted" or "from now on be counted out." McCarthy responded in his usual quiet but cutting way.

King did not relent. McCarthy, he said, represented "noisy and unruly" voices of extremism in the land. But McCarthy's mild response made King seem the extremist.

"The Communists in Vietnam are watching the New Hampshire primary," blared one administration radio commercial. "Don't vote for fuzzy thinking and surrender. . . ."

But McCarthy hardly seemed guilty of either, and people began to consider him with a new regard. And while the administration forces stumbled over their own rhetoric, a series of other events helpful to McCarthy were falling neatly into place.

On February 10, the national board of the Americans for Democratic Action endorsed McCarthy. The action itself was not particularly important, except that it prompted several pro-Johnson board members to resign, thereby emphasizing the Democratic split.

On February 28, Michigan Governor George Romney dropped his bid for the Republican presidential nomination, leaving McCarthy as the only anti-Vietnam candidate in the field and assuring a sizable switch-over vote by moderate Republicans.

In Wisconsin, McCarthy's name was officially placed on the primary ballot. In Nebraska, McCarthy leader Mark Acuff announced plans for a full slate of McCarthy delegates in that primary. In Florida, the Conference of Concerned Democrats voted to enter a McCarthy slate in the May 28 primary. In Pennsylvania, McCarthy leader Michael Malin disclosed that enough signatures had been gathered to enter McCarthy in the April 23 primary. In the District of Columbia, another McCarthy slate was announced. In Massachusetts, the March 5 deadline for President Johnson to decide whether he or any Democrat designated by him would run in the April 30 primary came and went; thus by default McCarthy was assured the entire seventy-two-vote Massachusetts delegation on the first ballot at the national convention. And, almost unnoticed at first, significant developments were occurring in Connecticut and Minnesota.

The Connecticut McCarthy organization was one of the most remarkable. Its mainstays were the Reverend Joseph Duffey, thirty-five, a Protestant urban theologian; Stephanie May, a member of the national board of SANE; Anne Wexler, wife of an eye surgeon; and Geoffrey Cowan, a Yale law student who for several months had been in touch with Curt Gans and Allard Lowenstein. It eventually included a roster of such luminaries as writers William Shirer, William Styron, Barbara Tuchman, Arthur Miller, and actor Paul Newman. But its main strength was the lesser-known, intelligent, white middle-class concerned citizen who predominated in my survey of McCarthy volunteers. Though students worked in Connecticut, it was not on the same scale as in New Hampshire or Wisconsin. Connecticut's was an Adult Crusade, and it represented the real strength of the McCarthy effort across the nation.

The Connecticut people sent much of the money they initially raised to national headquarters for use elsewhere and mounted their own drive at the same time. They printed their own literature and devised their own campaign buttons because Washington had nothing to send. (One button designed by a Connecticut housewife became a favorite nationally. It was a tiny blue button with the word "Eugene" in white letters. She designed it for her husband, who didn't want to wear anything too blatant to his office.) McCarthy national headquarters, in fact, had sought to discourage the Connecticut people at first on the grounds it was hopeless to try to buck the regular Democratic machine. But early in 1968, the Connecticut McCarthyites began making the very first inroads into traditional Democratic strength. McCarthy supporters took control in a string of small-town caucuses, a first step in selecting delegates to the national convention. In other towns, workers were circulating petitions to force primaries in their communities, a device never used before that turned up in Geoffrey Cowan's study of the state's delegate selection procedure.

This kind of participation had long been evident in Minnesota. It was certainly the key factor in the creation of the Democratic-Farmer-Labor party in the late 1940's by Hubert Humphrey and his friends. And it was certainly apparent in Eugene McCarthy's takeover of the Ramsey County (Saint Paul) organization in 1948 and in his campaigns for office. Yet by 1967, grass-roots politics in Minnesota was almost as withered as anywhere else: only a few citizens maintained year-round involvement, and these few controlled the precinct and ward organizations.

The evening of March 5, a full week before the New Hampshire primary, members of the Minnesota Democratic-Farmer-Labor party were to gather at precinct and ward caucuses held across the state. Delegates elected that night would go on to county and district conventions which would select representatives to the state DFL convention in June. Each of the eight congressional districts would select five national convention delegates, and the state convention would choose twenty.

Obviously, by winning large majorities at the lowest level of the process, the next steps might be controlled. Late in 1967, supporters of McCarthy began to prepare for March 5. Almost unnoticed, they concentrated on the Third, Fourth, and Fifth Congressional Districts, encompassing the Twin Cities and suburbs. They held precinct caucus schools similar to those that helped McCarthy take over the Ramsey County organization twenty years earlier. Even before Eric Schnapper headed through the sleet to New Hampshire, students were already canvassing in the Twin Cities door to door and by phone and, at night, pumping the results into a computer.

In the forefront of the effort were people like John Wright, thirty-four, a child psychologist at the University of Minnesota and chief spokesman of the Minnesota Concerned Democrats; Forrest Harris, DFL vice-chairman; Vance Opperman and Howard Kaibel, law students; John Connolly and James Goff, of Saint Paul; Alpha Smaby, a Twin Cities legislator; Jerry Eller, of the Senate staff; and David Mixner, of the national campaign staff.

The night of March 5, DFL regulars found themselves confronted by battalions of students, nuns, citizens of all economic levels who usually didn't attend precinct caucus meetings—whites, Negroes, and American Indians in one ward. This army voted the regulars out of precinct offices. Among those defeated were Secretary of State Joseph Donovon, who muttered, "Never before in fifty years of politics have I seen this happen"; Saint Paul Mayor Tom Byrne; millionaire Robert Short (Humphrey's finance chairman in his presidential bid); Humphrey's son Robert and his son-in-law Bruce Solomonson. "In the last couple of weeks I talked to every DFL-er I could find in my ward," said one DFL politician, "and every one of them said they were sticking with the administration. I couldn't find any support for McCarthy, not any. So I was sure they wouldn't get any. Then I went to my caucus. I have lived in that district all my life and I did not know 80 per cent of the people who were there."

To old-timers in Minneapolis, the events of the night reminded them of 1948 when young Hubert Humphrey, then mayor, helped organize the ADA and tried to dump Harry Truman. On caucus night city comptroller Earl Arneson, who had been there in 1948, wandered through the McCarthy headquarters on Minneapolis' old East Side. Arneson looked out of place with his slicked-down black hair, his tailored overcoat, and his crinkled skin. Everywhere were young people, most of them in their "Clean for Gene" garb. The buttons they wore didn't say "Support Your Vice President"—as those worn by the regulars, who tried to forget the night really had to do with Lyndon Johnson. Theirs said "McCarthy," "Resist," "Love." Mostly they were youth, but they needed no button for that. "Just like 1948," Arneson said. "There are probably some Humphreys and some Freemans and Mondales here."

He did not mention McCarthy. For it was not a McCarthy victory. McCarthy was its agent. It would continue this way, even though he would become a political personality in his own right a week later when the New Hampshire vote came in.

McCarthy rarely lost sight of this truth. He phrased it best himself May 15 in Sioux Falls, South Dakota. Glancing at his hands more than at the audience, McCarthy said with a half-smile:

You get somehow trying to be too humble. But I've got a reputation for reading poetry in this campaign. Which is a rather wild thing for a politician to do. I find some help in it.

I like to quote a Greek poet. He has a poem about three mules. In one part, a mule carrying the queen . . . slips and the queen falls and breaks her neck. But very soon thereafter, the spirit of the queen appears to the man who was handling the mule and says, "Do not punish the mule . . . I was full of the will of God and that was too much of a burden for any beast to bear."

So that if you understand my candidacy, I really don't want to let you believe that I'm carrying the whole burden for the country. I'm a kind of an accidental instrument, really, through which I hope that the judgment and the will of this nation can be expressed on these matters which I do think are of great import for the future of our country and also for the future of much of the rest of the world.

This judgment and will had begun to be expressed that night in Minnesota.

The McCarthy forces did not mount efforts in rural districts and thus were unable to control the delegation to the national convention. But what happened that night in the Twin Cities was a preview of developments to come in many ways. It marked the first determined steps of the Children's Crusade and the first major political expression of antiadministration sentiment. Minnesota was also a portent of the exclusionary tendency that developed in many McCarthy organizations; veteran party workers who had realized the importance of political involvement long before an issue came along were simply tossed out on their ears simply because they were old guard, even, in many cases, when they might have worked with the McCarthy effort. And, finally, the Minnesota story showed what Hubert Humphrey would be up against as a presidential candidate. His supporters that night tested, in effect, the argument that would become so prevalent in the autumn campaign: remember, remember all the great battles of Hubert Humphrey in the past. "They would look at you and say, 'Who's Humphrey?'" Robert Short said that night. "It just doesn't mean anything to them."

That same night in California another important event, as spontaneous as what happened in Minnesota, was unfolding. Nearly five hundred parties were held to get the 13,746 signatures necessary for placing McCarthy's name on the ballot for the June 4 primary election. Whichever candidate first filed the requisite number of signatures would get his name placed at the top of the ballot, and this could mean perhaps an extra 5 per cent of the vote. By law, however, the gathering of signatures couldn't begin until the first minute of March 6, and so the parties were scheduled for late in the evening of March 5. The petition party at the San Francisco home of Jack Morrison, county supervisor and unsuccessful candidate for mayor in 1967, was typical. People started arriving about 9:30 P.M. and talked politics while sipping beer or wine or coffee and eating the four cakes Mrs. Morrison had gotten from Woolworth's. At midnight, Morrison announced that it was time to start signing petitions. It took only a few minutes to get 117 signatures.

A deputy voter registrar was present to enable non-Democrats to change their party registration before signing the petitions. Mrs. Morrison estimated that about half of those who signed had switched their registration from the Peace and Freedom party, which many former Democrats had joined to protest the war before McCarthy became a candidate.

Across the state, some 28,000 persons signed their names. A party in the cavernous Hollywood discotheque called The Factory got a thousand signatures, one of them that of Los Angeles Mayor Sam Yorty's twenty-three-year-old son, a long-haired hippie film student at the University of California. A number of show-business figures threw parties, including Jan Sterling and Carl Reiner. At 9 A.M. the next morning, campaign leaders Gerald Hill, Edmund G. (Gerry) Brown, Jr., Mrs. Jo Seidita, and a number of aides toted cartons of petitions into the Los Angeles County Registrar of Voters office—the first to file. "This is a tremendous psychological victory for us," Brown said. "We have a complete slate, our petitions are in, we have a campaign rolling, and Johnson has nothing."

The week end before the New Hampshire vote, the momentum was dizzying. Newspapers, magazines, and television networks that had all but ignored the McCarthy story until then now sent in correspondents to catch up with things. In Concord young people toting sleeping bags streamed into headquarters despite last-minute pleas by the harried staff that they stay away. There was Joyce Sweet, twenty-one, wide awake and ready to go despite an all-night drive from Oswego (New York) State College. She was directed to a table where seven other volunteers sat listening to Mrs. Marsha Macey giving canvassing instructions.

"Now don't get angry at the people. If they get angry at you, leave. We don't want to antagonize anyone. Well, I guess that's about it. Oh—it's illegal to put anything in the mail boxes so don't put any of the literature there."

A young man with a wisp of beard approached the table. "You

can't canvass," Mrs. Macey said. "I'm very sorry; we can't have any beards."

Reporters circulated through the headquarters. Down in the basement were all those maps being pored over by all those beards. Upstairs in one corner was a bank of phones, and over there was a stack of instructions for canvassers:

You are to feel out the voter's opinions before pressing any of the issues (e.g. the pledge card, Vietnam, taxes and inflation, Johnson's credibility). You want to put yourself inside the voter's frame of reference and discover how he comes to the conclusions he comes to. Be a good listener.

The pitch will vary with your own style, but bear in mind certain things. . . .

Always identify yourself as a representative of Senator McCarthy. . . .

Never ask if he is going to vote for McCarthy. Your most direct bid will be, "I hope you will consider voting for McCarthy."

On a card for each interviewee, the canvasser was to note whether the voter seemed favorable to McCarthy, uncertain but possibly favorable, had no opinion, was uncertain but possibly favorable to Johnson, or was unfavorable to McCarthy. That week end the first alternative was most popular.

Similar activity was visible all over the state, and another look showed not only the largest number of students ever involved in a primary election campaign but also, for New Hampshire at least, the largest profusion of celebrities.

There was Tony Randall, talking at coffees and on street corners and giving the ladies kisses. Robert Ryan was there that week end. Myrna Loy and Jack Paar were said to be on the way. McCarthy radio spot commercials beamed a number of familiar voices: Rod Serling, Harry Belafonte, Robert Vaughn, Dustin Hoffman, Lauren Bacall, Jason Robards, Lee Remick, Joan Bennett, Joanne Woodward. And campaigning tirelessly throughout New Hampshire was Paul Newman, an actor no one disliked, one who came across to young and old, who radiated honesty and conviction. He had the star power that McCarthy lacked and imperceptibly was transferring a little of it to the candidate. He would approach women on street corners and pin a McCarthy button on them and tell each one, "I want you to be a listening woman. Listen to what Senator McCarthy says." Why was he, Paul Newman, helping McCarthy? He would disarm them as he looked directly into their eyes and answered: "I didn't come here to help Gene McCarthy. I need Gene McCarthy's help. The country needs it."

The combustion of student power and star power and concerned citizen power simply couldn't be missed that final week end. Even the candidate whom many had written off as lazy and uninspiring seemed uncharacteristically buoyant. That Saturday night in Manchester's Sheraton Carpenter Hotel, the ballroom packed to overflowing with New Hampshire people (students had specifically been ordered to another room), he made his final major appearance. Robert Ryan introduced him as the next President, and it no longer seemed totally implausible. McCarthy spoke of America's "eroded" image abroad; he spoke of the "general uneasiness" in the land; he spoke of the present "leadership of fear" and how it must be replaced with something different. "We're here tonight not just to light a bonfire of protest that will go out in the daylight, but a signal fire, a beach fire here in New Hampshire for the people in the United States and throughout the world."

The cheering was long and warm. Barbara Underwood would write in her diary: "There is a general feeling that everything that ought to be done has been done."

The administration forces became panicky. A significant vote for McCarthy would be greeted with "cheers in Hanoi," Governor King declared. Senator McIntyre, as he had before, sought to temper King's outburst. "Hanoi Jibe Splits Democrats," blared the banner headlines on the front page of the Boston *Globe*, which circulates heavily in populous southern New Hampshire, the Sunday before the election. Five Johnson delegate candidates repudiated the King statement, and a sixth switched to support of McCarthy.

Two days before the election, McIntyre suddenly withdrew his comment that King's statement might have been "a little unfair" and issued a belated unity statement. "Let me make it clear," McIntyre said. "Governor King and I are united in our support of President Johnson. . . . Governor King said that 'a significant vote for Senator McCarthy will be greeted with cheers in Hanoi.' I agree 100 per cent. . . ."

McCarthy had proposed that draft-age men who flee the country be allowed amnesty to return if draft laws were ever changed to permit selective conscientious objection. Now McIntyre, as if to underscore his regained purity, recorded a radio spot attacking the proposal. The commercial was hurried onto the air the day before election in a last-ditch effort to damage McCarthy. "This is Senator Thomas McIntyre," the spot began. It continued:

Senator McCarthy said Saturday he would ask for laws which would allow American draft dodgers, men who have fled to Canada or Sweden to avoid fighting in Vietnam, to return home scot-free without punishment. This is a cruel affront to those who have answered their country's call to duty. To honor draft dodgers and deserters will destroy the very fabric of our national devotion. This is fuzzy thinking about principles that have made our nation great. Support the loyal men who do serve this country by writing in the name of President Johnson on your ballot.

McCarthy, of course, had not recommended that draft dodgers go "scot-free." Youths seeking amnesty, he said, would still face the possibility of punishment. Even before the spot could be broadcast, McCarthy workers learned of it and got a copy. In the predawn hours of March 11, Richard Goodwin prepared a McCarthy rebuttal that was being broadcast on radio news programs even as the commercial was first being heard. Such swift response showed that a professionalism had developed in the McCarthy campaign totally unimaginable weeks earlier. Much of the professionalism was due to Goodwin.

McCarthy's message throughout the New Hampshire campaign was essentially what he had been saying since the start of his candidacy, but with greater emphasis, always implicit, on President Johnson's failure at leadership. And increasingly he linked his own effort to the interrupted work of John Kennedy. "In almost every field of action and concern we are rapidly losing the achievement of John F. Kennedy, and we must once again get America moving," McCarthy would say, while literature picturing him and Kennedy was circulated through his audience. He questioned administration tax policies, its international relations, the growing influence of "the military-industrial complex." When Johnson called up reserves in response to seizure of the *Pueblo*, McCarthy immediately charged that Johnson had overreacted, which proved to be the case. He criticized administration slowness on problems of the cities and was the first candidate to call without reservation for enactment of the recommendations of the Kerner Commission, formed after the 1967 race riots in Detroit and Newark.

Yet he continued to be called a one-issue candidate. The focus was on his challenge on the issue of Vietnam, though he spoke of much more. It was, in fact, McCarthy's opposition in New Hampshire that mounted a one-issue campaign. Said McCarthy as the campaign ended:

This may well be the first presidential primary campaign of the modern period in which supporters of the President have failed to defend the merits of his policies or discuss a single one of the great issues which confront this country as we move toward the decade of the Seventies. . . . The entire campaign for the President has consisted of a single shrill, irrelevant and false note, the implication that opposition to the President's policies is somehow disloyal.

And that heavy-handed implication made the McCarthy volunteers work that much harder, made them consider their cause that much more just. It did seem almost a crusade in this respect—a crusade for the simple right to speak out.

"There was a sense of exhilaration," Mary McCarthy would say later. "Everyone shared it, hopeless as they thought the campaign might be. We were saying what we'd been thinking. There was a sense of freedom." And so, individually, when they saw a chance, they would, one by one, come up to McCarthy and try to express their thanks.

"Thank you for giving us a choice," an elderly woman told Mc-

Carthy at the Knights of Columbus Hall in Nashua that final Sunday of campaigning. "That's what we want, a choice," added her husband. Later, as McCarthy conversed with me on a bench in a corridor of the Sheraton Wayfarer in Bedford, a young married couple from Rhode Island stopped to thank him. "We came up on our vacation to help out," said the woman. Moments after that it was a college student: "I just want to say, sir, well, I want to thank you for being in this, bringing this thing out, giving us some way of trying to answer this thing."

The people of New Hampshire began to answer the thing in the first minutes of March 12. In the little hamlet of Waterville Valley, just after midnight, ten Democrats and thirteen Republicans went to the polls. The Democrats voted eight for McCarthy, two write-ins for Robert Kennedy, and nothing for Lyndon Johnson. One Republican wrote in McCarthy's name. Thus, first returns gave Mc-Carthy a nine to nothing lead over Johnson. In the Manchester headquarters that Eric Schnapper had opened a little over a month earlier, students posted a new sign on the wall: "LBJ Has Met His Waterville."

Just how accurate that sign was became apparent about nineteen hours later, after the polls in the rest of New Hampshire closed. Snow had begun to fall, and exhausted campaign workers tried to relax, their exertions of poll watching, driving voters, baby-sitting, last-minute phoning, finally ended. Shortly before 7 P.M. a phone rang in one of the campaign staff rooms in the Wayfarer. Allard Lowenstein eagerly picked it up. It was the first major report: Portsmouth, with only one precinct missing. "Fifty-two per cent for Mc-Carthy," Lowenstein shouted. (Actually, the information was erroneous. The final Portsmouth count was almost 69 per cent Mc-Carthy.)

In a large room set up for an election night celebration, other reports began to come in, relayed from campaign workers to Concord state headquarters to the Wayfarer: 101 votes for McCarthy, 60 for Johnson. (Cheers from the knot of students crowded behind television cameras and reporters.) At 7:25 P.M., it was 460 to 402 McCarthy; at 7:30, 523 to 564 Johnson. The system broke down as the flood of returns increased and volunteers simply read latest reports from news wires or television, the crowd chanting excitedly with each new report. "Latest NBC figures show McCarthy as carrying forty-three per cent. . . ." (Applause; shouts of "go, go, go, go.") "As of 8:37 AP reports McCarthy leading for twenty-four convention delegates." ("Goodbye, Lyndon. Goodbye, Lyndon.")

At 9:11 P.M. McCarthy entered the room where the television lights glared, and his supporters closed in on him. At that point, projections had McCarthy getting perhaps 35 per cent of the vote. McCarthy told the crowd the results looked "encouraging." "We can now go on to the nomination in Chicago." Bedlam broke loose, and Isabel Reiff and Susan Spar, of Mount Holyoke, and Beth Dunlap, of Vassar, and Barbara Gould and Stuart Forster, of Brandeis, and all the others in the room went wild.

He appeared again when it was apparent he would get over 40 per cent of the Democratic vote. He had been relatively subdued the first time, but now he was fitting into a new role entirely unimagined when he announced his candidacy. "We said 1968 was the year; but March 12 is the day," he declared exuberantly.

"Vic-to-ry, vic-to-ry, vic-to-ry!" screamed his supporters, and with each syllable they shot up arms sprouting fingers making the V sign.

"I remember early in the campaign when I said I didn't want to lead just a Children's Crusade," he declared. "But I've concluded if they had Sam Brown and Ann Hart, the Children's Crusade would have succeeded." He hugged two pretty young workers close to him.

"We're prepared to negotiate a surrender if we can find a neutral ship . . . in the harbor of Chicago."

"Chi-ca-go, Chi-ca-go, Chi-ca-go, Vic-to-ry, Vic-to-ry, Vic-to-ry," the V-signs thrusting up militantly, McCarthy even feebly trying out this curious new sign, fingers bent tentatively, not wanting, apparently, to seem too emotional, then his fingers becoming more certain as the shouting continued.

"If we come to Chicago with this strength," McCarthy told them, "there'll be no riots or demonstrations, but a great victory celebration."

The cheering was deafening now. No one this night could realize what Chicago really would be, that it would be as much a nightmare as this night seemed a dream. They had done this thing, and they sang and celebrated as McCarthy walked back through the snow from the hotel to the house behind. There he sat with his friends long into the night while the votes mounted. The totals would show that McCarthy polled 42 per cent, or 23,280 votes, in the largest Democratic primary turnout in the state's history. Lyndon Johnson got 27,243. Adding Republican write-in votes, McCarthy polled a total of 28,791 to Johnson's 29,021, bringing McCarthy within 230 votes of beating Johnson. The McCarthy vote was more anti-Johnson than anti-Vietnam, later surveys showed. It included hawks who wanted out of the war by quick victory as well as doves who simply wanted out. Senator McIntyre would assess the results this way:

We caught hell over the Viet Cong uprising. And we didn't imagine how many students would come in or how well they would do. We didn't count on how fast the McCarthy people would respond to some things. The biggest thing I didn't expect was the amount of money spent. And McCarthy came across as a gentleman and a nice man. His appearance, his demeanor, helped his cause.

McIntyre didn't have to review the administration forces' mistakes. By far the greatest was to not limit the number of candidates for the convention delegate slots, as the McCarthy forces did. The vote for the administration candidates was split; thus the McCarthy slate won. "How do you tell the President that even though he got most of the vote he got only four delegates?" McIntyre moaned. There was no way. What if Robert Kennedy had been running instead of McCarthy? "He would have beaten the President two-to-one," said McIntyre.

Shortly after midnight Robert Kennedy phoned McCarthy in New Hampshire to congratulate him.

21. REASSESSMENT

Robert Kennedy did not tell McCarthy he now would enter the race, though Kennedy friends would say later that he had decided he would about March 4. Kennedy had asked Richard Goodwin to tell McCarthy that he probably would enter, but somehow the full meaning of the message never got through to McCarthy. At his announcement, McCarthy had said he had no commitment from Kennedy to stay out, and at the low point in his campaign in December, McCarthy told a reporter he would probably move aside if Kennedy came in. Shortly before the New Hampshire vote McCarthy told Kennedy he wanted only one term as President, but he did not ask Kennedy to hold back or promise to support him in 1972.

"Yes, it was great," McCarthy said into the phone New Hampshire election night. "It was rough. Those factories—man, I tell you, I went through more factories than I've been through in twenty years in politics."

Thus McCarthy went to bed early the morning of March 13 with Kennedy's phone call in his mind, and when he appeared before reporters several hours later to review his "victory," McCarthy found questions about Kennedy overshadowing all.

Did McCarthy think Kennedy might be unhappy at the election

outcome? "I don't know if he's unhappy. I'll let him continue as he has been, speaking out on the issues."

Might McCarthy step aside? "It wouldn't be voluntary," McCarthy said with an edge to his voice. "I have no intention of stepping aside. . . . I expect to win in Wisconsin. . . . I think I can get the nomination. I'm ahead now."

He testily cut off a questioner when the name Kennedy came up again. Kennedy came up again later that day, on McCarthy's return to Washington. At National Airport, Jerry Eller hurried onto the airplane to tell him Kennedy had said he was "reassessing."

McCarthy was still considering this piece of news as he stepped from the plane. His supporters surged forward shouting, "We want McCarthy, we want McCarthy!" and waving their signs ("Unforeseen Eugene," said one). McCarthy hesitated a moment. He was still fitting into the new role of important figure in American politics. The moment quickly evaporated. Like a jet blast, the questions came from reporters about Kennedy. What did he have to say about Kennedy's reassessment? His smile began to fade. "Well, that's something you should ask him." Would he withdraw if Bobby entered? Microphones jabbing at him; reporters swearing at each other and swinging their elbows; McCarthy's face grim now; an uncharacteristic stammer in his voice. "I don't intend to withdraw." What was said in the phone conversation the night before? Would he talk with Kennedy again? When? Kennedy Kennedy Kennedy Kennedy. The afternoon paper said Kennedy in the banner headline; McCarthy got lesser type. He was a secondary story before even a full day of headlines had been his. "It was like someone had stolen all the Christmas presents," Roberta Melia said forlornly at the McCarthy Washington headquarters. But they kept their sense of humor and cranked out a fresh news release that said: "If Bobby wants to join us, the first thing he's got to do is get a haircut."

McCarthy and Kennedy met briefly in the Old Senate Office Building still later that day at Kennedy's behest, and Kennedy told McCarthy he would probably become a candidate. McCarthy said that Kennedy was free to do what he wanted; as for himself, he was staying in.

"That Bobby; he's something, isn't he?" McCarthy commented to me the next morning.

Kennedy and McCarthy appeared before a meeting of the International Fellows of Columbia University that Thursday, March 14, to answer questions. The graduate student group also presented McCarthy its annual foreign policy award with "gratitude for his courage in expressing his convictions in this election year." They asked each of the Senators about the gold drain and the balance of payments problem. Kennedy prefaced his answer by saying he had gotten a D in economics. McCarthy prefaced his by noting he had been an A student, and the warm laughter showed whom the students were with. So, too, did a question asked of McCarthy after Kennedy had left: "If tomorrow morning President Johnson said he was opposed to the Vietnam war, do you think by tomorrow afternoon Senator Kennedy would be for it?" The laughter was louder now. He still had the students. There was no need to answer. The question had been answer enough.

At 2:30 A.M. Saturday, March 16, 1968, Edward M. Kennedy paid a courtesy call on Gene McCarthy in the Northland Hotel, Green Bay, Wisconsin. Kennedy told McCarthy that his brother Robert later that morning would officially become a candidate. Kennedy started to give some details of his brother's plans, but McCarthy steered the conversation to banalities. They talked of the Boston Saint Patrick's Day parade; the value of a good driver in a campaign. Kennedy carried a heavy brief case with an open latch. McCarthy suggested that Kennedy fasten it so no one would think it had been opened while the two conversed. Blair Clark, Curtis Gans, Richard Goodwin, and Sam Brown were there. They had discussed among themselves whether McCarthy and Robert Kennedy might share some of the remaining primaries, one man running here, the other there, to avoid a confrontation that might hurt the antiadministration drive. Not until California would they go against each other. Ted Kennedy had listened to the idea with interest. But no one raised the possibility with McCarthy. It angered him when he finally learned that some of his aides had seriously entertained the idea. If Ted Kennedy had wanted to bring it up early that Saturday morning, McCarthy never gave him a chance. Thirty-five minutes after he arrived, Kennedy left, his brief case tightly closed. A lot of people had lost a lot of sleep for nothing. "It's something to be said against easy travel," McCarthy would say of Ted Kennedy's trip that night from Washington to Green Bay and back.

In his announcement of candidacy, Robert Kennedy said he hoped to cooperate with McCarthy, stressing that "my candidacy would not be in opposition to his, but in harmony." An audible guffaw arose from reporters watching Kennedy in Washington. In answer to questions, Kennedy repeated again that had he entered earlier, the race would have been interpreted only as a personal struggle against Lyndon Johnson. New Hampshire, he said, showed that division existed in the party anyhow. No, he said, his candidacy wouldn't split the antiadministration vote. He would increase it because, he said, he and McCarthy had different strengths.

McCarthy watched part of the performance on a TV set in a Green Bay television studio and went on the air himself as soon as Kennedy was through. There was scorn in his words as he answered questions: "This challenge against the Johnson administration came at a time when it seemed to me that a lot of other politicians were afraid to come down on the playing field," McCarthy said. "They were willing to stay up on the mountain and light signal fires, bon-fires, and dance in the light of the moon, but none of them came down." It had been "lonely in New Hampshire," he said. "I could have used some help. . . . I kept waiting . . . but they didn't come in. They just threw messages over the fences."

Kennedy thought McCarthy's candidacy would crumble quickly. But he had waited too long. The young people he thought would rally to him had cast their lot. "Bobby Kennedy wasn't there when we needed him," said Sam Brown, the McCarthy student co-ordinator. "Gene McCarthy was."

The gracelessness of Kennedy's entry raised anew the specter of Kennedy as ruthless. So did garbled reports over that week end that

Kennedy might have stayed out if Lyndon Johnson had agreed to appoint a blue-ribbon commission to investigate Vietnam policy.

Even before he left Green Bay that Saturday for a stop in Indianapolis, telegrams and telephone messages with fresh promises of heavy financial support from anti-Kennedy Democrats were piling up in McCarthy's hotel and in Washington. "I don't need a stalking-horse at this point," McCarthy said later that day. "We don't need money. We don't need organization. I just need running room." And next day McCarthy flatly rejected a Kennedy offer to campaign in Wisconsin on McCarthy's behalf.

Some McCarthy aides feared that any accommodation with Kennedy could rob their campaign of the spontaneity so important in the McCarthy effort—a spontaneity that came from the people and not because of a man, a spontaneity that directly demonstrated the extent of popular feeling about Vietnam, the President, and what was happening to America. Even as press and television attention fastened on Kennedy, this constituency continued to grow. Little people in little, and big, places were still responding in untold numbers to the quieter beat of Eugene McCarthy.

In Wellfleet, Massachusetts, Mrs. Cal Kolbe Nossiter, who most of her adult life had harbored a profound distaste for politics, found herself organizing the Lower Cape Citizens for McCarthy. "The New Hampshire result shocked me into political mobility," she said later. "With all Senator McCarthy had at stake, it seemed to me the least the private citizen sharing his views could do was take the considerably less consequential risk of commitment to his political campaign."

In Benton County, Oregon, Harvey Williams had been downright discouraged by initial reaction to his call for a McCarthy organizing meeting he had scheduled for March 14. Only a half-dozen lukewarm responses had come in before the New Hampshire primary. The night of the meeting, however, two days after the New Hampshire election, thirty people showed up to hear a spirited presentation by Judy Allman, wife of the state McCarthy chairman. The

Benton County chapter of Oregonians for McCarthy was off and running.

James A. Johnson, a Princeton graduate student, phoned Sam Brown and Curtis Gans a day after the New Hampshire primary, wanting to go to work. Johnson quickly recruited more than thirty fellow students from the Woodrow Wilson School at Princeton to aid in the Wisconsin campaign.

Joel Berger, a young law school graduate from New York City, suddenly realized that "anyone with political campaign experience had an obligation to participate to defeat Johnson." He headed for Wisconsin.

In Anchorage, Alaska, Wendell Kay, a former state Democratic chairman, volunteered. He became state McCarthy chairman, operating out of a headquarters in a sparsely furnished one-time dance hall. Petitions went out. In Juneau and Anchorage, some three thousand persons eventually signed.

In California, Gerald Hill's California Democratic Council, at a meeting at which Dr. Martin Luther King, Jr., praised McCarthy as an "outstanding, brilliant" Senator, finally voted total active support of McCarthy. (King also praised Kennedy at the meeting.)

In Maine, some housewives, professors, and other concerned citizens, led by Robert J. Fitzpatrick and William F. Stone, hastily threw together a state McCarthy committee and began working to get delegates elected at the state convention in May.

In Caldwell, Idaho, Dean E. Miller, forty-five, a lawyer, volunteered and became state chairman. In Huntsville, Alabama, Mr. and Mrs. John Stephens set up a headquarters on their kitchen table. In Decatur, Georgia, Marc Brown, a seventeen-year-old high-school senior, set out on his own personal McCarthy quest; it would include selling doughnuts and collecting empty bottles for deposit refunds to build a campaign treasury. Douglas A. Wiken, twenty-four, a political science graduate student of Volin, South Dakota, began building in Clay County and was enlisted as temporary state leader. R. Douglas Averitt III, twenty-six, a prep-school teacher, and his wife, Kaye, sought, with modest success, to stir things up in sleepy

Lumberton, North Carolina. (The Lumberton *Robesonian,* which usually steered clear of that sort of thing, went so far as to print three pro-McCarthy letters that spring.)

The mushroom revolution had clearly intensified with the New Hampshire success, and nowhere was it more evident than Wisconsin, where on April 2 McCarthy would next challenge the President.

22. FULFILLMENT

By the New Hampshire primary, the Wisconsin organization numbered nearly three thousand adults. Led by such people as Don Peterson, Ted Warshafsky, Arnold Sewer, Frank Campenni, Jay Sykes, Midge Miller, Mike Bleicher, and scores more in their towns and counties, this army had raised close to $200,000 and created their own radio and television commercials, newspaper advertising, billboards, campaign literature. A force of some four thousand students from state colleges was building under the direction of George Wilbur, a senior at the University of Wisconsin. Some four hundred women banded together as the Concerned Women for McCarthy under Mrs. Jeanne Galazan and would prove as effective in their largely unseen roles as groups of women in other states.

Postmaster General Lawrence F. O'Brien was unimpressed. "The peace movement's backers in Wisconsin are mostly amateurs," he said to one reporter. "They are going off in all directions."

They were, indeed, and from certain vantage points it did seem directionless. For many weeks after McCarthy's announcement of candidacy, the Wisconsin leaders were unable to get the candidate or any of his aides to sanction them as his official organization for that state.

Bleicher, Peterson, and Sykes flew to Washington in December to try to straighten things out, but they were unsuccessful. Blair Clark seemed even more reticent to do business with them when they proposed a $670,000 campaign. "Silly," was McCarthy's reaction when he learned of the figure. (As it turned out, the Wisconsin campaign cost about $600,000.)

Sometime later, a check for $10,000 from Clark, made out to Wisconsin McCarthy for President, arrived in Wisconsin. "Oh, don't worry about that," Clark said when Jay Sykes reminded him that his group still hadn't been officially anointed.

In January, Midge Miller and Bleicher flew east for marching orders: What kind of campaign would it be? What should be its tone? How many days would the candidate be in the state? They got no answers. Disheartened, they flew home. "Mike and I had the feeling we'd have to do it ourselves," said Midge Miller. "We had assumed we would have a campaign manager and take his directions. From then on we ran our own campaign. By the time the national staff got there, we didn't want them. They came like swarms. They thought we needed them. We were already over the top."

Inevitably, when the young national staff did swarm in some antagonisms developed. Some of the newcomers, cocky in the flush of their New Hampshire success, performed at first as though nothing had occurred in Wisconsin before they arrived. One local leader quit. Others threatened to. "Never trust the locals," became the motto of some of the newcomers, and they took no pains to conceal it from the Wisconsinites. The hard-working locals did not like it.

As aggravating at first to the Wisconsin people was the candidate. Not until a day after the New Hampshire primary did they know definitely whether McCarthy would come to Wisconsin that week end. Until then it had been on and off, compounding the scheduling problems monumentally. At one point, Sykes, Sewer, and Peterson angrily dispatched a telegram to McCarthy: "We respectfully decline to cancel scheduled appearances in Wisconsin as you have requested and we cannot continue to cancel long-made plans. Too many arrangements have already been made. If you insist on cancellation, please send a man here authorized to speak on your behalf."

McCarthy national campaign officials read the telegram as a threat by the Wisconsinites to drop McCarthy, and they finally forced the candidate to end his vacillation. "Well, you won," Blair Clark said testily to Sykes over the phone. "You had us over a barrel, but that trick won't work again."

Until the day after the New Hampshire primary only a small number of out-of-state students had arrived, and only $12,000 had filtered in from national headquarters. The Wisconsin primary, up to that point, was strictly home-grown grass-roots.

Tom Hickey, forty-seven, a Beaver Dam (population 13,000) real estate dealer, is looking around the living room of the Burt Boyer home. Quite a cross section, he thinks. Two Lutheran ministers, a Methodist minister, a Catholic priest, teachers, a farmer, liberals belonging to no party, and a number of registered Democrats (like himself and his wife, Mary, and his brother Jim Hickey), people there at this McCarthy meeting early in 1968 like Jim and Ellie Dallman, who really started things in Beaver Dam and surrounding Dodge County, Fran and Doris Ingres, Don and Joan Yelineck, Mrs. Shirley Ghilardi, the Reverend and Mrs. Gordon Sorensen, Father Norman Frederick, John Hieleman, Tom Hansen, the Reverend and Mrs. Oz Anderson, of nearby Waupan. Hickey can speak for all of them as to why they are there: "Dissatisfied with the Johnson administration; disgusted by the brutal Vietnam war. Senator McCarthy's candidacy offered me, a lifelong Democrat, a legitimate means of dissent."

But has McCarthy offered a legitimate means of dissent? That is just what they are discussing in the Watertown law office of David J. Fries. It is the evening of December 28, 1967. Dave Brye, the college professor who started out in the campaign painting walls in the Madison headquarters, is there, one of his first organizing attempts. About six others cluster in the office. Brye appears to Fries to look increasingly disappointed as the discussion bogs down on the question of whether McCarthy has been antiwar enough to justify support on this issue in 1968. The session breaks up with general agreement McCarthy has not been as vocally antiwar as they might have hoped. Let's think it over. January 20 they meet again in Fries's law office and, despite their doubts, form the Jefferson County McCarthy for President Committee. Reluctantly, they throw in with the only legitimate means of dissent in their own or any other town that season.

January 23, 1968, six persons gather in the home of Mr. and Mrs. Dennis Green, on East Lincoln in Oshkosh. Mrs. Midge Miller, an early McCarthy supporter from Madison, and Charles Uphoff, a graduate student from the University of Colorado, outline plans for the Wisconsin campaign. On February 29, when the Oshkosh group meets again in a local YMCA, forty persons attend. They open a headquarters.

Here is Charles Uphoff again. This time he is knocking on the door of Don Belleau, thirty-five, a Sheboygan advertising man who has never really been politically active before. Uphoff is looking for someone to help organize Sheboygan. He has been driving all over the state for days in a 1958 Rambler, sometimes sleeping in it, making similar appeals. Belleau, though not really convinced, allows his dining room to be turned into an office for Uphoff, surrenders his telephone to the cause and his den for Uphoff to sleep in. This young man seems to be doing so much that Belleau decides he himself should be doing more, and he becomes county McCarthy chairman, half wondering if he is in some kind of un-American conspiracy. Then comes the New Hampshire election, and sometime later Belleau tells how he felt then: "We were suddenly out in the sunlight with fresh breezes blowing around us. We were in. We were part of the system. Pass the hot dogs. We're Americans."

. . .

In River Falls, Richard K. Darr, forty-seven, an economist at the River Falls branch of the University of Wisconsin, who has become interested in the campaign, is discussing it one winter night in a saloon with a friend, Bud Frederick, from nearby Woodville. They suddenly realize that all the big veterans groups support the Vietnam war. They set about to counterbalance this. Both are veterans, and soon a number of Veterans for McCarthy groups are in existence, with members from thirty states, three air force bases, Vietnam, and one naval vessel.

Gordon Shipman, sixty-seven, chairman of the sociology-anthropology department at the Stevens Point branch of Wisconsin State University, and his wife, Agnes, are standing in their home watching a socioanthropolitical phenomenon. It is after New Hampshire now, and the students are multiplying. They are carting huge cartons of supplies into the Shipman home. A couple of students are sleeping there at night. The phone never stops ringing. Now a couple of the young people are mounting a loud-speaker on the Shipman Volkswagen microbus, and now it's going down the street with someone inside yelling at people to vote McCarthy. (It drives into Wisconsin Rapids and somebody starts shouting, "Vote McCarthy," but the police there run it out of town.) Agnes Shipman cooking, feeding, washing dishes, linens, running for the telephone day and night. This is what it means to be wife of the Stevens Point McCarthy chairman?

Despite their unprecedented do-it-yourself effort, the Wisconsin people had not carried their campaign all the way over the top by mid-March, as some would later contend. The New Hampshire success uncorked several hundred thousand more dollars of outside money vital to the effort. The wave of new students helped make the difference in untold communities. And the small core of national campaign leaders for the first time could devote their attention to this next challenge. In the end, what happened in Wisconsin was a joint effort, as it was throughout the campaign.

. . .

When McCarthy finally arrived in Wisconsin the week end of March 15–16, the Wisconsin people weren't prepared for the hordes of newsmen who were now following him. The airplane they had chartered couldn't accommodate all of them. A local campaign official ruled that television equipment should be shipped by bus, even though the bus ran hours behind the plane. "Television won't be running this campaign," he declared. The television people exploded, and four extra smaller planes were quickly chartered. Later the same official clashed with TV newsmen again. "Are you sure you're not working for Lyndon Johnson?" one of them finally shouted. It clearly seemed that this was a presidential campaign in which television coverage wasn't wanted. This in itself would make one hell of a story, the newsmen decided.

"No, no," pleaded Ted Warshafsky, "that's not the story. The real story is how far we've come with such ineptitude. Isn't it great when you think how far we've come? This is a visible demonstration of the inherent strength of our position."

Another in the untold foul-ups of the McCarthy campaign was allowed to pass unreported.

The press dwelt in the first days of McCarthy's Wisconsin campaign on questions about Robert Kennedy. Would McCarthy support Kennedy if it came down to a choice between Bobby and LBJ? McCarthy had to say in all honesty he would, but there would be no accommodation, no concession, no compromise before such a hypothetical occurrence.

At the same time an accommodation of sorts seemed to be building. In Washington, D.C., McCarthy backer Joseph L. Rauh disclosed that McCarthy and Kennedy supporters were forming a fusion slate of delegates to oppose an administration slate in the May 7 District of Columbia primary. McCarthy at first agreed to the arrangement, insisting nevertheless that it not be considered a "coalition." Several days later, however, even though McCarthy supporters were given a majority of places on the slate, McCarthy, without notifying Rauh, withdrew his support, stating:

I have decided to dissociate myself from the unpledged delegate slate in the District of Columbia opposing President Johnson. Originally, I lent my name to this slate . . . in order to afford the voters the opportunity to choose between my policies and those of the Administration as a single endorsement.

Since the emergence of this slate a series of events have occurred that cloud the intent of the endorsement and give the impression of an arrangement with Senator Kennedy or his campaign. I have made my position on this matter very clear. I cannot allow any impression to be created that my effort will be any other than an independent one. The voters in the District of Columbia still have the opportunity to vote on this slate. It is not my slate nor a shared one.

Several days later, McCarthy's stand was emphasized by New York supporters who rejected overtures from Kennedy aides to run a joint slate of delegates in that state's June 18 primary.

Jay Sykes, a Kennedy hater of the first water, made his own gesture to keep McCarthy's independence unpolluted by Kennedyism. He discovered that a draft of instructions for student canvassers advised: "If anyone suggests a preference for Kennedy, tell him that Kennedy favors a vote for McCarthy." In the Madison *Capital Times* Sykes told what he did: "I picked up about 5,000 copies of the page, lying on a table awaiting stapling, poured water on them, threw them in the trash can, told the drafters what I had done and why." (Sykes's independence on this and many other matters ultimately brought him in disfavor with Wisconsin as well as national staff leaders, but he stubbornly persisted and was as effective as anyone else at that stage of the campaign.)

McCarthy's position became apparent in his speeches. Immediately on Kennedy's entry, McCarthy dropped the references to John F. Kennedy that had sprinkled his talks in New Hampshire. Kennedy's willingness to support him in some primaries while planning to run against him in others, McCarthy said, was "kind of like fattening me up for the kill." On the eve of Kennedy's announcement of candidacy, McCarthy told a Sheboygan audience how for a time he had been "concerned that some people who should stand up had not." Gradually, though, they did. Academicians, then women, then businessmen, and, finally, "some politicians who should have been among the first to protest have now concluded it's time to take a firm and consistent stand." He paraphrased the Bible: "While the lamp holds out to burn, the vilest sinner can return."

For most of the Wisconsin campaign, McCarthy dealt with Kennedy playfully. The bitterness would become more apparent later.

"I think we're more or less agreed in terms of the issue," McCarthy responded to a news conference question about whether he thought the question of personalities would be raised between him and Kennedy. He went on:

If you can't do that, the campaign becomes a question of personality, of competence and qualification. I don't know what else you argue about. If he wants to pick on us over our size, I'm willing to use that as a determinant. Or age. I don't think those should be standards, however. He plays touch football; I play football. He plays softball; I play baseball. He skates in Rockefeller Center; I play hockey. . . . If these are the bases on which you are going to make a decision, why, I mean, it'll become abrasive, I suppose.

A much more basic difference between the two men, however, was already coming to the fore. Kennedy appealed to Negroes. McCarthy did not especially. The reason was simple: Negroes knew Kennedy because they had known his brother; they did not know McCarthy from Barry Goldwater. This fact traumatized many of McCarthy's idealistic young followers throughout the campaign. They wanted him to make like Kennedy on the race issue: talk passionately, charge into crowds of blacks, *show* his concern. Many of them always wondered whether he truly was concerned.

This feeling was acute in late March as television and newspapers told of Kennedy's emotion-filled meetings with young people and blacks and other minorities across the land. The McCarthy idealists were filled with a love-hate for the man who had let them down by not entering the campaign sooner. Seeing him now talking to the black man began to soften the intense anti-Bobby feeling that had swelled up in many of them with Kennedy's entry into the campaign. To many of them, the real overriding issue of 1968 was the plight of the black man in America. They began to notice that their man, McCarthy, had not campaigned in a Negro area, except for a speech at predominantly black Howard University in Washington, D.C. It did not seem to matter that he had been speaking out on civil rights in his un-adrenal way, that he had been the first presidential candidate to recommend enactment of all the suggestions of the Kerner Riot Commission. It did not matter that there had been little opportunity to campaign in a ghetto. New Hampshire had one of the smallest Negro populations in the nation, and it was scattered. Wisconsin's nonwhites comprised about 2 per cent of the population.

There were several stages in the development of this tempest over McCarthy's not having campaigned in a ghetto. It began when Frank Campenni, Milwaukee vicinity organizer for the Wisconsin McCarthy organization, realized there was no campaign literature in Wisconsin laying out McCarthy's position on civil rights. He decided to create a McCarthy civil rights pamphlet on his own. But he soon discovered that what strategy there was for the Wisconsin campaign involved playing down the race issue by ignoring the Milwaukee ghettos. Curtis Gans, among others, felt that too big a play for the black vote might alienate the larger blue-collar ethnic vote (which went to Lyndon Johnson, anyway). The race issue in Milwaukee was delicate in the wake of the civil rights marches of Father Groppi. The McCarthy campaign, thus, would not roil the waters. Student canvassers sent into blue-collar neighborhoods were specifically instructed not to raise the race issue. If asked McCarthy's position they were to say only that "McCarthy's position is the same as the Democratic party's." Gans's view was shared by Richard Goodwin, who after the Wisconsin primary would move to the Robert Kennedy campaign, and Ted M. Warshafsky, vice-chairman of the Wisconsin organization. It amounted to a cold political judgment that seemed slightly out of kilter with the pristine nature of the new politics.

Gans at first tried to veto the idea of the pamphlet. Campenni, with Jay Sykes backing him up, moved ahead despite threats from Gans. But he soon found that the national staff would not let him, a McCarthy campaign official, see copies of McCarthy speeches so he could extract passages for the pamphlet. A meeting of about thirty campaign aides was held to resolve the matter. Instead, it broke up in bickering, with those opposed to seeking the Negro vote being accused of sellout by others. Among those who urged an intensive ghetto campaign were press aides Sy Hersh and Mary Lou Oates.

The tempest might have died there had Hersh and Oates not suddenly resigned over this and other matters. They leaked their decision to Ned Kenworthy of the *New York Times* in the middle of one night. His story stressed McCarthy's failure to campaign in the black ghettos as a prime reason. Even before the story was in print, McCarthy began to be besieged with questions about the resignations and civil rights. In Stevens Point, a reporter asked McCarthy about the lack of Negroes on his campaign staff. "Some of you fellows are frustrated campaign managers," he said coldly.

The tempest had hurt. "I couldn't . . . say anything that would do the damage that story has done," McCarthy said. It was true that some McCarthy campaign aides were trying to play down the race issue simply by not playing it up. But McCarthy was not part of this strategy decision. It was true two aides had resigned. But they had resigned over more than the civil rights matter. The message that came through, however, was that Eugene McCarthy didn't really care about the Negro. This was not true. He simply refused, from the start, to make special appeals to any group. It took a while for many supporters to get used to this. Clearly, many were willing to believe the worst about their candidate.

The story also triggered an outpouring of phone calls to the McCarthy headquarters from chagrined Negroes who had been sympathetic to McCarthy's candidacy and from liberal contributors threatening to cut off the flow of money. Richard Goodwin, juggling phone calls in his hotel suite, promised that McCarthy already had a forceful civil rights statement planned, that the issue had been blown out of proportion. Two Negroes were hastily recruited to travel with McCarthy as "advisers" the rest of the Wisconsin campaign. Two young black girls were cornered and cajoled into becoming McCarthy girls for a couple of days. McCarthy gave a rights speech in which for the first time he acknowledged that "white racism" was a fact of life in America. Otherwise, he said essentially what he always said when discussing civil rights.

And he went into the ghetto. It was a travesty. He purposely underscored the fact, for this thing had been forced on him. He pointedly made his ghetto tour not for the black man but for the critics and the press, and for a couple of hours he performed like a traditional candidate, doing, with exaggeration, things a candidate was supposed to do by the often ridiculous unwritten rules of of the game. He started from the Sheraton-Schroeder Hotel in Milwaukee toward evening. He bulled into crowds of late shoppers, grabbing hands and smiling as he worked through the downtown. At a furious stride, he headed toward a ghetto area. The stride broke into a trot. He was running—reporters, photographers, television crews, campaign workers, celebrities puffing to keep up. Motorists screeched on their brakes to watch the curious spectacle of a bunch of white people in suits running toward the black ghetto. One motorist, watching in fascination, slammed his car into the rear of another auto. As the mob moved into a public housing project a group of children at play dashed off in fear as they saw the mob approach. McCarthy stopped on a basketball court and shot a couple of baskets, teenage blacks looking at this gray-haired man in puzzlement. He ran on to another housing project and tossed a football with other boys for a moment, then raced on toward a blue-collar neighborhood, no longer running, but still striding furiously. He ducked into a delicatessen and ate a corned beef sandwich. That's what you're supposed to do, isn't it? Eat foods generic to the neighborhood while everyone watches? It proves you care, doesn't it? The "ghetto walk" finally ended after about four miles as dusk settled over Milwaukee and city police threatened to arrest the whole bunch if they didn't stay out of the streets.

.   .   .

The foul-ups, the diversion of attention to Kennedy, the civil rights matter, and scheduling problems, however, could not obscure the fact that McCarthy's Wisconsin campaign, after a wobbly few days, was going well. Some fifteen thousand persons jammed Madison's Dane County Coliseum, the largest McCarthy audience of the campaign to that point. The students were still his. At Beloit, Saint Norbert's, Marquette, whatever campus he visited, the reception was warm. These were listeners, not squealers, and McCarthy's voice would ring through the halls and auditoriums with a message little different than in New Hampshire, though now he talked more about reconciliation in America that a spirit of trust could bring.

If we are prepared to move in this spirit, then I think we can work out the reconciliation of generations in this country, a reconciliation, really, of the present drives and scattered purposes of this nation; a reconciliation of reason and a reconciliation in hope; and if we do this with dedication, despite the criticism directed against us, despite suggestions of disloyalty and lack of patriotism, we shall in 1968 perform at the highest level of patriotism: which is to serve one's country not in submission, but to serve it in truth. This is the call, this is the challenge, to which I ask all of you to respond in 1968.

The applause would build. There would be few cheers. The audience would stand respectfully and clap, apolitically. At Beloit, this applause went on for two full minutes. A washed look was on their faces, a look of awakening from a bad dream to find hope calling; to find that maybe the good in the nation which this sober, gray-haired Senator said was still there could yet be rediscovered. In these moments, thoughts of Kennedy and politics seemed forgotten. Each person present looked as if he had received a call to a crusade.

As April 2 neared, McCarthy began to talk of his concept of the presidency, a limited presidency, a people's presidency that "recognizes that the potential for leadership exists in every man and woman." And for the first time since he announced his candidacy, it seemed he was actually running for the office itself.

"What we're doing is laying down a challenge to control the presidency of the United States," he told a Milwaukee audience March 24.

"I entered New Hampshire because I thought the case against the war had to be personalized," he recalled in an interview at about the same time. "It was always in the back of my mind that Johnson could be beaten, but now the chances are growing increasingly strong that Johnson will not be re-elected."

In Milwaukee, all one had to do to see how badly the Johnson campaign was going was to walk over to 800 Plankinton Street, Johnson headquarters. Leslie Aspin, young Pentagon aide returned to Wisconsin to lead the Johnson effort, presided over a store front with almost no one there. Workers had to be hired, and only five were working through phone books and voters lists one afternoon when I dropped in. Two of them were complaining over the absence of a water faucet to fill their coffeepot. Aspin was annoyed. "Why don't you just take the damn pot down to the river? It's full of water." Things were clearly going badly, and he made no bones about it. Johnson had sent a string of Cabinet officials and the Vice-President into Wisconsin, and if they hadn't been booed they'd been received coolly and by small crowds. A $50,000 federal rat-control grant for Milwaukee was hurried through before the primary, but failed to control the vote. The Agriculture Department suddenly announced a hike in milk support payments to take effect the day before the primary. McCarthy quickly took credit for it. "The first tangible benefit to the people of Wisconsin of my candidacy," he declared. Television crews taking films of the Johnson headquarters were hard put to find action. One crew was reduced to asking William T. Chapman, a Washington *Post* reporter, to walk through the door a couple of times so they could photograph some motion. In a partitioned-off area Neil Staebler, former Democratic chairman of Michigan, one of several out-of-state pols shuffled in for the Johnson effort, sat disconsolately at a desk scribbling figures on a yellow pad. I still have a sheet of paper with his doodles on it, which purported to show that McCarthy's anticipated victory wouldn't mean much because of an expected large Republican crossover in the primary he couldn't count on in a general election.

And I still have notes of my conversation with another carpet-bagger from Staebler's state of Michigan come to Wisconsin for politics. He was Martin Hanna, an eighteen-year-old freshman at

Kalamazoo College. While Staebler was working at his figures, Hanna was several blocks away in the McCarthy headquarters in the Wisconsin Hotel, being put to work as a "runner" just a half-hour after arriving in town. I ran into Hanna before visiting Staebler. I ran into Hanna again four hours later. He had been promoted in the interim. That night he was to open a new McCarthy headquarters on Milwaukee's southwest side. Hanna had never done anything like this before, but he felt he had things in hand. "You just go there and clean it up and sort of get it ready," he told me. "The phones will come in sometime tomorrow. Then the literature, and we hope we will be ready by the time most of the volunteers come."

And once again they came. The boiler room operation on the Wisconsin Hotel's mezzanine, under the direction of Marge Sklencar, of Chicago, was a whirl of activity as she and her helpers sought to coordinate who would go where in what numbers. The motion was always indescribable. There's Marge Sklencar pivoting from phone to blackboard to map, to guide another covey of students heading this way. There's Mark Siegel, twenty-five-year-old Columbia law school student, rushing up and down corridors arranging for more headquarters openings—fifty in three days, ten of them in the Milwaukee area, two of them rented from a Nixon supporter, another from a Rockefeller man at cut rate. There's Joshua Leinsdorf, twenty-two, Columbia graduate student in literature, hair still down to his shoulders, just arrived, heading to a barbershop. He would end up chartering most of the planes and buses used in the rest of the campaign—doing it all by phone because to see him with his boyish face you wouldn't think he had the authority—a $250,000 expenditure when toted up. Belle Huang, twenty, a pretty pre-medical student at Wellesley, is first here, then over there, doing who knows what, but doing it very well. There's Paul Gorman, who became acting press secretary when Seymour Hersh stalked out, phoning Smith College to get Mary Davis out of exams until after the Wisconsin vote. Now he's helping Cindy Samuels with a thesis. There the young people are all over the state: Jan Goodman in Janesville; Charles Negaro in Eau Claire; Paul Wiberg in Watertown. The supervisor from the telephone company, who has handled many political campaigns, is in the Wisconsin Hotel smoking furiously, going out of his mind. He has never heard so many orders changed as soon as they are spoken. Lines, extensions. Here. No, there. Fifteen phones at the Eau Claire store front. No, ten.

It was the same on the road, as the young people tried valiantly to keep the traveling reporters up to date on the latest schedule change. All through the night came a swishing sound as yet another revised schedule was slipped under each correspondent's hotel room door, awaking him briefly, until the swishes became part of the rhythm of this unusual campaign and it was no longer surprising to get on a bus after a night of swishes and be handed yet another corrected schedule labeled "addenda and errata."

There was a certain intensity that had not been there in New Hampshire. It was new in New Hampshire, and so very much smaller. They had been surprised by their success. Now they had something to live up to, and Wisconsin was so *big*. "It was fun before we started winning," said one young staff member. And so in Wisconsin, despite gratifying indications from the canvassing, the improbable dream seemed as remote as ever.

What happened on April 2, when the people in Wisconsin went to the polls, was anticlimax. For the record, Eugene McCarthy received 412,160 votes, or 56.2 per cent, to 253,696, or 34.6 per cent, for Lyndon Johnson.

Again, McCarthy was the lesser story. The entrance of Robert Kennedy had overshadowed McCarthy's success in New Hampshire. Now the withdrawal of Lyndon Johnson two days earlier captured the major attention.

The McCarthy campaign would change now. He would gain in personal appeal as the next months passed. The little people in the little places would continue with the fresh idealism that had started them. But the campaign itself would take on an ugly aspect, for it would become a contest between two men who disliked each other. And in June, the improbable dream would turn to absolute nightmare.

VI

White Horse of Victory
Pale Horse of Death

★

Life is Russian roulette. . . .
Things have a way of changing
very fast.

ROBERT F. KENNEDY, IN CONVERSATION
WITH REPORTERS ABOARD A PLANE
THE NIGHT OF APRIL 2, 1968

23. CONTRASTS

Eugene McCarthy's candidacy was 106 days old when Robert Kennedy entered the race. Kennedy's first objective was to display the Kennedy drawing power; persuading politicians would come later. And so Kennedy drove himself particularly hard the two weeks after his announcement, traveling the country to be mobbed at every stop by crowds that sometimes seemed out of control. A child almost crushed. Later, a man yanking Kennedy from his open car, Kennedy's face banging against the bumper, cutting his lip and chipping a tooth. Another man in another city crashing through the crowd to try to attack Kennedy. Hatred was in the mobs as well as adoration. One wondered even then where it might lead.

Kennedy seemed to feed on the raw emotion of the crowds and even encouraged it. "Which of these men lost in Vietnam might have written a symphony? Which of them might have cured cancer? Which of them might have played in a World Series? . . . Which of them might have taught a small boy to read?" he would implore. "The failure of national purpose . . . is not simply the result of bad policies and lack of skill," Kennedy shouted in Los Angeles. "It flows from the fact that for almost the first time the national leadership is calling upon the darker impulses of the American spirit."

Criticism of his approach soon led Kennedy to temper his emotionalism and drop some misstatements he had freely used, but he continued attacking Lyndon Johnson more directly than McCarthy did at any time.*

In private, administration leaders began praising McCarthy's "responsible tone" while deploring Kennedy's "embittered" personal attacks. And McCarthy frequently drew attention to Kennedy's emotionalism. "In a way, it's almost an offense, I think, by way of a judgment of the people, to approach them as though you had to stir up their emotions to deal with problems which are as serious and as emotion-laden as issues like poverty and also the war," McCarthy said. Conveniently forgetting his use in New Hampshire of John Kennedy's get-the-country-moving theme, McCarthy added: "[We must] give consideration to what we are and to what we want to be and how we are going to achieve that purpose—instead of a kind of general projection that this country has to be in motion some way, that we have to have a kind of flow of movement of some kind some way, agitation and more distraction instead of a deep consideration."

McCarthy compared Kennedy's and his own approach trenchantly: "Do you know the difference between a grass fire and a fire in a peat bog? A grass fire just burns off over night. A peat bog fire holds on for months."

But McCarthy could use emotion, as his Adlai Stevenson speech proved. "In the name of God, let the killing be stopped," he would quote South Vietnamese bishops as saying. "In the name of humanity it must be stopped," he would quote the poets and artists of Vietnam as saying. And then McCarthy would add, "The time has come to say, in the name of America let the killing end." The

---

* McCarthy almost attacked President Johnson by name once. A speech text handed out before a February 21 McCarthy appearance said, "Lyndon Johnson is to blame for the deaths of our boys in Asia." McCarthy did not deliver the line and was annoyed it had been included in the text; he had not checked the text beforehand. Such inattention to detail was responsible for McCarthy's being reported as endorsing a "guaranteed annual income." A speech text in March had McCarthy supporting the concept, though he actually had not. McCarthy's relations with his speech writers were always strained.

inflection he used, his subdued delivery, gave the words an emotional impact McCarthy could very well have avoided.

The earliest noticeable differences between the two candidates were much less subtle.

Kennedy would arrive at an airport with a huge entourage in a huge airplane to be greeted by a huge crowd. McCarthy would land in a smaller plane with a smaller entourage to be greeted by a smaller crowd.

Kennedy would move to the airport fence to touch the hands stretching over it and to be touched, eagerly and without stopping until he had gone the length of the fence. Then he would jump into a convertible and stand in the back seat as it wound through shouting, grabbing crowds. McCarthy would not stay long at the airport fence if he went to it at all. Then he would climb into a closed car and drive to wherever he was going through peopleless streets.

Kennedy liked most of the reporters who traveled with him, enjoyed their company and conversation, listened to their views and sometimes learned from them. McCarthy could take them or leave them alone, preferably the latter. "It's not good to stay too close to these fellows all day," McCarthy informed a Wisconsin volunteer who sought to place McCarthy in the press bus for a day of campaigning so he could be more accessible to the newsmen. "Play them some soft music," he muttered to an aide on another occasion when told reporters expecting him at a press conference were getting impatient.

Kennedy's humor was usually directed at himself; McCarthy's was usually directed at others.

Kennedy would ask each crowd for their help; McCarthy almost never made such direct appeals.

McCarthy had no unseen enemies across the land; Kennedy had many.

Kennedy soon found he had to campaign against many of his brother's actions as President. "Bobby's tragedy is that to beat me, he's going to have to destroy his brother," McCarthy remarked. As we flew to California April 4, McCarthy told me how the campaign would unfold with Lyndon Johnson's exit and Humphrey's predictable entry:

> Bobby's problem with Lyndon out is that he can no longer run Jack against Lyndon. Bobby has to run himself against Hubert. He has to pretend McCarthy will fade out of the picture eventually, so there is no reason to attack McCarthy and risk antagonizing his supporters. If Hubert forces Bobby to take off Jack's mantle, he'll spare McCarthy the task of doing it. Bobby's strength was running Jack against Lyndon. Bobby has to change and McCarthy doesn't. Any time a candidate has to change, it hurts.

With Kennedy initially ignoring McCarthy, it was left to McCarthy to underline the differences between the two. In Indiana, he would say that he and Kennedy really had no major differences on the issues, just a point here and there: slightly differing views on what to do about the draft; on, possibly, the farm question; perhaps on how to handle the economy. He asked Hoosiers to examine his and Kennedy's personalities—a "Hey Look Me Over" appeal so successfully used by Senator Birch Bayh—and to choose which one they thought more qualified to be President, which one showed more potential for truly unifying the country; and if they could not decide it would be proper to vote for Governor Roger Branigin, the administration stand-in candidate. (Kennedy told the voters a vote for Branigin would be wasted.) In Nebraska, McCarthy added another difference, pegged to local interests. Kennedy had voted against beef import quotas; McCarthy hadn't. The issue obviously didn't have the effect McCarthy hoped for. He also pointed out for the first time in Nebraska a truism that sounded crass in the stating of it: McCarthy got the better-educated voters; Kennedy the less educated, a fact borne out by polls as well as election results. Similarly, McCarthy got the A students; Kennedy the B and C students.

By Oregon McCarthy had developed a full string of lesser points of comparison that he would tick off with relish:

—McCarthy had gone into New Hampshire, while Kennedy worried about his political future.

—McCarthy urged the resignations of Secretary of State Rusk, FBI Director Hoover, and Selective Service Director Hershey. Kennedy didn't.

—McCarthy questioned the growth of military influence under the Pentagon leadership of Robert S. McNamara, while Kennedy bought television time to air an endorsement by McNamara.

—McCarthy felt it irrelevant to campaign with his dog and an astronaut by his side. ("My dog's better than his dog," McCarthy would joke, and probably he was right. McCarthy taught his dog, Eric, a lugubrious boxer, to snarl when McCarthy said, "What do you think of Mayor Daley?")

By the Oregon vote, McCarthy had delineated more significant differences that nullified any thread of similarity, apart from the challenge of both men to the administration.

McCarthy offered a subtle perspective on a very basic difference between himself and Kennedy by applying passages of one of his poems, "Lament of an Aging Politician," which goes:

> The Dream of Gerontion is
>   my dream
> and Lowell's self salted
> night sweat, wet, flannel,
>   my morning's
> shoulder shroud.
>
> Now, far-sighted I see the distant
>   danger
> beyond the coffin confines of
>   telephone booths,
> my arms stretch to read, in vain.
>
> Stubbornness and penicillin hold
> the aged above me.
> My metaphors grow cold and old,
> My enemies, both young and bold.
>
> I have left Act I, for involution
> and Act II. There mired in
>   complexity
> I cannot write Act III.

"You know the old rules," McCarthy was quoted as saying in the *New York Times* after the poem was published in *Life* in April, 1968. "Act I states the problem. Act II deals with the complications, and Act III resolves them. I'm an Act II man. There's where I live—involution and complexity.

"Lyndon only really cares about Act III. What does history say about the Great Society? What will the future think of Lyndon Johnson? . . . Bobby is an Act I man. He says here's a problem. Here's another. He never really deals with Act II, but I think maybe Bobby's beginning to write Act III now."

McCarthy clearly felt that Act II was where it's at. In campaign speeches he sketched more immediate differences. Domestically, he questioned Kennedy proposals for attacking the urban crisis. In foreign affairs, McCarthy said, Kennedy was guilty of something far more serious than admitted mistakes in development of the policy that led to the initial escalation in Vietnam. Kennedy, McCarthy declared, shared much deeper misconceptions of America's global role—misconceptions that had sent foreign policy in the wrong direction since John Foster Dulles.

Even before the Wisconsin election, McCarthy was chiding Kennedy for setting up twenty-six separate campaign committees to deal with as many varieties of Americans: Irish, Polish, Negroes, Mexican, "retired former public officials," and so on. On the surface, it seemed a rather innocuous point to bring up. But McCarthy considered it a part of the whole erroneous premise of Kennedy's approach, of his thinking. A few special committees did arise in the McCarthy campaign—women, doctors, scientists, Black Americans for McCarthy (BAM), and so forth, but they arose in spite of Mc-Carthy, not because of him. He felt creation of BAM in particular contradicted the approach he had chosen, which he elaborated as the campaign progressed. "I don't have in mind to set up any special committee of any kind to deal with any one special group of Americans, but rather to offer my campaign and my candidacy for the separate and personal choice of each one, as far as can be reflected, of the 200 million Americans that live today." Though special interest, or ethnic, politics may have been viable, even use-ful, twenty or thirty years ago, it no longer was in 1968. Such an appeal today, he would say, represented "a kind of digging in in fear . . . a digging into whatever group you may belong to, a kind of defensiveness in which you try to hold on to whatever you have and do not venture very far from the entrance to the burrow, the kind of thinking reflected in people who wear the company jacket, or who wear the pin. . . ." It amounted not to a "constituency of conscience," but "a kind of composite American," a "constituency of special interests," a Johnsonian consensus. This was not real unity, not real reconciliation, McCarthy would say. It was

a false unity which we have achieved at some times in the past by putting together combinations of separate interests or separate groups, a kind of jigsaw arrangement out of which sometimes you can get a majority by virtue of the separate units' saying, "In order to get what we want we will help someone else to get what they want." This is not a genuine unity. It may have the appearance of it, but it is more organizational and physical than it is organic or than it is a unity of judgment and of commitment.

The Kennedy people would never forgive Eugene McCarthy for his attacks on Bobby. The attacks became increasingly personal through Oregon and California, but none was any worse than the distortions of McCarthy's Senate voting and attendance records that Kennedy supporters began placing in Negro and college newspapers as early as the Wisconsin campaign. And there was a bitter truth to much of what McCarthy said. Kennedy in his tragically short cam-paign had not really brought anything to the vague concept of New Politics so many of his admirers idealized. He was in political and personal transition when he died. The personal man had evolved farther than the political Kennedy, and so his campaign was tradi-tional, and no more so than in his frequent use of a dual approach to the blacks on one side of the tracks and lower-income working whites on the other. In the blue-collar neighborhood, he was former At-torney-General Kennedy, "chief law enforcement officer of the United States for three and a half years," as he spoke the clichés of law and order. In the black ghetto, he was a man visibly moved by an understanding of the black man's condition, the plight of each deprived minority.

The wild crowds that greeted him on both sides of the track and then voted for him suggested to many Kennedy admirers that this was the only politician of the day who might bridge those tracks. But was saying one thing to one group and something else to another, with opposite thrust and tailored appeal, really serving the end of reconciliation? McCarthy did not think so. He explained:

The test I am making is basically moral. It has, to be sure, its political aspects. We need imaginative and practical programs to respond to the cry from the ghetto. We certainly need something more lasting, substantial and productive than televised political tours through the slums, or vague promises that if the ghetto dwellers will only pull on the right lever on election day, all will be well for them. Promises like this have been made in every campaign. But after every campaign the slums have grown slummier, the desperation of the ghetto has grown more intense—and more justified than ever. . . .

In all the frantic discussion of the racial crisis and calculations about which minority is likely to vote for which candidate, this simple fact can be easily obscured, just as in the Vietnam controversy the fact that the war implicated all of us in immorality was obscured by political considerations. . . .

I will not make racial appeals, to either black or white. I will speak the same to all—and there is no reason not to, for all are men and all are Americans.

Even before Kennedy's death, a growing number of more militant black leaders began to question Kennedy's sincerity because of his dual campaign, and they began to identify themselves with McCarthy, the only presidential candidate in 1968 who did not make a law-and-order speech. "They saw him as a man who didn't play the Great White God," said Herbert O. Reid, black law professor from Howard University who traveled with McCarthy, helping set up private meetings with black leaders from city to city. "They respected his honesty. They began to think of Kennedy as a flim-flam artist on this issue."

But this was decidedly a minority view among the minority and among white liberals who, while they might have become accustomed to McCarthy's low-key style in relation to Vietnam, still felt a display of passion was necessary to truly convey a feeling about the injustice to the black man. By comparison with Kennedy, McCarthy always seemed indifferent.

After the slaying of Martin Luther King, Jr., on April 4, 1968, this seeming indifference amounted to a crime in the eyes of those inclined to question McCarthy's sincerity. The outward reaction of the two men at King's death seemed to underscore this opinion. Kennedy made two of his most eloquent speeches, one in Indianapolis and another in Cleveland the next day. McCarthy, to listen to him, seemed unmoved. His speeches—jokes and all—remained unchanged with but brief acknowledgment of the tragedy, except for a stop at the Compton Day Care Headstart Center near Watts. There he spoke movingly of Martin Luther King, Jr., though what he said was essentially his standard civil rights speech to that time adapted for the occasion. I remember listening to a McCarthy luncheon speech in Los Angeles the day after King's death. The reporters at the press table were specifically waiting for what McCarthy would say about King. The words came and went by almost without having been uttered. "What does that son of a bitch think has happened?" said a veteran television correspondent.

McCarthy knew what had happened and was reacting characteristically. It was his standard reaction of trying not to compound emotion in an emotional moment. It was one of McCarthy's faults, in my mind, that he negatively overreacted. He didn't simply rip off what there might have been of his heart on his sleeve; he also seemed to throw it away and say good riddance. McCarthy's approach was totally cerebral. He did not need, he felt, sensual contact as Kennedy did to understand and appreciate the problems. Moreover, his record had been consistently on the side of minorities from his first campaign for Congress in 1948. And he had done landmark work in the problems of unemployment and of migrant farmers, though without fanfare.

One traveling with him sensed a diffidence in dealing with or discussing blacks, especially early in his campaign. It took him several weeks to shift into an uneasy accommodation with the term "black," in place of Negro. (Very early in his campaign he sometimes slipped into the rather dehumanizing term "these people.") While he did not at first accept at face value the finding of the Kerner Riot Commission on "white racism" in America, by the end of the Wisconsin campaign he had, with subtly worded qualifications, embraced it.

From the start, McCarthy understood the new cry for self-determination by militants and other blacks and their deepening antipathy toward the patronizing paternalism of white liberals. And so he made no special appeal to blacks, allowing them in this way a kind of political self-determination. They could examine his record if they wanted and take him or leave him. In most meetings with Negroes, though, it appeared to be McCarthy who had chosen to do the leaving.

"Why should black people vote for you?" cried a Negro in Atlanta. "I never said they should," answered McCarthy. In the Steeltown ghetto of Pittsburgh, another black called out: "We see you now, but what'll you do for us if you're President?" McCarthy did not respond. "This man really needs educating," muttered another Negro in Detroit after an unsatisfying session with McCarthy. At a meeting in the District of Columbia, a black identified with Robert Kennedy asked McCarthy what he had ever done for the Negro. McCarthy suggested that the questioner examine his record. "Record, hell," shouted the Negro. "Tell us what you *feel*." "McCarthy has no soul," declared a Baltimore Negro. In Indianapolis, one Negro spoke for many when he said "that Kennedy cat is able to relax," but McCarthy "didn't put himself into it."

It was obvious in such situations that one was judged not so much by what he said as by how he said it. It defied the kind of reason McCarthy had based his campaign on. And so he overreacted in a negative way. He presented himself as unnecessarily mute. One could not help feel that he would have served the goal of reconciliation a bit more had he bent a little.

At the same time, he knew he could not hope to compete with Kennedy for the mass of the Negro vote. Kennedy was known; his appeal was built in. The picture of his slain brother adorned the walls of countless Negro tenements across the land. It did not matter that both Kennedys had not fulfilled promises to the Negro from the 1960 campaign and had delayed in the actions they did take, nor did it matter that Robert Kennedy as Attorney-General had been responsible for the electronic bugging of Martin Luther King, Jr. These facts were little known in the ghetto. What mattered was that the Kennedy family had suffered an unjust death, just as a ghetto family suffers countless daily unjust deaths of the spirit. They saw Robert Kennedy fight on despite the injustice, as they fought on each day. Call it identification, transference, communication. It was a spiritual thing that McCarthy could not even try to duplicate. It had nothing to do with issues. "I can't compete with Bobby or Hubert on this stuff in the primaries. It's too late, and it's just not my way to carry on," McCarthy said in early May. Knowing he could not draw the black crowds Kennedy did, McCarthy instead tried to reach the ghetto through private meetings with Negro leaders.

McCarthy correctly argued that the Negro and blue-collar vote would, in the end, go to almost any Democratic nominee for President. But while he lived, that vote was Robert Kennedy's, and primarily because of his name. The appeal passed on to Ted Kennedy after Robert's death. A Harris poll late in the summer of 1969, after Ted Kennedy's auto accident, showed the same strong poor, Negro and blue-collar support for Kennedy for President that had gone to his two brothers. Among other voters, however, Kennedy's popularity had dropped precipitously. Before Robert Kennedy was slain, a Gallup poll found that Kennedy's support came primarily out of personal loyalty. He could have taken a stand on nothing and polled the same, Gallup suggested. It was amazing McCarthy did as well in black precincts as he did. But by the Democratic convention he was getting formidable Negro support.

McCarthy's messages on the issues of race and poverty followed the pattern of most of his talks. At one moment they seemed to plumb depths; the next, shallows. There was always that delicate line, one more difficult to discern because he approached the issue without visible feeling.

Very early he began to speak of the condition of the Negro in America in terms no other major presidential candidate used in 1968. He phrased it this way April 3 in Hartford, Connecticut:

> We in this country since the Emancipation of a hundred years ago, have used the Negro people as though they were colonials, not allowing them the same opportunities, economic or educational or cultural; not allowing full participation in the politics of this country. This is essentially the same relationship that existed between the colonial powers of Europe and their colonies in other continents. . . . And so we come now to say this must end. . . . The time has come for us to respond to what is both a moral obligation and a very pressing demand of our own time.

Really it was the language, considerably restrained, of Black Panther Eldridge Cleaver; James Forman, the reparations crusader; Jerry Varnado, Black Student Union leader from San Francisco State College; and black militants everywhere in America. "We see ourselves as a group of colonized people," Forman had declared, "and we must ask what are the techniques of control that operate on us to accept the political servitude, the economic exploitation, the cultural degradation, the humiliation, the racism."

One of the factors, of course, was powerlessness. Both Kennedy and McCarthy spoke of hoping to begin to change this situation. "It is time," a McCarthy speech text said, "for a new administration to address itself to the condition of powerlessness. For the fact is that poverty among black people is no accident. Black people are poor because they are powerless and powerless because they are black." It was indirectly an endorsement of Black Power, which he had spoken of before, once in Watts just before the California election. "There has been Irish Power and Italian Power and there never has been a group in America who had more reason to organize themselves to get their rights," he told the small group of blacks who came to listen to him. "The question becomes one of how you organize and what you do. But there's nothing un-American about it, nothing contrary to the traditions of this country."

He always spoke of "four new areas of civil rights" that, he declared, must be recognized. He had been using variations of the line in speeches for years, and it was distressingly similar to several points in a "Second Bill of Rights" proposed by President Franklin D. Roosevelt in 1945.

On Roosevelt's list was "the right to a useful and remunerative job in the industries or shops or farms or mines of the nation. . . ." On McCarthy's was "the right to a decent job—one that is becoming to you as a man and as a woman, and which also returns to you the income which you need in order to live in dignity and to support your family. . . ."

Roosevelt spoke of "the right of every family to a decent home." McCarthy spoke of the right "to a decent house—not in a ghetto, not in isolation, but in a neighborhood and in a community which is a part of the United States itself."

Roosevelt recognized "the right to adequate medical care and the opportunity to achieve and enjoy good health." McCarthy recognized "the right to health . . . the right to be free from unhealthy conditions and the right to medical attention when some disability and sickness or accident comes upon you."

Roosevelt spoke of the "right to a good education." McCarthy spoke of the "right not simply to equal education, but to the amount and kind of education which is necessary to develop [every American's] full potential . . . for the most talented among us, for the least gifted, and for those who are of average gift."

In very general detail he would outline how he would seek to fulfill these rights. Better education would be accomplished, essentially, by upgrading existing programs. A job for everyone who could work would be accomplished through vastly expanded training by both the public and private sectors and the promise of government employment if no other work was available. For those unable to work, a program of an assured minimum income would be established, financed, primarily, through changes in a number of existing programs. He would develop a federally subsidized insurance program modeled on auto liability insurance to provide health care for all. To provide decent housing, he would seek to meet the goal urged in the Kerner Riot Commission report: six million units over five years. He proposed financing this through a government-industry partnership patterned after the interstate highway program.

None of what he proposed was revolutionary. It was as good as or better than any of a dozen other strategies advanced by other politicians. Not until late in May did he begin to expand, and then the object was primarily to set him apart from Kennedy's thinking on race, poverty, and the urban crisis.

He criticized Kennedy's emphasis on rebuilding ghettos through private enterprise. In doing so, he rejected the trend toward racial separatism that had become a part of the rhetoric of militancy by 1968 and was served, he felt, by Robert Kennedy's own renovation project in the Bedford-Stuyvesant section of Brooklyn. The Kennedy approach, McCarthy said, amounted to a kind of apartheid that had no place in America. McCarthy stressed creation of new towns as well as ghetto redevelopment, with the major share of financing left to government. Here is part of what McCarthy said May 28 at the Davis campus of the University of California while Oregon voters were going to the polls:

Any policy for rebuilding our cities must take into account the growing isolation of the poor in America. It will be important to bring industry into the central city, to create new jobs and make sure Negroes can be hired. But developing our central cities will not in itself be adequate. There is not enough land, there are too many people, and there simply will not be enough jobs and housing. In these circumstances, to offer programs for the ghetto alone is another form of paternalism. For the crisis of the ghetto is bound up with the structure of our entire society as a whole. . . .

That is why I am disappointed by Senator Kennedy's overemphasis on rehabilitating the ghettos through private enterprise. Certainly private industry has a role to play in the cities, but that role can never be sufficient. The ghetto may have a few more factories and a few more jobs, but it will remain a colony, it will retain its economic and political dependence as long as its citizens are foreclosed from participation in the life of society at large. . . . Private programs designed solely to rehabilitate the ghettos leave open to question our commitment to an integrated society. Rehabilitation financed by a profit-making outside organization can easily become paternalism.

Of course, all this conveniently ignored the fact that Robert Kennedy had long favored more than mere ghetto redevelopment. But by the end of McCarthy's speech, anyone who might have thought that McCarthy and Kennedy were a Tweedledum-Tweedledee match on the issues would certainly have had to revise his thinking. In two months, McCarthy had drawn the distinctions sharply, while Kennedy sought to ignore McCarthy altogether in the mistaken belief McCarthy would quietly go away—a belief fortified by what happened in Indiana and Nebraska.

24. DEFEAT

As Eugene McCarthy sauntered through these two states he found Indiana cold and unfriendly, and he lost. Nebraska he found warm and friendly, and he lost even worse.

In Indiana, Lyndon Johnson was no longer an issue. With the partial bombing halt and a first step toward negotiations, the issue of Vietnam had been somewhat diffused. The two major objectives for McCarthy's running in the first place had all but disappeared. Now he was in nothing more than a personality contest with another Democrat. What there was of a McCarthy campaign structure was not geared for this kind of contest. The absence of the old issues left the army of student canvassers with nothing compelling to talk about in a state unreceptive to strangers knocking on the door, and so they were ineffective.

Though it was spring, everything seemed gray. It was almost as if the whole McCarthy campaign had been transported back in time to the bleakest days of New Hampshire in January, when the people whose hands McCarthy would shake would look at him oddly and wonder who he was. Snow even swirled one dreary day, though it was late April, as the small McCarthy motorcade (two cars and a lagging press bus) proceeded through the countryside, sometimes getting lost, to places like Kokomo, Wabash, Peru, Gas City, and Muncie. Simply change the road signs to Berlin, Manchester, Nashua, Concord, and you would have had New Hampshire. In Gas City, McCarthy was suddenly caught up in a fleeting moment of *déjà vu* as he told a sparse courthouse audience: "Here in New Hampshire you like to talk about the big issues." In Wabash, the mayor introduced him to a gathering as "Senator McCarthy from Wisconsin."

The day was typical of the whole Indiana campaign, which did not get any better. Scheduling seemed to have been done by throwing darts at a map. McCarthy estimated that he wasted 80 per cent of his time talking to too few people in out-of-the-way places. For some reason, Curt Gans had devised a "rural strategy" that tended to deemphasize some areas where McCarthy, scheduled better, might have polled better. Even in those areas things went wrong. The advance man for a Notre Dame appearance approved for McCarthy's performance a hall that held only 350 persons, and even then a third of the seats were empty. The advance man had understood the appearance would simply be a lecture and so he didn't try to scare up a crowd or get a bigger hall. A high-powered New York ad man, Carl Ally, hired near the end of the Wisconsin campaign, was dismissed just as suddenly when it was felt he had flubbed the buying of advertising time. Campaign literature was in short supply in parts of the state. Some, inexplicably, was kept locked up in warehouses. In some instances, pamphlets pertaining to Wisconsin were distributed.

Chaos reigned in the main McCarthy headquarters. State supporters seeking answers more often got insults. "At times we were ready to shoot ourselves," said one Indiana McCarthy leader. Funds dried up. Scores of young people who had been placed on a small allowance of seven dollars a day went unpaid for days at a time, many of them going hungry, many of them coming down with colds and viruses. Furniture couldn't be rented, nor could cars for a time, and when cars were obtained, often there wasn't money to buy gas, and so they stood idle. Mailings were delayed because of no money for postage. At one point, $30,000 in emergency funds for Indiana were transferred instead to Oregon. A young man who had joined the campaign as comptroller in Wisconsin suddenly departed in Indiana as finances became more and more tangled. Kited checks would be written on the promise of fund raisers that certain amounts of money would soon be deposited. An atmosphere of despair developed. It was reflected in the language of the young people. The state McCarthy chairman, Jim Bogle, became known as Jim Bungle. The main Indianapolis headquarters hotel, the Claypool, a partly burned-out monstrosity landmark scheduled for demolition, became the Cesspool. The hotel where many of the young people slept, the Antlers, became the Ant Hill. (The Indiana McCarthy organization had its headquarters in the Essex House, and this, inevitably, became known as the Sex House.) On one particularly bad day, one of the pretty young student campaigners looked at me balefully with her brown eyes and said in utter dejection: "Everything seems so fucked up, Mr. Stout." (The free use of the word by the McCarthy Generation was something older reporters, and volunteers, took some time getting used to, though most of them did.)

Moreover, there was the Kennedy juggernaut to think about. Richard Goodwin had switched to the camp of his friend Robert Kennedy, and there he was now with all those people: Salinger, Teddy, O'Brien, O'Donnell. It was simply intimidating to consider, when the young people would look around their cavernous Cesspool at each other and wonder, who are we? They imagined the Kennedy people had bugged the Cesspool and ordered a security check, but nothing was found. Some of them made sick jokes about Kennedy, and one of the sickest was that they expected him to stage some sort of attempt on his life to get publicity.

Publicity. That was another thing. The Indianapolis newspapers, the *Star* in the morning and the *News* in the afternoon, both owned by a troglodyte named Eugene Pulliam, at first treated McCarthy almost as if he didn't exist, which was much better than the treatment Kennedy got, some of the most vicious, biased reporting a modern campaign had ever seen. In one cartoon, Bobby and Ethel Kennedy were depicted as Bonnie and Clyde driving across "Indianer" in a roadster tossing money to the wind. In another, Bobby was pictured as Little Lord Fauntleroy dragging a bag. "Bobby with Lots and Lots of Papa's Money," the cartoon was captioned. Both had to do with what Governor Roger D. Branigin had settled on as one of the big issues in the campaign: that Kennedy was trying to buy the presidency. "Presidential campaign slush fund," were the words printed on mock $3 million checks signed by "Robert Ruthless," which Branigin distributed as a campaign gimmick.

Branigin, of course, was the third candidate in Indiana. Hubert Humphrey had cajoled him into a stand-in candidacy before Johnson dropped out. After that, Branigin decided to continue as a favorite son candidate, aware Humphrey would probably make a move later and wanting to get Indiana in a position to bargain at the national convention. The state Democratic chairman, Gordon St. Angelo, rejected a plea from Ted Kennedy that Branigin drop out so that Robert Kennedy could dust off McCarthy right away, and so the sixty-four-year-old Harvard-educated millionaire governor campaigned vigorously in his folksy way ("A drop of cow piss falls in the milk can and you can ladle until hell freezes over and never be sure you got it all out"). His issue, besides Bobby's heavy spending, was the right of Hoosiers to control their own destiny. "Outsiders," Branigin would charge, were trying to "take over" the Indiana primary and, of all things, were raising national issues. "The only issue is who is going to represent Hoosiers at the Democratic National Convention in Chicago." Certainly it mustn't be one of those "guests among us campaigning for their own interests. They remind me of a deputy sheriff who can't find a man to serve a warrant on." Branigin was handed another issue when a wild story came out of Washington that he was on a list of potential vice-presidential candidates on a Humphrey ticket. "I'm a serious candidate [for Vice-President]," Branigin began saying. "Indiana is the mother of Vice-presidents. We've had four, and almost a fifth." Such statements demanded front-page attention from the Indianapolis newspapers, while Kennedy and McCarthy were back near the funnies, until late in the campaign.

For Kennedy, Indiana was everything. It was to him what West Virginia had been to Jack in 1960, a cliché that developed almost immediately. Kennedy had to win this first one, preferably by more than 50 per cent. Kennedy made clear in many of his speeches just how vital he considered Indiana. "Whoever wins here could be the next President of the United States," Kennedy told a breakfast meeting in Fort Wayne early in April. "That's how important Indiana is."

Though ostensibly he ignored McCarthy, Kennedy had one prime objective. Said an aide: "Win or lose, the main objective in Indiana is to drive McCarthy out of this thing so we can concentrate on the rest of the primaries."

The Kennedy forces developed an army of students patterned after McCarthy's, though with notable differences: adults for the most part directed their activities; many were lured by payment of close to two dollars an hour; transportation was provided. More than one young McCarthy volunteer put in time as a Kennedy canvasser (though doing little actual work) to earn money enough to stay in Indiana for McCarthy. The Kennedy student canvassing instructions were a rewrite of the McCarthy instructions prepared for Wisconsin by Ben Stavis, who had devised canvassing maps in New Hampshire.

Despite a monumental organizational undertaking by the Kennedy people, they began too late to do the job needed. Kennedy's victory was primarily a personal one. He campaigned effectively despite the confusion over issues that developed with Lyndon Johnson's withdrawal. It was a campaign with life, and nothing was more lively than an old-fashioned barnstorming tour through Indiana corn country on the Wabash Cannonball. Kennedy and his aides began the campaign with an age-old tactic: spreading the word they expected to lose, just as had been done in 1960 in West Virginia; but polls soon showed Kennedy to have a solid lead. And more and more McCarthy's effort seemed like a bus stalled smack on the crossing as the Cannonball roared toward it.

Everything seemed to be going so badly in Indiana that I became convinced the McCarthy thing was doomed. Everything that happened seemed worse than the thing before, so I passed up a seat on a small plane that took McCarthy into Bedford, preferring to stick with the press bus and pick him up at a later stop. I was convinced the plane would crash and did not want to be in it, and therefore I missed meeting Frances Morrow that day. The plane didn't crash; McCarthy endured Indiana, finding solace in such things as the fact Hoosiers would plow a furrow around a single tree in a field. It showed, he surmised, a reverence for living things, but I think he was wrong. Such a tree would be something for a farmer to swear at each time he plowed, otherwise his day might be ruined, and McCarthy understood what that could mean. Outside a plant gate in Muncie a man took McCarthy aside. McCarthy later told a reporter what the man wanted. "He was worried about the Communists. I told him to be worried, but not too worried. I didn't want to ruin his day."

And so McCarthy plodded through Indiana, seeming as much on a quest to stay in every Van Orman hotel in the state (and they weren't too spiffy) as running for President. "They kept talking about the poet out there," he would say later. "I asked if they were talking about Shakespeare, or even my friend Robert Lowell. But it was James Whitcomb Riley. You could hardly expect to win under those circumstances." I am a Hoosier and enjoy quoting Riley, and one night in a Van Orman hotel bar, to an audience that included McCarthy, I was reciting Riley's poem "Joney," about a disfigured young man made fun of until he drowned rescuing some children from a pond at a church outing. "Purty is as purty does," went the last line, but McCarthy was not around to hear the finish.

A presidential campaign? Through Indiana and Nebraska it was sometimes hard to believe: a McCarthy aide dickered with a high-school teacher to borrow a bull horn the rest of the day after McCarthy used it to address students on the street outside the school one morning. He had come this far without a bull horn, as unheard of in presidential politics as not making law-and-order speeches. Sorry, said the teacher, but we need it this afternoon for a school track meet. To another stop. A tire of the chartered plane suddenly collapsed with a loud hiss as McCarthy addressed an airport audience. Later there was a much bigger plane, four engines, late at night veering into Gary airport as word rushed through the cabin that really the runways were too short for such a big craft. A broken windshield wiper grounded the plane later on, threatening to strand everyone in Sioux Falls, South Dakota. Then another chartered plane with an Iranian pilot who did not speak English well, setting this two-engine job down on grass *beside* the runway, nearer the cattle, because the runway was not built for such a heavy plane. I like to fly, but I was becoming a nervous wreck.

A presidential campaign? The unreality quotient was high through Indiana and Nebraska, and so one preferred to stay on the ground, better still in the raucous but cozy press bus, a rolling happening supervised by college students like curly-haired Parker Donham, pretty Mary Davis, happy Cindy Samuels, thoughtful Steve Cohen, frail Tom Saltonstall. They said outlandish things (Mary Davis whistled louder than any kid on any block) and sang and often had to borrow typewriters and paper from the reporters to prepare their schedules and news releases. Where's the luggage? They stayed up much of the night doing various chores until one night, in Vincennes, Tom Saltonstall collapsed and was hurried to a hospital in an ambulance. Somehow, he revived, jumped out of the ambulance before they could even give him an aspirin, and was back in the bus the next morning.

The bus rolled along through the days and nights almost as if apart from what was commonly known as reality, and sometimes the young people played tapes of Beatles music and the strains floated through the bus:

> The Magical Mystery Tour is coming to take you away
> Coming to take you away
> The Magical Mystery Tour is dying to take you away
> Dying to take you away—take you today.

It was like no other campaign bus I had ever seen; like the campaign itself. They said it was a different bus in each state, but in retrospect I'm sure it was the same bus, from Gas City to Studio City to New York City, and the same driver, though they said the driver I have in mind worked only for the company that provided busses in the New York area. He was known as "the groovy bus driver," and driving this bus got him caught up in this thing and he wrote a campaign song for McCarthy (it was never used). The groovy driver was sneaked into the McCarthy Day Rally in Madison Square Garden wearing a spurious identification badge. For the sake of the story, let us say the badge bore the name Blair Clark, which was the case with another driver along the way. A groovy bus driver named Blair Clark? It did not seem implausible. "Dying to take you away—take you today."

McCarthy began commenting in this period that politics was not just the "art of the possible" but more exactly "the art of attempting the impossible, or at least the seemingly impossible."

He seemed to be practicing that art in Indiana and Nebraska, as he had in January in New Hampshire, and by most customary signs not very well. Yet it couldn't be gauged simply by how he seemed to be doing in relation to another candidate. He said a lot more than one traveling with him at the time realized, much of it in side trips outside Indiana and Nebraska. He was developing themes he had touched on earlier, but which, up to March 31, always seemed submerged in the larger issues of Lyndon Johnson and the war. With Johnson out of the race and Martin Luther King, Jr., dead, he stressed domestic issues more than he previously had: In New York he made a forceful civil rights statement. In Cleveland, he began to assail more extensively the "growing and dangerous involvement of the military establishment in the domestic affairs of the United States." In Philadelphia a McCarthy speech text, most of which wasn't delivered but was reported, criticized United States dominance of the North Atlantic Treaty Organization as a military bureaucracy playing "imaginary, anti-Russian war games." Said the text: "The Cold War in Europe is over. There's no need to go on fighting it." In New York, he declared the dollar crisis had become a new issue in American politics, a "kind of total test of our whole culture and our whole government." He maintained a vocally critical stance on Vietnam despite the President's move toward negotiations, the only candidate to ignore the charge he might hamper progress by speaking out. Red China should be recognized; campus rioters were following an understandable course despite their excesses; fire Hoover, Rusk, and Hershey.

"I'll tell you one thing about that fellow," said a southern Indiana farmer after hearing McCarthy say some of these things. "He's no radical." Such was the style of this mild-appearing, low-key man that he could have walked into a bank and said, "This is a stick-up," and the cashiers would have responded, "By golly, he's right!"

He sensed that many Hoosiers were appalled by the sight of the wild mobs Kennedy drew. New Castle City Attorney James White was typical. At a Henry County courthouse appearance by Mc-Carthy, White told me: "Kennedy's tried to associate himself with this . . . this, young, wild bunch," and you could see in White's eyes fuming disgust over long hair and dirty bare feet and . . . and *beads!* And so McCarthy repeatedly sought to spread serenity like a Johnny Appleseed dispensing tranquilizers. "Be patient with my campaign workers who will be covering the whole state, mostly college students," he said that day. "And also with my own radio or television programs which will interfere somewhat with your own plans. As you know, this is the 1968 presidential election year— a year in which, I think, the country is called upon to make probably the most important decision they've made in a long time—I go back at least to 1932. So I ask your patience, your attention. . . ."

More often McCarthy began putting into words what he, at least, meant when referring to the phrase "new politics." He would speak movingly of the importance of people being political. Very little of this was ever reported, though it was one of the most important aspects of McCarthy's campaign. For 1968, he told one Indiana audience, "has been a year of the people of this country so far as politics is concerned, not of political leadership, not of organized politics, but a politics of participation and a politics of personal response on the part of the citizens of this country."

And this essentially was the McCarthy New Politics. It involved a constituency of conscience, a spirit of participation, a politics "which indicates a basic confidence in American democracy, a genuine hope in the future, and fundamental to all this a willingness to use reason and knowledge which are the only instruments we have by which we can give direction to life and history; to use these also as instruments to make important political decisions."

When you got down to it, this wasn't really new politics, he would say. On April 22 in Cleveland he continued with these words:

It is a politics as old as the history of the country, because it's clearly consistent with what Adams described as the spirit of this country at the time of the American Revolution. He said that at that time there was abroad in the colonies what he called "a spirit of public happiness." He didn't use happiness in quite the same way that we use it today. I think he used it in the same sense in which it's used in the great document . . . the pursuit of happiness. They were not talking about a kind of general joy or gleefulness or irresponsibility, but rather satisfaction. And he said that that spirit was manifest among the people who lived in this country back in 1776 in this way: they were willing to take on the responsibilities of self-government, willing to participate in public discussion, willing to make decisions about what should be done to the commonwealth; and having made those decisions, to take responsibility for them and then to take whatever action was necessary or possible in order to carry out those decisions. He said this spirit was so strong then that in fact the Revolution was won before it was fought. . . . The spirit Adams described as existing before 1776 is not dead in this country.

These were astoundingly optimistic words for a politician to utter in 1968. McCarthy differentiated the historic "public happiness" he spoke of from modern concepts of "joy and gleefulness" just five days before Hubert Humphrey announced his candidacy and spoke of "a politics of joy." McCarthy understood what he was saying. Humphrey didn't.

What McCarthy was doing in his campaign, he would say, was to try to "set free the energies, intellectual and spiritual or moral" within the American people. He would explain:

What we are doing is giving the people of this country the right to pass judgment on vital political issues, not just the right but it is something they want to exercise, which they had come to conclude could not possibly have been offered in the American political process. And in addition to that, it is an action which part of our people may have felt that they wanted and is something which this country needed: something to revitalize the political processes of America with hope; beyond that, to revitalize the government, and beyond that, to provide a new kind of spirit and inspiration to the country itself. Because . . . these are the significant conditions which stress that a democracy is called upon to do two things: one, to support an act of public judgment; and secondly, an act of public approbation.

This amounted to nothing less, actually, than calling on the nobler impulses of the American spirit. His audiences responded to these philosophic, inspirational interludes better than the press, many of whom were never quite comfortable with a candidate who talked this way. They stared vacantly when he gave a Hammond audience this charge:

In these final days of the campaign, be as fully political as you can; beyond that, no matter what happens, continue throughout the rest of the campaign to honor all of your obligations and to carry all of your burdens in your professions and in your special callings. In addition to that, be more intensely and deeply political, more fully citizens of the United States than you perhaps have ever been in the past.

"The Man the People Found," as McCarthy was known on his Indiana billboards, did not ask their help; he did not ask their vote. He expected the main things from them.

Despite the results, many of the people of Indiana and Nebraska had been more deeply and intensely political than they had been in the past.

Frances Morrow, of Bedford, was a case in point. Her physician husband, Robert, was pulled into the act, flying Garry Moore, the television personality, around the state for campaign appearances. Mrs. Margaret E. Rach and her seventeen-year-old daughter, Carol Ann, helped keep things moving in Bedford, and a respectable crowd turned out the day McCarthy stopped through. In the crowd was a very pregnant woman in a red dress holding a sign that read, "McCarthy is the Dominant Gene."

In Terre Haute, Dr. Eugene I. Dyche, fifty-eight, a philosophy professor at Indiana State, had been political in the past, but never as intensely as in 1968. He had been a volunteer chairman for Stevenson twice, worked in Citizens for Kennedy in 1960, had been a state ADA chairman, and sponsored campus groups of Young Democrats and SDS. He was involved in the Hoosiers for a Democratic Alternative before McCarthy announced, and when the New Hampshire results came in Dyche felt something heavy lift from inside him. "McCarthy freed us all of the psychotic frozen circle we were in before New Hampshire," he said when it was over. No, there was no big success in Terre Haute, none you could point to, though a definite sense of fulfillment of, perhaps, public happiness. "We accomplished absolutely everything—and literally nothing in my area," said Dyche, undismayed.

Dr. W. W. Renke, fifty-six, psychology professor of Muncie; Raymond V. Wells thirty, of Richmond; Mrs. Nancy Salmon, of Bloomington; Mrs. Dee Rossman, Indianapolis; Mrs. Marjorie Eisinger, West Lafayette; Michael Downs, of the political science department of the Fort Wayne Purdue University extension—all were intensely political in 1968. Mrs. Ronald Giere, wife of an Indiana University faculty member and herself a doctoral candidate, ignored all else for a time to supervise the petition drive to get McCarthy's name on the Indiana ballot. The Tippecanoe County registrar paid a dime to deputy registrars for each new name added to the voter lists, and so the Lafayette area McCarthy organization, directed by Dr. Robert Toal, thirty-nine, associate professor of clinical psychology at Purdue, launched a registration campaign and got fifteen of its members named deputies. Nearly two hundred Purdue students rounded up unregistered voters, most of them university graduate students, and before long had 2,500 names. The $250 in dimes went into the campaign treasury. In Monroe County (Bloomington and Indiana University), the McCarthy group, led by James Dinsmoor, also a psychology professor, with the help of numerous local people, hundreds of local students, and some from out of state—like Peter Kolchin and Mike Burlingame, both Johns Hopkins University graduate students and veterans of New Hamp-

shire and Wisconsin—registered 3,000 voters and to facilitate canvassing fed names of 40,000 Monroe County voters into a university
computer. The Tippecanoe and Monroe County operations were
the best in the state for McCarthy and operated autonomously.

Many other young veterans of New Hampshire and Wisconsin
poured in, and there were many newcomers. John McIlwain up in
West Lafayette helping Bob Toal along with Mary Beth McCarthy,
a niece of the candidate from the University of Colorado. Dan
Wilson, seventeen, a high-school student from Sedalia, Missouri,
working in a slum store front in Indianapolis. Allison Teal stationed
in the Cesspool. Joshua Leinsdorf suddenly helping with TV when
Carl Ally was dispatched. Douglas Wachholz in Fort Wayne and
John Bennett in Evansville. Tony Podesta in Gary. Scores from
Ohio State recruited by actor Paul Newman. Lydia Gross, from
Earlham College, chairman Jim Bogle's girl Friday. Mary Perrone,
state student chairman, trying to communicate with the national
people through all the static and chaos. David Wilson, a Bard College English major, suddenly finding himself the field comptroller
trying to keep track of money, which went out faster than it came in.

Example of unseen, heroic endeavor: Eli Segal, inexperienced
advance man, is remembering instructions from advance chief Bob
Terry about making sure no trains cross the candidate's route at the
time he is scheduled, to avoid enervating delays while 46,000 freight
cars pass by. Also, make sure the windows of the car are clean so if
the candidate is photographed through them there will be no spots
on his face. Horrors! A train is due at a crossing in Fort Wayne at
5:50 P.M. McCarthy is due to land at 5:30. This should put him at
the crossing about fifteen or twenty minutes later. Eli Segal, twenty-
five, a graduate of the University of Michigan Law School, somehow gets the railroad to delay the train until 6:30. But McCarthy is
late. He lands at 6:15. The McCarthy cars and bus and the train are
converging. Movie house pianos are playing chase music in Segal's
brain. The motorcade moves closer to the tracks. Segal at this
moment is simply trying to disappear in broad daylight. Almost to

the tracks now. Oh, why did the railroad agree to delay the train? Just a few more feet. He can't look. What's this? We're past the tracks? No train? We made it? A mighty omen. He could have died in that moment, Eli Segal. Instead, he went on to become one of the prime legal minds behind the revolutionary change in delegate selection voted narrowly by the Democratic National Convention four months later.

Something weird happened in the Marott Hotel where McCarthy and top staff people stayed in Indianapolis the day before election. A giddy optimism became apparent. "There's something in the air," one young staff member said mystically. "I feel something in my elbows," said another. "What do you think?" I said I didn't know what to think. Every prediction about McCarthy had been wrong up to then, and they could be wrong again, but on the other hand. . . . "I think something's happened; we might squeak by," one of the young people said.

The McCarthy people had been saying they felt that anything over 20 per cent in the three-way race would be good. They hoped the spread between Kennedy and McCarthy would be no greater than five or ten points. It ended up 14.6 points. But Kennedy had not done as well as predicted; he had not achieved a majority. McCarthy had done better than predicted. Together, he and Branigin trounced Kennedy. The figures: Kennedy 328,118 votes, 42.3 per cent (about a fourth of this Negro); Branigin 238,700, 30.7 per cent; McCarthy 209,695, 27 per cent.

The lapses in the Indiana campaign did not have to be reviewed that night. McCarthy said his biggest problem had been to get known. Obviously, all those McCarthy signs on the sides of Indianapolis busses—"The Kind of Man Hoosiers Feel at Home With"—had not done the job.

Everyone, in effect, had been a loser, McCarthy felt. "I don't quite see this as Alice in Wonderland where everybody has run and everybody has won," he said. But if it could have been a head-on contest with Kennedy, McCarthy thought he would have won, he said. "We had Governor Branigin between us all the way." He also said: "I think the direct confrontation that was denied us in Indiana will be given us in Nebraska." (However, when the Nebraska results came in a week later McCarthy determined that it, too, had not been a head-on contest because Lyndon Johnson, still on the ballot, together with write-ins for Humphrey, polled about 15 per cent. He did not voice this complaint after the Oregon victory.) With the state of McCarthy's campaign in Indiana, McCarthy for practical purposes well might have been wiped out, had Branigin not run. The folksy governor turned out to be an unwitting stalking-horse.

Whatever gloom McCarthy may have felt the night of May 7, it was dispelled when he visited the Cesspool briefly to speak to the young people in the Riley Room, a large cavern with quotations from James Whitcomb Riley adorning the walls. Suddenly, the memory of New Hampshire returned: not of the cold, bleak days, but of election night when the bad days had been forgotten. They received McCarthy warmly there in the Riley Room, with the spirit that had first escaped the night of March 12. It was loud and long and more moving than even Wisconsin had been, and it seemed to be for the man this time. There were few regrets. "God was on our side; we should have done better," said one girl. But mainly there was a sense of having stood up to this new thing, the vaunted Kennedy thing, and having done well enough. They would leave hating Indiana. But the campaign came of age that night. The dream had passed, and now it was day and one must rise up and greet it. "I didn't come here to dismiss the troops," McCarthy said. They let loose then, and probably their spirit, if not their shouts, could be heard across the street in Robert Kennedy's headquarters hotel where they toasted victory, but felt somewhat empty.

Kennedy's objective for the night had gone unfulfilled. He had not crushed McCarthy. The early edition of the *New York Times* in the East was already stressing this fact, proclaiming that McCarthy had come up smelling roses. Kennedy had not stopped McCarthy and he had not won McCarthy's young troops, and this never ceased to pain him. Kennedy ran into two young McCarthy people after midnight in the Indianapolis airport where he had gone for a snack before returning to his motel nearby. The two were Taylor Branch, twenty-one-year-old Atlantan and student at the University of North Carolina, and Pat Sylvester, of the University of Massachusetts. They were waiting out the night for flights home, the Sylvester girl wearing a McCarthy campaign hat, and Branch, his McCarthy staff identification pinned to his jacket. He hadn't slept for two nights and was dozing off when Kennedy tapped him on the shoulder.

Kennedy asked them what they felt about the events of the night. "We're going to stay with McCarthy," the girl told him. Branch was frustrated over the dismal results of his own canvass of Negro areas for McCarthy.

"That's not your fault. Why wasn't McCarthy effective for you in those areas?" Kennedy said. Pat Sylvester reminded Kennedy he was a Kennedy. "You have the name."

"Look, I agree I have a tremendous advantage with my last name," he said. "But let me ask you, why can't McCarthy go into a ghetto? Why can't he go into a poor neighborhood? Can you tell me that he's been involved in those areas?"

"He kind of neutralized me," Branch said later. "I still worked for McCarthy, but I was drawn to Kennedy because of his flair and passion for the black people." But Branch would not switch allegiance.

Here it was, nearly 2 A.M., the vote all counted, victory in hand, and Kennedy was campaigning for two souls he could never win because he had not moved when he should have. In the quiet moments of the campaign, a haunted look sometimes came over Kennedy. Taylor Branch and the honest young people like him were one of the reasons. McCarthy had them.

The troubles of Indiana multiplied in Nebraska. The Kennedy effort was better organized; the McCarthy effort worse. Scheduling almost collapsed completely. National and state leaders operated in total antipathy to one another. Money, promised for months, never arrived until the last minute. Local efforts at fund raising had been dismal. The candidate was as unimpressive as at any time in the campaign. His rebuttals to distortions of his Senate record by the Kennedy camp took on a petulant tone. These distortions, Kennedy's refusal of a TV debate, and Kennedy's vote against beef import quotas comprised the main McCarthy pitch in Nebraska.

Local leaders like Mark Acuff, David Evans, Eugene Pokorny, Michael Oldfather, Mrs. Marion Youngquist, Robert Hans, William Campbell, Daniel Christensen, Bernard Clark, David Stevenson, and Mrs. Janet Freeman did the best they could, but their efforts obviously fell short.

And, once again, the student operation faltered. Little canvassing had been done until the final week end because of the stress till then on Indiana, and then not enough students came, and those who did were still hampered by the loss of Vietnam and Lyndon Johnson as issues. In Lincoln, they worked out of a dingy one-time dance hall over a bowling alley, and in Omaha out of a one-time auto agency showroom. Because of a telephone strike no switchboard could be installed. Students ran crazily from one room to the next to find which of the many individual phones was ringing. Morale was good, but not as spirited as in the past. The money squeeze had already brought cancellation of the happy idea of chartering a train to move the young people westward after Nebraska—a train they would call "The Little Engine That Could." It would have stopped in communities along the way, and the young people would have gone into the byways briefly to spread the word. But it didn't happen, which was too bad.

The word circulated that the money squeeze would also mean dismissal, after Nebraska, of some of the troops who had migrated there from New Hampshire via Wisconsin and Indiana or Connecticut and Massachusetts. About three hundred of them had developed over the primaries into an elite corps of young supervisors, most of them no longer eager to canvass themselves, preferring to order the one-shot student canvassers around and, where possible, the local people. The supervisors went on per diem of seven dollars, at other times five dollars. They had clearly, in their minds, become the more equal among equals in the Children's Crusade and, in some cases, came to believe *they* were the entire campaign. An elaborate system of evaluation developed to institutionalize who was more equal. Different-colored sheets of paper in each crusader's personnel file meant certain levels of competence, of acceptability to the record keepers who, without fully wanting to, became the most equal of equals. The inevitable resulted: competition; cliques; stand-off; struggle; rejection; acceptance; *Lord of the Flies.* Enough new students answered the call in Oregon and California to obscure this creeping perversion among a minority at the core of the Children's Crusade. And so the spirit of youth remained a meaningful symbol, and most of the young people continued to contribute mightily, but they were never the entire campaign.

On election night when the worst was known—Kennedy 51.5 per cent, McCarthy 31.8—McCarthy stood before his glum supporters and spoke of that spirit: "I think we ought just to sing tonight," he said. "Nothing has happened to change the spirit of our campaign." He did not thank them. He rarely did.

But Peter Yarrow, of the Peter, Paul, and Mary folk trio, had told them why there was really no need for thanks, the Sunday evening before the election, when he performed for them and then spoke of the campaign as he saw it.

"Don't expect anyone to thank you for what you've done," he said. "This is it. You've been a part of it."

A young girl named Pat Jenkins was not one of the 130 Children's Crusaders selected to move to the coast after Nebraska. So she hitchhiked there, despite the fact she had to wear a leg brace. And she went to Chicago, too. This was it, and she was determined to be a part of it.

25. KAFKAIANA

By looking beyond the horizon of Indiana and Nebraska one could see happier signs here and there. On April 10 in Connecticut, the McCarthy army did surprisingly well in the thirty cities and towns where they had forced primaries to select delegates to the state convention. On April 23 in Pennsylvania, the McCarthy army got out some 428,259 votes for their man, unchallenged in the Democratic presidential primary. (Total write-in votes for Johnson, Humphrey, and Kennedy amounted to 23.4 per cent.) On April 30 in Massachusetts, McCarthy, again unchallenged except by write-in votes, won 50.7 per cent of the vote in the state's primary. In the "Choice '68" campus elections, McCarthy came out on top—a victory he often boasted of. The vote: McCarthy 285,988; Kennedy 213,832; and Nixon 197,167. The ADA reaffirmed its support of McCarthy right after Nebraska but also endorsed a statement commending candidates Hubert Humphrey and Robert Kennedy.

It could also be reasoned that Indiana and Nebraska were valuable exercises. Both uncloaked weaknesses in the McCarthy effort that were ironed out by Oregon—weaknesses in organization and approach which might have gone undetected. Indiana kept attention on McCarthy that would have been forfeited had he ignored that race. The aura of the Kennedy juggernaut became less formidable as McCarthy performed better than expected. And as Kennedy had tooled up in Indiana and Nebraska to knock McCarthy out of the picture immediately, he and his strategists shortchanged Oregon in attention and skilled help. All of these were factors not visible in the immediate aftermath of defeat, and so almost to a man the national McCarthy leaders felt Indiana had been their biggest mistake and Nebraska a disaster too, though one that could not have been avoided. Nearly a million dollars and considerable energy had been blown that, properly used, might have made the difference in California, or so most of them thought. To put it mildly, there was consternation in the McCarthy camp after the two defeats. Shake-up was clearly necessary.

Primarily at the insistence of major financial supporters, McCarthy removed Curtis Gans from active supervision of the campaign and installed an older, more experienced man, Tom Finney, forty-three, a long-time McCarthy acquaintance and a partner in the law firm of Defense Secretary Clark Clifford.

Gans had become a controversial figure in the campaign through his free-form spending and his frequent tactlessness. He had built a campaign staff out of whoever there was at the time, and these had been mostly recent college graduates or graduate students. As the campaign grew, Gans more and more needed help, but he was reluctant to share authority. The work finally became too much for him. Moreover, in Indiana, the stress began to shift away from the grass-roots canvassing effort Gans had concentrated on and toward media. (It always rankled the young staffers that most of the contributions resulting from newspaper ads which portrayed McCarthy's "machine" as made up of young people who survived on peanut butter and jelly went to pay for television time and not their efforts.) It also did not help Gans that McCarthy disliked him.

Finney would become no less controversial within the campaign. The young people and Blair Clark never stopped suspecting that Finney, because of his close ties with the administration, was a double agent for Hubert Humphrey, despite McCarthy's assurances he wasn't. It did not matter to them that Finney had opposed the administration's policy from the outset and had made his stand known in memos to White House aides. The McCarthy aides either did not know or did not care that Finney had urged both the White House and Humphrey aides to give behind-the-scenes help to Mc-Carthy in Oregon and California.

Finney recruited new hands for the final two major primaries: Tom Morgan, a New York writer who had handled press for Adlai Stevenson at the 1960 convention; David Garth, who had been the producer for Stevenson's television appearances as UN ambassador and had guided John Lindsay's television campaign in his race for mayor of New York; and Ruth Jones, a media space buyer for J. Walter Thompson advertising agency who had worked in other campaigns (and who after the McCarthy effort joined the team of Richard Nixon). Tom McCoy, fifty, who like Finney had been associated in the past with the CIA, became a chief Finney aide.

Even before Finney joined the campaign, McCarthy had moved to improve his scheduling. Scheduling had been the responsibility of just about anyone who wanted to make it his responsibility. Now he approved Gans's suggestion that Norval Reece, thirty-three, a former Philadelphia ADA executive who had directed the Pennsylvania McCarthy effort and had worked in other campaigns, should take sole responsibility for it.

Reece quickly found what chaos the scheduling was in. Full days of McCarthy appearances for May 23 had been scheduled for both Oregon and California, for example. He discovered that McCarthy's administrative assistant, Jerry Eller, adhered to a list of guidelines that seemed better suited for a hermit than a man running for President. Large rallies were out; also smaller ones at airports. The feeling was that McCarthy couldn't compete with Kennedy for crowds, so comparisons shouldn't be encouraged. Press conferences were also discouraged. They always seemed to disintegrate into questions about Kennedy and eventual accommodation. Similarly, invitations to network television interviews, even those that would provide good exposure, were to be turned down. There was to be nothing hokey, and this included appearances on late night television programs like the Joey Bishop or Johnny Carson shows.

Eller maintained he had retained veto power over any Reece decisions. Reece quickly threw out the Eller guidelines. He proved McCarthy could get large crowds and compete favorably with Kennedy. He accepted invitations to every TV show he could get for McCarthy, particularly in California, since an extensive media campaign was necessary there. And he settled once and for all with McCarthy whether Eller had veto power. No, he didn't, said McCarthy. "But be nice to him. He thinks of himself as campaign manager," McCarthy told Reece.

The campaign had already developed spheres of influence, but now they multiplied, and eventually there were a dozen or more campaigns within the campaign. One was that of Curt Gans and his two hundred or so young aides. A handful threatened to resign after learning Gans was being moved aside in favor of Finney, but they stayed on when Gans was dispatched to Los Angeles to help run things there. Finney and the group he brought into the campaign became another sphere of influence. Abigail McCarthy was yet another, with her women's organization and her status as the candidate's wife.

There was the shadow axis of Maurice Rosenblatt in Washington and Stevensonians Larry Levine, Jack Shea, and Russell Hemenway in New York. This group had been instrumental in Finney's entering the campaign. Rosenblatt himself had recruited a number of others, including Mayne Miller, who had led McCarthy's 1964 campaign for the vice-presidential nomination, and Tom Mechling, who worked for a time with Gans, mostly at loggerheads.

There was also McCarthy's Senate staff, primarily Eller, Jean Stack, and Charlie Callanan, who decided on the campaign trail who could and who couldn't see McCarthy—and very few people got to see him. Arthur Michelson, a former McCarthy Senate press secretary, was part of this group, though he floated in and out of several spheres.

Finally, there was the circle of sycophants and friends who

traveled along with the candidate: notably, poet Robert Lowell; Dr. William Davidson, a psychiatrist who had worked in McCarthy's 1964 campaign as a volunteer; Shana Alexander the writer; Mary McGrory the columnist. The group served as McCarthy's relief and sometimes protection from the campaign. They read poetry and sang Irish songs with the candidate and sometimes offered diverting comment on other members of the traveling circus. Lowell, for example, a dark look coming over his face, his sibilance more pronounced than ever, would declare that Ned Kenworthy, of the *New York Times,* was not to be trusted. I sat down one evening at a table in a bar at the Beverly Hilton Hotel in Los Angeles with McCarthy, Theodore White, and Mary McGrory. "Don't nibble at him," Mary warned me. "You mustn't nibble at him." I swore I would not nibble at the candidate. In Sacramento one day, William Davidson, a short, pixyish man with a raspy voice, had become mildly outraged because McCarthy's room was next to a noisy elevator. He busily scurried about shushing anyone who came near the McCarthy door: the candidate was resting. McCarthy's secretary, Jean Stack, wandered out of a nearby room in her stocking feet, a drink in one hand, a cigarette dangling from her lips, a comfortable scowl on her face, and was immediately confronted by a shushing Davidson. "Forget it," said Miss Stack. "He's not in the White House yet."

It was in the company of Lowell that McCarthy seemed most relaxed and indifferent to the dictates of the campaign. Tom Finney instituted daily briefings for the candidate in Oregon to give him details about each day's stops and insight on any new aspects of the issues. Tom Morgan was the director of these briefings. Lowell would often interrupt, with either *non sequitur* or disdain. On one occasion, Morgan recalled, Lowell broke in with: "You know, Senator, this reminds me of the situation that existed between King James I and the Archbishop of Canterbury in 1604." Spasms of chuckling ensued, and the briefing went down the drain. On another occasion the disruption was a simple "You don't need to do this kind of thing" from Lowell. It was as if Morgan were nibbling at

McCarthy, and nibbling was a no-no. Discussion of politics was nibbling. Lowell and McCarthy would discuss it only obliquely. One afternoon in Wisconsin, Ned Kenworthy was riding in the McCarthy car and having little success questioning McCarthy, who was in deep discussion with Lowell. "Can they draft monks?" Lowell asked gravely. "No," McCarthy said. "Well," said Lowell, "that's a loophole." "Do you suppose we could get some bishop to give all our students minor orders?" asked McCarthy.

Each new Lowell outburst would bring new laughter from the candidate; the more disjointed the outburst, the better. "Life is a hypothesis," Lowell proclaimed one day as the campaign was progressing along a Los Angeles freeway. "Who asked you?" demanded Mike Campbell, a young college dropout who became McCarthy's driver and court jester for part of the campaign. McCarthy, in the back seat, began his quiet laughter. Several days later in a similar situation, Mike Campbell suddenly proclaimed, "Life is a hypothesis." Lowell considered this earnestly, then declared: "That's a good line. Where'd you get it?" Mirth rocked the rolling auto.

Campbell, as the jester, would be the efficient waiter, dusting crumbs from plates, from the jacket of the candidate, from the candidate's face, from guests, the swipes of the cloth becoming wilder as Campbell would circle the table whisking imaginary crumbs and dust away, then the room, the floor, the walls. This would unsettle any politician in the room—if indeed any was present, for McCarthy usually would dine in his hotel suite with a few friends. Campbell would mix the salad with his hands, tossing it, churning it with exaggerated strokes, then clump it on plates in fistfuls as the candidate chortled. Once, in Arizona, McCarthy told an audience how aged Arizona Senator Carl Hayden had once disproved a scurrilous rumor by a political opponent that he was dead by calling photographers into his hospital room to get a shot of him raising one hand from the sheets. That night Campbell stopped the waiter bringing dinner to the McCarthy suite, placed all the food on the floor in the corridor, then climbed on the rolling table

and folded the table cloth over him. He ordered the waiter to roll
him into McCarthy's room and announce, "Senator Hayden to see
Senator McCarthy," at which point Campbell slowly raised one
arm from beneath the linens. Laughter, of course, though McCarthy
ultimately tired of the court jester and he was banished by being
set to work planning the floor demonstration for McCarthy's nomination in Chicago. No demonstrations were allowed, of course, but
Campbell put together some fine plans, among them fifty banjo
players strumming while everyone would sing "Battle Hymn of the
Republic." Campbell did not mind that he was shunted aside, for
he had become a True Believer, as those who never—or rarely—
questioned an act of McCarthy were known. When the campaign
was over, Campbell did not mind that the candidate never thanked
him. "I should thank him," he told me. "He let me make him laugh."

Throughout the campaign there was competition between the
True Believers and everyone else. By California, for example, two
separate and sometimes competing television campaigns were in
existence. One was run by Bill and Kay Nee, a Minneapolis couple
who worked in previous McCarthy efforts. They could be classified
as True Believers. The other campaign was created by David Garth,
who was brought in by Tom Finney. Garth was not a True Believer.

Just as often the competition was simply a clash of personalities
that flourished in the free soil of the McCarthy hierarchy like weeds.
There was Stephen Quigley, Abigail's brother, who, in the Krem-
linology of the young people, fitted into the circle with Finney,
though his style of operation was uniquely his own. Richard Goodwin, when with the McCarthy effort, was a power unto himself,
though he worked well with the young people.

In New York, people associated with the Coalition for a Democratic Alternative, led by Sarah Kovner and Harold Ickes, who was
at odds with Gans, became an independent power in the national
campaign during the summer after their success in the June 18
New York primary.

The money people operated more as individual powers than as
a team. Arnold Hiatt and Howard Stein overthrew June Degnan as

nominal finance chairman early in the game—she continued her operation just the same—and often squabbled among themselves. Stein created his own committee to channel funds he and friends raised into the campaign. His interest was television and so most of his money went to that. By midsummer there were several major, autonomous, and competing fund-raising entities: Stein's in New York, Degnan's in Washington, another in Los Angeles, another in Boston, and one in Chicago.

At the same time, a network of unauthorized, and also competitive, "bootleg" bank accounts was established in the name of the McCarthy presidential effort. Into them poured money for projects the young people, whose role was diminished after California, wanted to carry out. When they couldn't get authorization or money from the official campaign comptrollers, they merely raised their own money in McCarthy's name from such sympathizers with their effort as Martin Peretz, one of the campaign's heaviest contributors. Tom McCoy, charged after the campaign with trying to settle outstanding bills and otherwise straighten out the tangled finances, discovered no fewer than a half-dozen of these accounts, all in the McCarthy campaign name but unknown till then to most campaign officials in charge of money. Fittingly, three were in the Freedom National Bank in Harlem. Two others were in Georgia, to finance the Georgia delegation challenge. Another, in Washington, which Blair Clark discreetly supervised, helped pay the costs of the young people's summer operation and kept young people on the payroll who had been cut off the regular payroll. (Clark was forever dipping into his own pocket to buy dinner for hungry young staffers, supplies, plane tickets, even to rent furniture for a second national headquarters set up in the summer by the young people.) Werner Kramarsky, a top aide of Mayor John Lindsay, of New York, one of several Lindsay aides to take part in the McCarthy effort, declared that "bootleg fund raising developed to the highest skill I've ever seen." He should know. He took to doing it himself during his brief period with the campaign.

Somewhere among all these various centers of power was Blair

Clark, the campaign manager who did not manage, buffeted by affronts and slights, wallowing in inaction, but tenaciously staying. He would learn Mayne Miller had been ordered to Milwaukee and call him asking: "Why are you going and who asked you to go?" He would storm at Arnold Hiatt for trying to recruit a new press secretary. (There were at least six through the campaign.) "Hiatt, you have no right doing what you're doing. You move into vacuums where you don't belong." "Blair, you create those vacuums," Hiatt would respond. David Garth would shout at Clark: "You're an imbecile, a stupid incompetent." And Clark would smile and say, "Dave, you've a great sense of humor." Arthur Michelson would actually slug Clark in one dispute. Clark would roll with the punch.

It was an atmosphere that gave ultimate truth to McCarthy's frequent statement: "We may not be very well organized at the top, but we're the best organized campaign at the bottom that there's ever been in the history of the country."

Nowhere was the second half of that statement more true than in Oregon.

26. VICTORY

Hours after the results from Nebraska were known, Blaine Whipple, a leader of the Oregon McCarthy organization, hurried letters to two thousand volunteers around the state urging them to work even harder, for now everything rested on Oregon. The messages went to people like Harriet Civin in Eugene, Barbara Ryberg in Ashland, Philip Nikkel in Grants Pass, Bruce K. Alexander in Beaverton, Mary Davison in La Grande, Walter L. AuCoin in Forest Grove. Since winter these people had been meeting, organizing, planning, mailing, campaigning, each separate local group in its own way with only loose coordination at state headquarters in Portland.

The beginning of the Oregon effort can't be pinpointed. Probably it started after President Johnson's initial escalation of the war February 6, 1965, not in any formal sense, but in the gnawing of spirit that brought people together in living rooms to discuss what might be done with increasing frequency and deepening concern as the weeks, months, years, passed with this thing growing ever worse. Their senior Senator, Wayne Morse, had been the most outspoken elected official in Washington, and he spoke for the much more quiet concerns of people like Mrs. Phyllis Zweig, of Eugene, Edward

F. Kienstra and Jane Foerst, of Grants Pass and Mr. and Mrs. Harry Shaich, of Portland, among others who in 1968 worked for McCarthy.

The 1966 United States Senate election in Oregon had hinged on Vietnam to a large degree. Though the election involved other factors, it was the first important one involving Vietnam that presented an antiadministration choice to the people on a state-wide basis. Thus in 1968 many Oregonians were already somewhat organized for an antiadministration campaign.

Curtis Gans traveled into this fertile valley about midway through October, 1967, with his pocket full of dimes. He first visited Bill Muir, of Eugene, a University of Oregon student and president of the state's Young Democrats. Muir told Gans he should talk to Blaine Whipple, a thirty-eight-year-old suburban Portland real estate broker and politician for ten years, who had managed Howard Morgan's 1966 effort. Whipple, naturally, included Morgan on a list of persons Gans should see. Whipple and Morgan both felt something should be done to tap the anti-Johnson sentiment in the state. They agreed to call a meeting and invited the eighty persons who had been most active in Morgan's 1966 Senate campaign. On October 29, seventy-five of the eighty gathered at 3 P.M. in the Salem YMCA. Allard Lowenstein arrived halfway through the meeting and made a moving presentation; then the group adjourned, committed to mounting a campaign for an antiadministration candidate in the May 28, 1968, presidential primary. They discussed Robert Kennedy, but accepted his statements that he would support Lyndon Johnson's nomination and dismissed him. That left, it seemed, only Eugene McCarthy, who Gans and Lowenstein had said would soon announce his candidacy. Who was Eugene McCarthy? Most knew little about him apart from his Adlai Stevenson nominating speech. A delegation of three went to Washington to urge McCarthy to run for President. "He didn't commit himself, but he didn't turn us down," Whipple said later.

The group that met in the Salem YMCA that Sunday was only one facet of the organization that ultimately developed. In fact, the group that met with Lowenstein almost fell apart before McCarthy's first Oregon visit. The dreary reports of the McCarthy campaign in that period had a discouraging effect on some supporters, but by no means all.

In Roseburg, A. C. Roll, sixty, a lawyer and long-time Democratic party worker, had no contact at first with the group that met in Salem, nor did the McCarthy organization that he and a number of acquaintances began in their area until close to the Oregon election. They turned out their own literature and copied ads from eastern newspapers for their own local publications; and though the Whipple-Morgan group may have seemed on the brink of disintegration through much of the winter, that was not the case around Roseburg or many other places in Oregon. "Some of us would never have quit," Roll noted.

In The Dalles, Ruth Stovall, a middle-aged housewife and Democratic precinct committeewoman, wrote McCarthy's office when she learned McCarthy was thinking of running, and held a meeting in her home; and soon yet another circle of support was growing.

In the area around Bend, people who had worked for Wayne Morse and Mark Hatfield met informally to talk about McCarthy, and finally, when the main McCarthy offices opened in Eugene and Portland, it was they who called the offices before the offices called them. Late in February, some sixty of them gathered in the Superior Cafe in Bend and organized formally, with Dr. J. E. Hyatt and Mary Katherine Swearingen as cochairmen but with the work to be shared by people like Mr. and Mrs. Michael J. Shannon, Dr. and Mrs. George D. McGeary (lifelong Republicans), Ralph Stevens, Dr. Raymond Graap, Mae Killen, Natalie Smiley, Mr. and Mrs. Mike Hollern, and Hildur Niskanen, who probably wrote more letters to delegates and editors than any other McCarthy volunteer in the country.

In La Grande, in sparsely populated eastern Oregon, two students at Eastern Oregon College, Mike Troyer and Maurice Barclay, walked into the office of history professor Mary Davison one day and said something ought to be done to help McCarthy; and soon something was being done, with great help from Mr. and Mrs. Winston Saunders, who were important in linking the efforts of town and gown. When Blaine Whipple came through for an organizing meeting March 28 in the afterglow of New Hampshire, there was no holding back the people from La Grande and the campus.

In the meantime Joseph Allman, an assistant professor of political science at the University of Oregon in Eugene, was elected state McCarthy chairman and Whipple vice-chairman, and around the state, sometimes through the efforts of Allman and Whipple, just as often spontaneously, the organization that became known as Oregonians for McCarthy began to grow.

In the Portland area, Paul Emery, the Chris Wrenches, Dr. James Watson, John Callahan, and Bruce K. Alexander were building toward May 28.

In Corvallis, a McCarthy headquarters opened March 28 in a store front in the New Julian Hotel, and the door kept swinging as they came and went and returned again: Spencer L. Baird, Jr., who became finance chairman for Benton County, Carol Krakauer, Jean Heath, and Joanne Anselone, who staged an art auction which raised $1,000 (later a "McParty" raised $200), Marilyn Holsinger and Alan Wong, who painted signs, Barbara and Bob Baldwin, who ran the mimeograph machine, Elaine Winters, Martha Brookes, Harvey Williams, Barbara Rohde, Nan Culver, Judith Baird. The Corvallis group did not match two stereotypes of the McCarthy campaign: that it was a crusade of, one, mostly very young, and, two, politically inexperienced people. The average age of the Benton County executive board was 40.75 years, and among them its members had a total of 146 years of political experience. In fact, the whole Oregon McCarthy effort was primarily an Adult Crusade.

The McCarthy people had the state well organized by the time Kennedy announced his candidacy, and the pace did not diminish. By the Indiana election, forty-two McCarthy groups were operating in Oregon, compared to ten for Kennedy.

It is May 10, four days before the Nebraska primary. McCarthy is in Oregon, his plane landing in Pendleton, the closest airport to La Grande, where he will make two speeches, his only appearances in eastern Oregon. If February 6 was the day his campaign in New

Hampshire got off the ground, this day and the next are when his Oregon campaign begins to click.

Brian Doherty is only sixteen, a Pendleton high-school junior, but he is Umatilla County McCarthy chairman, and in that role he has lured a hundred people to the airport to greet McCarthy. Doherty even gets the airport attendants out by the runway to cheer McCarthy. He has alerted all the newspapers and radio and television stations for miles around, and their representatives are there. Everyone is shouting "We Want Gene," and Gene smiles but does not make a speech, and ten minutes after the plane lands, McCarthy is heading for La Grande to speak at Eastern Oregon College. In the college paper, an editorial praises McCarthy to the skies, and in his column "Confetti '68," Mike Eastman writes, "Spring is not here. Robert F. Kennedy just rented the sun for political purposes." (Later, when Kennedy appears at the college, the faculty is so pro-McCarthy that the college president has to *draft* a faculty member to sit on the speaker's platform with Kennedy.)

La Grande, it turns out, is the town that the Bloomington, Indiana, McCarthy group adopts. The Bloomington people send $1,461 out there, and a graduate student from Indiana University at Bloomington, Clark Glymour, accompanied by his wife and their three-year-old child, travels to La Grande to help the local organization. Glymour notices that people who wander into the headquarters ask questions about McCarthy's views, which Glymour recalls they did not do in Indiana and Nebraska. They read the McCarthy position papers, and they stay at the headquarters for a long time discussing the issues.

McCarthy next day makes two stops in Portland, where 250 persons are turned away from one meeting, and another organization, the Chamber of Commerce, which has unsuccessfully sought Ronald Reagan and Richard Nixon, has the biggest attendance of any meeting in its history.

"That was the beginning," said Blaine Whipple later, speaking of those two days. "They really lifted Gene."

. . .

Mrs. Martha Lewis, of Washington, D.C., experiences the spirit in Oregon. She is one of the many women Abigail McCarthy has dispatched about the country with a round-trip plane ticket and a half-hour of advice: "Go out and try to get away from the headquarters and the population centers, because these are being covered. Try to see groups that aren't being seen by others. Don't forget the want ads as a way to get to people. . . . Look up anybody you can; follow any contacts you can." And so Martha Lewis goes to Oregon, where she gets the name of Kathy Swearingen in Bend. Mrs. Lewis calls Kathy Swearingen, who replies, "We're out here. Nobody comes here. We're very active. We want desperately to feel that we're noticed. We need the encouragement. I can schedule you every day for all the time you can give." So before heading into central Oregon, Martha Lewis and some McCarthy women working in Portland open their purses and take up a collection and write up a small want ad, which says: "I am very concerned that we keep politics in the hands of the people. It is important that Senator McCarthy wins in Oregon. Please help in these few remaining days by telling your friends to vote for Senator McCarthy. The country needs McCarthy's integrity, courage and quiet good sense."

The ad is signed, "Mrs. Herbert Park, Portland," and the copies are sent to weekly newspapers in the areas Mrs. Lewis will visit with a sum of money and a note saying that if the enclosed money is not enough, write Mrs. Park and she will send the rest; if it's too much, please send Mrs. Park the change. Very professional? Martha Lewis arrives in the Bend area and is the symbol of the national McCarthy campaign. Though Robert Kennedy drops through for a perfunctory visit, Martha Lewis is there day in and day out for six days, appearing at high-school current events classes, at women's groups, teas, before local McCarthy groups; and she finds as she moves to other nearby little towns that the people know of her and what she has been doing in the other towns, and a letter to the editor appears in the Bend paper noting that though Robert Kennedy may have visited in person, Mrs. McCarthy sent Martha Lewis, and this shows how much the McCarthys care. "You were encouraged to use your own creative resources, with very little direction and specific guidance, with very little checking. I found I had many more creative resources than I knew," Martha Lewis said later, for she had discovered what countless others found in themselves across the country in 1968, and she did it without compromising her own ideals. She is strong for gun control, though McCarthy in Oregon has said it should be largely up to states, and Oregon, a land of hunters, is against strong controls. She frankly does not know McCarthy's position, she tells listeners, but she, personally, hates guns, and though this doesn't go over well, the people seem to respect her honesty.

Is it hokey to send the candidate floating down the Willamette River in a canoe? Norval Reece decides it might be a good stunt. He is trying to schedule something pictoral each day. He breaks it to the candidate. "Do I have to paddle?" says McCarthy. "They've got wet weather gear for you and everything," says Reece. "I suppose no one would go in a motor launch," says McCarthy. The night before the canoe ride it rains, and Rick Kaplan begins to worry about the river bank where McCarthy will get into the canoe next day. Rick Kaplan is a student at the University of Illinois in Chicago, where he is also a precinct captain in, of all things, Mayor Daley's organization, but he is in Oregon as a McCarthy advance man, and it is his duty to make sure the canoe thing comes off right. He is worried about the river bank because it looked slippery when he checked it out during the day. So in the dark of night Kaplan goes out to the river bank, sliding on the mud, his legs alternately slipping into the river, to dig steps in the river bank for McCarthy to have proper footing to get into the canoe. The next day, the skies threatening rain, Kaplan holds his breath as McCarthy gets in and finally goes off. The next week, just before the California vote, McCarthy shows up on the cover of *Life* paddling down the Willamette River. "Voyage of the Loner," says the caption.

The McCarthy headquarters in Portland originally occupies part of one floor of the Dekum Building and is manned mainly by housewives. As the thing grows, it takes over the sixth floor, then the seventh, then the eighth, and finally when the lease expires May 1 the army moves to a cavernous five-story building that has once been an Elks Temple. Rent: $500 for one month. The stream of young national staff people begins, and other student volunteers pour in, and the nursery on the first floor is filled with children while their mothers work. "RFK Spies," proclaims a sign on a bulletin board, "we know you will see this—we think you must be pretty scared to start the rumor that a vote for McCarthy is a vote for Humphrey. You have some nerve."

Robert Kennedy had problems, it soon became apparent as he began to hold his finger to the Oregon wind. The wind did not blow as it had in Indiana and Nebraska. The make-up of the state was not right for Kennedy's type of campaign. Ethnicity barely existed. There were fewer than 20,000 Negroes in the 2 million population and only 50,000 union members, many of whom were anti-Kennedy from Kennedy's Hoffa-hounding days. Larry O'Brien looked and did not find the kind of blue-collar vote that had existed in 1960, when John Kennedy defeated favorite son Wayne Morse. "The guys who were blue collar then are white collar now," O'Brien said. "They've got a $7,500 equity in their house, 2.3 kids, 1.3 cars." Moreover, the educational level of Oregonians was among the highest in the nation, and the higher the educational level, the campaign had shown, the less Kennedy's appeal. "Everybody here is either taking a course from somebody or giving a course to somebody," said one Kennedy aide in dismay. The face of Oregon in 1968 was less troubled than much of the nation except on the issue of Vietnam, and McCarthy owned that issue. "Oregon may be the microcosm of the new America to come," O'Brien grumbled. "How do you get a handle on a state like this? Where you have Negroes and blue-collar types, you can use them to give your campaign some cohesion." How, he wondered, do you shake up the people of Oregon?

"You *can't* shake them up," responded Representative Edith Green, who helped direct the Kennedy effort.

Kennedy sought mightily to reach the people of Oregon, but the harder he tried, the more he seemed to turn them off. He had not been campaigning for this type of voter before. "Once the pattern is set in a campaign, you can't change it. We set the pattern in Indiana and we couldn't start playing to the middle class here," explained a Kennedy strategist. And so Kennedy bulled through Oregon: sixteen-hour days freckled with sparse crowds; 320,000 letters sent out; 50,000 homes canvassed; 150,000 homes telephoned; a tabloid newspaper, the Oregon *Campaigner*, widely distributed in six regional editions; fifteen days of campaigning to McCarthy's eight. "If I get beaten in a primary I'm not a viable candidate," Kennedy blurted in San Francisco seven days before the Oregon vote. People looked at this grown man up there who at times became forbiddingly cute—if he didn't win "tears would run down the little cheeks" of his children—and they just didn't respond. Suddenly polls showed Kennedy with just a two- to four-point margin, and McCarthy had made up more than that in the final days of the Indiana and Nebraska campaigns. The smell of defeat.

In the McCarthy camp there was the smell of victory. Scheduling, media, the organization clicked. Norval Reece delegated much of his scheduling authority to Blaine Whipple in deference to Whipple's knowledge of Oregon and its politics. Whipple, in turn, was guided partly by intensive studies that young Steve Cohen had made of crowd and television potential. For the first time a crowd-gathering team was at work, another forte of young Cohen. The television campaign was the best of the primaries to that time, outshining Kennedy's. All over the state the Oregonians for McCarthy responded to the message of Indiana and Nebraska: that now it all rested on them.

Arthur Herzog, a New York writer older than most of the young national staff people, had been sent in as the national campaign's main presence in Oregon. He worked well with Blaine Whipple. A quiet, thoughtful person, Herzog took pains to learn something about the state and the McCarthy organization in it, and he recognized the need for as little interference from the national staff as possible. Thus frictions were relatively few. Herzog did resign in a huff after one dispute with Whipple, then thought better of it later. But disputes were not the rule, as in Indiana and Nebraska. Herzog, moreover, was blessed with some able help from the national staff. Susan Thomases was his right hand. Philip M. Friedmann, twenty-three, set up the best-organized system of controlling money to that time.

As important as scheduling, media, and organization was the candidate. After a faltering start, McCarthy seemed more consistently forceful, his mien more confident, as the crowds remained large and responsive. But just a week before the election it almost came apart.

In an air-borne television interview between campaign stops on May 21, McCarthy offhandedly indicated he would prefer Humphrey over Kennedy if he himself did not get the nomination, providing Humphrey altered his position on Vietnam. Within hours, the statement had been aired nationally. McCarthy seemed to be giving truth to the Kennedy claim he was but a stalking-horse for Humphrey. Phone calls shot into the California McCarthy headquarters from across the country, demanding clarification. The reaction was so instantaneous that before the day was out McCarthy held a clarifying session with reporters, again aboard his plane. This time McCarthy stressed he had no preference between Kennedy and Humphrey. Whom he supported should he not get the nomination would depend not only on Humphrey's Vietnam stand but also on Kennedy's conduct in the campaign, which McCarthy thought had been unfair.

The incident underscored McCarthy's disinclination to attack Humphrey with the same verve as he did Kennedy. Already annoyed by this, some McCarthy staffers began to talk resignation. "If McCarthy hadn't disavowed Humphrey, he would have lost some very important workers, possibly including myself," Norval Reece said later.

The full disavowal came the following night in a speech at the Cow Palace in San Francisco in which McCarthy drew the sharpest distinction between himself and Kennedy, and also Humphrey, to that time. Kennedy, said McCarthy, was as much a slave to the outmoded concepts of foreign policy promulgated by John Foster

Dulles as Hubert Humphrey, Lyndon Johnson—and John Kennedy. Though an appearance of policy change may have occurred after Dulles' death, actually there had been none. "Its foundation has remained the same as it was in the early '50's and in the '60's," McCarthy said. "Containment, and a continuation of the Cold War; some new language; some new sails on the ships; some new rhetoric —instead of containment it is counterinsurgency. But no difference in the policy—essentially the same diplomacy assuming for itself the role of the world's judge and the world's policeman."

Finally, McCarthy got to the guts of the speech, the explicit demarcation, the demanded disavowal. He said:

Any man who played a prominent role in developing the policies of the early '60's, I think, can be called upon to explain his role in those policies and not just in those policies but in the development of the process out of which those policies did develop. The policies are not the product of specific misjudgments—they grew from a systematic misconception of America and of its role in the world.

I am not convinced that the senator from New York has entirely renounced those misconceptions; nor is the vice-president prepared to say that the process is wrong as well as what it produces. If they did—in the case of the senator from New York—I would find it difficult to explain why he would use an endorsement from the former Secretary of Defense, who was one of the principal engineers of those policies. I have not yet heard him criticize . . . the role of the military in this nation, nor the Department of State, nor the Central Intelligence Agency. . . .

At the very time when American foreign policy was growing more disastrous, the vice-president became its most ardent apologist. This may have been in service to the President, but there are other considerations of service to the country. Not merely did he defend the war but he defended the assumptions which produced it—America's moral mission in the world; the great threat from China; the theory of monolithic Communist conspiracy; the susceptibility of political problems to military solutions; the duty to impose American idealism upon foreign cultures especially in Asia—all of these myths and misconceptions, so damaging in their consequences, have had, I must say, the enthusiastic support of the vice-president. And those who thought, in the best American tradition, to question those policies have been subject, all too often, to ridicule and to scorn.

Though the speech was intended primarily to disassociate him from Humphrey, McCarthy again concentrated his attack on Kennedy. He always found it hard to attack Humphrey. To him Humphrey was not venal; dumb, maybe, but not a bad man. Kennedy was, to him, the opposite. Moreover, the very realities of the campaign dictated that McCarthy make his prime attack on Kennedy. He was in no position to ignore Kennedy as Kennedy sought to ignore McCarthy through Oregon. And so McCarthy's personal distaste for Kennedy was served by the very demands of the campaign. He had to go after Kennedy. Kennedy was his major opponent.

McCarthy pursued him with ever-increasing wit and bitterness into the last week end of the Oregon campaign when, finally, he stood before his most enthusiastic audience since he had announced his candidacy. It was on Saturday evening, May 25, in Portland Memorial Coliseum. Some five thousand persons were there. McCarthy seemed to feast on this audience. It was the only time in the entire campaign that one might have felt compelled to apply to McCarthy that creepy phrase of the year that found its way into presidential politics: "Sock it to 'em." McCarthy socked it to Humphrey and Kennedy as he had in the Cow Palace, but primarily to Kennedy who, said McCarthy, added up to nothing but old politics in every way.

"He really hasn't brought in any new issues," McCarthy said. "Nor has he thrown any light on the old issues. . . . He's not brought any New Politics to the scene in 1968. We had something going, and still have in New Politics in this year, but it doesn't consist of adding up somehow a consensus or a composite of minorities who have special problems and saying this is the New Politics, because this is as old as the history of politics in this century."

Kennedy's very rhetoric was old politics, McCarthy declared. "No new language—we're going to do better, we're going to get the country moving, we're going to do more—but beyond that no specification as to which way the country's going to move, or what we're going to do more of, or what or who we're going to do better. . . ."

Use of a "cocker spaniel" (actually Kennedy's dog Freckles was an Irish cocker) was as old politics as 1952, when Richard Nixon and Checkers went on TV, McCarthy said, and he didn't see that it clarified the issues when Kennedy suddenly stripped to his shorts and took a plunge into the cold Pacific off the Oregon coast one day.

"This is all old politics," McCarthy said. "Nothing new, nothing surprising," and with almost each phrase came the shouts and applause, and by the end of that Saturday evening Oregon had settled on who would win and was ready to go to the polls.

Robert Kennedy that night did not appear for a joint television appearance with McCarthy in Portland. McCarthy had bought a half-hour and invited Kennedy, not expecting him to appear, simply squeezing a bit more out of the debate issue. There had been some talk in the Kennedy camp of accepting. The polls were dismal. Defeat was very possible. But no, there would be no confrontation. Nor was there the next day at the Portland Zoo.

By chance the two candidates visited the zoo about the same time, Kennedy running late in his schedule, McCarthy on time—as he was in most of the campaign, but especially in Oregon. McCarthy speech writer Jeremy Larner noticed the Kennedy press bus by an entrance to the zoo and learned Kennedy was riding a small train about a quarter-mile from a garden McCarthy and his small party were strolling through. He ran to the garden shouting, "Kennedy's up there," and pointing in the direction of the train. Vainly at first, Larner tried to steer the McCarthy party toward the train, hoping for the long-awaited Kennedy-McCarthy confrontation here in the zoo among the animals. Slowly, the McCarthy party began to move toward the entrance to the train where Kennedy's convertible waited. Larner ran ahead, ordering three young people wearing McCarthy buttons to stand in front of Kennedy's car to prevent a hasty exit.

McCarthy was closing in as Kennedy started toward his car. About fifty yards now.

Kennedy became aware of the situation. "Let's get out of here," he commented to an aide, and stepped up his pace.

Forty yards. Kennedy got in the car. The motor started. The three McCarthy youths backed slowly as the car began to inch forward.

Thirty yards. Larner raced to the side of the car. "Senator McCarthy is coming," he shouted.

Twenty-eight yards. "Why don't you stick around and have a talk with him?"

Twenty-six. "That's too bad," Kennedy said, his blue eyes ice.

Seventeen. The car moved away, and the TV cameras caught McCarthy approaching as Kennedy fled.

"Chicken! Coward!" came the shouts, and the TV sound men picked up the shouts, among them Larner's voice shouting the two words, and the words beautifully matched the footage. It was probably the most dramatic footage of the Oregon campaign, much better than a direct confrontation, the McCarthy people felt when it went on TV that night. Bobby Kennedy running away.

McCarthy paused with a smile on his lips as Kennedy's convertible sped off, so fast the Kennedy press bus was still in the process of loading. McCarthy boarded it and joked with the reporters. "Why don't you come over to my campaign?" he said.

There had been twenty-six election nights for the Kennedys since John Kennedy had first run for the House, and they had all ended victoriously. On each one Pierre Salinger had been involved in, he had worn his lucky pink shirt, and on the evening of May 28 he again wore his pink shirt. As the returns came in, it was wilting, and the Kennedy invincibility with it.

The Kennedy headquarters was in Portland's best hotel, the Benson. As the returns began to be broadcast, Kennedy was flying back to Portland after campaigning in California. The Kennedy suite on the Benson's seventh floor was grim. William vanden Huevel, a Kennedy aide, sat in a chair constantly switching the color TV channels with a remote control device he held in his hand—maybe there was better news on the next channel. Patrick Lucey stared at the constantly shifting picture that was all the same no matter how often vanden Huevel pressed the button. Edith Green sat quietly, as unshaken as any of her constituents. Ted Kennedy called from South Dakota, where he was working on the primary a week hence, and spoke to Larry O'Brien. No, the margin is holding here, O'Brien told Ted Kennedy, only it's McCarthy. The final spread would be McCarthy 44.7 per cent; Kennedy 38.8; Johnson 12.4; Humphrey 4.0; and others .1 per cent.

Robert Kennedy finally arrived, and the silence became more telling than the noise that had greeted him on the first foray of his campaign in mid-March. "You did all you could," he told the people in the suite. "*I* lost it." Soon, Richard Goodwin, Fred Dutton, Pierre Salinger, and Adam Walinsky, seated or standing around a French provincial canopy bed in the suite, began to draft a valedictory to Oregon, a congratulation to McCarthy. Those closest to Kennedy could not forget that McCarthy had never sent the customary congratulatory message in either Indiana or Nebraska. There were some niceties of the old politics that the New Politics might have borrowed.

In victory or defeat the McCarthy election night celebrations were much the same. But the one this night in Oregon outdid them all.

"Tonight," a voice boomed over the loud speaker in the third-floor ballroom in the old Elks Temple in Portland, where the McCarthyites were jammed waiting for their man, "represents the first time in twenty-seven elections a Kennedy has been defeated."

The cheering and screaming became deafening: the young hands and many older ones shot up in the McCarthy victory sign. The fact ripened in that moment, and a chant arose: "Gene in '68; Bobby'll have to wait; Gene in '68; Bobby'll have to wait."

"What about Hubert Humphrey?" the loud-speaker said. "Boooo."
"Gene in '68; Hubert'll have to wait. Gene in '68; Hubert'll have to wait." And finally: "Gene in '68; they'll *all* have to wait."

The candidate arrived about 9:30. The band played "Happy Days," and Eugene and Abigail McCarthy pushed to the stage through the path that had barely been kept open for them.

He thanked them all, which was usually an afterthought with McCarthy, but this time he did it right.

"I said in Nebraska election night," he told them, "the record of the westward movement shows that almost every wagon train got as far as the Missouri River. But the real test began once you crossed the Missouri and started up the Oregon trail."

"We overcame," shouted someone.

"We proved who had the best horses and the best wagons and the best men and women. We proved that, here today in Oregon."

The cheers kept interrupting, and the smile on McCarthy's face broadened, and he gave them the V sign they liked to see, though still a little restrained, the fingers slightly crooked, the arm not quite straight up.

"Here we had the right issues and the right candidate, and here it was just a question of finding our constituency. . . .

"The campaign here not only bridged the generation gap; there wasn't any generation gap; it was solid all the way. . . . It will be solid all the way to Chicago and on beyond Chicago. . . ."

Constant cheers.

"I said early if I were the candidate we wouldn't have riots, we'd have singing and dancing in the streets." Words from that night nearly three months ago in New Hampshire.

"We'll have a short inauguration speech." (YEA!) "Take down the fence around the White House." (YEA!) "And have picnics on the lawn." (YEA!)

Skip Bracken, a handsome young Negro who had worked the black area of Portland with some success, stepped forward and led the crowd in what had become one of the songs of the McCarthy campaign, "The Battle Hymn of the Republic." It made the white McCarthy people feel good every time they saw a black out front in the campaign, but that was not a consideration this night as their voices rose. Tears welled in the eyes of many of them as they sang.

It had barely ended when the band broke into "California, Here I Come," and the McCarthys, threading a route bulled open for them by a cadre of young volunteers, moved out of the ballroom through a rear door. But the jubilation continued long after, for this was the highest point of the campaign since March 31, 1968.

27. DEATH

California is the plum of the electoral Chautauqua circuit. This is the one to take, above all others, at least under normal conditions. McCarthy's strategists, ironically, thought it would benefit them most to lose. They had convinced themselves, after Oregon, that if McCarthy defeated Kennedy in California, Kennedy would drop out, and Kennedy had said as much. But, they figured, McCarthy, to have any chance at Chicago, needed Kennedy. So it would be advantageous to lose in California, though narrowly, by no more than a few points—enough to stay in contention. If Kennedy could go into the national convention with 600 to 800 delegates and McCarthy with 500 or 600, they thought, then Hubert Humphrey could be stopped for at least one ballot, after which a move toward McCarthy might begin. An unspoken element of this thinking was that in a deadlock, Lyndon Johnson would use what influence he had to deny the nomination to Kennedy. This scenario rested on a lot of *if's* that might well never have developed. And by the end of July, McCarthy himself would concede in private conversation that had Kennedy lived, Kennedy would probably have gotten the nomination. He also came to believe that even had Kennedy lost in California, Kennedy would have found some way to stay in the race despite his assertion his only course would be to withdraw.

All of this is not to say that McCarthy pulled punches or sought to lose in California. The campaign was run with every intention of trying to win. When Tom Finney arrived in San Francisco just two weeks before the California primary, McCarthy was down some nineteen points to Kennedy by the most reliable polls. In a 2 A.M. staff meeting on May 21, the day after his arrival, Finney declared: "We're going to win in Oregon, and we're going to win in California." Some who heard him already suspected his loyalty. This statement made them suspect his sanity. Morale was low, and the phrase McCarthy had dropped when passing through California on May 11 seemed more realistic. "My strategy," he had said, "is to walk through the Red Sea dry shod. Any of you who want to follow before the waters close in are welcome to do so." But then May 28 came, and Finney proved to be at least half right.

It was always difficult to say with confidence who in the end was responsible for what in the McCarthy campaign, good or bad. The only reliable barometer throughout was the local organizations. Where they were good, McCarthy did his best. Where they were not, McCarthy did badly.

California had been organized even longer than Oregon. The core of the McCarthy army was formed by the network of clubs affiliated with the California Democratic Council. The CDC was stronger in the northern part of the state, and so the McCarthy organization there was stronger. In the south, things were more diffuse, in keeping with the very character of that part of California. Industrialist Martin Stone, in charge in the Los Angeles area, and his young assistant in the campaign and in business, thirty-year-old Peter Dybwad, worked diligently, but out of inexperience were inclined to wait for directions from the national staff rather than to move boldly ahead on their own. Thus many things lagged in the populous Los Angeles region.

Whatever the disparities between north and south, the McCarthy organizing kept progressing, and by election day there were nearly two hundred McCarthy headquarters and neighborhood centers up and down the state. There were people like Jack Lowe, fifty-five, a farmer who helped start a group in the Hanford area; Richard Holdstock, thirty-four, who became county McCarthy chairman out of Davis and, among other things, helped raise $3,000 from Davis alone, all of it in contributions of $10 or less; Gordon Reed, forty-five, of Strathmore, who with his wife formed a Tulare County Democratic Club in October of 1967 to oppose the war; Russell Millsap, fifty-two, a lawyer of Woodland, father of a conscientious objector; Mrs. Darlene L. Pritchard, of Covina, wife of a machinist, who claimed to have opened the very first McCarthy headquarters in the entire state; the Reverend Richard Weston, thirty-two, of Whittier, Richard Nixon's home town; Mrs. Ethel Longstreet, of Beverly Hills; Harvey Forgasch, of San Diego; Ray Banks, of Hermosa Beach; Richard W. Hart, thirty-five, of Bloomington; Mrs. Jeanne Eger, of Richmond; Oliver A. Baer, forty-nine, another of the many never-before-politically-active, who became treasurer of the West Contra Costa County McCarthy group; Mitchell E. Abbott, eighteen, of Kings Beach, a high-school senior who organized in the Lake Tahoe area; Professor Cheryl Peterson, of Santa Rosa.

Fred Knauer, thirty-seven, owner of an Oakland curtain company, deserted his firm to work in the campaign. Peter L. Besag, thirty-seven, of Carmel, a department manager for Litton Industries, quit his job. John J. Barton, forty-four, a lawyer from Torrance, watched his law practice dwindle to half its size from the time he began working against the administration in September, 1967, to the time of the California election.

All worked selflessly in a cause that had been launched to depose Lyndon Johnson but now was aimed at defeating Robert Kennedy and electing Eugene McCarthy. And Kennedy now recognized publicly that McCarthy was really in the running. He agreed to the long-sought TV debate. Newspaper ads attacking McCarthy began to appear. The hostilities beneath the surface in both camps became more and more apparent. In the zeal to sell their man and undermine their enemy, McCarthy aides made one of the unfortunate mistakes of the campaign. A newspaper ad linking Kennedy to the decisions that resulted in United States intervention in the Dominican Republic inadvertently slipped by Tom Finney's scrutiny. Kennedy had not even been in the administration when the Dominican Republic crisis occurred.

Kennedy immediately countered: "This great crusade that began for the future of the United States is now involved in a campaign to distort and stop me."

McCarthy TV commercials generally took on a more aggressive tone and led to yet another dispute behind the scenes.

Through Oregon, most of McCarthy's TV campaign had been handled by William and Kay Nee, television and public relations experts from Minneapolis who had worked in McCarthy's two Senate campaigns. Their philosophy of presenting the candidate on television was to feature him as he was, with excerpts from speeches, short statements or half-hour monologues. It was not flashy television, but then their candidate was not a flashy man. They thought it best to display him calmly as a man who needed no fancy packaging. His credibility would come through, they reasoned. David Garth, the talented New York television producer brought into the campaign by Finney, thought differently. Particularly in California, he and Finney felt, McCarthy should be sold more forcefully. Rather than having McCarthy speaking alone, Garth produced a package of "voice over" TV spots, commercials with an unseen announcer talking about McCarthy, the way beer, cigarettes, and soap are often sold on television. They were very good television, but Nee felt some of them to be too aggressive and unrepresentative of the candidate.

One, produced by a California firm, Norman Rose Associates, and endorsed by Garth, featured actor Eddie Albert stating:

When it seemed that the Vietnam war was going to go on forever, who stood up to President Johnson in New Hampshire? Who put his career on the line because he had guts? Eugene McCarthy. I'll tell you why I'm for Eugene McCarthy: because he's got more brains than any other candidate, and more guts. That's why I'm going to vote for him.

It fitted the tone Garth and Finney wanted to establish: that Eugene McCarthy was a man of action, a man with "balls," to use a word prevalent in the argument that ensued, not just a handsome philosopher. But the "brains and guts" spot, as it was called, angered McCarthy True Believers, including one close friend who stormed at Garth: "You can't use the word 'guts' to describe Eugene McCarthy." "I'll say you can't," responded Garth, who quickly became disenchanted with the candidate and the campaign and quit when his California work was completed.

Nee and others, including CBS newsman David Schoumacher, successfully urged McCarthy to order the spot kept off television, though it still appeared here and there in California up to the election. The Nee circle was also violently disturbed over a Garth commercial that pictured in succession campaign posters of Humphrey, Kennedy, and McCarthy with an announcer stating:

This man [Humphrey poster] wants to be President of the United States. Qualifications: four years as apologist for an escalating war. Four years as participant in forming the Johnson Administration policies. Four years of rising racial disorders and division.

This man [Kennedy poster] also wants to be President although he supported President Johnson for the job until the New Hampshire primary changed his mind. He has a slight edge. The best financed political machine in the history of American politics.

And this man [McCarthy poster] wants to be President. His credentials: He's fed up. He's fed up with all the political opportunists who didn't speak up when they were needed. He's fed up with a senseless war. He's fed up with the rottenness in the cities and the cause of despair in the ghettoes.

Are you fed up with these things too? Vote for Eugene McCarthy.

This, too, was ordered off the air, though it, too, continued to be played here and there until the election. Ultimately, Garth included some Nee spots in the California TV effort because there was not time enough to create entirely new material.

Regardless of who was right, whether Garth or Nee, McCarthy was an exceptional TV presence, and he exploited the many radio and television talk shows throughout California. While the voters almost daily were seeing Kennedy on television being mauled by mobs, they also saw McCarthy speaking to them quietly. Blair

Clark had recognized McCarthy's television personality early. In my very first conversation with Clark, in December, 1967, he mentioned this McCarthy talent. Richard Goodwin felt McCarthy was the best television candidate since John Kennedy. And to watch him perform extemporaneously was evidence of it.

In Wisconsin, the final half-hour program on election eve was to have been excerpts from a speech McCarthy had given in Madison several days before Lyndon Johnson dropped from the race. But Johnson's withdrawal made much of that speech inappropriate. Goodwin, together with New York ad man Carl Ally, began preparing an alternative program, a staged rally in a hotel ballroom at which McCarthy would make an election eve statement. Nee, learning of the plans, argued for a more "cool" approach, fearful that a "hot" rally might spur a backlash vote for Johnson at the last minute. Less than three hours before McCarthy was to go on the air in a $72,000 nationally televised broadcast, Nee changed the whole format. He ordered Curt Gans to round up a small audience of attractive people who would sit around McCarthy in a TV studio. They would serve as a backdrop as McCarthy told of himself and the reasons for his campaign. Nee's preshow warm-up stressed the need for "cool." "Those taking part were to think of themselves as being in church or listening to a wise philosopher in a forest dell," he explained later. "There was to be no sound whatsoever from the audience. No applause. No chuckles. No groans. Absolutely no sound."

And that's how it came off: the wise philosopher in the forest dell speaking calmly, glancing occasionally at nearly illegible notes scrawled on large cue cards, turning casually from one camera to another, speaking right into the machines, right into the cables and the wires that led to the homes, to the TV sets, right out at the people sitting in their living rooms silently like the studio audience, the timing exact, introduction, body, conclusion, all as if planned and rehearsed for days.

The program near the end of the Oregon campaign to which Kennedy had been invited as a participant was the same, McCarthy with his uncanny timing finishing right on the dot. I once watched him in Indiana, on election night in fact, after the returns were in, sitting calmly in a hotel room making a string of radio spots for Nebraska. "How long?" he would ask the young man with the recording machine. "Twenty seconds for this one." "What subject?" "Oh, the farm issue." Twenty seconds later the spot would be completed. No watch had been used. No script.

Yet when the long-awaited television confrontation between McCarthy and Kennedy finally came off in San Francisco on Saturday, June 1, 1968, the man with the remarkable TV presence seemed to many who watched to be partially absent.

It was not that he wasn't prepared. For most of three days and nights a McCarthy research and speech-writing team worked, following the procedure of John Kennedy's staff before the 1960 Nixon debates. Tom Morgan, Paul Gorman, Jed Shilling, Susan Bodenheimer, Jeremy Larner, Sam Ostrow, among others, put together two booklets of material. One contained specific pieces of information McCarthy asked for, such as National Aeronautics and Space Administration spending since 1960 compared to public housing, and a comparison of McCarthy's 1959 unemployment committee's recommendations with those of the Kerner Commission. The other booklet contained questions that might be asked by the panel of three ABC newsmen, summaries of the Kennedy and McCarthy positions on each of the questions, potential Kennedy answers and points of weakness, and potential McCarthy answers and rebuttals.

What happened before the debate became a point of contention among some members of the campaign staff. Tom Finney took the material to McCarthy's suite in the Fairmont Hotel on Nob Hill late in the afternoon and spent about forty-five minutes reviewing it with McCarthy. It was a good session. Finney came out pronouncing: "He's in fighting trim." McCarthy was then going to rest and perhaps sleep a bit before the debate. But some of the McCarthy court paid him a visit—poet Robert Lowell, Shana Alexander, Mary McGrory, also Blair Clark—and for an hour or so before McCarthy left for the studio he joked with them, and they sang Irish songs and read poetry. Lowell scoffed at the elaborate preparations and belittled the idea McCarthy had to match Kennedy little fact for little fact, for McCarthy was above such things. Their intention, Abigail McCarthy said, was to help McCarthy to relax and to express their hope he would not treat Kennedy too bitterly in the debate. However, others, like Tom Morgan, felt they took the drive out of McCarthy. "They castrated him at this point," said Morgan in yet another of the many allusions to genitals that graced the California campaign vocabulary. "No one is ever castrated if he doesn't want to be," retorted David Garth, who came to feel McCarthy was afraid to be President. (After the debate, Garth would tell Finney in a moment of exasperation: "The next time we pick a candidate, when his opponent goes for his jugular, our boy will go for his balls.")

Whether the visit from friends had indeed unwound McCarthy is problematic. Had he done much better in the debate it could have been pointed to as a stimulant. But McCarthy clearly seemed down, perhaps tired, extra restrained. The little bags under his eyes, more pronounced when he was tired, were very pronounced as he left his suite to go to the TV studio. Blair Clark offered another explanation for the performance McCarthy was to give: "He was caught by an intense dislike of Kennedy; yet he didn't want to show it. He wanted to destroy him in one way, but without wanting to be so tough. And so he held back."

When Kennedy suggested that McCarthy was in favor "of forcing a coalition on the government of Saigon, a coalition with the Communists, even before we begin the negotiations," McCarthy rejoined mildly: "I didn't say I was going to force a coalition. . . ."

McCarthy knew Kennedy would make him concede the Dominican Republic newspaper ad had been erroneous, and he was prepared to hit back with an attack on distortions of his Senate voting record. He had carried to the studio a copy of one of the Kennedy circulars, which he would pull dramatically from the pocket of his jacket and then, in effect, push down Kennedy's throat. But when Kennedy disclaimed any knowledge of the distortions, McCarthy reached toward the circular he carried and said quietly, "I have it in my pocket." And he left it there.

When Kennedy suggested that part of McCarthy's platform on the race issue was to take ten thousand Negroes out of the ghetto and place them in white and very conservative Orange County, McCarthy let the remark pass.

And so the debate went, and thus ended the McCarthy momentum from the victory earlier that week in Oregon. One poll of viewers of the debate indicated that 55 per cent thought Kennedy came off better to 38 per cent for McCarthy.

Not until the next day did McCarthy say what he might have said during the debate. Kennedy's statement that McCarthy planned to move ten thousand Negroes to Orange County was, said McCarthy, "a crude distortion of my proposals. It could increase suspicion and mistrust among the races." Negro writer and television commentator Louis Lomax jumped in on the side of McCarthy. During a McCarthy stop in Watts, Lomax announced his endorsement with a stinging blast at Kennedy. Declared Lomax:

We cannot solve the problems of poverty in this country as long as we are spending $40 billion a year in Vietnam. Robert F. Kennedy admits he was one of those who made the decision to involve us in Vietnam. Eugene J. McCarthy is the only presidential candidate pledged to get us out.

I marched with Martin Luther King, Jr., in Birmingham, Alabama. I know that Robert F. Kennedy, then United States Attorney General, refused to use his authority and power against the white racists who unleashed dogs on black and white women and children. I am convinced that Eugene J. McCarthy will not play footsie with southern bigots as Robert Kennedy did with George Wallace.

I have copies of the official documents involved and, after studying them for several days, I am convinced that then Attorney General Robert F. Kennedy did order and approve "bugging" on August 17, 1961. I was amazed when Kennedy denied this fact during the TV debate last Saturday night. I was appalled by Kennedy's statement last Saturday night to the effect black people should remain in the ghettos until they were properly educated and job orientated and thus would be "accepted." I seek justice, not "acceptance"; Eugene J. McCarthy is correct when he says we must break up the crowded ghettos of this nation, and not practice apartheid as they do in South Africa. Robert F. Kennedy may have won votes in racist Orange County by what he said but he lost mine and I suspect he lost the support of thousands who expected more of the man. I am going to vote for Eugene J. McCarthy.

Part of the Lomax statement was used in a radio spot placed on Negro stations. And it gave new emphasis to the question of whether Kennedy had indeed ordered the bugging of Martin Luther King, Jr., an issue McCarthy had been handling gingerly since Oregon, when Drew Pearson had resurrected the old Kennedy-King bugging story in his column. At first, McCarthy would condemn FBI bugging without direct reference to Kennedy. By the end of the California campaign, he was belittling Kennedy's assertion in the TV debate that he did not discuss individual cases and had merely *approved* FBI wiretap requests while Attorney-General. "The Attorney General ought to know what wiretaps he's approved," McCarthy said. "He shouldn't say, 'The FBI asked me to do it and I did it.'" This, McCarthy went on, "was a little like Adam and Eve saying, 'He gave me the apple and I ate it.'" Kennedy's denial that he knew anything about the distortions of McCarthy's voting record was "a little bit like his knowledge of wiretapping." So the jousting went, needle-sharp, always with the prick of a truth. Kennedy's statement that he might be forced to quit the presidential race if he lost in California became a favorite McCarthy target. "It's a little bit like the child who if he doesn't get what he wants threatens to hold his breath. He might turn a little pale. But you always find at the last moment they always take another breath. . . . I expect if [Kennedy] doesn't win here, he'll reassess." The Bobby-haters rejoiced at the simile, but in the Kennedy camp the anger grew.

Kennedy, nonetheless, continued the charade of being receptive to some form of accommodation with McCarthy. "Perhaps, after the California primary, we can somehow join together," he said two days before the vote. But from Kennedy's first offer of coopera-tion during his announcement of candidacy, McCarthy had read Kennedy's statements as so many offers to swallow him whole. Even as Kennedy made these statements, his people were seeking defectors from the McCarthy staff. Two of the recruiters were Frank Mankiewicz, the Kennedy press secretary, and Richard Grand-Jean, a young Saint Louis lawyer who had been Curt Gans's hand-picked leader for the Indiana primary, but had left the McCarthy campaign. Grand-Jean informed Mankiewicz that a large number of young McCarthy staffers had soured on their candidate after Nebraska and were talking of leaving the campaign. According to Kennedy campaign sources, a number agreed to move to the Kennedy camp after the Oregon primary—if McCarthy lost. When he didn't, the defection effort focused on the post-California period. As the California campaign ended, Grand-Jean circulated through the Beverly Hilton Hotel in Los Angeles, the McCarthy headquarters in that city, bearing a list of McCarthy staff people supposedly wanted by the Kennedy camp. The Sunday night before the California vote, Kennedy speech writer Jeff Greenfield and writer Jack Newfield, a *de facto* Kennedy staff member, sought to persuade their close friend Paul Gorman, a McCarthy speech writer, to join the Kennedy campaign if McCarthy lost in California; but Gorman, who regarded Kennedy more highly than McCarthy, demurred. He had cast his lot and would not desert. Similarly, speech writer Jeremy Larner rejected a Kennedy offer. A handful of young McCarthy aides were to have had breakfast with Robert Kennedy the morning after the California election. But, said Sam Brown, there would have been no defections. At the same time, a number of young McCarthy people, unhappy at the antagonism between McCarthy and Kennedy, talked of leaving the campaign after the California vote to start an independent operation dedicated to whichever candidate could do most to end the war. Some ultimately did do this and helped Allard Lowenstein form the Coalition for an Open Convention in the summer. And some young McCarthy staffers who liked Kennedy more than their own candidate nonetheless stayed with McCarthy because their responsibilities were so much greater than would have been the case with Kennedy.

But now it is still late May. Think of a light show and a psychedelic rock band with Crazies swaying and grinding all over the place. Now squint your eyes a little so the scene is blurred. There it is: the fantastic Los Angeles-Westwood McCarthy headquarters. A large old place, a one-time Sears Roebuck building, suddenly dolled up with pop art, colors clashing and flashing, housewives and students by the hundreds intermingling in this dance of politics, shouting, sending more peanut butter, bologna, potato chips, and Cokes down to the bearded ones in the basement where the literature is kept and pictures are developed. A line a mile long at the duplicating machine. Mobs of children the women brought wandering through this cavern that rented for $3,500 a month, plus fifty parking spots at $12.50 a month each, plus seven dollars a day for more than three hundred people. My gosh, the money people said; this was almost a $20,000-a-week operation; they must be on pot! And one could imagine, as one wandered among the colors and the people, the faint scent of "grass" in the building. (Indeed, two young McCarthy men were busted for possession in Los Angeles—a constant fear in the campaign—convicted and quietly shuttled out of town on probation without the press ever learning.)

Westwood. They could never get anything done there so the leaders would troop across the street to the delicatessen for their meetings. Westwood. The great mimeograph machine caper happened there. One of the Finney men wanted a sheet run off, comparing McCarthy and Kennedy positions. The operators of the machine read the copy and found it misrepresented Kennedy's record, or they thought it did, and they would not duplicate it until it was rewritten, and so it was rewritten, twice. Westwood. The McCarthy daisy first blossomed there—the wonderful flower that blossomed all over California almost overnight, and then all over the nation, and still blossomed on the Volkswagens of McCarthy people into 1970.

One day someone showed a design of the daisy to someone else and he liked it, so it was shown to Peter Dybwad, and he didn't like it at first, but other people liked it. Sam Brown liked it very much and, with Curt Gans's blessing, ordered 100,000 of them for $4,200. When the money people saw a bill that size for 100,000

"Rickie-Tickie-Stickies," which was the brand name of the daisies, they went through the ceiling, but they quickly came down when a television newscast devoted several minutes to shots of McCarthy Rickie-Tickie-Stickies going up all over the place. More truckloads were promptly ordered.

June 4, election day, McCarthy flew briefly from Los Angeles to Phoenix for a meeting with supporters there. The only thing memorable about the trip was something Robert Lowell said. Swirling yet another martini in his hand as the McCarthy campaign plane flew through the air, Lowell suddenly proclaimed: "I keep thinking I'm going to have a hallucination of Richard Goodwin walking through the plane advising people." It was incongruously funny, as many things were in the McCarthy campaign, but it hardly seemed even remotely prophetic at the time.

The evening had a melancholy to it. Though an intensive nine-day campaign in New York still lay ahead, California was the symbolic end of the long road from the snows of New Hampshire. It seemed that everyone I had ever met in the campaign was now suddenly milling around the lobby of the Beverly Hilton, subdued, for the first returns had not yet started to come in. Soon they would begin to move to various rooms throughout the hotel and turn up their TV sets to live the moments with Huntley and Brinkley, Cronkite and Reynolds, maybe wandering to nearby rooms, conversation competing with the noise of the TV sets, ice beginning to be broken out, the liquid starting to flow, the crescendo rising. In the two large halls on lower floors of the Beverly Hilton the faithful began to gather to hear the candidate, whenever it was he would appear. Humorist Carl Reiner, who presided at almost every dinner and rally for McCarthy in the Los Angeles area, kept the crowd loose in one of the halls, the one where McCarthy would come first. A band played and finally Jack Jones sang, and when he did the room became suddenly quiet. He sang "The Impossible Dream" and, indeed, each supporter, each worker, each student there could feel that at one point in this crusade he had overwhelmed the unbeatable foe, no matter what this night might bring, for it was becoming apparent that the night would bring a form of defeat.

McCarthy kept thinking the final results would not show quite the gap between him and Kennedy suggested at 9 P.M. by the first CBS projection: 52 to 38 per cent in favor of Kennedy. First returns showed McCarthy ahead, though these returns had included nothing from the populous Los Angeles area, where Kennedy was stronger.

The ritual of the television interviews began, and soon McCarthy was facing David Schoumacher of CBS. Really, nothing had gone wrong, McCarthy said. "This has gone about as we expected." He was sliding into an assessment of convenience as he had in each primary. If it was good, it was an important primary; if bad, not really important. "We've made our real test in Oregon, where there were no bloc votes, and we made the case as clear as we could there, neglecting California in order to run in Oregon, and expected it would go about like this."

What he said was true. California would come out as expected when the full vote was in. By then the margin would shrink to 46.3 per cent for Kennedy, 41.8 per cent for McCarthy, and 11.9 for the administration slate headed by State Attorney-General Thomas Lynch. (The same night, in Humphrey's home state of South Dakota, Kennedy won another primary with 49.7 per cent to 20.4 for McCarthy and 29.9 for Humphrey, a resounding victory.) In California, Kennedy would again prove to be the candidate of the black and brown masses, though McCarthy got 19 per cent of the black vote and 13 per cent of the Mexican-American vote state-wide. And McCarthy's constant assertion, repeated again that night on television, would not be disproved: that Kennedy couldn't get votes McCarthy would in a general election, but that McCarthy could get the Kennedy vote.

The ritual of the evening progressed, and McCarthy made brief appearances before the two halls of campaign workers. At the second, one of the new McCarthy black supporters, Rufus "Catfish"

Mayfield, a young Washington, D.C., militant, took the microphone long enough to call Robert Kennedy a honky. They sang the "Battle Hymn of the Republic":
Mine eyes have seen the glory. . . .
Not long after that, Sirhan Sirhan shot down Robert Kennedy.

The suddenly remembered signs flicked through the mind like the television footage that ran over and over again:
A sniper scare in Lansing; a near plane mishap in Columbus, Indiana; Martin Luther King, Jr.; John Kennedy; a crazy man in Oregon trying to burst through the crowd to grab Robert Kennedy; "life is Russian roulette"; firecrackers popping like gunshots in Chinatown; Los Angeles—"my Resurrection City"; the wild mobs, that first visit to Los Angeles in March, correspondent John Lindsay, of *Newsweek,* watching them with mounting fear and saying that night, "This country is going to kill another Kennedy; he's going to get shot; somebody's lying out there waiting for him."
In the McCarthy camp, they suddenly recalled that incident of a few days earlier in south Los Angeles: A neatly dressed young man forced a soft drink into McCarthy's right hand, then a supposedly lucky coin into his left, and as McCarthy stood there holding these two objects, the young man let go a haymaker that grazed McCarthy's chin as he deftly pulled back. The young man was quickly thrown to the ground by McCarthy aides, the incident was forgotten, and the name of the young man never learned. A haymaker and a bullet: degrees of insane hatred.
I was in Tom Finney's room at the Beverly Hilton. Finney left with Blair Clark to go to McCarthy's suite (McCarthy was reading poetry) to work on final wording of a congratulatory telegram, the first McCarthy would have sent during the campaign. In Finney's room the television was on, but most of the stations were just ending their election night coverage. Tom McCoy switched through the channels to try to get any last bit of election coverage. He flipped past a fleeting scene of people in pandemonium, going two or three more clicks of the television dial beyond. I yelled at him to turn

the dial back; something had happened. The reporter's rule to stick with the candidate, which I had followed since New Hampshire, was suddenly meaningless, and I hurried from the hotel room to cover the new story. As I ran down the corridor, a McCarthy campaign aide grabbed my arm. "They won't try to blame us for this, will they?" he asked. And then he paused as if to say, "What am I saying?," shook his head, and walked away.

Finney and Clark had arrived at the McCarthy suite and were working on the telegram to Kennedy. The draft referred to Kennedy's "splendid" victory based on early returns and overstated predictions of the Kennedy margin. McCarthy did not like the word "splendid." "I think we should say 'fine' instead of 'splendid' because I don't think the margin will go that high," he said.

At about this point, David Schoumacher appeared at the door announcing Kennedy had been shot. McCarthy put his hands over his eyes with a look of disbelief. "Maybe we should do it a different way. Maybe we should have the English system of having the Cabinet choose the President. There must be some other way," he said.

McCarthy asked where his other children were—Mary and Ellen were in the suite—fearing for their safety. They were quickly rounded up. McCarthy's face was ashen as he watched the TV set, at the continual replay of the moment of tragedy and the confusion in the Ambassador Hotel ballroom. "There wouldn't be that confusion in our campaign," he muttered at one point. "Someone would take charge. A Steve Cohen. . . ."

Abigail McCarthy sat on the edge of a bed murmuring. "Oh my God." Blair Clark, Tom Finney, others, lined against the walls like statuary gazing at the television. Mary McCarthy did not want to be with all these people. She went to Dr. William Davidson's room nearby and sat alone. At one point, Ellen McCarthy cried, "This means he'll be President. This means he'll be next. They'll smother him."

McCarthy spoke of the young people in the campaign. What would this do to them, he wondered. He knew despite their loyalty to him that most of them liked Bobby Kennedy. What would this do to them? Their first election. The idealism . . . then this. His basic reaction as best anyone could read it was horror at what this tragedy represented. He would not pretend hypocritical personal sorrow. He had not liked Robert Kennedy. He would not try to pretend now that he did. Quietly he would feel sorrow for the Kennedy family. But he would have to remember the spoken bitterness of the campaign and wonder whether had some things not been said, had there been no television debate, this thing might not have happened. All the *ifs* . . . a child holding his breath.

Robert Kennedy had a call put through to Allard Lowenstein in Long Island shortly before he went to the Ambassador ballroom but did not have a chance to talk to him. Lowenstein had been waiting for Robert Kennedy to call again when Kennedy was shot, just as Lowenstein had waited those months through the end of 1967 for Kennedy to say he would run.

Eugene McCarthy went into his bedroom alone sometime around 3:30 A.M. One person who was in the suite thought he saw the gray glow of a television set burning from under the door as the hours passed.

Near dawn, a Secret Service man came. Young Mike Campbell and Jean Stack were sitting in the living room of the suite when he came, and he said he was there by order of the President to guard Senator McCarthy. He asked them who they were and then asked them to show their identification.

Someone said that when McCarthy learned in the morning that a bullet was lodged in Kennedy's brain he wept.

Tom Finney had been in touch with some Kennedy people during the night to express McCarthy's distress and to ask whether they felt it would be appropriate for him to visit the hospital. The lingering bitterness of the campaign later caused some of the Kennedy people who learned of the call to feel Finney was interested only in whether Kennedy would be able to resume campaigning, and one or two allowed themselves to imagine that McCarthy was probably sitting with Finney as Finney phoned, grinning a vulture's grin; but this was not the case. Finney in the McCarthy camp and Dick Goodwin in the Kennedy camp previously had arranged a secret means of communicating with each other on election night in the event the results would lead one of the candidates to drop out. This would have allowed both candidates to know the situation quickly so that a proper public response could be made. At McCarthy's request Finney made use of that arrangement to contact the Kennedy camp after the shooting. McCarthy had only wanted advice on how he might react in a way that would not add to the burden of the family.

Tom Finney and Tom McCoy returned to the McCarthy suite at 7 A.M. and told McCarthy, who was in his pajamas, that Kennedy would not make it.

"Well, what do you think we ought to do?" McCoy remembered McCarthy's asking.

"Well," said McCoy, "you don't know how long he's going to live. If you stay here you're going to be bothered by the press all day long."

It was decided to leave Los Angeles on the first possible plane, but there was the question of whether McCarthy should go to the hospital first. He did not want to go. He did not want to seem a looming presence; there was nothing he could say when he arrived; someone was sure to view it as a tasteless political act. No, Norval Reece vehemently insisted. He had to go. And he had to say something. Before he left the Beverly Hilton, McCarthy read a statement to the press in the corridor outside his suite. It said in part:

No words can fully convey the feeling that I have toward the Kennedy family in this time of their particular tragedy or the feeling that one must have for the nation in the face of this new tragedy.

It's not enough, in my judgment, to say that this is the act of one deranged man, if that is the case.

The nation, I think, bears too great a burden of the kind of neglect which has allowed the disposition of violence to grow here in our own land, or the reflection of the violence which we have visited upon the rest of the world, or at least part of the world.

All of us must keep vigil with the nation in prayer and hope that Senator Kennedy will recover. . . .

He went to the hospital then.

Take-off time was nearing. There was to be a police escort, and the police were asked not to use their sirens, but when they neared the hospital they turned the sirens on because traffic was getting bad. There was no radio connection to the car McCarthy rode in so he could not ask again that the sirens not be used, and some of the Kennedy people heard the sirens and they would say later that McCarthy came with the sirens on so the world would know, and that would be another mark against him in their minds. McCarthy arrived at the Good Samaritan Hospital at 11:25 A.M. and left by 11:47 after speaking briefly to Pierre Salinger and Richard Goodwin. They were the only ones he saw. He said he did not want to disturb members of the family and so he did not see Ted Kennedy. Ethel Kennedy was sleeping. He had come with the sirens on. Goddman Eugene McCarthy, he came with the sirens on, they would say. Even in their sorrow, the hatred of some of the Kennedy people against this man who stood up when Robert Kennedy had not and then refused to sit down deepened to unreason. And so the McCarthy-Kennedy episode ended as it had begun, in bitterness.

There was some conversation on the plane on the way back to Washington. Tom Finney, Tom McCoy, Bill Davidson, and Jean Stack were the only ones McCarthy asked to come with him. David Schoumacher learned which flight McCarthy would take and was also on board. Finney and McCoy recalled parts of the conversation.

Finney and McCarthy talked aimlessly for a time until Los Angeles was behind. Finney said he thought that McCarthy must continue on, but Finney didn't know how McCarthy could do it, how his sanity had held up the long months, the showing in New Hampshire obscured by Kennedy's entry, the Wisconsin victory overshadowed by Lyndon Johnson's withdrawal, and now this. "Maybe the Lord's purpose in all this is to cure you of the sin of pride," Finney told McCarthy.

"You know, that's the deadliest sin," McCarthy answered.

Then, without passion, McCarthy said it. "It's all over, you know." Really, there was no chance now, McCarthy said. There would be no further need for the large campaign staff, all the people, all the plans. "It's not going to make any difference. What we have to do now is cut down and just see what influence we can bring to bear on the situation between now and August," said McCarthy. "It's all over."

The Whole World Was Watching

★

Who will be left to celebrate
a victory made of blood and fire?

FROM ''OUR GREEN GARDEN,'' BY
THICH NHAT HANH, A VIETNAMESE POET

28. PENULTIMA

Despite a rosier outlook by some of his campaign aides much of the summer, Eugene McCarthy was rarely shaken from his belief it was all over after Kennedy's assassination, so far as the possibility of his nomination went. But there was no way to bow out; the accidental instrument did not really have such a choice, for there was still the possibility he might be able to force something approaching a Vietnam peace plank at the Democratic National Convention. Having made the original decision to allow himself to be the focus for the issue, he must continue on, even though personal defeat—the execution of "the messenger who brought the bad news," as he often called himself—assuredly lay ahead in Chicago.

He thus approached the summer campaign not altogether positively (some would say he went at it as if with a death wish). He had never really been in control of his organization, and now it veered almost totally out of hand. Across America, however, far from the madding influence of the national staff, the people in their local situations worked with the spirit that had been a part of the campaign since precinct caucus night in Minnesota.

For the candidate, the summer became eternal. Though exhausting, the primaries had had stimulating new beginnings and climaxes. The summer did not. "It's as if someone gave you the football and you're running with it, but the field never ends," McCarthy observed. "There's no goal line. No opponent. You just run. And every time you reach a marker on the field it's always the fifty yard line."

Blair Clark picked out a word to describe this period. "We have entered the penultimate stage," he told a press conference early in the summer. "The last but one," Webster's *New Collegiate Dictionary* defines "penultimate." Indeed, that's what the summer was: last stop before the final act of Chicago, unless of course one were to get the nomination. But McCarthy was not going to get the nomination, and so Blair Clark chose his word carefully. The campaign was in penultima, or however you want to say it.

Over the summer, McCarthy kept up a fairly strenuous round of public appearances and meetings with potential supporters and groups of delegates. He visited thirty-eight states in the campaign and twenty-five delegations over the summer. Yet he could not tell delegate groups the main thing they wanted to hear: that he would support the party's nominee, Hubert Humphrey or whomever. To tell them this would have been to surrender his final weapon to influence the platform and possibly over-all policy. He had to maintain the threat of possible nonsupport, which his backers exercised much more loudly as state convention after state convention failed to give them what they thought their due in national convention delegates. And so McCarthy's meetings with delegates invariably ended dismally.

His efforts to bring some order into his campaign structure were minimal and destined to failure. He could have given more direction, but then, that was not his style; that's not what this educational exercise was about. The people, at whatever level, had to lead. It was up to them. Certainly in New York State it had all been up to them.

McCarthy had planned to campaign intensively throughout the state, but this plan was canceled at Robert Kennedy's death. McCarthy made but two desultory visits to New York City before the

June 18 election, one of those trips forced upon him. Thus he never got around the state to see the New York version of the McCarthy movement: people like Mrs. Diana Ruchelman, twenty-nine, of Alfred, wife of the head of the political science department at Alfred University. The Ruchelman home was the headquarters for activity in the Thirty-Eighth Congressional District, and Diana Ruchelman was the chairman, pausing just long enough one week to have a baby, then continuing on, the baby flung over her shoulder as she worked the phone. In Brockport, Mickey Messerschmitt, who helped her minister husband, John, run the local organization, waddled about clear to election day before she gave birth. Though a joyful event, it kept her from voting. Her husband left her side long enough to do so. He and enough others got to the polls June 18 to pull off a startling upset.

Sixty-two national convention delegate candidates supporting McCarthy were elected. Most remarkable, in accordance with state law they had run on ballots that did not identify their allegiance to McCarthy. His workers in New York State had had the added job of making sure his supporters knew which delegate candidate was for which presidential candidate. They also won the Democratic nomination for the United States Senate for McCarthy backer Paul O'Dwyer, who got 36.1 per cent of the vote over Kennedy backer Eugene Nickerson (33.7 per cent) and administration supporter United States Representative Joseph Y. Resnick (30.1). (O'Dwyer lost to Republican Senator Jacob Javits in November.) The New York effort had been led, as much as anything was ever led in the traditional sense in the McCarthy campaign, by three state cochairmen: Mrs. Eleanor Clark French, Clarence B. Jones, and Richard Lipsitz. They were backed up by Harold Ickes, Jr., and Sarah Kovner, of the Coalition for a Democratic Alternative, which became the McCarthy group.

How the election might have resulted had Kennedy not been killed will never be known. He had also planned an intensive campaign, for there were signs he was in trouble in New York. The CDA had organized, and organized well.

.   .   .

The New York victory seemed to augur well for the McCarthy summer effort, but in the two weeks that followed, it became brutally apparent, to these who had forgotten, that winning primaries was not necessarily the way to win the nomination. The final rounds of delegate selection conventions were held in the states that did not employ elections for this purpose, and the regulars controlled them.

What with the pickup, hand-to-mouth nature of the McCarthy campaign, relatively little attention had been given to nonprimary states. David Mixner for weeks worked the nonprimary states almost alone, shuttling from Minnesota to Iowa to Pennsylvania to Maryland, North Carolina, Kansas, Kentucky, Texas, Georgia, trying to make some sense out of things, at first phoning Washington headquarters regularly to Curt Gans's wife, Genie, for instructions, enduring the stream of swearing that usually greeted him, and finally hanging up, the instructions bounding around inside his head: "Do your own thing." Regularly, he would resign, but Blair Clark would never accept his resignations. ("Now, now, David. Cool down.")

McCarthy himself would tell supporters from state to state essentially what Mixner would hear over the telephone from Genie Gans. "It has never been a question of a very orderly sort of an organization," McCarthy said in understatement to Iowa supporters in June. "We haven't had a single mastermind. It has been a kind of peasants' revolt from the very beginning. Don't wait for any kind of organized instructions. . . . Don't hesitate for instruction. We know what our case is. We know what we are concerned about. And we just ask everyone to carry on within the organization where we have it. But don't wait for instructions. Just go out and make the case to the people."

In April, Don Green, who had helped organize a dissident Democrat group in the District of Columbia, joined the campaign staff and found himself coordinating nonprimary-state efforts. He, Mixner, Genie Gans, Eli Segal, Thomas Mechling, and Jim Goff did as much as a handful of people with little experience could do, but it was

not enough. Even in the few places where early grass-roots organizing won significant portions of state convention delegates, there still
were not enough in almost all cases to grab control of the delegate
selection process, once the conventions met. In state after state,
McCarthy people found themselves being shut out. They responded
with a string of noisy demonstrations and convention walkouts that
only stiffened resistance of the regulars to the McCarthy insurgents.

The curtain raiser for what happened around the country occurred
in Pennsylvania late in May. An unusually early caucus of the
Pennsylvania delegation to the Democratic National Convention
was held the day before the Oregon primary in Harrisburg's Penn-
Harris Hotel, even though the delegates hadn't yet been officially
certified. The caucus had been plotted by Humphrey campaign
strategists, who had no primaries to preoccupy them and could
undertake a major nonprimary-state delegate-hunting operation
from the start, something John Kennedy had done but Robert
Kennedy hadn't had time to do. The object of the early caucus:
quite simply to lock up a big northern industrial state right away
for a show of strength that might offset whatever happened in the
remaining primaries. Moreover, it could help influence caucuses in
two other important states, Michigan and Missouri, scheduled a
few days later.

The Humphrey strategy was aimed at Robert Kennedy more
than at Eugene McCarthy, despite McCarthy's good showing in the
April 23 Pennsylvania primary. The caucus, which inevitably became known as "The Pennsylvania Railroad," was merely to make
official what was already fact: Humphrey would control the delegation overwhelmingly. To make sure, Senators Walter Mondale and
Fred Harris, Humphrey's top two preconvention strategists, had
wooed Pennsylvania Democratic leaders for weeks, the Vice-President himself chatting with them on the phone. For the caucus,
they established a command post in the presidential suite of the
Penn-Harris, the Pennsylvania delegates flowing in and out con-
tinually.

An unsigned memo prepared by the Humphrey camp was circulated among delegates as a hedge against Kennedy. "Bobby cannot win the 1968 election," it was titled. It cited the "unanimous view of southern Democratic leaders that Bobby would lose seven southern states carried by John Kennedy in 1960." The memo declared:

With the loss of these states alone, Bobby Kennedy's electoral vote total would be 208—or less than the 270 required. . . . Indeed, his role as party-splitter and as the candidate of the most extremist elements in the country would damage his effectiveness to the point that a full-scale Democratic Party debacle, both as to the presidency and as to the House of Representatives, would be the bleak certainty if he should be nominated in August.

No need was felt to prepare a memo on McCarthy. After all, he had lost in Indiana and Nebraska and certainly was washed up. The McCarthy supporters who appeared at the Penn-Harris Hotel were of different mind. Housewives and students toted in their placards ("Don't let them steamroll," "Vote in Chicago, not in Harrisburg") and glumly listened to the politicians announce the heavily Humphrey result of their caucus. Fred Harris privately characterized the result as "the first of our big dominoes." For the McCarthy people, it was a lesson. "Well," said one McCarthy housewife to another as the politicians held forth in the hotel's crowded, walnut-paneled Governor's Room, "now you've seen how politics is *really* played."

John Bailey, the Democratic national chairman, tried to play it in his own state of Connecticut, where he was also chairman, at the party's state convention. McCarthy supporters, led by Anne Wexler and Joseph Duffey, at first demanded a fourth of the forty-four national convention delegates to be selected by the state convention. Bailey offered five during preliminary negotions with Duffey that began weeks before the convention in Hartford. Duffey adamantly refused to take less than ten, the McCarthy supporters having made clear to him they would storm out of the convention if they got less. Bailey just as stubbornly refused to go higher than nine. In a final negotiating session that lasted till near dawn on convention day, June 22, Bailey offered Duffey a high-paying job on the Democratic National Committee and a chance to run against Abe Ribicoff for the Senate, if he would just be reasonable. Even without such inducements, Duffey was ready to settle for nine, but the McCarthy supporters still refused to let him. It was yet another example of the independence of the McCarthy campaign. As the convention got under way, Curt Gans and Donald Green of the national staff frantically phoned the Connecticut leaders trying to prevent a walkout, but the Connecticut leaders refused to take the calls. A representative of the national staff sent to oversee what happened was ordered by Connecticut McCarthy leaders to stay away from the convention. The national organization had had nothing to do with their success and had even discouraged their activity as hopeless in the stronghold of John Bailey, but the Connecticut people had gone ahead, forcing primaries in thirty towns, taking about 43 per cent of the vote. They weren't about to relinquish control of their campaign now to outside meddlers. And so the moment of truth came and Duffey led his 250 or so troops from Bushnell Auditorium in Hartford. "We walk out not to leave this party, but to work to change it. This is a political act, not just a gesture of indignation," declared Duffey. Eugene McCarthy was a bit indignant. He later told Duffey he should have accepted the nine delegates, which Duffey belatedly did. But Duffey also made sure McCarthy supporters would have Connecticut representation on the rules and platform committees—committees that McCarthy delegates across the country were striving to get on.

The old-style politics was played in Indiana. Delegates selected by a state convention normally would have been required to vote for the winner of the primary. Robert Kennedy's death changed this. June 20, the night before the convention in Indianapolis, delegates caucused by congressional district to nominate slates of national convention delegates. In the Seventh, Eighth, and Ninth District caucuses, McCarthy supporters found themselves being ignored as they rose to place names in nomination. Chairmen took nominations from party regulars and quickly rammed through their acceptance. None of the three meetings lasted longer than five minutes. Charles Schuee, who chaired the Seventh District caucus, banged an ash tray on the table muttering "meeting's adjourned" while McCarthy supporters still shouted for recognition.

In the Eighth District caucus, McCarthy supporter Nancy Elmes, twenty-six, of Evansville, screamed at caucus chairman Edwin H. Pieper, "Pieper, you stink!" as the meeting abruptly ended. Another McCarthy backer, Sidney Berger, also of Evansville, jabbed an index finger at Pieper: "You're driving away kids who have more integrity than anybody else in the Democratic party!" he shouted, and the two men started scuffling.

Tempers flared on the convention floor the following night when McCarthy backers still sought to place some of their own in nomination. Mrs. Nancy Salmon, of Bloomington, stood implacably in front of the chairman's platform seeking recognition along with other McCarthy supporters. At one point, Berger jumped to the microphone and tried to nominate himself and another man, but was shoved aside by convention chairman Ray J. Madden, an Indiana Congressman. Another McCarthy supporter, Dennis J. Shorthouse, of Indianapolis, tried to fight his way onto the speakers' platform but was hurled to the floor and dragged out by state police. Some McCarthy supporters' names were finally put forward, but without success.

In Minnesota the same week end, the situation was similar, except that both Hubert Humphrey and Eugene McCarthy appeared before the state Democratic-Farmer-Labor party convention. From the audience in the Saint Paul Hilton Hotel as Humphrey addressed the convention came derisive shouts from McCarthy supporters. "You do your candidate a disservice," Humphrey declared, not backing down. "I suggest to supporters of Minnesota's illustrious senior Senator that you be as polite and as decent as he is." When the convention began to consider a proadministration Vietnam resolution, hundreds of McCarthy supporters donned black arm bands and demonstrated in the aisles. Carrying pictures of injured and burned Vietnamese children, they marched by the dais to deposit in a cardboard box petitions calling for "a return of the party to the people" and urging the party to work for "peace and new priorities." The proadministration resolution passed. When it came time to designate twenty at-large national convention delegates, the Humphrey regulars ignored the McCarthy backers' plea for at least eight as representative of McCarthy's showing in the precinct caucuses in March. Instead, the state convention gave McCarthy no additional delegates. McCarthy supporters stalked out.

At the meeting of the New York State Democratic Committee in the Commodore Hotel, more McCarthy supporters walked out, shouting "Nazi!" and "Fascist!" at the regulars who remained behind. The committee had failed to give the McCarthy forces the number of at-large national convention delegates they thought they deserved to add to those won in the primary.

"In the name of intelligent politics," shrilled Allard Lowenstein, "I implore you not to be so stupid as to select a candidate whom we will not be able to support."

There it was, the threat. Similar statements were becoming a part of the McCarthy movement litany elsewhere: probable defection of large numbers if Humphrey were nominated.

At the Illinois Democratic convention, Mayor Richard J. Daley, of Chicago, was roundly booed and McCarthy supporters waved signs saying, "Let the people elect the President," when Daley refused to recognize McCarthy supporter Dick Mudge for the purpose of nominating delegates. "We'll hear from you later," snarled the mayor when Mudge sought the floor.

In Louisville at the Kentucky state convention, hundreds more McCarthy people walked out when the delegate tide went against them. "We want Gene, we want Gene!" they chanted as they left. In Texas, three hundred liberals departed from the state convention in a rift over the unit rule, by which a delegation's total vote was cast in accord with the majority sentiment of a delegation. In the case of Texas, the unit rule was to be used to bind the delegation to the favorite son candidacy of Governor John Connally. "We want the nation to know that John Connally is no favorite son for all of us," cried liberal leader Mrs. Billie Carr, of Houston.

In Washington State some 177 delegates to the state convention, whose credentials were challenged by McCarthy backers, were permitted to vote on the legality of their own seating. Naturally, they voted to seat themselves, and in the closely divided convention, their own votes provided their margin of victory. The situation that had provided the major challenge was that of populous Pierce County. More votes had been cast than there were delegates at the county convention, and the ballots were burned, making a recount impossible. "Shame on Pierce County!" came the chant from the galleries at the state convention, "shame, shame, shame!" Soon the chant turned into, "We want Gene, we want Gene. . . ." And when delegates from across the nation gathered in Chicago, one of the many pieces of literature handed them was a poem called "The Ballad of Pierce County":

> From the shores of Puget Sound
> The story's going round
> How they burned the evidence
> To hide their crime from view
> One-thirty-seven cast their votes
> Hubert won but it was close
> But the ballot was one-forty-two
> (Very strange)
> So they burned all the ballots
> Burned up the ballots
> So no one could ever see
> They burned all the ballots
> Burned all the ballots
> In Washington's Pierce County. . . .

In Comanche County, Oklahoma, home of Humphrey leader Fred Harris, they did not burn ballots. They simply changed the basis for casting them at the last moment. Legally, only delegates to the county convention selected earlier at precinct meetings could vote. State Senator James Taliaferro quickly moved that the rules be suspended and that *all* registered Democrats at the county meeting Saturday afternoon, June 15, be allowed to vote. Humphrey backers had packed the meeting, and Taliaferro's motion was quickly approved. The initial step in the national convention delegate selection process, the precinct meetings, had suddenly become meaningless. One Humphrey supporter, outraged by the highhanded actions at the county convention, filed a suit against county chairman Allan D. Sasser, charging that her civil rights had been violated. In Cleveland County, Oklahoma, the tack was slightly different. The county chairman, Dan Rambo, brought 123 proxy votes to the county meeting, enough to control it. Though many of the proxies were not properly filled out or notarized as required, state chairman William Kerr, a Humphrey backer, ruled by telephone that the proxies were valid. Thus one man with 123 votes determined the support of all of Cleveland County's Democrats.

In New Mexico, though Humphrey backers controlled the state convention, McCarthyites by a narrow vote were able to get the convention to adopt "proportional representation" for selecting national convention delegates. The solidly Humphrey nominating committee had offered the McCarthyites only six national convention delegates, but with proportional representation McCarthy won eleven. Humphrey got thirteen. Police were present to guard against violence.

McCarthy researchers soon began examining the delegate selection process rather closely. Fifteen states, they discovered, selected delegates two to four years before the national convention. Thus about 600 votes, almost a fourth of the 2,622 total, had, in effect, been selected before the Vietnam war had become a major issue. This included 159 who were picked by state convention delegates who themselves had been chosen by state committees two and four years before, or by state committees constituting themselves as a state convention to pick delegates; 110 members of the Democratic National Committee elected in 1964; 65 selected by state committees elected in 1966; 125 selected by state convention delegates picked by county, district, or precinct caucuses two years before the national convention; 86 selected by district committees or individuals chosen by precinct caucus winners elected in 1966; and 41 tapped by the state chairman with the advice and consent of the governor—with no direct access to the people.

A McCarthy staff study depicted the overwhelming Humphrey

strength in these fifteen "closed states" by extracting midsummer *Newsweek* and Associated Press delegate projections for Humphrey and McCarthy in those states:

	Associated Press	Newsweek
McCarthy	30	38½
Humphrey	327½	455½
Uncommitted (includes Kennedy and favorite son delegates)	203½	112

"In these closed states," the McCarthy study exclaimed, "Hubert Humphrey's delegate strength is roughly twelve times as great as Eugene McCarthy's! !"

The study also pointed out that only 446 of the votes cast at the convention would reflect the primary elections, since Pennsylvania's vote was not binding and the death of Robert Kennedy made the results in several other primary states inconclusive. "Stated another way, delegates selected, in effect, two and four years ago will cast 160 votes more than delegates who will be most responsive to the public will." These "nonresponsive" delegates made up about a half or more of Humphrey's estimated delegate strength at that time. Less than 10 per cent of McCarthy's estimated strength at the same time came from "closed" states, the study said.

The findings fortified the growing anger in the McCarthy camp at the "steam-roller" tactics and "bossism" laid to Humphrey in state after state. Humphrey responded late in July by calling for an end of the unit rule—rather tardily, McCarthy said—and ordering his supporters to allow McCarthy a fair share of delegates in the few states, most of them relatively unimportant, where the selection had not been completed. Then Humphrey tried to seize a small bit of the initiative on the issue:

I would hope that Senator McCarthy would join me in this effort to obtain a truly open convention by releasing all delegations bound to him. To those who have been looking upon the unit rule as a one-edged sword which is of benefit only to me, I might note that all seventy-two votes of the Massachusetts delegation are bound to Senator McCarthy by law on the first ballot in an equivalent of the unit rule, just as all thirty-five of the delegates in Oregon are pledged to him although he won only forty-four per cent of the vote in the state primary. I want an open convention. I want a chance at the Massachusetts delegates and the Oregon delegates just as he wants a chance at the others.

However hollow Humphrey's words, there were definitely two sides to the question. For not far beneath the righteous indignation of the McCarthyites were plently of examples of the same kind of highhandedness blamed on Humphrey and his supporters.

It had been seen on precinct caucus night, March 5, in the Twin Cities area of Minnesota, when party regulars in many cases were ruthlessly dropped from long-held party positions. In New Mexico, one of the relative McCarthy successes, McCarthy supporters imposed a unit rule at precinct meetings throughout Los Alamos County to select a unanimous slate of twenty-two McCarthy delegates to the state convention, despite the fact Humphrey people had approximately 46 per cent of the precinct meeting attendance. At the Colorado state convention, a coalition of McCarthy and former Kennedy supporters flatly opposed sharing representation as suggested by the Humphrey camp, for the McCarthy-Kennedy coalition was in control. Leaders of the coalition circulated a memo to members with this instruction: "Vote *against* proportional representation in the selection of delegates." Similar actions were seen in a number of county conventions leading to the Colorado state meeting. In Cascade County, Montana, the McCarthyites pulled the same trick. There were many other instances, and they lent some truth to a statement in yet another Humphrey campaign memo:

In general, wherever the McCarthy forces have had the majority, however slight, they have chosen to adopt a winner-take-all policy. And where they have been in the minority, they have appealed for a rule of proportionality, often with the implication that unless they get what they ask for they will bolt the party in November. This should be recognized for what it is: perfectly sound tactics to maximize McCarthy voting strength. What is not involved is "boss rule" or "distortion of the will of the people" to the benefit of Humphrey.

Nonetheless, the system had been found wanting in state after state. It was the nature of the McCarthy campaign that someone would begin to wonder how to do something about it.

In Connecticut, the McCarthy people were still unhappy over what had happened to them at the state convention and determined to bring a credentials challenge at the national convention. A number of them, including Anne Wexler, Joseph Duffey, and Geoffrey Cowan, gathered for lunch one day in the office of Louis Pollak, dean of the Yale Law School in New Haven. It was agreed that it would be helpful to have some nonpartisan group document their grievances. It was a natural leap from there for someone to suggest formation of a commission to study delegate selection nationwide. One thing about the Connecticut McCarthy people: they never thought small. They agreed on one more important thing: such a commission should not have a McCarthy label. It should represent all factions of the party interested in reform.

Anne Wexler was soon on the phone. She talked to Eli Segal, a McCarthy staffer who had been assigned to further McCarthy's interests with the rules committee. She called William Sueppel, Iowa Kennedy chairman, and, like her, a member of the rules committee, to see if Governor Harold Hughes might be importuned to chair such a commission. She called McCarthy supporter Howard Morgan in Oregon and Mrs. Arie Taylor, who had been a Colorado Kennedy supporter, two members of the national convention credentials committee, for their thoughts.

The idea began to jell. Cowan enlisted the aid of a number of young attorneys and began to build a staff headed by Washington lawyer Thomas P. Alder. Hughes readily accepted chairmanship, and a panel of big-name commission members was pulled together: Representative Donald M. Fraser, Minnesota Democrat, vice-chairman; Harry Ashmore, of the Center for the Study of Democratic Institutions; Alexander Bickel, of the Yale Law School; Julian Bond, black leader and a member of the Georgia House of Representatives; Frederick G. Dutton, who had headed Robert Kennedy's campaign; and Mrs. Doris Fleeson Kimball, former nationally syndicated newspaper columnist. On August 4 in Chicago, formation of The Commission on the Democratic Selection of Presidential Nominees was announced, with Mrs. Wexler, Sueppel, Morgan, and Mrs. Taylor as sponsors. New York publisher William Johnson raised much of the money for the commission and published its report.

In less than three weeks, the hard-driving staff examined delegate selection procedures in the fifty states and came up with a series of recommendations which helped shape reforms adopted at the national convention.

"This convention is on trial," the Hughes commission report declared. "We have concluded that state systems for selecting delegates to the National Convention, and the procedures of the Convention itself, display considerably less fidelity to basic democratic principles than a nation which claims to govern itself can safely tolerate."

Two recommendations were most immediately important:

—That the 1968 convention abolish the unit rule, which it did.

—That all delegates be selected relatively near the time of the convention. The Hughes commission suggested no earlier than six months before. The 1968 convention voted to require selection within the calendar year before the next session.

A number of other recommendations for more democratic convention procedure and delegate selection were left for further study before the next convention by two special commissions established as a result of the 1968 convention, just as the issue of racial discrimination in delegate selection was dealt with by a special commission between the 1964 and 1968 conventions. But in 1968 itself, as an outgrowth of the work of the Hughes commission, which in turn was an outgrowth of the McCarthy campaign, the Democratic National Convention started toward revolutionary changes in the process of selecting its future presidential nominees.

This was the high point of the McCarthy summer. Nothing else that happened was as important, and at least part of what else happened was counterproductive. At the very bottom of the barrel was the sick wrangling within the national staff. It is worth mentioning if only to reemphasize how this unusual campaign could go so far without, it often seemed, really trying.

Now that the primaries were over, how did you convince delegates that the enigmatic McCarthy should be nominated?

The young, newly trained political technicians led by Sam Brown and Curt Gans favored a huge national grass-roots organizing and petition drive whose vastness would intimidate delegates into supporting McCarthy.

Tom Finney favored the more traditional, quiet, individual approaches to delegates by seasoned political operatives who spoke their language, and selective polls to show McCarthy's strength.

Proponents of both strategies felt they had McCarthy's endorsement, but then McCarthy decided to begin cutting the costs of his expensive campaign, at that time close to a million dollars in debt.* This meant many of the young staff members would have to go.

They, of course, were indignant. And they were doubly angered when they read McCarthy's explanation. "It's a combination of things," he told Gloria Steinem, who reported the conversation in *New York* magazine. "Partly an economy move, partly a normal cut-back after primaries. And then, some of them are like ski bums in the summer. They ought to go home and get jobs. They just like to hang around." Well, no, not *all* of them were like ski bums, he corrected. "But they really should go home. Sometimes you have to get rid of a few good ones, too, because you can't just separate out the ones you'd like to go."

The words were telling of McCarthy's relationship with the young people who had flocked to his campaign. Their relationship was symbiotic, a word plucked out by Joshua Leinsdorf, the Columbia graduate student in literature who supervised travel arrangements for the campaign—symbiotic in just about every

* The McCarthy campaign ended about $1.3 million in the red. Most of the largest bills were settled by negotiation, with actual payments averaging about thirty-six cents on the dollar.

nuance of the word: an intimate association of dissimilar organisms, sometimes destructive, antagonistic, reflecting aspects of parasitism, but mostly a highly advantageous and necessary blend. "Oh, it was helpful," said McCarthy at his press conference the morning after New Hampshire election night when asked how important the student volunteer effort had been. "You can't measure it in any way." Despite the validity of the statement, it seemed a monumental put-down in the afterglow of the night before. From the start, he coldly sought to keep things in perspective. Some of the ski bums, and even some of the good ones, were not always able to do that.

First news of an impending staff cut coincided with a meeting of state McCarthy leaders called by Curt Gans for the week end of June 22 in Chicago.

The meeting itself was a disaster, in view of its $20,000 cost. The state leaders, who came from as far away as Hawaii, had thought they would get firm outlines of a summer strategy, but they did not. At the same time, most of them were on guard against any of the national leaders' trying to assert too much control over them. The meeting wandered into a review of grievances against the national office and candidate himself that were like echoes from months before. "He acts like he's half asleep," said an Illinois man of McCarthy. "He's not getting through to the blacks," said a Negro staffer.

Some had come expecting to see McCarthy, but they only heard him in a brief telephone speech. McCarthy had cooled on the meeting after learning of its probable cost and had stayed in Washington. Deservedly the meeting came to be known as "Curt's Follies."

After the state leaders left, a much more intense discussion over ramifications of the staff cuts arose among the forty or so young staffers who had also gathered in Chicago. Their initial shock at the news had turned to outrage and then suspicion. Was this really a money problem, or a power play by others in the campaign: Tom Finney and Abigail McCarthy's brother Steve Quigley, who had begun to hold an iron fist over campaign spending?

"We couldn't tell what it meant or why it was being done," said John O'Sullivan, a law school student volunteer. "You felt if the worst was true you wanted to stay together; if not, you'd never get back together again. It was as if the first-stage rocket was being jettisoned. It came down to a fight for the right to campaign."

And they definitely felt they had a right. "How could McCarthy fire them?" Don Green asked when it was over. "He never hired them. They came when no one else would. It was as much their campaign as his."

By that week end in June, the Children's Crusade had splintered into any number of often competing factions because of a string of personality clashes, the theoretical impersonality of New Politics having been lost somewhere along the way as the old politics took hold. But now, as they debated their problem long into the night, they were suddenly reunited in a parochial cause aeons removed from the cause that had originally brought them together. It was the cause of self-preservation.

Their discussion developed into perhaps the most remarkable hen session in presidential politics as they hashed over the faults of the often acerbic Curt Gans, whom many now blamed for their being discarded. Out poured the grievances of months, the remembered slights, the failures of communication, the complaints of secretiveness; and once they had drained themselves, they resolved that the object of their scorn must be preserved as a symbol of their own stake in the campaign. "Gans did make mistakes," declared David Mixner with passion at one point. "He did screw up. But if we let ourselves become the instrument of the Quigleys in Washington, we've thrown it all away."

They worked through the rest of the week end drawing up a summer plan for a number of regional desks in Washington and field men touring the states to coordinate grass-roots organizing and collect delegate information.

The plan, which stressed that Gans should lead, was placed before a staff meeting in McCarthy's Senate office the following Monday, June 24—an unusual meeting, for it was one of those rare times when McCarthy sought to delegate authority. "It was the only time I ever saw him all business," said a participant. "He had worked on an agenda at his house the night before, and when we met he ticked off responsibilities and made assignments."

The meeting might just as well not have been held, for almost as soon as McCarthy's orders were uttered they were ignored. "Nobody ever stayed in his own bag," Tom McCoy said when the campaign was over.

Repeated efforts to pare numbers of young people from the staff failed. When dropped from the official payroll, they would immediately move to an unofficial payroll financed by bootleg contributions from backers sympathetic to their cause. Others were supported by a kind of foster-parent program. "We sold young people out in the field, by description of who they were and what they were doing, to little old ladies who sent them weekly food checks in return for letters describing what it was like to be a McCarthy worker in the field, starving," said Wendy Robineau, a Washington staffer.

Not only did the young people go right ahead with their plans for regional desks and field operations, though on a reduced scale, but they opened a new Washington headquarters as a way of getting out from under Quigley's nose. This was a formidable task in itself since Quigley ordered incoming mail, private as well as official, opened and inspected for contributions he wanted to keep the independent young staffers from squandering. Sometimes he prowled hotel corridors to make sure dismissed staffers were not continuing to live off the campaign. Another time he threatened prosecution of a young staffer who without permission took pay checks for himself and several friends from Quigley's office so they could eat. The young staffer, Parker Donham, just as angrily threatened to sue the whole campaign for withholding pay.

But Quigley was correct in his concern about costs. Spending had gone wild; waste was monumental. The young staffers shared air travel and telephone credit cards freely, and often for noncampaign purposes. (One phone call to Hong Kong showed up on the records.) Some forged Quigley's name to get such things as rental autos. An older staffer parked a rented car in a hotel garage after driving it only from an airport and forgot about it as the bill mounted. Another staffer bought an expensive sports wardrobe on the campaign. Another young staffer, just two weeks before the convention, ordered a million post cards after being told not to. They were to be sent to delegates as one last plug for McCarthy, but time ran out. After the election in November, 850,000 of the cards still sat unused in the attic of a Washington hotel.

More than an example of waste, the post card incident illustrated the disintegration of what loose command structure there had ever been. "There was only horizontal authority," said one young staffer. "It was easy to go down the line until one was found that thought your way. Suddenly this became *your* authority. . . . 'Well, Blair said I could. . . .'"

And there was little coordination among these "horizontal" authorities. Both Tom Finney and Dick Goodwin, who returned to the McCarthy camp after Robert Kennedy's death, ordered expensive polls, a duplication that cost an extra $25,000. Neither poll was ever put to optimum use. One set of findings, mailed to Blair Clark at the McCarthy headquarters in Washington, was returned to the pollster marked "addressee unknown."

The "horizontal" authorities just as often clashed. Dick Goodwin and Blair Clark differed with Bill Nee and Art Michelson over how to present McCarthy on a costly national telecast. The dispute got so heated that Michelson actually hit Clark at one point, and at another stole and destroyed a tape of McCarthy that Goodwin liked but Michelson and Nee didn't. Even as the taped telecast finally went on the air, a young staffer sent by Michelson was on her way to the New York studio to make one last attempt to switch tapes. The broadcast was not memorable.

At a more important level, Finney and Stephen A. Mitchell clashed on convention strategy. Mitchell had joined the campaign in May with the understanding he would plan for the convention. Finney thought he was to plot strategy. Another collision. Mitchell's strategy was simple: "Fight every step of the way. We'll try to make

Hubert look bad and hope for the best." He would fight with credentials challenges, rules challenges, the platform challenge, possibly even a challenge of the convention leadership.

Finney saw no point in such an all-out assault. It would merely confirm what too many delegates already believed: that McCarthy was dangerous. If McCarthy hoped to get any support from them, he should put on a conciliatory face, or so Finney felt. But Mitchell went ahead and established a staff in Chicago in midsummer that in many ways duplicated efforts under way in Washington. Delegate-hunting efforts were even more confusing, with, once again, no one ever staying in his own role.

One of the more successful events of the summer—M-Day fund-raising rallies in a multitude of cities August 15—came about only after heated disagreement among the McCarthy staff. It was finally carried out by the excellent New York organization.

And so the summer went. Endless inconclusive meetings, conflict, disagreement. "The summer was few steps forward and many steps backward," said a young staffer.

After a month of continued chaos, McCarthy once again asked Finney to take over-all charge. Finney demanded that McCarthy announce the assignment in a press release so there would be no question about his authority. McCarthy said he would, but a day later decided he couldn't. Finney dropped from the campaign, though he later performed some secret tasks for McCarthy. It was the last time McCarthy even tried to bring order to his strange crusade. Blair Clark would insist that all campaigns reflected as much disarray. Certainly most develop competing factions and bitterness. But probably never in presidential politics had these natural tendencies burgeoned to such gargantuan degree.

McCarthy's efforts to impose order were feeble at best. But there were other significant impediments. The very way the campaign grew, from nothing to a great deal in a very short time, was the biggest. The volunteers were in it not for personal gain but because of an issue. The subconscious discipline that comes with possibility of reward if victorious was not a consideration. And the people who came to this campaign were, as a whole, probably the most intelligent and highly educated large group of people who had ever joined together politically in the history of civilization. They were a group antiauthoritarian by nature. Leaders were not designated so much as developed by chance. Within most local organizations, leadership was diffuse.

Mrs. Reese Palley's home in Margate, New Jersey, near Atlantic City, served as headquarters for about sixty students who worked the area for McCarthy during the summer. She saw happening in her house what had happened months earlier in the Concord, New Hampshire, McCarthy headquarters, when the Children's Crusade was taking its first steps and was at its most effective. What she observed was the birth of the basic organizational form that served the McCarthy campaign, whether among students or adults, wherever groups sprang up:

> They resisted bureaucracy, hierarchy, all the normal methods of organization. Things got done without vote taking. Projects were initiated independently. Responsibility was assumed without appointment. Formal committees, structure and coercion were not the order of the day. When the youthful co-chairman resigned, there was no effort to replace him.

It was not significantly different in Fayetteville, Arkansas, in a largely adult McCarthy group. Eloise Jones, forty-one, wife of a University of Arkansas professor and herself a part-time student, wrote a paper on the local McCarthy organization for one class. The paper, titled "A Description of the Dynamics of a Political Action Group," earned an A. It said in part:

> This group displayed a rather stable structure without there ever having been any explicit description of that structure or any formal agreement concerning structure. . . . Some people like to assume responsibility while others prefer to be told what to do. The roles taken by members of this group seemed to evolve rather naturally around the people who assumed them. . . . This group could be characterized as symmetrical. . . . The mobility of this group . . . could flow freely in both directions. . . .

In the national headquarters in the summer little flowed any more in any direction. Things just sloshed. Oh, there were some delightful incidents that would never have happened in any other presidential campaign. The young people held a couple of seminars in their new headquarters to discuss philosophy and things. One day the headquarters all but shut down while the young people went off to picket a Safeway Supermarket that sold California table grapes. But for the more meaningful glimpses of what yet was happening in 1968 because Eugene McCarthy stood up, it was better to look away from Washington.

July comes and John Brightley, thirty-two, and his wife, Ellen, twenty-seven, of Bennington, Vermont, pitch a tent in Perry, Maine, and begin canvassing Washington County in their decrepit 1956 Volkswagen, 3,000 miles of driving before they finish. Months earlier, Brightley quit a job as a well-paid electrical engineer, and he and his wife went to work in the McCarthy campaign. He operated in Poughkeepsie, New York; she traveled through Wisconsin, Nebraska, Oregon. Now they are working together getting out the vote in a private presidential primary organized by Albion Goodwin, national convention delegate from Maine. Whoever wins the primary, Goodwin has proclaimed, will get his vote in Chicago. The Brightleys receive ten dollars in expense money and do not seem to mind, though they have drifted several thousand dollars into debt for the cause. Working closely with residents of the county, they open small headquarters in Calais and Machias and for four weeks canvass the entire county. Election day, 207 vote for McCarthy to 57 for Humphrey and 5 for other candidates. Albion Goodwin has allowed the people to make up his mind.

The word "deal" ricochets through the mind of Mrs. Jess P. Miller, thirty-two, of Hampton, Virginia, for she and her group have just entered into one with an old-line Virginia politician from her area. They're at the state Democratic convention. Mrs. Miller, wife of a physician, mother of six, including two sets of twins, has never been in politics before. "I never thought it was very important, until this year," she says. She becomes chairman of the Peninsula Citizens for McCarthy and goes to the state convention, helps break the unit rule, and suddenly finds herself involved in a *deal*. If she does something first, the *politician* will support her on another point. What she has to do seems harmless. She simply has to abstain from voting on one small issue in a caucus. She does not have to vote on the side of the politician; just relinquish her vote, her right to speak out, her duty to speak up. What she will give up grows bigger and bigger in her mind as she sits in the caucus awaiting the moment to not act, to fulfill her part of the *deal*. She begins to think of her *children*. Is she teaching them to grow up to make *deals*? The moment comes. She plunges headlong into abstention, cringing inwardly, suddenly feeling herself the fallen woman. The politician does not keep his end of the *deal*, of course. He misunderstands, he says. A politician always says that when he does not keep his end of a *deal*, though Mrs. Miller is unfamiliar with this rule. She cries all morning. Surely, she feels, she has betrayed her family, the group she represents, just about everything and everyone. She has never been in politics before. Will she stay? The tears dry. She resolves she will. Deals she will try to keep away from.

For weeks, Mary Schramm, of Washington, D.C., wife of a minister named John, has been waiting for the question as she and her husband travel the country for McCarthy. "What are you—a Lutheran clergyman and his wife—doing campaigning for a candidate?" The question never comes. And by the end of summer a more pertinent question would be why a clergyman hadn't campaigned in 1968. Never before in American politics have clergy played such a large role as in the McCarthy campaign. In the summer fifty prominent Protestant, Roman Catholic, and Jewish clergymen announce a Clergy for McCarthy Committee headed by Dr. Robert McAfee Brown, Stanford religion professor, who has been a McCarthy admirer since the congressional campaign of 1952. The Reverend John Boyles, assistant chaplain at Yale, is given space in McCarthy headquarters and starts sending out mailings, the first to 100,000 churches and synagogues. "The campaign has set out to make the professed moral values of our nation a reality," says one letter. "Some of us are also communicating with local delegates to the Democratic National Convention to discuss the issues and our urgency concerning the crisis in our democratic process." All over the country, men of the cloth are engaged in a new kind of proselytizing, men like the Reverend L. Douglas Throckmorton, thirty-five, of Brookings, South Dakota, the Reverend Kenneth A. Young, thirty-one, of Pastor Dunn's Corners Community Presbyterian Church, Westerly, Rhode Island, and Richard W. Hart, thirty-five, of Bloomington, California. Hart is a fundamentalist, director of the Evangelical Christian Churches, and his church has always considered politics outside its realm. Now the thinking is suddenly different. Politics. Morality. Spiritual responsibility. Maybe these things are related. In August, Hart contacts seventy-four congregations and 164 ministers of his church, asking them to present the candidacy of Eugene McCarthy to their 14,971 members.

Maybe it's all over in McCarthy's mind, but it is not all over across the nation as the summer passes. In the summer colony of Provincetown, Massachusetts, a band of scruffier than usual young McCarthyites open a store front. Actually, it is a card table in front of a store. They have to take it down each night. They sit there through the summer, raising money: $650 in small change. In Asheville, North Carolina, the big sign on the McCarthy headquarters attracts a steady stream of vacationers who drop in to chat with Mrs. Demaree Bess and the other volunteers, a couple of them students who saw the sign on the way home for summer vacation, stopped, and simply stayed. In London, England, David Golding, an American motion picture executive, opens a McCarthy headquarters with a goal of raising $10,000. The months-old Overseas Americans for McCarthy, headed by Professor Robert Blood, Jr., of the International Christian University in Tokyo, Japan, still meets every other Monday evening. A press release from Lynne Abraham: "In the first nine hours after a New York *Post* advertisement announced the debut of New York's 'Telephone Revolution,' more than 5,000 calls were registered. Dr. Susan Fine, a 'People for

McCarthy' spokesman in New York, said that at least 3,000 of the callers pledged funds to the campaign." The fine Iowa organization that includes such people as John Garfield, Ann Hogsben, Mary Jo Small, and Harry Beardsley is collecting ballots at county fairs all over the state, McCarthy coming out on top, and Governor Harold Hughes coming out for McCarthy. Some fifty thousand inside and outside Fenway Park in Boston to hear McCarthy, some spectators even sitting on the props of the huge Gilbey's Gin billboard above the bleachers (crowd builder Steven Cohen gives out two and three tickets for each seat to make this the biggest political rally in the city's history); twelve thousand in Pittsburgh's Mellon Square at noon for McCarthy; twenty-five thousand in Detroit's Tiger stadium despite an evening rainstorm; in Richmond several thousand more than greeted George Wallace; in Saint Louis's Kiel Auditorium, twelve thousand standing, cheering, applauding for seven minutes before McCarthy can say his first word. McCarthy sees these responses across the country, and he cannot help but think how it all won't do any good. He thinks of another year. "I remember the cheers for Stevenson in 1960; but there were not many votes," he would say.

The important votes during the summer did not appear at stadia or rallies. They sat in back rooms or dark restaurants or their law or insurance or real estate offices waiting to be come after. "The campaign was never planned as a delegate-gathering effort," McCarthy would say afterward. He never said this to anyone during the campaign, least of all the various people who considered themselves responsible for trying to hunt delegates. So it was that McCarthy all summer long never directly asked a delegate to the national convention to support him. If any were to come to him, it would have to be through reasoned judgment, through the processes of thought, the way the people had come in the primaries. It would require a degree of courage for those tied by so many strings to the administration. But perhaps they would make the right choice, as Tom Jefferson said was the habit of the people if given a chance.

McCarthy would leave what happened to the truest spirit of American democracy, "that spirit which calls forth the 'uncommon man' in every citizen and offers him a chance to shape the present, to create a better future," to quote a McCarthy speech which paraphrased Ralph Waldo Emerson. Some of his more hardheaded campaign aides began to feel McCarthy had finally succumbed totally to a mysticism that said if he did anything the usual way what little chance there was of success would evaporate and all he had accomplished would mean nothing. "I couldn't help but feel sometimes that someone up there was watching him," said one campaign aide. "This thing couldn't have gone this far if that weren't so." It had come this far through the efforts of a lot of people. McCarthy was not going to change his approach now. He would urge delegates to "reserve judgment" while studying the candidates and issues. "I have to assume that the delegates are just as intelligent as the rest of the people of the country, and just as responsible," he said early in the summer. "I think they are just as subject to education as the general public."

Perhaps, but they found McCarthy too eccentric a professor to learn much from. When he met with them in public or private meetings, he spent his time talking about *issues*. Delegates like to hear some promises, some words that give them the feeling a candidate fully appreciates the unwritten rule of reciprocity in political back-patting. They never heard these things from McCarthy. McCarthy recognized his approach was not making much of a hit with these people. "It was a typical delegates' reception," he said after one session. "They generally are not very excited." And he would speak of his progress with them whimsically. "Oh, I think we'll have some strength with the Ohio delegation," he said with a straight face after meeting with part of the 115-member Ohio contingent. "We know of three votes we have." He assessed another session this way: "I may have made an impression on about ten of the New Jersey delegates." How could he tell? By the way they smiled or shook his hand, he would say.

Many came out of sessions with McCarthy shaking their heads, one delegate thinking he had heard McCarthy stress one thing, another thinking McCarthy had stressed the opposite. A session with the Massachusetts delegates before his fantastic reception in Fenway Park was typical. State Representative David Harrison, of Gloucester, left the reception disturbed because McCarthy had told the delegates, said Harrison, that "if the platform isn't right on Vietnam he could support the Republican or a fourth party." Representative David Bartley, of Holyoke, left the session gratified. "As a partisan Democrat myself, I was pleased to hear him say that he would stay within the framework of the Democratic party." Actually, both statements were accurate. It was the individual listener who supplied the emphasis. McCarthy constantly repeated that he was testing the Democratic party, had no real interest in a splinter movement in 1968, and absolutely would not lead such an effort. Yet under certain conditions he could see himself supporting the Republicans or even a fourth-party candidate. It was the wrong thing to admit if one wanted to sway delegates. But it was the truth.

This candor cost him possible support of perhaps a dozen delegates in Michigan when he was asked at a meeting in East Lansing whether he might support Nelson Rockefeller, were he the GOP nominee. Many if not most of the delegates came out of the meeting thinking McCarthy was actively considering support of the New York governor. Delegates across the country read the stories of the Michigan meeting and found it difficult to appreciate McCarthy's explanation. "This answer came in response to a question which had about five conditions on it," McCarthy said, once the damage was done. "If Hubert Humphrey is the nominee, and if his foreign and domestic policy is not any closer to Senator McCarthy's than it now is, and if his nomination results from some kind of exclusion as practiced in the New York delegation, and if Nelson Rockefeller is the Republican nominee, it is conceivable that I could support him."

It was a classic McCarthy response to questions he felt unnecessarily hypothetical. He would usually criticize the question and the questioner, then launch into an acidulous answer composed of a multitude of conditions which he did not always delineate as clearly as he imagined he had; and when he would be misunderstood, he would then implicitly criticize his listeners for not having listened closely enough. This is not to say he could not have fun on occasion with such questions. Again and again he would be asked whether he would accept the vice-presidential candidacy on a Humphrey ticket. He might, McCarthy once said, if Humphrey altered his position on the war, let McCarthy select the Secretaries of State, Defense, Agriculture, and the heads of the FBI, CIA, Voice of America, Civil Aeronautics Board, and the Equal Employment Opportunities Commission and a few others, and agreed to some private considerations.

Delegates, however, wanted straight answers to what they felt to be simple questions. Though McCarthy aides would vainly try to assure them that McCarthy would stay in the party and support the nominee, McCarthy would inevitably sweep away this ground-work when he would meet with the delegates, who learned one thing about McCarthy if nothing else: no one spoke for him; no one could dispel the doubts he raised in their minds except McCarthy himself, a man who didn't even sound like a politician.

"So I ask you to take this burden of citizenship in a very special way," McCarthy said at the North Dakota Democratic convention, "and to understand it as clearly as you can, and to be committed to meeting all the obligations that go with being a delegate to a Democratic convention, to making the kind of decision you are called upon to make for the people whom you represent. . . . I am not asking you to give me any particular number of delegates here today. I do hope that the delegation will be somewhat representa-tive of the position which you hold."

Jeez. What kind of talk was that? Delegates looked at each other vacantly.

He would go on to remind many of his audiences at state con-ventions of the milestones in Democratic party history: Thomas Jefferson, the founder, who instituted participation politics through a network of clubs and "grass-roots" organizations which overthrew the "cloakroom rule of state legislatures" that had kept property as the sole test of voting rights; Andrew Jackson, who invented the national convention as an instrument for more democratic politics, replacing "King Caucus" by which a few congressional and party leaders would hand-pick presidential candidates; Woodrow Wilson, who advanced the idea of primary elections for candidates and convention delegates; Franklin Roosevelt, who led the fight to abolish the rule requiring a man to get two-thirds of the convention vote to be nominated—a rule which, in effect, gave every regional group or sectional bloc in the party a veto on the nominee; Adlai Stevenson, who in 1956 left selection of his vice-presidential running mate to the convention, an example of "putting more trust and more responsibility upon the convention delegates than had ever been done in the past." McCarthy would add: "Then came John Bailey. Last year he said that the convention was already over. He said the nominee had been picked; and the platform had been written; and that whatever the rest of us might do throughout the next six or eight months would be . . . an exercise in futility. . . . Well, there have been some changes since then."

McCarthy might speak of the challenge by his campaign on the structure of the Democratic party itself, as he did at the Iowa Democratic convention:

We shall show whether that party is, as we have claimed it to be, an open institution, belonging not to a few, but belonging to the Democrats of this country. We will show whether or not, as we have asserted in the past, we as Democrats truly believe in the judgment of the people. The party will show respect, if it does these things, for the rights of Americans to affirm good policies and to reject bad ones; to affirm acceptable leaders and to reject others. And if we fail in these actions, then this party of ours can no longer claim, as it has been able to claim with justification in the past, that it is the party of the people, the party which trusts their judgment and which has responded to that judgment in the past.

In Sacramento, California, August 12, he proposed a number of reforms that would move the party even more into the hands of its individual members. "Party functions and machinery must be enlarged to bring into politics—all year round, every year—all the people of our party," for, he said, the party had become "a kind of empty shell without much power and without much vitality."

These things got but passing notice in the press and among those who heard him. In California, what the delegates heard most loudly was something McCarthy did not say. Not once did he mention the name Robert Kennedy, the man whose banner these people had carried with an abnormal love. Why he did not was but another of the unanswerables about the man, and there seemed to be too many of these unanswerables for those who had not already accepted him.

Thus, much of his message over the summer fell on partially deaf ears that did not always hear the more important things he said. For during this penultimate period, McCarthy from time to time spoke of an issue that was not altogether apparent in 1968 but would become the major issue in years to come. It was an issue, or a bundle of issues, that added up to "matters of the spirit," as McCarthy put it, of the very quality of life. It was tied up with an erosion of honesty in the country, an impossible gap between the promise of America and the reality, tied to the feeling that technology was gelding the individual, that the individual had lost control over things from Vietnam to pollution to what went on in his own block. The issues were becoming psychological for a large part of the population in 1968 and less and less economic and physical. Matters of the spirit began to replace matters of the body and of the pocketbook.

The hope that America's unequaled technology could help end the problems of ignorance and poverty and ill-health and tyranny and provide a richer, fuller life, McCarthy said, had not been borne out. "We have learned that these were false hopes; that science offers tremendous potential for exploitation and abuse of humanity; that the new political forms are subject to new forms of demagoguery; and that mass communications can pervert as well as educate."

Material production and consumption, he declared, had become the center of human activity, profoundly changing the nation's value system. "We accepted the principle that one *ought* to do what is technically *possible* to do. If it is possible to travel to the moon, we ought to do so, even though at the expense of many unfilled needs on earth; if it is possible to build ever more destructive weapons, we ought to do it, even if they threaten to destroy us and the whole human race." And what of man himself in this process? Said McCarthy:

Man, totally concerned with the production, sale and consumption of things, becomes more and more like a thing himself. He becomes a total consumer engaged in the passive taking in of everything from cigarets and liquor to television, movies, and even lectures and books. He feels lonely and anxious, because he does not see a real meaning to his life beyond that of making a living. He is bored and overcomes his boredom by more and ever-changing consumption and the thrills of meaningless excitement. His thinking is split from emotions, truth from passion, and his mind from his heart. Ideas do not appeal to him because he thinks in terms of calculations and probabilities rather than in those of convictions and commitments.

This indifference to life, he said, was manifest in the potential for violence and destructiveness in America. The nation professed values of reverence for life, love, compassion, reason, brotherhood, the boundless possibilities of man, but too many had become motivated by greed, selfishness, material hunger, an indifference to life "which allows us to conduct a war against a small nation, destroying and maiming human beings day after day, because we have made it part of our political creed that we must save the freedom of these people even if we destroy them in the process." America's justification for acting became national defense. "We were the first leading nation of the world in history that had looked upon its role largely as a defensive one," said McCarthy. The United States had developed "a punt on first down" mentality. "The danger of the defensive approach is that there is no limit to what one needs to protect himself. It is Kafka-like. It is the burrow: If you listen carefully, you can always hear the scratching sound." And in the hearing came a self-inflicted curtailment of spiritual as well as national freedom. McCarthy said:

We cannot for long in a society such as ours, in which we make such clear and continuing claims to be both free and responsible, restrict democracy and deny freedom in any area of our lives without the most serious and damaging consequences—either the growth of hypocrisy and frustration and ultimate dishonesty, or the kind of open protest which has characterized too much of American life in recent years.

We seek a new kind of freedom: again to be ourselves and to be honest within ourselves and also with the rest of the world.

Not many people listened carefully when McCarthy said these things over the summer. People like Frances Morrow, of Bedford, Indiana, did, for these were things she had been thinking about for some time, and she could appreciate the deeper meaning in McCarthy's more memorable lines, as when he said if elected he would take the fence down around the White House. It was another way of saying this new freedom, or a renewed sense of freedom, must return to America. To do this, America must look into itself, as McCarthy had suggested when he first spoke out on Vietnam in the Senate in January, 1966; as he was saying when he suggested in New York in 1968 that

the time may have come for us to turn the Statue of Liberty around—and turn it to our own nation for the next five years and see how we respond to the needs and demands of our own who are tired, who are poor, who are huddled, who yearn to breathe free. Then, having satisfied ourselves with having responded to it, having proved something about Americans, we can turn it around again to the rest of the world. As of now, we should drape it, I think, until we are prepared again to show it in a shining light.

Other things he said got more attention. In June he gave the opinion, in answer to a question, that he thought the American people would accept unilateral withdrawal from Vietnam. "The people seem to think, well, we've made a judgment against the war now. We don't have to do anything more about it. Their conscience is clear." At the same time, the mood of detachment on the issue was so paradoxical the people might also tolerate further escalation, McCarthy noted. Political opponents quickly began saying McCarthy advocated unilateral withdrawal, which was not at all what he said.

Members of the Kennedy following who could not abide

McCarthy but were perhaps willing to give him a chance were turned off when, in answer to another question in another interview, McCarthy belittled the need for stricter national gun-control laws. "It's been my experience in twenty years in the Congress that you really ought not to try to put through legislation under panic conditions, and that to say we'll need a different gun bill today than the one we needed yesterday or the day before is not a good way to proceed." It was another example of the McCarthy cool seeming to be callousness, though his position on gun control, enunciated during the campaign in Oregon, a big hunting state, remained consistent. He favored national registration of hand guns and heavy guns, but would leave control of rifles and shotguns to the states. The fact of Kennedy's death would not panic him into advocating more.

When he talked for a time of going to Paris to confer with Hanoi's peace negotiators, he was charged with meddling, the same indictment Roy Wilkins, of the National Association for the Advancement of Colored People, leveled at him for visiting Atlantic City during the supposedly nonpolitical NAACP national convention. Said McCarthy:

There is a rather good tradition in this country of meddling. It goes back to Thomas Jefferson and some of his friends, who decided to meddle a little bit with the British empire back in 1776. And I have been doing a little meddling myself in the year 1968. I think 1968 is a year in which all of us ought to meddle with politics just a little bit.

Some of his critics, as well as some of his supporters, thought he was being unnecessarily capricious when one day he announced names of the kind of people he would like to have in the Cabinet if elected. His choices weren't at all bad, better certainly than Nixon's, even though they gave very little due to politicians and, jotted down hastily as they were during a flight from Washington to New York, contained one or two errors of spelling or middle initials when released to the press. The list included: Secretary of State—Senator J. W. Fulbright, Senator Thruston B. Morton, a one-time Assistant Secretary of State, or Senator John Sherman Cooper, like Morton a Kentucky Republican, who had served as ambassador to India; Defense—John W. Gardner, former Secretary of Health, Education, and Welfare, and director of the Urban Coalition; Treasury—Thomas J. Watson, Jr., president of IBM, CBS president Dr. Frank Stanton, or Donald C. Cook, head of the American Electric Power Company; Attorney General—David Lindsay, a lawyer and twin brother of New York's Mayor John Lindsay; Commerce— William Clay Ford, vice-president of Ford Motor Company, or former Georgia Governor Carl E. Sanders; Labor—Representative John Conyers, Jr., Michigan Democrat; Housing and Urban Development—Governor Nelson Rockefeller of New York or Governor Richard J. Hughes of New Jersey; Health, Education, and Welfare —Mitchell I. Ginsberg, New York City's Director of Human Resources, or Walter P. Reuther, head of the United Auto Workers; Agriculture—Republican Senator James B. Pearson, of Kansas, whom McCarthy had jokingly promised a Cabinet post before even announcing his candidacy; Postmaster General—Patrick J. Lucey, former lieutenant-governor of Wisconsin and a long-time Kennedy associate; Transportation—Howard W. Johnson, president of the Massachusetts Institute of Technology; Interior—Vermont Governor Philip Hoff or Mount Everest climber James Whittaker; United Nations ambassador—Mrs. Martin Luther King, Jr.

One can only imagine the political impact such a list would have had in a general election. The list was more than a third Republican (including at least one ex-Goldwater supporter); it had two of the most prominent Negroes in the nation, a number of important political and business figures, and representatives of the South. And the South was not an area McCarthy ignored in his campaign.

He toured several southern and border states in July and was greeted by enthusiastic crowds wherever he went. McCarthy had once commented that his philosophy embodied "the essence of conservatism." And in the South his supporters emphasized just this. Franklin Ashley, a professor at the Citadel and a leader in the Charleston, South Carolina, organization, sought to compare Eugene McCarthy to California Governor Ronald Reagan after canvassing showed strong Reagan support in his area. They both had integrity, Ashley would stress. Neither McCarthy nor Reagan had very much to apologize for—unlike Humphrey and Nixon, he would add. While McCarthy was calling for an end to the unit rule and favorite son practice, a southern operative in the campaign, Hugo Sims, an Orangeburg, South Carolina, lawyer-politician, urged southern delegates to hold to favorite son positions, flatly telling some that if the South stuck together it could have its way in choice of a vice-presidential candidate on a McCarthy ticket. Sims sold McCarthy as a man interested only in purifying present legislation, not in introducing sweeping new laws. "These are the things we here in the South have fought for," he would say. "He told me he would treat the South as any other section of the country," said Sims, which, he stressed, was a part of McCarthy's philosophy of making no special appeal to interest groups or sections of the country, or to races. McCarthy, declared Sims, was definitely right of center on many issues and so Sims, a hawk on Vietnam, could support him. "He's not a peace at any price candidate," Sims would proclaim. A visitor from the North could not help but sometimes think that it was George Wallace whom Sims was talking about. But it definitely was McCarthy, or "Snowstorm" as he became known in the coded jargon of the Secret Service.

His trouble in reaching black Americans suffered to some degree from Secret Service zeal in protecting him. His two dozen agents were nervous about every ghetto visit and caused a number to be canceled, acting frequently on local police intelligence often compiled with little understanding by officials of what actually was happening in black neighborhoods. McCarthy was rarely disturbed, however, when appearances in ghettos or with black militants were scrubbed at Secret Service suggestion. He felt scheduler Norval Reece was putting too many such appearances in the schedule. Not only did he not want to appear to be making a special play for the black vote but he was tired of the rows that accompanied each cancellation with local supporters who felt the appearances essential. Moreover, he had had enough of being challenged about his record in crude language by persons who did not know his record. He had begun to get important black support, as he always maintained he would, without having to try to act like Robert Kennedy. Julian Bond rejected lucrative offers from the Humphrey camp to go to work instead in the McCarthy campaign late in the summer. Some preconvention polls showed McCarthy even with Humphrey or only a few percentage points off in black support when pitted against Richard Nixon.

The impression persisted, though, that McCarthy was not comfortable when dealing with blacks. An appearance before a Negro audience in Newark one night in August was canceled when the Secret Service warned that it did not have time to secure the meeting hall properly. Another stop was substituted: at the Tammy Brook Country Club in Cresskill, New Jersey, a lush club with wealthy-looking suburban types abounding, holding their glasses under fountains that spewed martinis. It was like going home, more than one reporter on the press bus noted—going home to the suburbs where McCarthy seemed to belong.

Only at the end of the summer when McCarthy visited the South Side Chicago church of the Reverend Jesse Jackson, the dynamic young leader of the Southern Christian Leadership Conference in the North and director of the successful Chicago-based Operation Breadbasket political and self-help project, did a black gathering respond to McCarthy with something close to total enthusiasm. It was on a Saturday morning in August, and Jackson's church was sweltering, the two thousand persons gathered there cooling themselves with fans as the program droned on: the collection, long speeches, singing. Finally McCarthy, perspiring as he hadn't done during the whole campaign (some reporters had come to believe he had no sweat glands), stood to speak. Even at his best, how could McCarthy match the cadence and emotion of Jackson, the fire of the Reverend Calvin S. Morris, one of Jackson's assistants? Robert Kennedy could, but how could McCarthy? He did it that day. That day McCarthy showed something he rarely displayed. "Soul Power," they called it at Jackson's church.

"What about us?" McCarthy repeated in a soft but evangelical beat. "Civil rights begins when you resist the politicians. What about us?

(Yes, yes, A-men.) What about us? I have no obligations and no Maddoxes. What about us? (Yeah, man.) I don't ask for any easy judgments. What about us—the *people*?"

They sang "We Shall Overcome" when he had finished. McCarthy sang with them, or, at least, he moved his lips. He swayed with them as they sang, and hesitantly at first, he grasped the hand of a black girl who came to stand beside him, and with the other hand he held to the black man on the other side of him. Then it ended and the campaign moved to another well-to-do suburb, this time on the classy Chicago North Shore. A man introduced McCarthy as "the candidate for America's suburbs." "That's where the vote is, you know," McCarthy told me on the flight back to Washington late that afternoon. But for a time that day he showed he could also be a candidate of the ghetto. He was reaching a stride as the campaign was ending. It was the final bright moment of the campaign.

The final low point of the summer before Chicago came a few days later when Soviet and other Iron Curtain troops moved into Czechoslovakia to muzzle the liberal Prague government. McCarthy had not wanted to make a statement about the incident, but aides insisted he must. What he came up with was an honest but cold statement which criticized Lyndon Johnson for overreacting by calling a midnight National Security Council meeting regarding an incident that McCarthy accurately felt was not a major world crisis. But he omitted any expression of sympathy for the Czech people. "That goes without saying," he said testily when asked about the omission at a press conference where he read the statement August 21, 1968, in Washington. "Do I have to say it every time?"

This time, yes, almost all of his aides thought. Criticism showered in, not only from opponents but from fervent supporters like Paul O'Dwyer, New York Senate candidate, John Kenneth Galbraith, and Jesse Unruh, who was nearing a McCarthy endorsement. McCarthy was finally forced to make one of his few clarifications of the campaign. But the damage had been done. McCarthy's initial reaction confirmed for many what his detractors had been charging: that McCarthy suffered from an immense passion gap. The invasion itself had strengthened the hand of anti-Communist hard-liners at the national convention, dealing, perhaps, the final blow to passage of a Vietnam peace plank.

Hubert Humphrey, of course, was also touring the country in the summer of 1968, and George McGovern, in an afterthought candidacy, joined in the final couple of weeks. But Humphrey was the main show, for he would get the nomination.

Humphrey had been the first administration official publicly to criticize McCarthy's announcement of candidacy, and now, in the summer of 1968, he was saying the same thing. McCarthy had not made his alternative to Vietnam policy clear, Humphrey repeated; yet in another breath Humphrey would suggest that his differences with peace advocates were so small he would have no difficulty accepting a platform plank they might write—a statement he backed away from rather quickly. At another point, he suggested his Vietnam position was very close to that of Robert Kennedy, whose position Humphrey had once criticized as like advocating putting a fox in a chicken coop. And at yet another point, Humprey said his and Richard Nixon's positions were very much alike. "A Man for All People," was the title of a Humphrey campaign picture book, and indeed it often seemed he was striving to live up to that slogan, so industriously, in fact, he diminished even further what was left of his own identity. "Where does *he* stand on Vietnam?" McCarthy asked with justification.

Both his unequaled loyalty and a gnawing fear that Lyndon Johnson might yet somehow pull the rug out from under his candidacy kept Humphrey from the clear break with Johnson that Democrats across the country were praying for. And so he went through the summer, and the fall, not really his own man, always Number 2, a role he had learned to play so well that some of his aides worried lest he had lost the ability to think or act as Number 1. Indeed, Humphrey looked upon the office of Vice-President as had perhaps no other man in America's history. John Nance Garner, Franklin Roosevelt's first Vice-President, considered the office not worth even "a jugful of warm spit." But as Hubert Humphrey once said: "I'm proud of the fact, and I love the country that made it possible, that a poor boy who grew up in his daddy's drug store in Huron, South Dakota, could rise to be the Vice-President of the United States. Of course I'd like to be President some day—who wouldn't? But if this should be the end of my career I would think it well spent. Just think: I occupy the second highest office in the land." It was vintage Humphrey: effusive, corny, sincere. But for Humphrey, 1968 was definitely a season to start sounding more like Number 1, like his own man.

He tried to deal with the problem with jokes or hints of future independence. Entertaining a group of mayors who had endorsed him at his lake-front home in Waverly, Minnesota, Humphrey pointed to his speed boat. "It's an eighty-five horsepower Johnson motor," he grinned, "but it's going to be a 100 horse Humphrey." At a National Press Club luncheon he reminded his listeners that "there's a lot of difference" between being a "member of the team and captain of the team." Before the New York Liberal party, he emphasized he would not hypocritically run away from administration policy but also emphasized: "The Vice-President of the United States does not make the policy."

He was caught in one of those boxlike rooms with shrinking walls, and when White House political operatives selected the roster of convention committee chairmen and officials completely shutting out the McCarthy forces, the onus fell on Humphrey—who was not free to protest that he had no say in the selections or to argue with them. "I think the President ought to set [Humphrey] free," McCarthy commented late in June. But Humphrey wasn't free. And so he frantically stacked up the delegates in the nonprimary states right and left, with an effective organization and the currency of loyalty and future reward, and in doing so donned the mantle of steam roller and boss in the eyes of the McCarthyites.

"I'd like to feel that when I went to Chicago that there were enough delegates in hand so that we had some degree of security, so that I could be a serene and pleasant man while I'm there," Humphrey explained.

Humphrey dropped his "politics of joy" slogan quickly after his entry into the race, but his message still was strung on phrases that seemed hollow coming from the 1968 Hubert Humphrey:

Peace making is delicate business. Peace talking is easy business. Peace booing is ridiculous business. . . .

I am a man of hope and progress. I am a man of unbridled and unlimited faith in the capacity of the American people. . . .

. . . The nation is not sick. There are a few pimples on the body, but it is a sign we are growing up. . . .

. . . I'm asking you as a private citizen and a public official that we have the same willingness to make sacrifices at the conference table for the cause of peace as we have sacrificed on the battlefield.

He intended to "awaken and arouse the silent majority of American people."

He still maintained Vietnam had not drastically hampered domestic programs because even with Vietnam, spending for social purposes had increased more rapidly than at any time in history.

It is true Vietnam is a very heavy cost item, but with no Vietnam we didn't do anything for our youngsters in Head Start. With no Vietnam we had no food stamp plan, except the one that Hubert Humphrey offered. . . . With no Vietnam we didn't have a thing going for the consumers . . . with no Vietnam we didn't have any war on poverty. . . . So it isn't the war that is the excuse here. What is the real fact is that we have done more despite the war. . . .

But it sounded almost as if he were daring to suggest America had done more *because* of the war. His logic seemed jumbled, in this and other matters.

"You young people have failed to take a good look around you," he told a group of collegians he met with privately, which was a sappy thing to try to tell them. They had taken a look around them, as had many, many others in the country, and it did not help Hubert Humphrey to tell them they had not.

Humphrey ran scared through the summer, despite his mammoth delegate edge, trying to balance his crucial southern support with his northern support in a way that would not disturb Lyndon Johnson and also leave a way for the McCarthy people eventually to embrace him. His aides sought to counter the growing impression Humphrey was a loser with still another memo that concluded that the primaries didn't mean anything. In New Hampshire, it said, many hawks had voted anti-Johnson because they wanted a stepped-up war. Indiana represented nothing more than Kennedy charisma. Oregon, and California to a lesser extent, was anti-Kennedy sentiment at work. In New York, fewer than 25 per cent of registered Democrats voted. In the polls, Humphrey was clearly the choice of Democrats. The fact the Kennedy and McCarthy primary vote totaled about 80 per cent was not meaningful because of other factors. "In short," the memo said, "the presidential preference primaries did not indicate a public rejection of Humphrey or of the Administration as the McCarthy camp and some writers would like people to believe today."

That may have had at least a grain of truth to it. McCarthy himself placed the 80 per cent argument in perspective when he said it was "a bit misleading. Some Kennedy support was just pro-Kennedy and had nothing to do with the issues. Some of it will go to Humphrey.* Some of mine was just anti-Kennedy, and it'll slip too. I think we could hope that a majority backed us."

The primary vote may not have meant outright rejection of Humphrey, but neither was it anything like acceptance, and the McCarthy supporters continued, as did McCarthy, to drive home the message of the primaries: the people wanted nothing more to do with the administration, including Humphrey. Humphrey was a loser, and McCarthy a winner. Just look at the polls.

The polls through most of the summer showed McCarthy stronger than Humphrey against Republican candidates. A McCarthy-financed survey by John Kraft showed McCarthy stronger than Humphrey in fifteen states where there had been primaries. In California, he topped Humphrey by 15 per cent, 20 per cent in Oregon, 17 in Nebraska and Illinois. The major independent polls, Harris and Gallup,

---

* A *New York Times* survey shortly after Kennedy's death indicated about 400 of the Kennedy-leaning delegates would move to Humphrey and 75 to McCarthy. The figure proved to be high, but represented the nonideological basis of much of Kennedy's support, a factor the McCarthy campaign could not deal with.

had narrower findings, but still McCarthy led, though during August his gains in the major polls were not as steady. A McCarthy staff analysis blamed this on faulty sampling by the pollsters. All year long every poll had underestimated McCarthy's strength. There was every reason to believe it was being underestimated now. But *hari-kari* mentality seized too many regular Democrats. "I'd rather lose with my guy than win with yours," Pittsburgh Mayor Joseph Barr told Tom McCoy. Barr simply preferred to be aligned with someone he knew and felt he could trust rather than with mysterious McCarthy and his clamorous crowd who seemed bent on shoving every long-time party worker out to pasture.

McCarthy considered contacts with such politicians rather pointless. "I got with the Ohio people a couple of times, and I went to see Joe Barr. . . . I saw Bill Green in Philadelphia and I saw what's-his-name in Cleveland." That was another thing that troubled the regulars. McCarthy did not even seem to care what their names were. What's-his-name, Bert Porter, Cuyahoga County Democratic leader, was receptive to McCarthy's candidacy. But no one, for a long time, even thought of talking to him, not even the "young fanatics," as Porter called them, on the campaign staff.

This failure to ask for support was a convenient excuse for politicians who had other grievances against McCarthy. Had McCarthy been a different kind of candidate and appeared headed for the nomination no one would have waited to be asked. The excuse was particularly useful to men who shared McCarthy's view on the war, like George McGovern, of South Dakota. It seemed to them justification for not acting. McGovern also had other reasons. He simply did not like McCarthy. He felt him ungenerous and arrogant, and he undoubtedly could not get it out of his mind that had he himself acted on his convictions rather than in regard for the safety of his reelection he might have done what McCarthy did.

Another useful excuse for many Kennedy supporters was that they were certain McCarthy would be a rotten President. At least one from the Kennedy inner circle, Pat Lucey, investigated for himself the validity of this conclusion. He spoke with McCarthy friends and associates of his misgivings about McCarthy as President. They dispelled enough of his doubts to prompt him to get an appointment with McCarthy in Washington. Their conversation bantered on for about twenty minutes without McCarthy's trying to enlist Lucey, the conversation dwelling on Saint Thomas College, where Lucey had been a student. Lucey finally offered his help and it was readily accepted. Most of the rest of Kennedy's major political supporters held back and began to look for another horse, and their gaze soon fell on Kennedy friend George McGovern.

Ironically, it was Pat Lucey who helped plant the seed for the McGovern candidacy. While riding from New York to Washington, D.C., on the train carrying Robert Kennedy's body on its last ride, Lucey introduced Jesse Unruh, of California, to William Dougherty, South Dakota Kennedy chairman. Unruh and Dougherty conversed by phone a number of times after that. Dougherty also spoke with other Kennedy backers around the country. In California, Unruh talked up a McGovern candidacy, always hypothetically. The idea began to blossom.

It first surfaced publicly in the form of a Kennedy memorial dinner the evening of Saturday, July 13, in Huron, South Dakota, Hubert Humphrey's old home town. The date coincided with a meeting of South Dakota delegates to the national convention. The guest list was impressive. It included Ted Sorensen, Jesse Unruh, Pat Lucey, Kennedy Iowa leader Donald O'Brien, Massachusetts Kennedy backer David Harrison. McGovern was in Europe at a World Council of Churches meeting. South Dakota McGovern supporters had hinted the evening before that Unruh and Sorensen would announce their support of McGovern's candidacy, and so an Unruh-Sorensen press conference in Sioux Falls before the dinner was well attended. Both men feigned surprise that the question should arise and insisted they would remain uncommitted until the convention. That night at the dinner, Sorensen urged all Kennedy delegates to do the same in the hope yet another candidate would arise. So far, he said, no candidate had yet arisen "who can lead in the future to fill Bob Kennedy's legacy."

The dinner ended in some confusion, many of the participants wearing McGovern for President buttons that had mysteriously appeared, but without a candidacy having flowered. That night Dougherty rammed through a favorite son vote for McGovern, on the unit rule, at a caucus of the South Dakota delegation. But the McGovern candidacy seemed to have stopped there, for the same day in Ohio former Governor Mike DiSalle had announced he would place Ted Kennedy's name in nomination in Chicago. The news had broken before the Sioux Falls press conference at which the McGovern candidacy was to have gotten its lift-off.

In this period, it became increasingly clear that the refusal of many Kennedy delegates to support McCarthy might weaken the muscle of antiwar delegates hoping for a peace plank in the platform. The need to reach some unified position before the convention began to move those truly concerned about the issues.

In Washington, a group of Kennedy and McCarthy men finally sat down at lunch to discuss how to get together on a single peace plank. The group included Joe Rauh, Blair Clark, Fred Dutton, Kenneth O'Donnell, Frank Mankewiecz, Senators Wayne Morse and Claiborne Pell, and John Gilligan, of Ohio, who was running for the United States Senate. Gilligan's concern was similar to that of Anne Wexler in setting up the Hughes commission: it must not appear to be the child of any single candidate. This might also help Humphrey ultimately to move away from Johnson on Vietnam. "It would be like throwing a child in a swimming pool—he'd swim," Gilligan would say hopefully of Humphrey. Gilligan and O'Donnell, who had declined to join in the budding McGovern effort, became cochairmen of the group. Kennedy campaign chief Dutton, who had rejected Humphrey's invitation to join his campaign, was assigned to draft the unity peace plank.

At about the same time, another and partly overlapping group of antiadministration politicians met in Chicago and formed the Committee for a Democratic Convention. The committee aimed at building support for recommendations of the Hughes commission and a unified peace plank and, most important, sought to stake out—for several with races in the fall—a position independent of what figured to be a Humphrey-led ticket. Those at the meeting included McGovern, Governor Philip Hoff, of Vermont, Senator Claiborne Pell, of

Rhode Island, Governor Harold Hughes, of Iowa, Jesse Unruh, of California, Pat Lucey, of Wisconsin, Ken O'Donnell, Ted Sorensen, Larry O'Brien, and others. McGovern informed those present he planned to become a candidate. The news was greeted with mixed reactions. Lucey disclosed he had determined that support of McCarthy was the only way to continue to oppose the administration and rejected a suggestion from another participant that all there take an uncommitted stance. Cynics suggested later that Lucey's motives were colored at least partly by the obvious McCarthy strength in Wisconsin and Lucey's desire to run for governor in 1970 in a field that probably would include Wisconsin McCarthy leader Donald Peterson. Unruh, ever holding his cards to his vest, indicated he would eventually declare support of McCarthy. So, too, did Hughes and Hoff, both of whom were feeling pressure from McCarthy supporters in their states.

McGovern thus went away from the meeting only with the title of chairman of the new committee and the probability he would present the unified peace plank before the platform committee. But on August 10, spurred on by some Kennedy men who still could not bring themselves to support McCarthy, as well as his own sudden taste for the quest, McGovern announced his candidacy. The convention was two weeks away.

A few days before McGovern's announcement, Tom Finney proposed to McCarthy that a secret effort be made to find a party-unifying compromise candidate. McCarthy, more than ever convinced he had no chance in Chicago, agreed, and suggested Edmund Muskie or Governor Richard Hughes, of New Jersey, but preferably Muskie. For forty-eight hours Finney and Tom McCoy explored the possibilities in a string of phone calls, but the idea died when the White House failed to encourage the effort.

McCarthy moved in other ways, primarily through Finney, to try to lessen the split the convention would widen if Humphrey failed to move closer to the McCarthy position on Vietnam. Finney felt out Humphrey campaign manager Larry O'Brien about giving McCarthy some of Humphrey's convention votes, particularly from states like Illinois, Pennsylvania, and Texas, whose delegations did not reflect

McCarthy's popular support. The aim was to assuage McCarthyites angry over Humphrey steam-roller tactics. Finney added an incentive: McCarthy would campaign for Humphrey only in those states that gave up a few votes. "If I had [Humphrey's] margin," McCarthy said weeks before Finney went about his secret mission, "I'd give some away for the sake of party unity and appearance." McCarthy himself placed the proposition before Mayor Daley, of Chicago, by phone a week before the convention. About twenty or twenty-five Illinois delegates would do it, McCarthy told Daley. All told, the McCarthy camp was asking only about fifty additional votes, but the initiative failed.

Finney also arranged a breakfast meeting between Humphrey and McCartthy several days before the convention in Humphrey's Washington apartment. McCarthy wanted to discuss the Vietnam plank and to make clear that he did not want to be considered for the vice-presidential nomination. The Humphrey camp would regularly leak names of vice-presidential potentials in the age-old game of trying to corral support (something McCarthy never did), and McCarthy's name had been mentioned occasionally. McCarthy wanted this stopped. Such talk suggested possible arrangement between the two and might make suspect any future support McCarthy might be able to provide Humphrey. What little influence McCarthy might have on his independent-minded supporters to back Humphrey would be damaged. And, as McCarthy had already said publicly: "If I were to go on the ticket with Hubert it would be kind of like the captain of a ship getting in the first lifeboat and waving to those still on board saying, 'I hope it doesn't sink.' "

Finney also worked behind the scenes to kill the television debate with Humphrey that McCarthy had sought for so long. He did it with McCarthy's knowledge, even as Blair Clark went ahead trying to arrange the confrontation. If indeed Humphrey was edging toward a new stance on Vietnam, as it seemed for part of the summer, a debate might make more difficult Humphrey's final conversion and possibly hamper the peace forces in the platform fight. Negotiations for the debate had languished over the summer. McCarthy originally wanted three meetings. It fitted in with the campaign strategy, such as it was, of maximum television exposure over the summer. But agreement was not reached on a time and format until too close to the convention to have any impact, except possibly negative, McCarthy decided. It was agreed the Humphrey camp would plead conflict in schedule to get out of the debate, and McCarthy would not seek to make political hay out of it. Typically, McCarthy could not keep his part of the bargain. In Chicago, the Mitchell wing of the McCarthy campaign immediately leveled a blast at Humphrey for pulling out of the debate. McCarthy finally had to take the fall. It was too late for a debate, he pronounced.

All the secret activity had been for nought, except to implant still deeper among most other McCarthy campaign aides the belief that Tom Finney was a secret agent for Humphrey. McCarthy had been the secret agent, in effect, in a campaign to present the best situation possible to Humphrey as the Democratic nominee for President. McCarthy had gone more than halfway. He had been hampered by his own organization at times, but the main failure had been that of Humphrey and those around him.

For McCarthy personally, it was just as well that these moves remained secret. As the summer waned, the suspicions and bitterness within his own fractious staff began to fly off at everyone—at opponents, at themselves, at their own candidate. Many of the staff felt McCarthy failed to exert himself adequately during the summer. They complained when he went to Saint John's University to visit old friends for a few days, playing softball with nuns and reading poetry at a time some felt he should be giving attention to position papers. They complained when he spent a long week end in Maine with Robert Lowell and other acquaintances. They agonized when he went into Oklahoma and said he would settle for two convention votes after his workers thought they had lined up a minimum of eight. That was a hard one to explain, but his intervals away from the campaign were not. He had campaigned actively longer than any other candidate running in 1968. (Nixon had been running for two years, but through the primaries his lack of opposition allowed him a more leisurely pace.) By summer, after the emotional strain of the Kennedy slaying and the months of fatiguing effort, McCarthy was bone-weary. The few days at Saint John's were a needed rejuvenation for the tired candidate. The visit to Maine occurred as the Republican convention met, and attention was off the Democratic race temporarily anyway.

But the complaints did not abate. He left his supporters and workers at once frustrated and inspired, angered and gratified. It was as if he had given the campaign both everything and nothing.

McCarthy had known from the beginning he had very little chance to win. When Robert Kennedy entered, he felt the chance further diminished. Finally, when Kennedy was killed, he considered it all over. He went through the summer doing most of what was required, but without enthusiasm. "I sensed that we weren't going to win," he said in one interview. "Since that was the case, it was best to keep things a little bit on the cool side." Despite his comments about the young ski bums, he wanted the young people who had followed him to end their doomed crusade as unwounded as possible. And so he resisted the attempts of those who would make him a hero. He did it by simply remaining himself.

He had said the outlandish things in a calm voice: end the war, fire Hershey and Rusk and Hoover, recognize Red China, restore Cuba to the family of nations, institute selective conscientious objection, understand student protesters, admit our mistakes, and "take our steel out of the land of straw huts." He often said along the way that, if nothing else, his campaign perhaps had made people a bit more honest, had set people free. This was true in many subtle ways and quite a spectrum responded: latent George Wallace supporters in the farm belt; militant Negroes in BAM; William Clay Ford, biggest stockholder in Ford Motor Company and a 1964 Goldwater supporter; the Reverend Albert B. Cleage, Jr., one of Detroit's most militant black leaders. Their common denominator was a longing to control things affecting their lives, a desire for a return to honesty in things that the System had seemed to pervert.

McCarthy gave a valedictory in his last campaign speech a week before the convention. "We've tried to change the system," McCarthy said. "Whether we've changed it or not, we've given it one or two good shakes; we've brought it alive."

Not even the events in Chicago could change that.

29. EXECUTION

Nearly twenty thousand persons were waiting to greet Eugene McCarthy when he flew into Chicago's Midway Airport Sunday afternoon, August 25, 1968, for the Democratic National Convention. "Quite a few people have shown up for the execution," he commented to a friend as his jet lowered onto the runway at its last stop of the long campaign. Thus, McCarthy arrived in Chicago as a man going to the wall. Never mind the blindfold. Let's just get it over with.

It would take five days to get it over with—five days that would shake the Democratic party to its foundations and leave one wondering whether the executioners had not done in themselves as well.

DAY I: SUNDAY—MONDAY

This was the period of arrivals.

Cindy Samuels, twenty-two, arrived in Chicago, the smile on her round face and the sparkle in her green eyes still as refreshing to reporters who followed the McCarthy candidacy as the first time they saw her in New Hampshire. She had been a campaign press aide and traveled with the candidate through the primaries. A Smith girl from Pittsburgh, she missed her graduation because of the campaign, but her candidate sent her the traditional roses that Smith girls carry at graduation time. She came to Chicago and began to feel something bad happening inside her. Anger filled her, unreasoning anger, each time she saw someone wearing a Humphrey button. She wanted to go up to each one and shout, "Do you know what you're doing?" But she didn't. She could only realize that for the first time she understood prejudice, because she felt it.

The McCarthy delegates arrived in Chicago, and they too were out of a different mold. Many of them were new to politics; concerned with issues first, party second. Most were younger than the non-McCarthy delegates; made for the most part more money; could boast more postgraduate degrees—facts detailed statistically in a study of 187 convention delegates by Professors John W. Soule and James W. Clarke, of Florida State University's Political Research Institute. These McCarthy delegates were intent on reforming the party, and as they arrived a number of them—thirty-three in all—along with McCarthy campaign staffers quietly, virtually unnoticed, began laying the groundwork for a vote that would do just that.

This group of reformers included Eli Segal, a twenty-five-year-old lawyer who had been a McCarthy advance man during the Indiana primary; Anne Wexler, a member of the rules committee from Connecticut, who had sparked the whole effort to democratize the delegate selection process of the party; Joseph Crangle, an upstate New York Democratic leader and otherwise a Humphrey man who now became one of the stalwarts in the final drive for acceptance of the reform package; Howard Willens, of Washington, D.C.; and Robert Strout, of Kansas.

Also in Chicago was a team of lawyers headed by John Schmidt and Wayne Whelan, who, with the advice of Joseph Rauh and Herbert Reid, had helped prepare the credentials challenges of nineteen states, a record in party history, on a multitude of unprecedented grounds. Shouldn't *all* political views be given a voice among delegations, the kind of voice the party had already ruled must be accorded racial and national minorities? Should not this party of the people somehow adhere to the U.S. Supreme Court mandate of one-man, one-vote, in its representation at national conventions? Should one man or a small number of men have the power to pick the people who choose delegates from any one state? Shouldn't they be chosen near enough to a convention so that they might be more responsive to current issues than persons selected two or even four years ahead of time? These were the questions uppermost in the minds of the McCarthy rules and credentials challengers as they were stirred about in the caldron of Chicago.

There were the Wynken, Blynken, and Nod of the Vietnam fight: Richard Goodwin in McCarthy's corner, Pierre Salinger in McGovern's, Ted Sorenson in an ambiguous corner (some said it was Humphrey's). They had taken the words that the group of Kennedy, McGovern, and McCarthy men had fashioned in the weeks before the convention and with doves on the platform committee had shaped a tolerably decent peace plank for the Democratic party—a plank that sought to distill a multitude of positions into one and leave a small handle for Hubert Humphrey to grab, if only he would. The plank* they had come up with late Friday night, August 23, was not overly satisfying to anyone, including Eugene McCarthy (though he did not say so immediately), but it was all right. It was primarily a redraft of points from a speech Ted Kennedy had given August 21, a speech Goodwin had worked on.

And what of Ted Kennedy as the convention opened? He was there in essence, as was Lyndon Johnson. Kennedy's brother-in-law Stephen

* The final peace plank provided:

—An unconditional end to all bombing of North Vietnam, while continuing to provide in the South all necessary air and other support for American troops. (The plank adopted would stop the bombing "when this action would not endanger the lives of our troops in the field; this action should take into account the response from Hanoi.")

—A negotiated mutual withdrawal of all United States and North Vietnamese forces from South Vietnam, phased over "a relatively short period of time." (The plank adopted was essentially the same, but also spoke of negotiating with Hanoi "an immediate end or limitation of hostilities.")

—Encouragement of a reconciliation between the South Vietnamese and the National Liberation Front, looking toward a government which was broadly representative of these and all elements in South Vietnamese society. "The specific shape of this reconciliation will be a matter for decision by the South Vietnamese, spurred to action by the certain knowledge that the prop of American military support will soon be gone. In addition, the South Vietnamese will assume

Smith, surrogate for the legacy, was back in Chicago after a week-end flight to Hyannisport to talk to Teddy about what might be a boomlet forming in Chicago for the last of the Kennedys—a young man still torn by too much tragedy, yet intrigued by the budding opportunity; a young man with a life so full of history and stimulation and laughter and friends and children suddenly as lonely as a man had ever been. What was he to do? What should he do? What did he owe his party and his country? What did they owe him?

A man afflicted with a far different kind of loneliness arrived in Chicago Sunday afternoon: Hubert Humphrey, who had begun writing his acceptance speech two days earlier. He had wanted to come to Chicago with a measure of serenity, but instead found himself buffeted from all sides as he walked into the Conrad Hilton, even though he had a good 1,460 delegates already sewed up, and he needed only 1,312 to win the Brass Ring. He knew the President's man, John Connally, was disturbed about things Humphrey had been saying while wooing the McCarthy wing of the party, and he sent aides to soothe the tall Texan. Finally Humphrey himself confronted Connally. Yes, he would oppose elimination of the unit rule in 1968, even though he had written a letter to rules committee chairman Samuel Shapiro on August 21 reaffirming his statement of the summer that he wanted done with it. Yes, he would oppose the Texas credentials challenge: it charged that dissident political views had been excluded through use of the unit rule in 221 of the 241 Texas county conventions leading to the state convention. No, he wouldn't pick a running mate abhorrent to the South. No, he would not in any way retreat from Lyndon Johnson's Vietnam policy.

---

increasing responsibility for the resolution of the conflict and full responsibility for determining their own political destiny." The United States would offer economic help to rebuild war-ravaged areas. (The plank adopted urged all parties and interests to agree that a postwar government should be established by "fair and safeguarded elections," preferably with some international presence to facilitate transition from war to peace and protect minorities from reprisals. In the meantime, the United States should accelerate efforts to train and equip the South Vietnamese army so it could defend its own country and take over the burden from American forces. It also spoke of postwar economic aid.)

—A lower level of violence by reduction in offensive operations which would reduce casualties and enable an early withdrawal of a large number of American troops. (The adopted plank said nothing on this order.)

Representative Hale Boggs, the platform committee chairman, had been summoned to the White House, ostensibly for a briefing on the Czech crisis, but more pointedly for a stiffening on the Vietnam plank, which he passed on to Humphrey. Yet another emissary from the White House, Charles Murphy, former Civil Aeronautics Board chairman, was in Chicago to starch Humphrey more. A Vietnam plank draft put together by a team of Humphrey men led by Washington lawyer David Ginsburg, who had consulted regularly with doves, was too soft, Murphy informed Ginsburg and Boggs, especially on the matter of a bombing halt. (The draft said only that a halt was acceptable under certain conditions: it did not propose one.)

What remaining notion Humphrey may have had of a Vietnam position of his own died soon after he arrived in Chicago. He was still not his own man—though he would have to be, regarding Vietnam, by the night of nomination or he would surely never become President, Larry O'Brien was heard to say.

Now Humphrey worried about the immediate problems: breaking the southerners out of their favorite son stance; watching out for this Kennedy thing people were talking about; staying wary of the small undercurrent of support for a Lyndon Johnson nomination; wondering why Richard Daley was delaying announcement of his favorite, which Daley had promised for late Sunday. All of this was not the recipe for serenity.

And at 1:25 P.M. Sunday, Eugene McCarthy dropped into the caldron. The day had begun typically for the McCarthy campaign, with both minor and major crises. A car that was to take some of the McCarthy luggage to Washington's National Airport broke down minutes before take-off. Two students threw their sports cars into operation, stacking the bags in the cramped passenger seats and speeding off to the airport. Onto the runway they flashed, the Secret Service monitoring their approach, and screeched to a halt beneath the plane's wing. The two young volunteers deposited the luggage with a flourish characteristic of almost every motion in the campaign —a flourish that said this act was the most important of the effort, and who was to say it wasn't? One Secret Service agent watched in wonder, then, shaking his head, muttered to another, "Only Mc-Carthy."

Only McCarthy. Up one minute. Down the next. Never predictable. McCarthy had stopped at the Washington CBS studio en route to the plane for a "Face the Nation" appearance and had caused another crisis. The day before, McCarthy had been reported as endorsing the Vietnam peace plank the doves had agreed on. Now he seemed cool toward the compromise, since it failed to include two positions McCarthy had said he would demand: a statement admitting that the Johnson policy had been in error and a definite provision for an interim coalition government as a first step toward peace. He called the unity peace position "a mixed sort of plank" and added, "I haven't quite said I accept it." He would straighten things out in Chicago, he said. David Schoumacher, of CBS, one of the panel of questioners, would not drop the issue even as he and McCarthy stood together removing their make-up after the program. To Schoumacher, Mc-Carthy had retreated drastically from his original position.

"Dave," McCarthy said in a pained voice, "why don't you leave it alone? It's all over."

"But it's what the whole campaign was about," stormed Schoumacher. "Maybe McCarthy is over, but the reason for the whole thing isn't."

McCarthy was said to be down during the telecast, partly the result of a phone call from Chicago the night before outlining the desolation his effort faced at the convention. He did not particularly want to go to Chicago and for a time thought he might stay just a day or two, then go off alone some place, possibly to return for the closing. He had turned down numerous offers of accommodations away from storm of the convention hotels, including one at the Play-boy pad of Hugh Hefner.

As usual, one looking for clues to McCarthy's mood on the flight would have been disappointed. He wandered back through the re-porters' cabin briefly, joking a bit, seemingly at ease. He was still claiming his chances were fifty-fifty, though he knew differently. For the first time he disclosed names of several persons he had in mind for Vice-President on a McCarthy ticket: George McGovern, Senator Frank Church, of Idaho, Governor Richard Hughes, of New Jersey, Edmund Muskie, Ted Kennedy. (He did not mention former North Carolina Governor Terry Sanford, a Humphrey backer, who, he said two days later, would have been his choice.) Otherwise, the flight was like any other during the McCarthy campaign, reporters and staff alike still amazed that the campaign could have come this far.

As the plane came to a halt at Chicago's Midway Airport, Pat Lucey hurried aboard to intercept the candidate and try to cheer him up. Abigail had told Lucey that Eugene was depressed. "The important thing," Lucey recalled McCarthy's saying disconsolately, "is to make a good show for the kids." "I don't want to hear any more of that defeatist crap," Lucey responded, and he outlined what he felt were the few positive things that seemed to be happening.

Pat Lucey, another man in the caldron. Lucey, the Kennedy man, in the closing days of the McCarthy campaign became its mainstay. For two weeks Lucey had been making hundreds of phone calls to delegates in a last stab for the nomination. With Curt Gans, Don Green, Norval Reece, Marty Gleason, Steve Mitchell, and others he had pulled together the McCarthy convention floor operation. (There were lapses, however. When McCarthy delegate Bruce Mason, of Arizona, arrived in Chicago, no one had ever heard of him. The campaign staff had instead been concentrating on a Humphrey delegate believed to be a McCarthy supporter.)

Lucey felt more at ease in conversation with McCarthy than he had with either Jack or Robert Kennedy, and he had the ability to get McCarthy to do things he didn't want to do, like agreeing to a number of visits with convention caucuses.

Now, after McCarthy had addressed his supporters briefly at Midway, after flowers had been showered on him and the chants had died away, McCarthy got into a car with Abigail and Lucey and headed into Chicago—"a good place to start a revolution," McCarthy had said in speeches through the summer—past the police in baby-blue helmets, through traffic clogged because the city had chosen this day to repaint street crosswalk lines in the vicinity of the airport—a happening in character with the decision to ban ice cubes from soft drinks at the convention hall in the fear they would be used as weapons, with the decision to make delegates wear credentials around their necks like cowbells to stick in authoritarian machines to gain entrance or exit at the hall.

McCarthy began to seem cheerful enough to get to business, and Lucey plunged into Machiavellian hypothesis.

"I'm going to pose a question," Lucey began. "You can take twenty-four hours to answer it. Do you want to be President bad enough to have John Connally as a running mate?" (Richard Goodwin had spent two hours with Connally the night before beating about the bush, not offering anything directly but reminding Connally that Hubert Humphrey was the one man who could not possibly place a Texan on his ticket.)

Lucey's words had barely died before McCarthy answered. "I don't need twenty-four hours. The answer is no," he said.

The car moved on toward the execution, toward a meeting with one of the chief executioners, Mayor Daley, who waited in room 220 at the Sherman House in the Loop. This meeting was McCarthy's first obligation on arriving in Chicago, as it had been the obligation, the necessity, of every other politician of import who came to Chicago for the convention.

For days Mayor Daley's door had been revolving with politicians coming and going. On Friday, Stephen Smith had dropped in for an inconclusive fencing match about a possible Ted Kennedy draft. Pat Lucey saw Daley for twenty minutes Friday evening. Interestingly, Lucey thought, Daley never brought up the subject of Hubert Humphrey. That was up to Lucey, who stressed that Humphrey was a loser. Daley did not disagree. Lucey left with the impression that Daley's overriding loyalty was to Lyndon Johnson. Saturday, at Lucey's behest, Representative Charles Vanik and John Gilligan, of Ohio, visited Daley and got the same impression. Maybe Lyndon Johnson should come back into the race, Daley commented. We can trump that ace, responded Gilligan. You bring in Johnson and we'll bring in Teddy. How would Teddy do in November? Daley wondered. Senator Abraham Ribicoff of Connecticut, a Daley friend since 1956 when Ribicoff sought Daley's support of John Kennedy as Adlai Stevenson's running mate, visited for ninety minutes Saturday to feel him out about the last Kennedy. Humphrey's weakness was brought up again. Daley did not disagree. What about Kennedy? Daley had been on the phone to him that day without learning Teddy's intentions. Will he go? Daley wondered. Maybe you should stay uncommitted awhile, Ribicoff said. A phone call with Lyndon Johnson interrupted the visit: more talk about Humphrey's weakness; maybe Johnson should be nominated; no, was the response, Humphrey. A Daley-Smith phone call, Smith in Hyannisport with Teddy: Kennedy would make no overt move, nor, for that matter, a covert move. The next morning, Sunday, Daley had breakfasted with Jesse Unruh, of California. More talk of Humphrey's being a drag on the ticket. More talk of a possible Kennedy draft. More talk of Johnson. McCarthy? Unacceptable, Daley said. Unacceptable.

It is doubtful McCarthy would have visited the Illinois caucus and Mayor Daley had he been apprised of this breakfast conversation. He entered the caucus at 4:55 P.M., Abigail with him, a move calculated by Lucey, who thought that her matronly, Catholic presence might counter the downright fear and even hatred many non-McCarthy delegates had of McCarthy. He left after seventeen minutes of pleasantries. "He didn't say much," McCarthy said later. "It was what he didn't say, really. The members of the City Council came in. One of them gave me a Daley-for-Vice-President button."

McCarthy did not learn that Daley had finally stated flatly that he was unacceptable until he conferred with Unruh Monday morning. It came as no surprise. The knowledge, though, would make the necessary motions of the days to come that much more arduous.

Sunday night, police clashed with people north of the Loop in and around Lincoln Park in the neighborhood of Mother Cabrini, who rose out of labor strife to become America's first saint; the neighborhood where John Dillinger was slaughtered by J. Edgar Hoover's boys as he left the Biograph Theater, which still showed flicks; the neighborhood where the Saint Valentine's Day Massacre took place. Chicago.

DAY II: MONDAY–TUESDAY

The McCarthy people's public statements were hopeful all day Monday. Mayor Daley's delay of his endorsement, the seeming stiffening of the southern favorite sons, even the rumors of a Kennedy draft, were seen in McCarthy's favor. It was quite clear, Blair Clark declared at a press conference, that Hubert Humphrey would not be nominated on the first ballot. McCarthy did not allow himself to be as euphoric. "Campaign managers see things a little more clearly than candidates, generally, like fight managers," he said when asked about Clark's statement. "You don't challenge that. I mean, it's all right; you let them say that."

He visited caucuses of four states, submitted to some television interviews, and otherwise stayed out of the limelight.

What about this Kennedy thing? he asked Dick Goodwin, who had been in touch with Steve Smith. McCarthy commented rather hypothetically that perhaps together he and Kennedy could stop Humphrey.

He listened to various staff members who wanted him to make dramatic appearances before the convention. Norval Reece, for example, was among those who urged McCarthy to speak for the minority rules report on the convention floor. McCarthy considered and, as Reece later recalled his words, replied: "It's really a matter of whether we cross the moat and storm the walls or just camp out here in the woods. That's what it all boils down to, doesn't it?" Reece readily agreed. "If we go down, I want to go down fighting," McCarthy added, and he instructed Reece to clear his schedule for Tuesday afternoon so he could prepare a party reform speech. McCarthy worked on it a good portion of Monday night, but as events unfolded the next day, McCarthy determined that he should not go to the convention floor on that or any other issue.

Richard Goodwin, Steve Mitchell, and Tom Finney separately

urged McCarthy to speak out on the Vietnam issue at the convention. Finney worked a compromise into his idea. McCarthy, he said, should declare that if the convention adopted the peace plank he would agree in advance to follow the will of the convention in any way; to participate on the ticket in the Number 2 slot, or to give his support as an earnest and eager advocate in the event the convention wanted someone else. "It's not a bad idea," McCarthy said, though staff members who got wind of it considered it another example of Finney-style sellout. "Let me sleep on it." McCarthy did, and he decided against it.

He endured a morning staff meeting, the first chance the men running the various aspects of the convention for McCarthy had had to speak to him in a group since his arrival in Chicago. Predictably, it descended into acrimony when Tom Finney began to speak. The others did not consider him a member of the staff, though McCarthy had implored Finney to come to Chicago to act as liaison with Jesse Unruh. Steve Mitchell had refused to give him or Tom McCoy convention credentials. Finney began to inform the group that some members of the regular Georgia delegation had approached him, suggesting a compromise regarding the McCarthy credentials challenge of their delegation. Before Finney could explain the compromise idea, Mitchell cut him off. "Hell," stormed Mitchell. "What are you doing talking to the Georgia delegation?" Over the weeks Georgia had become the focal point of Mitchell's whole strategy for the convention, even over and above the Texas and unit rule challenges. He was not about to drop it now. Go ahead with it, McCarthy told Mitchell. This would be McCarthy's last campaign staff meeting.

Mitchell's convention strategy had not changed since originally enunciated earlier in the summer. "Yell foul at every turn of the screw," Mitchell's cohort Marty Gleason now outlined it. "Holler fraud generally. Put the politicians on the defensive. Put public pressure on them and get the mood of the country going against the system." This Mitchell had sought to do as he complained about poor convention facilities and called regularly for John Bailey's resignation as national chairman. Mitchell, however, had agreed to drop a plan to challenge the leadership of the convention. This meant the credentials fights would occur first. "What we hope to do with credentials," Mitchell said on the eve of the convention, "is to get the delegates in the habit of voting against Humphrey, then maybe they will vote against Humphrey as the nominee."

The strategy was almost ingenuous, for it ignored many things. It disregarded the fact that much necessary support for the peace plank might be alienated by too many challenges of too many delegates. The challenge of some northern delegates, often on shaky grounds, threatened support for the more solidly based southern challenges, Joe Rauh felt. (In the end, only three challenges, all of southern states, were argued on the floor.) And did it make sense to pin John Connally to the wall when any chance for the nomination hinged heavily on the southern favorite sons' holding firm from Humphrey? An ordinary campaign could have resolved these anomalies, but not the McCarthy campaign.

Actually, Mitchell's strategy had little to do with getting more delegates for McCarthy, and the noble end of dramatizing the undemocratic delegate selection system often seemed to get lost in the fight. Had all the McCarthy challenges been successful, he would have picked up no more than fifty additional votes. "That's an outside figure," Mitchell conceded. "I doubt that it would bring us that many."

What the whole thing really got down to was a strategy to try to embarrass Hubert Humphrey at every possible turn. This was not possible in the challenge of the Mississippi delegation on grounds of racial exclusion. Humphrey and McCarthy forces worked together on that one, a reprise, in effect, of the 1964 convention. In all the others, though, Humphrey was cast as the opponent of reform, the pal of the bosses and assorted unsavory politicians, even ones like Governor Lester Maddox, of Georgia, renowned for use of an ax handle to keep Negroes from his Atlanta restaurant. It did not help Humphrey that he had been photographed with his arm around Maddox, both of them beaming widely, after Maddox's election in 1966. The photo, blown up into a poster, was a favorite of McCarthy supporters even before the decision was made to focus on the Georgia delegation.

. . .

Washington lawyer Joe Rauh, until Vietnam one of Humphrey's stunchest supporters, had laid the Georgia plot before McCarthy during the summer: Negro leader Julian Bond and McCarthy against Lester Maddox and Hubert Humphrey. McCarthy readily agreed. "It appealed to Gene's exquisite sense of how to torture Humphrey," Rauh said later. Independently, the young national staff had come up with the same general idea and McCarthy staffer Charles Negaro was already in Atlanta working with local McCarthy supporters. Sam Brown and David Mixner flew there from Washington. Ivanhoe Donaldson, a black member of the McCarthy staff and a long-time friend of Bond, went too. Parker Hudson and Taylor Branch, the young Georgian whom Robert Kennedy had tried to talk out of the McCarthy campaign the night of the Indiana primary, joined in. Curt Gans flew in for the kill, which was to be on August 10 in Macon.

That day, a group called the Georgia Democratic Party Forum held a rump convention to select its own slate of delegates to the national convention, the first step in a challenge of Maddox's one-man rule of the Georgia delegation. The Forum had developed out of opposition to Maddox's race for governor two years earlier, its aim being to bring the Georgia Democratic party into the twentieth century. Racially mixed, the Forum was supported by substantial liberal Georgians and was, all in all, a good group. The top leadership, however, favored Hubert Humphrey. At the same time, Humphrey had not repudiated the Maddox slate. The aim of the McCarthyites was to take over the Macon rump convention and make it select a challenge slate favorable to McCarthy, thus shoving Humphrey into the arms of Maddox.

It was cold-blooded. It disregarded the risk of dividing and setting back a very important reform movement in Georgia politics. But it was successful. "Amoral," gruffed E. T. Kehrer, the convention chairman, as he stalked from the meeting hall after he had been dumped by the McCarthyites who had come from all over the state. Julian Bond and James L. Hooten, a white preacher from Savannah, were proclaimed cochairmen of the challenge delegation, made up for the most part of people who had not met before that day. Late in

August they went to Chicago, and Monday, August 26, they neared the showdown.

Julian Bond, the young, prep-school-bred, articulate, good-guy black radical who, like McCarthy, sometimes wrote poems, made a hit with the credentials committee when he testified in preconvention hearings. It quickly became apparent that any compromise would have to include Bond. Even Hubert Humphrey wanted him, though some of the regulars found this curious since they thought they had Humphrey's assurance the regulars alone would be seated. The regulars proposed sacrificing Bond if Maddox were sacrificed, which would not have been a sacrifice to party stalwarts. They had no love of Maddox either and tended to blame him for the credentials hassle. Governor Richard Hughes, of New Jersey, credentials committee chairman, refused the Maddox for Bond deal. It became moot when Maddox resigned from the Georgia delegation as the convention began to devote full time to his brief presidential candidacy.

The convention opened with the credentials committee recommending that both the full "Maddox" delegation and the full Bond delegation be seated and the Georgia vote be split between them. This would give each group twenty and one-half votes. Votes of the national committeeman and woman were not disturbed by the compromise. Both sides, however, moved to be seated alone. Thus the opening night of the convention promised the first major fight.

The opening gavel fell at 7:31 p.m., Monday, August 26, 1968, sixteen minutes after Hubert Humphrey passed through the lobby of the Conrad Hilton Hotel—through the aroma of freshly unleashed stink bombs, past the young faces jammed in the lobby yelling such things as "Humphrey is a Pig" and "We want Gene."

"The marching feet of youth have led us into a new era of politics and we can never turn back," Senator Daniel K. Inouye declared in an otherwise forgettable keynote speech.

Only a voice vote was needed to throw out the unit rule. The powers had decided that was all right, a small concession to the marching feet not only of youth but of the older McCarthy supporters, like those of the Wisconsin delegation far back on the convention floor busily dialing numbers at random on their one floor telephone. The powers had decided there was no need to provide directories. Who could possibly want to communicate at this convention? So the Wisconsinites were building their own directory of key numbers.

There had been an interim decision that neither the Bond slate nor the "regular" Georgia Democrats were to be seated before the convention voted on the compromise. But there on the floor were the regulars in the Georgia seats—handsome Lieutenant Governor George T. Smith, very relatively speaking a progressive of sorts; Bobby Pafford, a beefy crew-cut colleague of Bond in the legislature who still believed Bond was a draft card burner, which was not true; gaunt Joe Sports; national committeeman William P. Trotter, state chairman James H. Gray. The Bond contingent had found seats way back in the gallery, "like the old Jim Crow theaters in the South," Bond smiled.

Chairs on the floor were hastily provided when credentials chairman Hughes realized what had happened, and shortly before the unit rule vote, the Bond delegation slowly moved onto the floor, not totally without scuffling, a bit more of the Old South being advanced upon by marching feet. Bobby Pafford was seething.

At about this point, Jesse Unruh, of California, moved that the credentials challenges not be considered until the following day. They had originally been scheduled for Tuesday, August 27, but the powers had suddenly advanced them to early Monday, ostensibly in case Lyndon Johnson appeared at the convention Tuesday, his sixtieth birthday. The switch, Unruh complained, had left the challengers with insufficient time to prepare their cases. In the first roll call vote of the convention, Unruh's motion was defeated 1,691½ to 875. The vote was a gift to the Humphrey forces as an unexpected early test of strength on a point of no real moment, a silly mistake by Unruh, many felt.

Rapidly, by voice vote, the convention rejected challenges of the Washington, Pennsylvania, and Connecticut delegations and seated the Mississippi challengers.

At about 1:30 A.M., after two hours of argument and disruption, the convention, in its second roll call vote, seated the Connally Texans 1,368 to 955. At 2:37 A.M. the convention rejected by 1,413 to 1,041½ the effort to seat the Bond group as the sole Georgia delegation. The marching feet had been stopped. Booing erupted. The New York delegation chanted "No, no, no," gesturing with thumbs down. The Georgia regulars waved white handkerchiefs. Charles E. Anderson, a black California delegate, set fire to his credentials. Senator Inouye, temporary convention chairman, futilely sought order. John Bailey stepped to his side and glanced at his Connecticut delegation and got a motion for adjournment and the opening session was history.

North of the Loop, police clashed again with people.

DAY III: TUESDAY—WEDNESDAY

The remaining credentials contests were settled the following night to the benefit of the regulars—challenges involving Louisiana, Tennessee, North Carolina, Michigan, and Alabama. The credentials committee compromise on Georgia was accepted. There was some disruption, but it was obvious Steve Mitchell had not gotten the delegates into any habit of voting against Humphrey.

While the McCarthy people were preoccupied with the challenges, their candidate spent Tuesday doing what some thought were curious things, though they were consistent with the man. That morning in the LaSalle Hotel he was to take part in what promised to be the best show of the day: a joint appearance before the California delegation with Hubert Humphrey and George McGovern—the three candidates all in one package answering questions. McCarthy had not wanted to take part. What could he say that these delegates hadn't already heard from him in the long months of the campaign? Starting nearly a year earlier, he had visited California regularly.

"I suppose that this delegation needs to hear me less than it needs to hear any candidate in history," he told them.

Rereading the transcript of the caucus does not suggest quite the listlessness that some McCarthy diehards felt their man reflected. Norval Reece, in charge of preparing McCarthy for the caucus, listened to his man with growing despair as McCarthy declined to answer a question about his views on Vietnam because, he said, his views were well known. "I could feel my feet moving," Reece said later. "I wanted to walk across that platform and give him a note to get up and speak." Reece did not, nor did he when McCarthy prefaced his closing summary by remarking that to squeeze nine months into three minutes "is a little like building boats in a bottle." The critics gave McGovern the highest ratings. Though he said nothing remarkable, he said it well, and he was still a new figure for tired reporters to write about. Hubert Humphrey was Hubert Humphrey, and he passed the hour and forty-five minutes of the caucus without saying what McCarthy was listening for: some indication, however small, that he was willing to compromise in some way on Vietnam.

"The road block to peace, my dear friends," Humphrey said when asked about Vietnam, "is not in Washington, D.C. It is in Hanoi. And we ought to recognize it as such."

"It was a total defense of administration policy," McCarthy said later. "All he regretted was that it hadn't worked." Humphrey had closed another door on early support by McCarthy.

McCarthy made a couple of other stops that day, one at the West Virginia caucus, where he got off one of those statements that glazed many delegates' eyes. "I am here as one of those who is asking you to include me in your general examination of candidates and to consider me as you move on to make that most important judgment," he said. It was McCarthy's last formal pitch for votes.

That Tuesday he began to complain in private conversation about the peace plank turned out by Goodwin and the others. This was a curious development, since he had left the matter in Goodwin's hands and had not complained during the drafting. Not only had it excluded points he had once demanded, he said, but it was badly constructed. By this time he had no intention of appearing on the convention floor on any issue unless Lyndon Johnson showed up at the Amphitheater, but he would find it difficult to speak up for this plank in any event.

Pat Lucey, when it was all over, would list "six body blows" he felt helped beat the life out of the final McCarthy effort in Chicago. In no particular order of importance were:

1. McCarthy's Czech crisis statement. While honest and even accurate, it was not political. Lucey got feedback from wavering politicians across the country.

2. The California caucus. Again, McCarthy had disappointed.

3. A final Harris poll released late Monday night that showed McCarthy with no edge over Humphrey in a race against Richard Nixon. Both candidates and even Lyndon Johnson were shown trailing by six percentage points when pitted against the Republican candidate. The main argument of the McCarthyites, that McCarthy was a winner and Humphrey the loser, was riddled, though they had good reason to question the polls' accuracy, so consistently had their man been underpredicted through the year.

4. Collapse of the "southern strategy." Late Monday, the southern favorite sons began returning to the Humphrey fold as the Kennedy boomlet broadened.

5. Collapse of the Kennedy candidacy, which many McCarthy aides had counted on to help block Humphrey on the first ballot. Everything revolved around stopping Humphrey for one ballot—southern strategy, Kennedy strategy, the urgings of some McCarthy supporters that uncertain delegates support even George McGovern if they couldn't yet bring themselves to acceptance of McCarthy.

6. The "Knight interview," as it was called. In it, McCarthy as much as conceded publicly, a full day before nomination of the presidential candidate, that Hubert Humphrey had it in the bag. Again it was an honest statement, but of the sort that could drive political handlers mad, for your man just doesn't concede defeat before the fact at a national convention unless you have sealed whatever deal may be in mind.

But McCarthy abandoned the usual rules as he sat down in his Hilton suite before the large windows overlooking Grant Park Tuesday afternoon and propped his legs on a coffee table and started answering the questions of newspaper owner John Knight and several other members of the Knight organization.

At no time did McCarthy stipulate that his comments could not be used immediately, though he later sheltered himself from the fallout that developed by suggesting he had understood the interview would not be published until after the nomination, one of the few evasions he allowed himself during the campaign.

The interviewers had barely gotten through the opening pleasantries when McCarthy offered:

"I think it probably was settled more than twenty-four hours ago."

QUESTION: You mean it's wrapped up for Humphrey?

McCARTHY: I think so.

The Knight men realized instantly they had a journalistic scoop. They glanced at one another surreptitiously, and at the tape recorder to make sure it was still working. They could barely contain themselves as they returned to their office to transcribe the tape. They finished the job at 6 P.M. A short time later one of the Knight men leaked the copyrighted interview to United Press International. Not long after that, the UPI wires at the convention hall were setting off one of the many shock waves of the evening.

McCarthy said a number of other things in the interview; that Nixon would probably beat Humphrey in November, that he might retire from the Senate after his term ended in 1970 ("Once you've made the run for President out of a Senate job you ought to quit. Otherwise, you're like Lazarus coming back from the dead"), that he might run for President again. And he said he doubted that Ted Kennedy could win the nomination if his name were entered officially.

Shortly after the Knight men left, Stephen Smith entered the McCarthy suite. The two men talked about Ted Kennedy and the presidential nomination.

The Kennedy phenomenon had been building since Sunday, when a draft headquarters opened in the Sherman House and hundreds of volunteers out of nowhere began distributing Kennedy buttons and placards, many of them handmade. All through Monday and into Tuesday the wheels turned, Smith's suite at the Standard Club and even the McGovern presidential headquarters at the Sheraton-Blackstone becoming centers of activity. Disclaimers of sorts came from Kennedy people. It was disclosed that Kennedy had asked former Ohio Governor Mike DiSalle to drop his six-week-old intention of placing Kennedy's name in nomination, but the move was more to take nominal leadership of the draft drive from DiSalle's hands than to kill it. DiSalle, it was felt, was not the man to lead, should a real draft start blowing. Jesse Unruh played every bounce. Late Tuesday he formally reserved the right for California to make a nomination. He talked to Kennedy on the phone. One conversation with Abe Ribicoff even got to the point of discussing a Kennedy running mate. McGovern would be good, Unruh offered.

The man who mattered most in all this, Richard Daley, adamantly continued to refuse to commit himself unless Kennedy flatly gave a go-ahead. A good half-dozen phone calls between Daley and Kennedy failed to resolve the impasse. Political reporters who knew Daley best steadfastly maintained Daley would surely announce his support of Humphrey when the dust settled. They knew he rarely played his cards until the last moment, preferring to await the unforeseen event that might change everything. Some would suggest that Daley's main intent in Chicago was to add a bit of suspense to a foregone conclusion and perhaps euchre Ted Kennedy into a vice-presidential nomination, a ploy the Kennedy people were guarding against at each turn. Others felt his real hope was to pull a Johnson-Kennedy ticket out of the growing chaos, and there was some evidence of this.

In any event, by Tuesday afternoon, Daley was tiring of the game and becoming increasingly irritated at what he considered Kennedy's lack of resolve. He felt the draft lacked for direction and a solid assessment by Kennedy or his supporters of their potential strength. "That young man has got to learn to count," Daley said at one point, according to one good source. "Jack Kennedy knew how to count and Bob Kennedy knew how to count and that young man had better learn quick. That young man has got to learn to read a map or he's going to end up in the lake."

McCarthy could count, mainly with his senses. He sensed the peace position at the convention had about a thousand supporters, which was only a few votes off, and he figured that Kennedy could get only about nine hundred votes and probably no more, so locked up had the convention become by the hour of McCarthy's meeting with Stephen Smith.

It was with this conviction that McCarthy offered to urge his people to vote for Ted Kennedy if Kennedy were willing to run. McCarthy told Smith that he wanted his own name placed in nomination for the sake of the people who had campaigned so hard for him and have a run for it on the first ballot, even though he knew he couldn't make it. If it were felt this wouldn't work or would weaken the cause, he would forgo even this. "I did say," McCarthy wrote in his book *Year of the People*, "that because of the campaign which had been run against me, I could not have done the same for Senator Robert Kennedy." Again he had made an honest but impolitic remark. Kennedy support for McCarthy was not offered then, nor had it ever been. Smith went away from the secret meeting unconvinced of McCarthy's sincerity. Smith had asked McCarthy for nothing and had stressed Teddy's noncandidacy, but back at Smith's suite in the Standard Club, the wheels of the possible candidacy continued to move.

Young Kennedy supporters flowed about the convention floor as the second session convened that evening. California supporters circulated a petition calling for Kennedy's nomination. Allard Lowenstein continued to urge delegates to contact Smith to urge Teddy to run. The Kennedy "boiler room girls," working in Chicago for McGovern, began doing double duty. Groups of McCarthy supporters and staffers were actively drum-beating a Kennedy candidacy. Ribicoff and Unruh met again in the Amphitheater and decided to hurry to Smith's suite. Ribicoff had to invoke his status as a United States Senator to get Unruh out of the convention hall when Unruh's plastic credential failed to turn on the green light of one of the ominous entry-exit security machines. Unable to find Ribicoff's car in the parking lot, they bummed a ride in an American Airlines limousine. The Keystone Cops aspect of the whole thing was heightened by the fact that, unknown to the two of them, Daley had ended the whole affair shortly after Smith's visit with McCarthy.

In one final phone call to Kennedy, Daley angrily berated Kennedy's ambivalence and said he would wait no longer. Soon after, Daley phoned Humphrey to tell him that Humphrey had Daley's support. Even as Ribicoff and Unruh were arriving at the Standard Club, even as the pro-Kennedy floor activity heightened, Daley made it known he thought it looked as if Humphrey had the nomination, and Kennedy began drafting the unequivocal statement of nonavailability he would make public the next morning.

All this was not general knowledge when David Schoumacher at 8:27 P.M. reported on CBS that Stephen Smith, in a *two-hour* meeting with Eugene McCarthy a short time earlier, had *asked McCarthy support* for Ted Kennedy. Only the fact of the meeting, which lasted fifteen minutes, was accurate. Smith, infuriated, demanded a denial. Richard Goodwin, who with Pat Lucey had arranged the meeting, confirmed it on television but denied Smith had sought support. Before a further denial from McCarthy himself could be aired, the UPI leak of the Knight "concession" interview reached the convention floor.

The chaos of the convention hall now mounted. The television floor men sought to straighten out the reports while keeping up with still later ones: Kennedy won't turn down a genuine draft, says Lester Hyman, of Massachusetts; Humphrey man Delton L. Hutchens, of Missouri, says he has information Kennedy would accept the vice-presidential nomination if offered; McCarthy will come to the floor to speak on the Vietnam issue; McCarthy won't come to the floor to speak on the Vietnam issue. Violence outside the Conrad Hilton.

Each report broke on another, the entire evening suddenly a jumble of moments: Betty Furness makes a speech. Anita Bryant sings "Happy Birthday" to Lyndon Johnson. Shouts of "Peace Now" at the Hilton.

Out of this surrealism came the one bright moment of the convention. Near midnight, convention chairman Carl Albert announced that by a vote of 1,350 to 1,206 a minority report from the rules committee had passed. Thereafter, the unit rule was to be barred in selection of delegates clear down to the local level; delegates were to be selected within the calendar year of a convention; party processes were to be opened to public participation as a strict policy; efforts to improve the workings of the national convention were to be undertaken.

The voting had run wildly. Such states as Maryland and Missouri, which had systems as boss-controlled and closed to grass-roots participation as any, voted solidly for the reform position. On all other votes they were just as solidly anti-McCarthy. "Many of those delegates didn't realize what they were actually voting on," declared Eli Segal, one of the McCarthy workers who had quietly put together the winning package. Many delegates obviously thought they were merely outlawing the unit rule for the 1972 convention, as they had done the night before by voice vote for the 1968 convention. The McCarthy campaigners had purposely not sought to explain the full import of the measure to anyone not curious enough to ask. In spite of itself, the Democratic party had acted to democratize itself in the most momentous action since abandonment of the two-thirds rule in 1936.

The euphoria was short-lived. The powers sought to push ahead with the debate on Vietnam as the clock moved into the first hour of Wednesday. Shouting and jeering broke out, for if the debate were held at that hour no one would be up to watch on TV. Donald Peterson, of Wisconsin, yelled to be recognized. Carl Albert finally allowed him to speak.

"I think every delegate in this hall wants to go to bed," he cried, and moved for adjournment.

"The motion to adjourn is not a recognizable motion," Albert declared, setting off a louder volley of catcalls.

"The convention will be in order."

"No, no, no, no."

For two minutes the tumult resounded.

"Will the convention be in order?"

"No, no, let's go home, let's go home."

Albert, shouting, declared, "The convention will be in order. The chair recognizes the mayor of Chicago."

He stood now at his place on the floor in the Illinois delegation, which was right at the foot of the speaker's podium. Daley turned colors when he was angry, red deepening into purple. He was nearing purple now as he stormed: "This convention is held for delegates of the great Democratic party and not for the people in the balconies trying to take over this meeting. And if they don't . . . we'll turn them out. Mr. Chairman, they're here as guests of the Democratic party and let them conduct themselves accordingly or clear the gallery. . . ."

The shouting became louder now and the mayor more purple. For the shouting was not from the balconies. It was from the delegates at the rear of the floor where, it happened, most of the McCarthy contingents had been placed. Daley was used to ruly crowds, like the ones he would pack into the City Council Chambers when controversial issues were expected. This could never have happened in the council chambers.

"Will the convention be in order?" Albert implored. "Will the convention . . . will the convention . . . will the sergeant-at-arms enforce order in the convention. . . ."

Daley made a slashing motion across his neck with one hand. Albert immediately recognized him for a motion to adjourn.

At 1:17 A.M. Wednesday, August 28, the second session of the thirty-fifth quadrennial Democratic National Convention was officially gaveled to a close. The shouting did not die down until sometime later.

Eugene McCarthy was in his hotel suite as the convention was approaching this hour of tumult, the television set on, occasional shouts of "Peace now" floating up from the streets, the conversation in the room touching on many things, not all of them political. Robert Healy, of the Boston *Globe,* another of McCarthy's reporter friends, was there and captured the flavor. This is part of what Healy recorded:

McCarthy sat down on the green sofa and raised his feet to the coffee table. Across from him sat Robert Lowell, the poet. McCarthy suggested that the campaign had made Lowell look younger, and then he asked: "What new creaks have you heard in the morning?"

While Lowell thought for a moment, McCarthy remembered that some wild prairie flowers have a particular creak when they open in the morning, and that old houses have a special kind of creak early in the day, one that they do not have later on when the sun has dried their moisture.

It was 11:15 P.M. and two quiet men were casually discussing flowers, old houses and advancing age. . . . They talked easily about the sweater mills and sawmills they trudged through in New Hampshire.

And McCarthy asked Lowell if he knew that older men become far-sighted "so they can see the enemy coming," and older women become near-sighted. The explanation of this had something to do with saving them from seeing what goes on around the house.

They talked, too, about horses. "You didn't know that old horses never lie down until they're ready to die?" he asked rhetorically.

The chant outside continued and it grew.

"Peace now . . . peace now . . . peace now. . . ."

Blair Clark broke in and told the senator that he had told his aide, Sam Brown, to get his counterpart in Vice-President Humphrey's camp to go out in the streets and watch over the demonstrators to make sure their heads were not smashed as they were the night before.

"That's a good idea," said McCarthy.

Six hours earlier, Senator McCarthy's campaign for President had died in that same suite.

It came at a meeting between him and Stephen Smith of New York, brother-in-law of Senator Edward Kennedy. . . .

There was a trace of bitterness but no tears as McCarthy reluctantly talked of his meeting with Smith.

Now, six hours later, the senator spoke of Moses leading his people to the promised land. But, he said, Moses never took his people into the promised land. Aaron did. Aaron, McCarthy suggested, was the advance man for Moses.

"Moses made the long journey . . . but, you know, maybe he was lucky. The truth is, the promised land always looks better from a distance."

. . . He was bitter about newspapers. Someone warned him that if he said that publicly, it would sound like Richard Nixon's last remarks to the press after his defeat for governor of California.

"Why not? It's true," said McCarthy.

Then he turned to the subject of Ted Kennedy.

"Do you think he will have the guts to get in?" McCarthy asked. "He might get beaten, you know. He might not be able to win the nomination from Humphrey . . . even with my support. . . ."

Then he talked of Robert Kennedy. He said that if Kennedy had not gotten into the fight, he would be the nominee of the Democratic Party.

"Sure, you know, I would have been the fellow that brought down the President."

In the end "they would have turned to him [Kennedy]."

It was late now. McCarthy looked tired. It was suggested that he might go to the amphitheater and speak to the convention on the platform fight.

But he would not do it. The McCarthy crusade—which began in those New Hampshire hills where young men shaved clean for Gene and young girls wore longer than mini skirts for the cause—was over.

It ended in a suite of the Conrad Hilton. Twenty-three floors below his constituency sat on the grass of Grant Park and sang . . . inside an iron ring of Chicago policemen.

DAY IV: WEDNESDAY—THURSDAY

Early in August, McCarthy had publicly appealed to young supporters thinking of going to Chicago to stay home. He also had his staff contact numerous student leaders to relay the same message to their friends. Before the convention, he spoke to Mayor Daley by phone offering to be of any help he could in dealing with problems that might develop at the convention. Daley made no suggestions and never asked McCarthy for any.

Now, on Wednesday in Chicago, the day of climax, what with the Vietnam plank fight and the nomination scheduled, most of those who did come were prepared as best they could be for the finish. They roamed Grant Park as tourists, not yet a part of it. They would stay with their crusade at least through the moment of execution.

South Dakota delegates were passing out black arm bands within an hour after the debate on Vietnam began at 12:41 P.M. Wednesday, August 28, 1968. The conclusion was foregone. The words that had been labored over no longer meant anything. For the result would mean only that the administration had won.

Hale Boggs had the last word. He raised the Commie scare with remarks about Czechoslovakia and Soviet aid to the Arabs in the Middle East, and this led nicely into his final statement about Vietnam, which was to read the message from General Creighton W. Abrams on probable effects of a total bombing halt: " 'If the bombing now authorized were to be suspended unilaterally, the enemy in ten days to two weeks could develop a capability in the DMZ area in terms of scale, intensity and duration of combat on the order of five times what he now has,' " read Boggs.

"I cannot agree to place our forces at the risk which the enemy's capability would then pose. That, my friends, concludes our debate."

The violence was heating up in Grant Park across from the Hilton once again as Boggs put the exclamation mark on his last words. On the fifteenth floor of the Hilton, the young McCarthy people watched television screens disconsolately.

The roll call on Lyndon Johnson's war began. It got to New Hampshire. Twenty-three for the peace plank. Three against. "It's so nostalgic," murmured Nancy Perlman, remembering how she had helped get those twenty-three votes.

The roll call went on and it became obvious how it was weighted. "It's absurd," said Cindy Samuels.

A chorus of oinks, grunts, and snarls sounded when Mayor Daley's face appeared on the screen to say that 105 of Illinois' 118 votes were for studying war some more. Tom Saltonstall rolled over on a bed and covered his head with a blanket.

"It's unbelievable," said Mary Davis as the roll call continued down to Texas. John Connally announced a unanimous delegation for war. "There were at least fifteen McCarthy people in that delegation," one of the young people gasped. "Their lives must have been threatened."

"I wonder how many of those delegates really read the platform and the minority report," said Cindy Samuels. "I really wonder."

It was over by 4:39 P.M. Peace was defeated 1,567¾ to 1,041¼. Delegates from primary states, where the people had had a role in their selection, voted two to one for the peace plank. The states where the people had had less of a role—in some cases no role—in choosing delegates went three to one against.

"We Shall Overcome" and the "Battle Hymn of the Republic" rose from the New York delegation. California joined in. The voices grew and Carl Albert banged his gavel, and then the official convention orchestra blew down the voices of peace with military marches.

·   ·   ·

The condemned man looks out the window of his Hilton room. Another crowd is gathering in the park intending to walk to the Amphitheater for the evening session. "Look at them," McCarthy says:

The police have cut them off. They told them they could march, and they've surrounded them. It's the way we treated the Indians. We always told them we were taking them to a happier hunting ground and then we surrounded them. The country is like that. Milling around, ready to march, and nowhere to go.

I just told them downstairs this movement will go on because it doesn't depend on structure or organization but just on what is in people themselves. It's like striking a hammer on the anvil. It rings forever. It's like infinity.

Daley packs the convention galleries that evening with payrollers and their relatives carrying "We Love Mayor Daley" signs. The powers will not let authorized McCarthy signs in the hall. They have to be smuggled in. The band plays, "Hail, Hail, the Gang's All Here."

Outside the Conrad Hilton what comes to be known as the "police riot" is unfolding as dusk settles. Police are surging into the mobs, swinging their clubs indiscriminately. "The whole world is watching, the whole world is watching," chants the crowd on the fringe of the violence.

McCarthy is watching from his twenty-third-floor window. "It's worse than Prague," he says. Now the demonstrators are not like Indians surrounded; it is as if they are trapped in one of Hannibal's double envelopment movements, he says. There on Michigan Avenue is the main body, the police. He points out the window. Back in the trees east of Michigan Avenue, he says, is the National Guard. When the battle gets rough, the Guard will move around the flanks of the battlers in the classic double envelopment movement. "A ballet of purgatory," he says.

What he is seeing twenty-three stories below keeps his mind racing from allusion to allusion, almost as if trying to escape the reality of the sight. Now it is "rather like a medieval battle," he says. One can imagine hearing his voice coming over a radio, broadcasting what is happening, and it is compelling and frightening:

The police have surrounded the kids in the park and the kids can't get in or out. You'd think they'd have enough sense to open some kind of small funnel to let the kids out and stop the total confrontation. You know, I think a lot of these kids are already sick of this thing and would like to get out. If they could get out and go their own way and mind their own business. But the police are not prepared to let them. You know, the thing that concerns me as I watch this thing is that this country could become the first democratic police state. If this continues much longer—this sort of thing—you're going to find, I'm afraid, a violent reaction to the right. People are not going to tolerate this sort of thing. And there are going to be demands for repression which are going to destroy a large portion of the greatness of this country.

Kimberly Brangwin, nineteen, had not joined the campaign until it got to Oregon. She could not leave it after that. She returned to the University of Washington long enough to finish final exams, sell her books and clothes, and prevail on local McCarthy supporters for enough money to get her to New York for that primary. She worked through the summer in the Washington headquarters. Now she is in the lobby of the Hilton, gagging on the tear gas that has drifted in. She goes outside to see if she can help anyone. She sees someone with a battered head through the scuffling feet and legs, and she kneels down to try to help the person get to the makeshift hospital the young people have set up on the fifteenth floor of the Hilton. A policeman's club comes crashing down on her back.

David Mixner, twenty-three, who survived an auto accident in North Carolina and a plane crash in Texas while organizing for McCarthy, is suddenly trapped with other people against the big window of the Hilton's Haymarket Lounge facing Michigan Avenue. The blue helmets keep pressing in. It is not double envelopment, or being surrounded; it is massacre. The heavy window of the lounge caves in from the weight of the people. Mixner and several others fall into the lounge, the police running in over them, batting at them, chasing people who run through the window right through the bar where people are drinking. Mixner's leg is badly cut, but he pulls himself and a companion away from the police and makes it to State Street, where he ducks into the subway.

McCarthy is on the fifteenth floor now where his brother Austin, a surgeon, and his friend Dr. William Davidson are helping the injured who are being brought into the hotel by McCarthy staffers. There is rage in him as he looks at the bloodied young faces. "We're trying to heal the wounded. That's all we ever tried to do," he says softly. The rage suddenly bursts out of him. He yells at some photographers to get the hell out.

The violence is even in the convention hall. When McCarthy returns to his room, the television set is showing a scuffle of some sort inside the Amphitheater. A cadre of guards is dragging away Alex J. Rosenberg, Howard R. Moody, and Paul O'Dwyer of the New York delegation as helmeted Chicago police pour onto the floor. Rosenberg has refused to show his credentials to a security guard, and he is being expelled. They take away O'Dwyer and Moody when the two men come to Rosenberg's aid, and they shove them into a back room and question them for thirty minutes. Mike Wallace, the TV newsman, is pushed around and taken into custody temporarily.

McCarthy is beside himself as the violence continues. There is too much madness. Shortly after balloting for the presidential nomination begins, McCarthy calls Governor Harold Hughes, of Iowa, and says to remove his name. Maybe somehow this might end the madness, the violence. But it is too late. And he owes it to the people who have worked for him to stay in, Hughes tells him. McCarthy, a man who has "caused a clean wind of hope to blow across this land," Hughes says in his nominating speech, a man the Democrats cannot claim to have found because "the people found Gene McCarthy for us. They found him; they followed him; they have urged him on us. He is more accurately the people's candidate than any other man in recent history."

Tear-gas clouds rise outside the Hilton. Policemen on motorcycles drive right into a crowd. McCarthy will get 601 votes to Humphrey's 1,760¼ this night.

Julian Bond and Kenneth Galbraith second the McCarthy nomination. "The American people are demanding a fundamental change that, I think, is the great lesson of the campaign of 1968," says Bond. "They are demanding an end to the politics of unfulfilled promises and exaggeration, an end to the politics of manipulation and control...."

"He has shown that resort to violence first destroys those who employ it," says Galbraith. "His campaign has shown that this may not be the age of John Milton, but he has shown that it is not the age of John Wayne or even of John Connally."

The wounded keep pouring into the fifteenth-floor hospital. Young Anne Jackson watches and she looks out a window at what is still happening below. Finally she cannot stand it. Her hands shaking, she sits at the Telex machine that connects the McCarthy Hilton headquarters with the Amphitheater command post. Her fingers stutter on the keyboard as she tries to send the news of what is happening to the Amphitheater:

V
McCARTHY CGO
THIS IS ANNE

THE FRONT OF HILTON IS BLOODY   D PEOPLE ARE BEING BROUGHT IN HERE TO FIRST AID STATION WHICH IS ACRROSS THE HALL FROM US AND THEY HAVE GASHED GAPS AND GOD IT CANT BE DESCRIBED   THE Y ARE BEING POUNDED ON I   IS THE MOST UNSLIGHTLIEST MESS I HAVE EVER SEEN

PLEASE PLEASE PASS THIS INFO ON TO CURT AND DON TELL EVERYP EVERY ONE AND IT IS A SE SCEENE THAT SHOWS THE TRUE COLORS   THE NEWSMEN ARE GETTING IT MUCH WORSE THAN THE DEO DEMONSTRATORS BE CAUSE THEY DONT WANT THE THEM TO PUBLISH OR SHOW THIS SCENE SADISTIC OR MASOCHISTIC SCEENE   YOU WOULD NEVER BELIEVE YOUR EYES   OUR STAFF IS IN HYSTERIA   IT IS TOO MUCH   I JUST DONT BELIEVE THAT I SE   SEE O AL OF THIS   GOD PLEASE HELP US PLEASE HURRY UP

Little news of the Hilton violence has gotten to the convention floor. Because film footage has to be processed, the worst scenes are not shown on television immediately. On-scene radio and wire service reports are still sketchy. Anne Jackson's message is one of the first solid indications of the degree of the horror that is happening while the Democrats move toward nomination of a presidential candidate. The people in the McCarthy command post quickly duplicate Anne Jackson's dispatch and distribute it to delegates on the floor. The wire reports soon follow, and the television pictures soon flash in the amphitheater delegate lounges, and for the first time the delegates begin to realize what is happening. Favorite son Governor Dan K. Moore, of North Carolina, McCarthy, and Humphrey have been nominated by this time. The call of the roll has gotten to Colorado. Now, at 10:03 P.M., Colorado delegation chairman Robert Maytag asks the chair if there is any way "Mayor Daley can be compelled to suspend the police state tactics" used by Chicago police outside the Hilton. Carl Albert rules Maytag out of order.

Abraham Ribicoff stands at the speaker's podium now, at 10:07 P.M., to nominate George McGovern. "With George McGovern," Ribicoff declares, "we wouldn't have Gestapo tactics on the streets of Chicago." Cheers and boos break out. Mayor Daley's face is angry. His mouth is forming words that cannot be heard, but they are angry words. "How hard it is to accept the truth," says Ribicoff, glowering at Daley a few yards away. "How hard it is to accept the truth in facing the problems of our nation...."

The New Hampshire delegation seeks to have the convention adjourned until violence ends, but is ignored. Donald Peterson, of Wisconsin, moves that the convention be adjourned and reconvened two weeks later in another city. He is gaveled down, and shouting erupts once more throughout the convention hall.

Wendy Anne Robineau, twenty-one, a University of Connecticut dropout who has been in the campaign since New Hampshire, is working in the McCarthy Amphitheater command post answering phones, juggling fifteen or twenty calls at a time, outwardly calm, her voice steady, but tears streaming down her face as she watches the scenes of people being clubbed in the street on one television set and Donald Peterson being gaveled down on another. And all at once it seems it is Carl Albert pounding his gavel on the heads of the people outside the Hilton and the police gaveling down Peterson with their clubs in the hall. The tears pour from her eyes as the phones ring and helpless rage wells inside her and in this atmosphere Hubert Humphrey is chosen to run for President of the United States. The execution is completed. When the delegates return to the Hilton after midnight, the voices are waiting to tell them what they have done.

"The party is dead. You killed the party," the voices chant.

The McCarthy delegates and workers went to Grant Park in a candle-lit procession early Thursday while darkness still clung, the smell of the candles mingling with the tear gas yet in the air and the smoke from scattered bonfires in the park. Don Peterson and Paul O'Dwyer and Richard Goodwin were there. Midge Miller and John Meloney and Jed Shilling and Eleanor Slater were there. Lance Dublin from the mimeograph room was there, seventy-two sleepless hours behind him. John Shattuck and Ellen Perlmutter and Wendy Robineau were there. David Mixner had limped there from the subway where he had hidden from the police. They *all* were there, for this is where the long crusade had ended. It was not a wake, but an epiphany, and their voices rose strongly in song, drowning out the occasional sob.

DAY V: THURSDAY—FRIDAY

The young people wore a new campaign button Thursday morning. It was a blank white button, not even one word on it, designed by Don Green. They were through with presidential politics for the year, a few forever. They would never work for Hubert Humphrey. "How can I work for a war criminal?" Sam Brown would say when a Humphrey man approached him. Humphrey may have gotten the nomination at the Amphitheater the night before, but he lost the election in the streets outside the Hilton in the same hour.

There was no further reason for staying. But no one seemed to know what to do. How do you begin to say good-bye? From the snows of New Hampshire. Only yesterday.

Eugene McCarthy began the withdrawal process in the afternoon. He appeared before his volunteer army in valediction. The voices rose again when he came before them in the Hilton's Florentine Room, this man of the campaign poster that read, "He stood up alone and something happened."

"We want Gene, we want Gene!" the voices repeated, and once again the V signs were there.

What memories were evoked in this moment? "If elected I will go to the Pentagon," he had said. That had been a favorite, and there were others—how he'd take down the fence around the White House; that poster that said "A Breath of Fresh Air."

"We want Gene, we want Gene...."

Finally they quieted and the ex-candidate spoke.

"I may be visibly moved," he smiled. "I have been very careful not to be visibly moved throughout my campaign. If you people keep on this way, I may—as we say—'lose my cool.'"

Laughter and tears.

"I may not show active compassion; but I may show a kind of participatory joy," which, he added, was "kind of a dangerous thing."

They listened closely. He recited poetry. Lines from one of his favorites, Vernon Watkins—lines with a personal meaning for this fifty-three-year-old Senator.

> It was in the spring that all was sung.
> But it was the autumn that made me young.

He could not leave out his friend Robert Lowell:

> The sound of man thinning out his kind
> Breaks with the Sabbath noon
> The blind swipe of the pruner and his knife
> Busy about the tree of life.

He recalled once again the goals of his campaign: Vietnam, America's priorities, "a basic question about the processes of American government and of American politics."

"I think that the country has passed a judgment on the war," he said. "Our failure here was not with the people, not with reference to our not having accomplished our purpose—because we did accomplish that. It was only that the judgment of the people could somehow not be put through the procedures of politics in 1968. And I don't say that we have altogether failed as yet. But in any case, we have tested the process and we have found its weaknesses."

He mentioned the convention, and a voice in the back of the room yelled, "Forget the convention."

"We have forgotten the convention," McCarthy said. "We are beyond the convention. We have forgotten the vice-presidency. We have forgotten the platform. And we have forgotten the national chairman of the Democratic party."

The voices chanted for Gene again and the V signs reappeared, and McCarthy said:

So what we do is to go on, to continue to present to the people as best we can for judgment between now and November the issues we have been raising for nine months in this country. We will continue to demand explanations from the candidates. But more important than that, we will proceed as best we can to support those candidates, particularly for the United States Senate, who have stood with us, and to identify those issues with our candidates. . . .

We have not lost the fight on the issue. We have not lost it in terms of the potential of the American system to respond in a time of need such as this. We have had a great victory to this point, one which should reassure us about the system itself. But more important than that, if we had any doubts—and I think most of us really were without doubt early—about the people of this country, I think we are on the way in 1968 to preparing the way for the judgments that need to be made, perhaps somewhat less clearly, perhaps without getting less credit than we might have liked if we had the White House. But we are willing to share that, and to forgo it, if we can accomplish these things for the country. I think that the outlook is one that must be reassuring: one of confidence and one of optimism—not really of our own making, but by virtue of our having discovered it to exist in the minds and in the hearts of the people of this country. Your credit is not altogether in putting it there—excepting insofar as you yourselves had it—nor is my credit.

But I think that we can say that we were willing to open the box and to see what America was. We had that kind of trust and that kind of confidence. And when we opened it, we found that the people of this nation were not wanting.

A bit later, to the dismay of his Secret Service agents, McCarthy went to Grant Park. The sea of blue-helmeted policemen and olive drab National Guardsmen parted, and McCarthy crossed Michigan Avenue, dry-shod, to the park. One guardsman lowered his rifle with its sheathed bayonet to block a young supporter who followed a pace behind. Blair Clark flicked the bayonet aside. "Don't be a fool, my good man," he said.

After Dick Gregory had introduced him, calling him a "Soul Brother," McCarthy stood under an elm tree with a red balloon in its branches and held a microphone as he greeted "the government in exile." The throng, mostly young, sat in the dust of the battlefield and listened, shushing the inevitable derision that came from some.

Shouts of "No!" came when he said that they would continue to work within the system.

"Yes," McCarthy shot back. Then he turned the grumbling to cheers. "I will not endorse either of them." So much for Nixon and for Hubert Humphrey, who at that moment was telling a press conference in the Hilton his running mate would be Edmund Muskie.

"I am prepared to stay with the issues so long as I have a constituency," McCarthy said, "and I still have a constituency."

The sun shone and a refreshing breeze touched the park. They listened.

He recalled how he had said if he were elected that "instead of riots and protest we would have dancing in the streets. I haven't been nominated and elected; but I do hope that we are on the way of opening up hope and confidence and some spirit of optimism."

Words of optimism uttered on a losing battlefield? No castigation for the brutish victors? "I never tell them what they want to hear," McCarthy reminded an aide.

He closed with some thoughts that had ended many of his speeches over the nine months. The words rang like a chapel bell in a devastated village:

So let us be prepared to make mistakes, if we must make them, on the side of trust rather than on the side of mistrust in our fellow men or in other peoples around the world. Let us be prepared to make mistakes on the side of hope instead of on the side of despair and fear, whether we look to the present or whether we look to the future.

This should be your spirit. This has been the spirit of my campaign. And we can, I think, make it the spirit and the basis of action in the United States of America and in those things around the world in which we have some influence and some force.

So let us go from here to do the thing we can do, and not worry about what we cannot do; here this afternoon, to make the kind of commitment, as I made it to you and as you have made it to me.

It seemed the fitting way to close the book. Chicago would not have it so.

That night Jed Shilling, a McCarthy researcher, was taken into custody for carrying ripped sheets from the Hilton for use as bandages and gas masks in Grant Park, where sporadic violence had resumed as darkness fell. As he sat in the makeshift police headquarters in the basement of the Conrad Hilton, he heard some officers talking about the fifteenth floor and how troublesome it was and that they would have to do something about it.

Shortly after 5 A.M., Friday, August 30, 1968, the police did something about it.

A party had been going on in one suite, where twenty or thirty McCarthy staffers reminisced about the campaign. Others sat in a corridor, singing. Some played bridge. Others, exhausted, were asleep in other rooms.

A handful of policemen suddenly entered the room where the party was underway. Everyone would have to leave, the McCarthy staffers were told, because objects had been thrown from the windows of the room. A McCarthy staff man, George Yumich, thirty-one, began to argue. John Warren, twenty-four, cooled Yumich down. The matter seemed on the way to solution.

But then National Guard troops poured onto the floor. More policemen arrived and a hotel security man barged into the room and began ranting that these people must be gotten out because the room wasn't registered to them. (It had been registered to John Kenneth Galbraith and also used as a general working area.) A police lieutenant told the hotel man to calm down, that these people would leave peacefully. "Oh shut up," yelled the hotel official. "You're a bother."

The sudden appearance of an army in the corridors had set off screaming, and now the police snapped again. They began to hustle the McCarthy people out of the room to the elevators. Warren, becoming angry, asked a policeman to take it easy. "Don't complain to me," an officer barked. As he was shoved into the elevator well, Warren saw Yumich being clubbed to the floor.

Warren stumbled over a coffee table and reached down instinctively. He began to pick it up. "Put the table down," screamed Kathy Anderson, twenty, another young staffer.

In the next instant, Warren felt what he thought was Mace stinging his face and eyes, then a club coming down on his head. Police would say later he hit one of them with the table. Warren would say that wasn't true.

The screaming had become hysterical. The raid on one room now became a general expulsion of people from the floor. "Ninety per cent of you don't work for McCarthy," screeched the hotel man.

Philip Shear, sixteen, a Sherman Oaks, California, high-school student, had been asleep in one room when police pulled him from bed and dragged him to the elevators, clubbing him.

When she heard police shouts of "Get out," Ellen Perlmutter thought they meant to get out of the corridors and went to her room. A policeman followed her, yelling at her to pack and get out of the hotel. As she frantically threw things into a suitcase and tried to shut it, the policeman scattered papers and campaign records on a table with his club and took a swing at the shower curtain to make sure no one was behind it.

John Shattuck had left the chain on his door when he went to sleep. The police tried but could not get in. Another young staffer, Cherie Block, had hardly slept since Monday. The hammering at the door of her room spurred a half-waking nightmare that someone was pounding on a steel drum. The police went away without entering. She fell back into a fitful sleep.

George Yumich, his head bleeding, made his way to the twenty-third floor. At that moment, McCarthy, who had risen early, was about to stroll over to Grant Park to talk to the people still sitting around bonfires, and he ran into Yumich.

By the time McCarthy got to the fifteenth floor, most of his workers had been herded to the lobby and were sitting on the floor. Richard Goodwin had happened on the scene and was telling his campaign colleagues to sit quietly. All is being taken care of, all is being taken care of, he repeated in a soothing drone. Even so, at one point a policeman lunged at one young man on the floor and clubbed him until other police pulled him off.

McCarthy arrived and asked for the police officer in charge. When there was no response, McCarthy ordered his workers back to their rooms in groups of three and four. Stephen Cohen, meantime, had called Hubert Humphrey for help. An aide refused to wake the nominee.

Earlier in the week, fifteen-story-long petitions for McCarthy had been hung briefly from windows on the raided floor. Debris had come from windows on various floors of the Hilton, including the fifteenth, at various times during the violence. But it was never proved objects were coming from the room where the raid started in the early hours of Friday.

"All inquiries regarding the fifteenth floor failed to turn up any reason for the massive police raid," McCarthy wrote in *Year of the People*. "What did occur was a massive invasion of privacy—action without precedent in the history of American politics."

McCarthy delayed his departure from Chicago until Friday evening, after most of his young campaigners had left the city safely.

"We are leaving Prague," the pilot of McCarthy's campaign plane said as it lifted from Midway Airport.

"This is an America in which again there can be singing," McCarthy had said along the campaign trail.

One wondered in that moment of departure if that could be so.

30. REQUIEM

In Laconia, New Hampshire, in January, 1968, long before anyone took him seriously, McCarthy said in passing: "This is Nixon's year. No one can beat him but me."

After Chicago, it seemed clear Hubert Humphrey could not.

And Chicago made it impossible for McCarthy to move before he finally did, which was October 29, 1968, a week before the election, when he announced he would vote for Humphrey. Nor could he act too much before candidates he campaigned for, such as Paul O'Dwyer, finally said they, too, could vote for Humphrey.

There was a great deal of pressure on him to act sooner, though he diligently removed his name from ballots of twenty-five states. The pressure built after Humphrey's September 30 television statement on Vietnam in which he didn't really change his position but sought to convey the impression he had. McCarthy watched the speech and said afterward: "It's good openers for twenty-five cent poker." The pressure extended to his former staffers. Steve Mitchell signed on as a Humphrey citizens chairman almost immediately and spent his time trying to get McCarthyites active in the Humphrey campaign.

About thirty young McCarthy staffers got together on Martha's Vineyard after Chicago to discuss what to do and they decided to devote their energies to such candidates as Paul O'Dwyer, Wayne Morse, George McGovern, John Gilligan, George Brown, Don Edwards, Charles Vanik, and Harold Hughes, though they listened to the pleadings of Vermont Governor Philip Hoff, who flew there in a chartered plane in behalf of Humphrey. They must work for the ticket, they were told. There would be a budget of one million dollars if they would. But they wouldn't. A number of them accepted a ride in the chartered plane, however.

Before the convention, McCarthy would say in private conversation he felt that after two or three weeks, should Humphrey be nominated, he would probably make some kind of endorsement. It would depend, of course, on what Humphrey had done by then regarding Vietnam. McCarthy did not foresee the violence that would occur in Chicago —violence Humphrey was not fully aware of until after the fact, so preoccupied with pursuit of the Brass Ring had he been.

McCarthy was a candidate who liked to say he set people free, but in doing so he constricted his own freedom to act as he might have preferred. He had never enjoyed attacking Humphrey. He did not feel it necessary. He had been forced to use what harsh terms he did. Nor could he stop the threats of many backers not to support the ticket. "The problem I have is with the young people," he said while in Chicago. "I've been more insistent than I really wanted to be about not supporting the ticket. Because they'd figure this is a sellout. They're ready to accuse you of a sellout, anyway." (At the same time, McCarthy felt it was something of a sellout by George McGovern and Ted Kennedy to declare before the nomination they would actively support the party choice. Had they held back longer, McCarthy felt, perhaps Humphrey might have been moved on Vietnam.)

But, sure enough, McCarthy's endorsement of Humphrey, despite its tepid nature, brought sellout charges from a few former supporters. Others simply differed with him, observing that McCarthy had said his own supporters "are quite capable of making up their own minds."

Some of his key campaign staffers promptly issued a statement that they could not vote for Humphrey, for Humphrey shared responsibility for the war and the violence in Chicago.

"When a Democrat who bears responsibility for so much tragedy and error is nominated by undemocratic procedures for the presidency, the time has come for that faction of the party which won all major primaries to refuse to be taken for granted," the statement said. "If it does not do so now, it may never do so."

The statement was signed by Sam Brown, Paul Gorman, Harold Ickes, and Martin Peretz and Robert Pirie, important campaign financial figures.

Across the country came the same reaction. Most of the McCarthy supporters eventually came around, but a sizable minority did not, probably enough to have deprived Humphrey of the election. In the end, Humphrey was able to win back most of the northern defections to George Wallace. He was not as successful with the McCarthy diehards. I asked the several hundred McCarthy volunteer leaders in my survey whom they voted for in November. Here was the response:

Candidate	Per Cent
Hubert Humphrey	72.4
Did not vote for President	8.3
Eugene McCarthy	5.3
Dick Gregory	4.9
Richard Nixon	2.7
Other	6.4

The "other" category included votes for Edmund Muskie, Eldridge Cleaver, Socialist Labor, an assortment of liberal splinter groups, and two votes for comedian Pat Paulsen. Some surveys suggest George Wallace received a portion of the McCarthy vote, particularly in farm areas. My survey prompted no reply from anyone who said he voted for Wallace. This may be because my survey focused almost totally on "leaders," people assuredly more articulate and better educated than most Wallace people who, if active in the McCarthy campaign, probably did not take leadership roles.

In any event, more than a fourth of the McCarthy supporters in my survey could not bring themselves to swallow Humphrey. Eugene McCarthy could not tell them to. He did not lose the election for Humphrey. But the people he set free did.

VIII

Some Footnotes to This History

★

It will never happen like this again.

CURTIS GANS,
MCCARTHY CAMPAIGN AIDE

31. McCARTHY

Had the miracle sustained, had Eugene McCarthy been nominated, there is no question in my mind that he would have been elected President. The fence around the White House would still be intact: the Secret Service has some wondrous powers in this democracy that even a President cannot undo. But there would have been no candlelight peace marches past that fence, for this nation would more quickly have been on its way to getting out of Vietnam.

He would have, in effect, surrendered, for that is really what he had been talking about, and the Republicans would have made a mammoth issue of this, and a new White Knight would have come forth to reaffirm Apple Pie and all that McCarthy had sold down the river in the name of the Ultimate Weakness that, the Knight would insist, was not in the Marrow of Our Founding Fathers. A Great National Debate on America's Role in the World would have arisen, abetted by Polls and TV Specials. Cries for impeachment would have sounded, and history would have noted this fact; but it also would have noted, eventually, that Eugene McCarthy had tried to make the oldest democracy in the current world grow up, to make it more truly a member of the family of nations which, to be a family, cannot be dominated by a self-proclaimed cop, other than truth.

"Maybe you can do more for this country as a candidate than as President," McCarthy commented to a friend when it was over. Perhaps what he did accomplish would not have seemed so large had he won the Oval Office rather than lapsing not so gently into the quiet night of lame-duck Senator. Though he made few promises, his very election would have seemed a monumental one. Expectation again would have gone unsatisfied.

It is silly, of course, to try to project what kind of President McCarthy would have been. Where would the Other White House have been? Saint John's? That really was McCarthy's only other home besides his Senate office. He had no summer place, no other favorite retreat. Only a reporter who covers the White House regularly can appreciate the thought of date-lining his stories *Collegeville*, Minnesota, and staying in who knows which Collegeville motel, if there is one. Sunday feature stories about the nuns. It would have been a "passive" presidency, to be sure. "I think a little passivity in that office is all right—a kind of balance, I think," he told the California delegates in Chicago.

There would have been no aura of "doing," which, apart from Vietnam, would have made the senselessly inevitable First Hundred Days stories universally bleak. McCarthy's would have been a didactic, a dialectic presidency. Some commentator would eventually have struck on the fact that McCarthy seemed to be bent on undoing. "McCarthy is a brilliant negativist," one of his older and more critical campaign aides remarked in one of those flashes of insight that occasionally occurred.

There would have been a major rearrangement of America's foreign policy that, probably, would have received more acceptance abroad than at home. And, no doubt about it, McCarthy would have gone to the Pentagon to start to undo what had been done during the Cold War, which he would have declared ended.

J. Edgar Hoover would quickly have been committed to his scrapbooks.

For better or worse, McCarthy would have been America's first intellectual President since Woodrow Wilson. And he would, like

Nixon, probably have thrown a big White House party for Duke Ellington. McCarthy remarked after Nixon's Ellington bash that that had been a good thing.

And he would have been a one-term President, for, as he had said, that was all he felt necessary. If he couldn't do what he had in mind in four years, he could not do it in eight, he had said. Thus, he would have entered the White House after the Inaugural Parade with self-imposed limits on his power.

McCarthy's would probably have been a presidency somewhat like Richard Nixon's, though with notable differences. Certainly there would have been no Cambodia gambol. The civil rights revolution would have been allowed to progress, though McCarthy would have favored no single group, in accordance with his campaign speeches through 1968. No Spiro Agnew would have been allowed to emerge to make whoopee of baser instincts in America, though McCarthy would not have been unmindful of these instincts, some of them founded in legitimacy. There would have been no Warren Earl Burger, no Clement Haynsworth or G. Harrold Carswell, no flapdoodle over football, though there would have been over poetry. "No one who's insensitive to poetry and song can have respect for learning," McCarthy would say, paraphrasing an ancient Welsh poet. "And no one who has no respect for learning can have real respect for justice, and no one who does not respect justice can, in fact, manifest a true love for his country."

The week end before the Wisconsin primary, McCarthy began to discuss his concept of the presidency in a way no other Democratic candidate did, to give the people at least some notion of what to expect once they elected him. He returned to this theme over and over again in the following months.

Never, he would say, should the presidency be thought of in personal terms. "A President should not speak of 'my country' but always of 'our country,' not of 'my cabinet' but of 'the cabinet,' . . . not 'my ambassador to the U.N.' but 'the U.S. ambassador to the U.N.'" For the office belonged not to any man, but to the people. Out of their office should come these things: "One, under certain circumstances,

leadership; but for the most part I think this is almost a residual function. . . . Most important, I think, is to set free the energies, intellectual
and spiritual or moral, which do, as we know, exist in great strength
in America."

The presidency was an *office,* not a *job.* "It is a public charge. . . . I
don't look upon my Senate position really as a job," McCarthy would
say. "I look upon it more as an office."

But how to judge whether a man is suited to be President? "I
think," McCarthy said, "that anyone who offers himself or permits
himself to be offered or supported for the presidency must meet two
or three conditions of character and experience and understanding.
He must, I think, be able to read with reasonable judgment the needs
and aspirations of the people." He felt his two decades in politics had
shown he possessed that sensitivity. "I think a man who is presented
for the presidency must also know the limitations of power, and the
limitations that must be placed upon the exercise of power in that
office in which you do have the greatest concentration of influence and
power in any office in the modern world."

It was not an office a person should "*want* in terms of personal
desire or aspiration. I'm quite willing to be President," he would say.
But he had not run to fulfill any "boyhood dream, and not even a late
adult dream."

His critics would say McCarthy's lack of administrative experience
was a mark against him. "That's a little like saying the President
should be a plumber because there are fifty-three bathrooms in the
White House. You can be so much of an administrator that it prevents
you from making decisions," McCarthy said. He considered experience much less important than character and judgment.

He could handle the office adequately, he felt. He would shy from
saying he would be a "good" President.

He spoke of his concept of the Cabinet.

"For the most part, you ought to take the people into the Cabinet
who have some kind of constituency of their own, so that their ideas
have some political support. And, therefore, if they are in disagreement on a policy, it means that at least they can resist the policy which

a President might want to impose upon them; it could leave them in a position where they could dispute with some strength his policies." A McCarthy Cabinet would have had more individual responsibility, but also more accountability. "We ought to be able to drop a Cabinet member the way you drop a prime minister in England if his policies fail," McCarthy said.

These outlines of what a McCarthy presidency might offer troubled those who preferred a "strong" presidency. Pat Lucey was one of these, but he submerged this conviction in the deeper belief McCarthy would have been strong enough to get the United States out of Vietnam, which really couldn't be considered a weak man's task.

Arthur Schlesinger, Jr., among the first McCarthy supporters to jump ship when Robert Kennedy entered the race, felt a McCarthy-style "passive presidency" would lead to a Democratic party composed of "a semi-precious alliance of college graduates." He wanted a party that was "truly national, embracing the poor as well as the rich, the black as well as the white, the young as well as the old, the uneducated as well as the educated." He saw this possible only under the "strong" presidency that he said Robert Kennedy would have offered—a strong presidency which would be "the tribune of the disinherited and the dispossessed" and the "herald of change."

The doubts went even into McCarthy's personal realm. "Gene as President?" one person close to him is said to have remarked. "It would be a national disaster." The Kennedy people often used almost precisely the same words.

The critics would point to the usual things: McCarthy's "weak" Senate staff, his chaotic campaign organization (never mind its success), his seeming disinclination to listen to advice, his unpredictability, what they regarded as aloofness, arrogance, his lack of observable passion, his failure to communicate with the blacks (not as gigantic a failure as they supposed). Probably the biggest unstated criticism was that McCarthy was inexplicable. He began his crusade a mystery, and ended it a mystery.

The ambivalence over what kind of President he might have been extended to his supporters across the country. "He was cold, imperious; I would have been afraid of him as President, for I fear he would never have consulted with anybody and may have been a do-nothing Ike type," said Dr. Edgar Crane, fifty-one-year-old professor and a McCarthy leader in Houston. "He was too much of a loner to be effective in the White House," said Philip H. Elliott, Jr., thirty-eight-year-old Daytona Beach attorney.

Some aides ended the campaign with a totally negative view of McCarthy. "Whatever he was doing, he was not seeking the presidency," said one, "and since he wasn't, his attacks on Bob Kennedy were totally uncalled for." Said another: "To take as much money as he did and allow it to be used the way he did was grotesque mismanagement." Said another: "He was a demagogue. All that talk about not wanting to be a strong President—pure demagoguery. Huey Long could have made the same speech." "Every move McCarthy made was one of withdrawal and retreat from responsibility," said another embittered staffer, echoing several more. "A lot of the young people on the staff would not work for him again," said one young crusader.

These were minority views, however. Most spoke of him with a respect approaching reverence, though usually short of idolatry. Most recognized his shortcomings and accepted them, noting that had McCarthy been any different, probably he would never have stood up alone in the first place. "The characteristics which frustrated his supporters at times were also responsible for the degree of success he achieved," said Mary Jo Small, thirty-one, of Hills, Iowa. "He let us all be ourselves, or, rather, he insisted on it, and I suppose this was his greatest strength and his greatest weakness," said John Shattuck, twenty-four, a Yale law student.

Ted Warshafsky, Wisconsin vice-chairman, was typical of those who buried their doubts in ultimate respect.

He did many things with which I disagreed and demonstrated many attributes of which one might disapprove. But McCarthy never tried to inculcate a cult of obsequiousness to his personality, never presented himself as a god. Therefore, when he displayed human weaknesses, one could not complain of a god who had fallen. . . . The things that so many criticize—his view of the presidency, the Cabinet, and even the role of the individual

ersonal. His Cabinet seemed to have more freedom. At first, rela-
between the Executive and the Congress seemed more in bal-
, or so McCarthy felt. McCarthy almost accepted Nixon's offer
e post of United Nations ambassador. The President agreed to
arthy's stipulation that he be free to speak out as he saw fit.
n also agreed that a Democrat should be appointed to replace
arthy in the Senate. However, Republican Governor Harold
nder, of Minnesota, refused to go along with this condition, and
Carthy turned the job down.

ough he declined to run for reelection as Minnesota Senator,
st in McCarthy's plans did not abate. For a time he considered
le Senate contests in either New York or California. He kept his
for 1972, if he had any, shrouded in mystery. He would be
ally active "at least through 1972," was all he would say flatly.
es he would speak about chances for formation of a new liberal
for 1972. At other times he would comment that the Democratic
still seemed the best hope. It was impossible to predict what he
do next.

ugh he had disappointed many supporters both during and
is presidential campaign, by 1970 untold numbers had become
iled to his unpredictable nature and dreamed of a McCarthy
nce. "If he said the word, I'd be there again," said one young
thy worker eighteen months after the campaign. But would
he word?

arthy began to come out of his exile late in 1969. He began to
Nixon on Vietnam and other matters. He traveled to South
to confer with leaders of a number of countries. He met with
Kosygin in Moscow. His production of magazine articles
d. He closely watched political developments. His activity
seem that of a man who would end his time lying on a west-
ill writing only poetry, though his poems began to appear
en in magazines.

remained impossible to predict what was around the corner
ne McCarthy. He had been a man for one very important
American history. That was the only certainty.

in history—were to me strong lessons that will be rememberd. The fact he could run for President without, as he put it, having a physical need to be President, is the seed of humanity that I think must take root if we are to achieve a meaningful future.

A seed of truthfulness was ready to take root after four years of the Johnson Credibility Gap. "Those of us who had opposed the war for years and had fought for domestic equality and justice needed a candidate whom we could trust at least as much as we needed someone who could win," said Mrs. Mary Jean Lord, of Yakima, Washington.

Though he usually kept his private thoughts and those things he considered his own to himself, there was never a McCarthy for public consumption that was particularly different from the man friends saw in private. He was essentially the same whether going through his biting monologues at parties or on the stump, whether going into a funk in his office or on the campaign trail, whether criticizing a Kennedy in private or in public. McCarthy said in June, 1968, "This has been the character of my campaign: not to impose my personality upon anyone, not really to impose my ideas, or to give you any new information, but rather, simply, to give the people of this country a chance to act upon what they know to be true...."

But McCarthy did in a real sense impose his personality upon the campaign. It was the personality of a nonhero who, therefore, came off as a noncandidate. Of course, it was up to his supporters and his staff to take him or leave him, but since there had been no other candidate in 1968 until mid-March, they were forced to accept McCarthy's personality, and since he did not perform like other candidates, an aura of mystery surrounded him. Perhaps it should not have, for above all else McCarthy was amazingly consistent. He was less mysterious than met the eye. The trouble was, not as much of McCarthy as of most men in public life met the eye. And so some of his actions in the year after the 1968 election seemed to his former supporters to only deepen the mystery of the man and added to whatever doubts they may have harbored about what kind of President he might have been.

He voted against Ted Kennedy for the job of assistant Democratic

Senate leader. He dropped from the Foreign Relations Committee. He left Abigail to live alone.

"He really dived off that pedestal, didn't he?" Alice Krakauer, a young campaign aide steeped in psychology, commented at the time. "I guess he just didn't want people to expect so much of him."

That was certainly true. "This hero stuff scared the living daylights out of him," Jerry Eller commented after the campaign. But there were other reasons for McCarthy's moves, not all of them particularly admirable.

He simply could not abide the Kennedys. "To him Kennedyism was a chronic disease," one friend who had implored him to vote for Ted Kennedy said. Instead, McCarthy voted for Senator Russell Long, Louisiana Democrat, a blustery defender of the oil depletion allowance and all Mayor Daley had stood for in Chicago. Long, who then held the post of assistant leader, or whip, had never done anything to McCarthy. "Jack lied to me, Bobby smeared me, and Teddy never did anything to help," McCarthy commented to one acquaintance. Moreover, McCarthy thought the issue unimportant, the job unimportant, though other men, like Hubert Humphrey, had made something of it. He could not see why a man with presidential ambitions like Ted Kennedy "would want the job of washing out the jock straps [sanitized to "sweat shirts" in the retelling] when he wants to be quarterback." At the same time, McCarthy had been ready to help Edmund Muskie in a fight for the job.

McCarthy dropped from the Foreign Relations Committee, he said, to settle a dilemma only Senators would appreciate, and certainly not all of them. Chairman J. W. Fulbright had long wanted to restore the committee to somewhere near its original thirteen-member size to increase efficiency. Over the years it had grown to nineteen, which Fulbright considered unwieldy. The 1968 election results, however, meant no new Democrats could be added to the committee if the size were reduced to fifteen, the figure Fulbright settled on. Fulbright had promised Gale McGee, of Wyoming, the administration's most articulate Vietnam supporter, a place on the highly coveted committee. McGee had been bumped from a committee seat as a result of the 1966 election which changed the Democrat-Republican ratio.

McGee was ready to fight for retention of the n to insure his return. An impasse seemed to b McCarthy volunteered to resign, which enc Carthy supporters were shocked that he woulc to a man who espoused the policies he had fou found that a man did not need a Foreign Re to make his views on foreign policy known Fulbright reduce the size of the committee delayed aspirations of a number of other Sena to the committee. Among these was Ted Kenn

As an alternative, McCarthy accepted a Operations Committee. "Operations is polic Marshall McLuhan. And he hinted that he investigation of operations affecting foreign could he have done so because of problems

Finally, in the summer of 1969, McCarth of rumors that his marriage was on the roc marriage, friends would say, had been stra in an interview McCarthy had compared rather hard to pick because of the thorns." himself. Why they finally separated was rumor mongers would insist there was an not the case at the time McCarthy movec

And so in the first year after his 1968 bent only on disappointing. He said littl felt he had said quite enough during the retreat from the public eye both for per litical reason: he felt he had been overe to let other Democrats jockey for top bi voice on important issues, such as C Muskie, and, for a time, Ted Kennedy had a book to write; he felt the new ac a chance to get started.

At first, McCarthy viewed the Nix favor. Nixon seemed to be putting int McCarthy felt right for the office. Nix

imp
tion
ance
of tl
McC
Nixo
McC
Leva
so M
Th
inter
possil
plans
politi
At tin
party
party
might
Tho
after l
recon
resurg
McCar
he say

McC
questio
Americ
Premie
increase
did not
facing
more of
But it
for Eug
season i

32. PEOPLE

The war continued. McCarthy did not win. These cold facts seemed to demand assignment of the word "failure" to the McCarthy crusade. But that would be a mistake. For McCarthy did prove that an American President, or at least a Democratic President, could never again take the people or his party for granted. He must respond to the people, or they would have done with him. McCarthy also introduced a style of campaigning that would be felt for many years— a style based on the simple premise that the people have brains and a high regard for honesty and morality. It was a style that belied the assumption that some people considered proven in the 1968 campaign of Richard Nixon: that sophisticated gimmickry and manipulation and contrived electronic packaging of a candidate had become the most important factor in presidential campaigns. Nixon's fancy television didn't win him the election. The Democrats booted it. Finally, McCarthy gave form to a vital new force in politics that probably could not have arisen in a different campaign: the young people and quiet adults alike who learned the techniques of politics. For they had to learn them; McCarthy would not instruct them; and, having learned, they put their lessons to work again, whether in their communities or on the national scene. And together these people and McCarthy, though primarily the people, had forced the Democratic party to a new day of reform that, they hoped, might make it more responsive to more people.

To establish guidelines for party change, the Democratic National Committee formed two commissions: one on delegate selection and party structure, headed by Senator George McGovern, and one on national convention procedures, headed by Representative James G. O'Hara.

The O'Hara commission had not completed its work as this book was in its final revision, though it had, among other things, suggested limiting the number of convention delegates to 1,500 with 500 alternates. The combined number in 1968 had climbed to 5,611. Late in 1969, however, the McGovern commission, after many months of hearings and argument, settled on eighteen guidelines by which state parties could begin the difficult task of reform. The recommendations were marked by a number of compromises that left more intense reformist members not altogether happy with the final product.

First, there was the question as to whether state parties should institute "proportional representation." Proportional representation would assure national convention delegate strength to a loser in a primary or state convention roughly in ratio to his supporters' strength. Dissent, thus, would be institutionalized within the party. The ability of a Mayor Daley or a John Connally to arrive at a national convention with a solid bloc of votes in the hip pocket would be ended forever. The commission, however, decided to endorse proportional representation merely in principle and only to recommend it to the party. At the same time, a handful of states adopted it on their own.

Nor did the commission go as far as it might have regarding the principle of one-man, one-vote in delegate selection—a principle Eugene McCarthy had called necessary in his testimony before the commission. Instead, the commission accepted a compromise that would require state parties to apportion their national convention delegates on a basis that gave equal weight to the size of the Democratic vote in the previous presidential election and the latest reliable state population figures. States using a convention system would be required to elect at least three-fourths of their delegation at the congressional district level or lower.

With little dispute, the commission adopted standards of participation for racial minorities and women and persons under thirty, including eighteen-year-olds. The commission urged states to give these groups representation that bore "a reasonable relationship" to their presence in the population. At the 1968 convention, for example, women held only 13 per cent of the delegate votes, though they outnumbered men in the population. Sixteen state delegations had no one under age thirty; thirteen had only one member in that age bracket. But again, the commission conclusion was more a recommendation than a demand.

State parties were to be allowed to assess a member no more than ten dollars to run or participate as a delegate (Indiana required $500 from each delegate), and petition requirements for delegate candidates were to be standardized. Proxy voting was ordered outlawed in delegate selection, and times, places, and rules for public party meetings were to be publicized. Favorite sons were discouraged, and the unit rule was urged abolished as ordered by the 1968 convention. The convention provision calling for delegates to be selected within the calendar year of the convention was also among the guidelines.

"What we have done," George McGovern declared as the commission wound up its work, "is unprecedented for a major party—that is, to look very critically at our procedures and to make substantial recommendations for reform."

Some states approached the problem of reform vigorously. But many had not begun to do so by mid-1970. And though the McCarthy legions remained active in their individual situations, they had not achieved enough strength in party structures of many of the less progressive states to assure the reforms would be adopted. Adoption in many places would require a major struggle that could come to a head in the credentials battles of the 1972 convention.

Success would give new meaning to the Democrats' claim of being the party of the people. Failure to reform would increase the potential for development of a splinter party, one perhaps strong enough to insure defeat of the Democrats in 1972, depending on whom the Democrats would nominate and what the issues would be.

As the McGovern commission report stated: "If we are not an open party; if we do not represent the demands of change, then the danger is not that people will go to the Republican party; it is that there will no longer be a way for people committed to orderly change to fulfill their needs and desires within our traditional political system. It is that they will turn to third and fourth party politics or the anti-politics of the street."

Few of the people who made up the McCarthy movement in 1968 seriously felt he would rise again in 1972, though some dreamed he might. Most preferred to move on with their own business: continuing fighting the war in local organizations, trying to reform the party, working for candidates, or whatever. They would remember their year and the man who happened to lead them—fondly, for the most part, and with deep gratitude, but not necessarily with a sense of future obligation. "I took off my McCarthy button the day after the nomination," said Don Peterson, who in 1970 ran for governor of Wisconsin. He took it off, but what it had represented shaped the approach of his campaign even before he announced his candidacy, as it would shape the tone and honesty of countless campaigns for a long time.

The people learned politics with McCarthy, whether it was new or very old politics. They learned the music of public happiness. It was fitting that McCarthy sometimes closed his campaign speeches with lines from "I Hear America Singing," by Walt Whitman:

> I hear America singing, the varied carols I hear;
> Those of mechanics, each one singing his as it should
>   be blithe and strong,
> The carpenter singing his as he measures his plank or beam,
> The mason singing his as he makes ready for work,
>   or leaves off work,
> The boatman singing what belongs to him in his boat, the
>   deckhand singing on the steamboat deck,

The shoemaker singing as he sits on his bench, the hatter
    singing as he stands,
The wood-cutter's song, the ploughboy's on his way in the
    morning, or at noon intermission or at sundown,
The delicious singing of the mother, or of the young wife at
    work, or of the girl sewing or washing,
Each singing what belongs to him or her and to none else. . . .

McCarthy would fuse the poem at this point with Whitman's "Poets to Come," and he would say these lines, changing or adding a word here and there:

Poets to come! orators, singers, musicians to come!
Not to-day is to justify me and answer what I am for,
But you, a new brood, native, athletic, continental,
    greater than before known.
Arouse! Arouse—for you must justify me—you
    must answer.

There was more to that poem, some final lines McCarthy never spoke to his audiences, but which told more about the man in relation to his campaign and the people than anything else that was written:

I am a man who, sauntering along without fully stopping,
    turns a casual look upon you and then averts his face,
Leaving it to you to prove and define it,
Expecting the main things from you.

Frances Morrow does not think overly about Eugene McCarthy any more. The main things do not give much time for idle recollection.

AUTHOR'S NOTE

Particular thanks to Dorothy Stout Avels, my mother and first journalist in the family, who introduced me to the profession and made useful comments on the manuscript.

Also to Mel Elfin, Washington Bureau chief of *Newsweek*, who more than anyone made this book possible.

Special thanks to Peter Barnes, both an inspiration and a help; my wife, Barbara, a good editor; a long list of *Newsweek* colleagues whose work helped fill in gaps; Thelma McMahon, who prepared the manuscript; and Amanda Zimmerman, who introduced me to my fine editor at Harper & Row, Tom Congdon.

My gratitude to six hundred or so persons who provided information and insights on the man and the movement. I can name only a few, and am sure to have left out several who were a particular help: Mark Acuff, George Agree, Karl Andresen, Sam Brown, Blair Clark, Steve Cohen, Joe Duffey, Jerry Eller, Tom Finney, Sandy Frucher, Curt Gans, David Garth, Marty Gleason, Dick Goodwin, Don Green, Russ Hemenway, Arnold Hiatt, Gerry Hill, Bill Johnson, Joshua Leinsdorf, Pat Lucey, Abigail and Mary McCarthy, Tom McCoy, Larry Merthan, Art Michelson, Mayne Miller, Midge Miller, Dave Mixner, Tom Morgan, Bill Nee, Martin Peretz, Don Peterson, Norval Reece, Maurice Rosenblatt, John Safer, Cindy Samuels, Eli Segal, Howard Stein, Robert Toal, Barbara and David Underwood, Anne Wexler, Blaine Whipple.

INDEX

About the Author

Richard T. Stout is a political reporter in the Washington bureau of *Newsweek*. He was born in 1931 in Indianapolis and received an A.B. degree from DePauw University and an M.S. from the Columbia Graduate School of Journalism. After two years in the Army, he went to work for the Chicago *Daily News*, rising from reporter to assistant city editor to Washington correspondent. A housing exposé carried out by a team of reporters under his direction, in company with a team from a Chicago television station, won the 1963 Sigma Delta Chi public service award. At *Newsweek* he has covered such continuing stories as civil rights, urban affairs, and the peace movement. He has reported two presidential elections, traveling with Goldwater in 1964 and accompanying Eugene McCarthy in 1968 from the beginning to the end. He lives in Washington with his wife, Barbara, and their four children.

Design by Sidney Feinberg
Set in Linotype Caledonia
Composed, printed and bound by The Haddon Craftsmen, Inc.
HARPER & ROW, PUBLISHERS, INC.